S0-BFB-948

DRAMATISTS SOURCEBOOK

23RD EDITION

DRAMATISTS SOURCEBOOK

23RD EDITION

Complete opportunities for playwrights, translators, composers, lyricists and librettists

THEATRE COMMUNICATIONS GROUP
NEW YORK
2004

Copyright © 2004 by Theatre Communications Group, Inc.

Published by Theatre Communications Group, Inc.
520 8th Ave, New York, NY 10018-4156.

All rights reserved. No part of this book may be reproduced in any manner whatsoever without written permission from the publisher, except in the case of brief quotations embodied in critical articles and reviews.

This publication is made possible in part with public funds from the New York State Council on the Arts, a State Agency.

TCG books are exclusively distributed to the book trade by Consortium Book Sales and Distribution, 1045 Westgate D., St. Paul, MN 55114.

Manufactured in the United States of America.

ISSN 0733-1606
ISBN 1-55936-247-2

CONTENTS

PREFACE

Welcome to the 23rd edition of the *Dramatists Sourcebook.*

The *Sourcebook* was first published in 1981 and contained three hundred listings. Now, more than twenty years later, it hosts three times that many. This is good news. Though over the past few years there has been a decline in funding, and many organizations are in the process of redefining their programs (some being dropped altogether), there has also been a regrouping by others and an insertion into the theatre community of new development opportunities for the creation of new work. There are many reasons for playwrights to be hopeful—more listings are included here than in our last edition, published just two years ago.

We take great care in organizing and editing the *Sourcebook.* Each edition (published every two years) is fully revised. Every organization listed in this *Sourcebook* has been contacted directly, and the accuracy of their listing confirmed at press time.

Using the *Sourcebook.* The Sourcebook is published biennially. Because of this some deadlines may fall outside the publication years covered by this edition. It is always important to confirm a deadline before submitting work; an organization's website is an excellent source for this. All deadlines reflect the next upcoming submission deadline for an organization at press time. Because each edition of the *Sourcebook* is fully revised, it is important to always use the most recent version.

Study Tony Kushner's "A Simple Working Guide for Playwrights" (page ix, the Prologue). It's filled with great advice.

Select those listings your work is best suited for and follow the guidelines meticulously. The Special Interests Index is helpful in finding those listings that may be suited to your type of work. When instructed to write for guidelines, do so. This is a good idea in general, as sometimes dates and guidelines change after the *Sourcebook* is published. Most important is to **ALWAYS ENCLOSE AN SASE** with every mailed script, unless the entry specifies that scripts will not be returned. If a listing states that an organization accepts scripts, it should always be assumed that an SASE must be sent along; we do not restate this for every listing. Always assume the deadline dates in this book refer to the day materials should arrive, not the postmark date.

"Full-length play" means just that—a full-length, original work for adult audiences, without a score or libretto. One-acts, musicals, adaptations, translations, plays for young audiences, solo pieces, performance art and screenplays are listed separately. "Young audiences" refers to audiences age 18 or younger, "young playwrights" refers to playwrights age 18 or younger, "students" refers to students in college or in an affiliated writing program.

Entries are alphabetized by first word (excluding "the") even if they start with a person's name. So, for example, "Mark Taper Forum" is listed under "M." In the index, you will also find this theatre cross-listed under "T." Regardless of the way "theatre" is spelled in an organization's name, we alphabetize it as if it were spelled "re."

It is important to us at TCG that the *Sourcebook* continue to be a beneficial service to playwrights. With each edition, we take painstaking effort to ensure the accuracy of the listings and to make sure the book is clearly written and easy to navigate. Please let us know how we are doing, and if there are ways we can improve the *Sourcebook.* Throughout the years, your feedback has been an enormous help.

We thank all of the organizations included here, and appreciate their diligence in providing us year after year with their listing information. And, we thank you, the artists, for your great work. We are honored to be a part of your process and to support you in your lifelong career as theatre practitioners. We wish you all the best.

The Editors
July 2004

PROLOGUE

A Simple Working Guide for Playwrights
by Tony Kushner

A) Format: Most playwrights use a format in which character headings are placed centered above the line and capitalized:

LIONEL

I don't possess a mansion, a car, or a string of polo ponies...

Lines should be single-spaced. Stage directions should be indented and single-spaced. If a character's line is interrupted at the end of the page, its continuance on the following page should be marked as such:

LIONEL (CONT'D)

or a string of polo ponies...

There are denser, and thus more economical, formats; since Xeroxing is expensive, and heavy scripts cost more to ship, you may be tempted to use these, but a generously spaced format is much easier to read, and in these matters it doesn't pay to be parsimonious.

B) Typing and reproducing: Scripts should be typed neatly and reproduced clearly. Remember that everyone who reads your script will be reading many others additionally, and it will work to your serious disadvantage if the copy's sloppy, faded, or otherwise unappealing. If you use a computer printer, eschew old-fashioned dot-matrix and other robotic kinds of print. Also, I think it's best to avoid using incredibly fancy word-processing printing programs with eight different typefaces and decorative borders. Simple typescript, carefully done, is best. Check for typos. A playwright's punctuation may be idiosyncratic for purposes of expressiveness, but not too idiosyncratic, and spelling should be correct.

C) Sending the script:

    1)   The script should have a title page with the title, your name, address and phone number, or that of your agent or representative. Scripts are now automatically copyrighted at the moment of creation, but simply writing © and the date on the title page can serve as a kind of scarecrow for thievish magpies.

    2)   Never, never send an unbound script. Loose pages held together by a rubber band don't qualify as bound, nor do pages clamped together with a mega-paperclip. A heavy paper cover will protect the script as it passes from hand to hand.

    3)   Always, always enclose a self-addressed stamped envelope (SASE) or you will never see your script again. You may enclose a note telling the theatre to dispose of the copy instead of returning it; but you must have the ultimate fate of the script planned for in the eventuality of its not being selected for production. Don't leave this up to the theatre! If you want receipt of the script acknowledged, include a self-addressed, stamped postcard (SASP).

D) Letter of inquiry and synopsis: If a theatre states, in its entry in the *Sourcebook,* that it does not accept unsolicited scripts, believe it. Don't call and ask if there are exceptions; there aren't. A well-written and concise letter of inquiry, however, accompanied by a synopsis possessed of similar virtues can get you an invitation to submit your play. It's prudent, then, to spend time on both letter and synopsis. It is, admittedly, very hard for a writer to sum up his or her work in less than a page, but this kind of boiling-down can be of value beyond its necessity as a tool for marketing; use it to help clarify for yourself what's central and essential about your play. A good synopsis should briefly summarize the basic features of the plot without going into excessive detail; it should evoke both the style and the thematic substance of the play without recourse to clichéd description ("This play is about what happens when people lose their dreams…"); and it should convey essential information, such as cast size, gender breakdown, period, location, or anything else a literary manager deciding whether to send for the play might want to know. Make reference to other productions in your letter, but don't send thick packets of reviews and photos. And don't offer your opinion of the play's worth, which will be inferred as being positive from the fact that you are its parent.

E) Waiting: Theatres almost always take a long time to respond to playwrights about a specific play, frequently far in excess of the time given in their listings in the *Sourcebook.* This is due neither to spite nor indolence. Literary departments are usually understaffed and their workload is fearsome. Then, too, the process of selection invariably involves a host of people and considerations of all kinds. In my opinion you do yourself no good by repeatedly calling after the status of your script; you will become identified as a pest. It's terribly expensive to copy and mail scripts, but you must be prepared to shoulder the expense and keep making copies if they don't get returned. If, after a certain length of time past the deadline, you haven't heard from a theatre, send a letter inquiring politely about the play, reminding the appropriate people that you'd sent an SASE with the script; and then forget about it. In most cases, you will get a response and the script returned eventually.

One way to cut down on the expenses involved is to be selective about venues for submission. Reading *Sourcebook* entries and scrutinizing a copy of *Theatre Profiles* [online version (www.tcg.org) coming 2003; see Useful Publications] will help you select the theatres most compatible with your work. If you've written a musical celebration of the life of Phyllis Schlafly, for example, you won't want to send it to theatres with an interest in radical feminist dramas. Or you won't necessarily want to send your play about the history of Western imperialism to a theatre that produces an annual season of musical comedy.

F) Produce yourself! In *Endgame*, Clov asks Hamm, "Do you believe in the life to come?" and Hamm responds, "Mine was always that." The condition of endless deferment is one that modern American playwrights share with Beckett's characters and other denizens of the postmodern world. Don't spend your life waiting. You may not be an actor, but that doesn't mean that action is forbidden you. Playwrights can, with very little expense, mount readings of their work; they can band together with other playwrights for readings and discussions; and they can, if they want to, produce their work themselves. Growth as a writer for the stage depends on seeing your work on stage, and if no one else will put it there, the job is up to you. At the very least, and above all else, while waiting, waiting, waiting for responses and offers, keep reading, thinking and writing.

Tony Kushner's plays include *A Bright Room Called Day, Hydriotaphia, Angels in America, Parts One and Two, Slavs!* and *Homebody/Kabul*. His adaptations include Corneille's *The Illusion*, Ansky's *The Dybbuk*, Brecht's *The Good Person of Szechuan*, Goethe's *Stella* and English-language libretti for two operas: Krasa's *Brundibar* and Martinu's *Comedy on the Bridge*. In 2003, HBO presented a film version of *Angels in America*, directed by Mike Nichols. Mr. Kushner is the recipient of numerous awards, including the Pulitzer Prize for Drama (*Angels in America, Part One*), two Tony Awards for Best Play (*Angels in America*, 1993 and 1994), three Obie Awards (*Slavs!*, *Homebody/Kabul* and *Caroline, or Change*), an Evening Standard Award (*Angels in America*), two Dramatists Guild/Hull-Warriner Awards (*Angels in America* and *Homebody/Kabul*), an Arts Award from the American Academy of Arts and Letters, a Cultural Achievement Award from the National Foundation for Jewish Culture, the PEN/Laura Pels Award for Mid-Career Playwright and a Spirit of Justice Award from the Gay and Lesbian Advocates and Defenders. He was born in Lake Charles, Louisiana, but he doesn't live there anymore.

PART 1
SCRIPT
OPPORTUNITIES

Production

Prizes

Publication

Development

PRODUCTION

What theatres are included in this section?

The overwhelming majority of the not-for-profit professional theatres throughout the U.S., which accept submissions, is represented here. Theatres to which playwrights cannot contact or submit work, even through an agent, are not included. (These are theatres that directly solicit playwrights only.) In order to be included, a theatre must meet professional standards of staffing, programming and budget; most have been operating for at least two years. Commercial and amateur producers are not included.

How should I go about deciding where to submit my play?

Don't send it out indiscriminately. Take time to study the listings and select those theatres most likely to be receptive to your material. Find out all you can about each of the theatres you select. Visit the theatre's website. Read *American Theatre*'s "OnStage" section to see what plays the theatres are currently presenting and what their other activities are (see Useful Publications for more information). Whenever possible, go see the theatre's work.

When I submit my play, what can I do to maximize its chances?

First, read carefully the Simple Working Guide for Playwrights in the Prologue of this *Sourcebook* for good advice on script submission. Then follow each theatre's guidelines meticulously. Pay particular attention to the Special Interests section: If a theatre specifies "gay and lesbian themes only," do not send them your heterosexual romantic comedy, however witty and well written it is. Also, bear in mind the following points about the various submission procedures:

1) "Accepts unsolicited scripts": Don't waste the theatre's time and yours by writing to ask permission to submit your play—just send it. If you want an acknowledgment of receipt, say so and enclose a self-addressed stamped postcard (SASP) for this purpose. **Always enclose a self-addressed stamped envelope (SASE) for the return of a script.**

2) "Synopsis and letter of inquiry": Never send an unsolicited script to these theatres. Prepare a clear, cogent and *brief* synopsis of your play and send it along with any other materials requested in the listing. The letter of inquiry is a cover note asking for permission to submit the script; if there is something about your play or about yourself as a writer that you think may spark the theatre's interest, by all means mention it, but keep the letter brief. We've asked theatres requiring letters and synopses to give us two response times—one for letters and one for scripts, should they ask to see one. All response times are approximate, and theatres may take longer to respond than stated. Always enclose an SASP for the theatre's response, unless the theatre specifies that it only responds if it wants to see the script.

3) "Professional recommendation": Send a script (not a letter of inquiry) accompanied by a letter of recommendation from a theatre professional. Wait until you have obtained such a letter before approaching these theatres.

4) "Agent submission": If you do not have an agent yet, do not submit to these theatres. Wait until you have had a production or two and have acquired a representative who can submit your script for you.

5) Do not email your submissions, unless specifically stated to do so. Email and web addresses are included for the purpose of general inquiries and, when noted, to obtain guidelines or applications.

6) Deadlines: Some deadlines for special programs may fall outside the publication period of this book, which is biennial. All deadlines reflect the upcoming submission deadline for a theatre at press time. It is always best to confirm a deadline before submitting work (a theatre's website is an excellent resource for this).

ABOUT FACE THEATRE

(Founded 1995)

1222 West Wilson, 2nd Floor; Chicago, IL 60640; (773) 784–8565,
FAX 784–8557; email faceline1@aboutfacetheatre.com;
website www.aboutfacetheatre.com

Literary Department

Submission procedure: no unsolicited scripts; brief synopsis, 10-page dialogue sample and letter of inquiry. **Types of material:** full-length plays, one-acts, adaptations, musicals, performance art. **Special interests:** queer scripts only, with a particular interest in lesbian plays; material that challenges self-conceptions, moral expectations and ideas about gender and sexuality in historical or contemporary contexts; imaginative scripts of literary caliber with strong dramatic action, theatricality and dynamics; unpredictable characters that break traditional ideas about dramatic form, structure, presentation and characters. **Facilities:** no permanent facility. **Production considerations:** no fly space, limited backstage space. **Best submission time:** year-round. **Response time:** 3 months letter; 6 months script. **Special programs:** writers workshop, readings, rough stagings with audience response.

THE ACTING COMPANY

(Founded 1972)

Box 898; New York, NY 10108–0898; (212) 258–3111, FAX 258–3299;
email mail@theactingcompany.org; website www.theactingcompany.org

Margot Harley, *Producing Director*

Submission procedure: no unsolicited scripts; professional recommendation. **Types of material:** full-length plays, translations, adaptations. **Special interests:** mainly classical repertory but occasionally produces new works suited to acting ensemble of approximately 8 men, 3 women; prefers works with poetic dimension and heightened language. **Facilities:** no permanent facility; touring company which plays in New York City for 1 or 2 weeks a year. **Production considerations:** productions tour in repertory; simple, transportable proscenium-stage set. **Best submission time:** year-round. **Response time:** 3 months.

ACTOR'S EXPRESS

(Founded 1988)

King Plow Arts Center, J-107; 887 West Marietta St NW;
Atlanta, GA 30318; (404) 875–1606, FAX 875–2791;
email jasson@actorsexpress.com; website www.actorsexpress.com

Jasson Minadakis, *Artistic Director*

Submission procedure: no unsolicited scripts; 1-page synopsis and bio. **Types of material:** full-length plays, musicals. **Special interests:** contemporary, socially relevant material; minority and gay themes; works with poetic dimension; multi-ethnic works. **Facilities:** Actor's Express, 150 seats, black box. **Production**

considerations: modest production demands; no fly space. **Best submission time:** Apr-Jan. **Response time:** 6 weeks letter; 6 months script.

ACTORS' GUILD OF LEXINGTON
(Founded 1984)
141 East Main St; Lexington, KY 40507; (859) 233-7330,
FAX 233-3773; email actorsguild@qx.net;
website www.actorsguildoflexington.org
Richard St. Peter, *Artistic Director*

Submission procedure: no unsolicited scripts; synopsis and letter of inquiry; prefers email submission. **Types of material:** full-length plays, solo pieces. **Facilities:** Main Stage, 200 seats, black box. **Production considerations:** cast limit of 6; no fly space; prefers single set. **Best submission time:** year-round. **Response time:** 1 month letter; 6 months script.

ACTORS THEATRE OF LOUISVILLE
(Founded 1964)
316 West Main St; Louisville, KY 40202-4218; (502) 584-1265,
FAX 561-3300; website www.actorstheatre.org
Adrien-Alice Hansel, *Literary Manager*

Submission procedure: direct solicitation to playwright or agent; for Humana Festival (see below): no unsolicited scripts; accepts synopsis and dialogue sample; prefers agent submission. **Types of material:** full-length plays, translations, adaptations. **Special interests:** plays of ideas; language-oriented plays; plays with passion, humor and experimentation. **Facilities:** Pamela Brown Auditorium, 637 seats, thrust stage; Bingham Theatre, 320 seats, arena stage; Victor Jory Theatre, 159 seats, thrust stage. **Best submission time:** Apr-Oct. **Response time:** 9 months (most scripts returned in late fall). **Special programs:** National Ten-Minute Play Contest (see Prizes); Humana Festival of New American Plays: annual presentation of new work in rotating rep; *deadline:* ongoing; *notification:* fall 2004; *dates:* Feb-Mar 2005.

ACTORS THEATRE OF PHOENIX
(Founded 1985)
Box 1924; Phoenix, AZ 85001-1924; (602) 253-6701,
FAX 254-9577; email info@atphx.org;
website www.actorstheatrePHX.org
Matthew Wiener, *Producing Artistic Director*

Submission procedure: no unsolicited scripts; professional recommendation. **Types of material:** full-length plays, translations, adaptations. **Special interests:** plays dealing with the Southwest. **Facilities:** Herberger Theater Center, Stage West, 300 seats, proscenium stage. **Production considerations:** cast limit of 8. **Best submission time:** year-round. **Response time:** 10 months.

ACT THEATRE

(Founded 1965)

Kreielsheimer Place, 700 Union St; Seattle, WA 98101-4037;
      (206) 292-7660, FAX 292-7670; website www.acttheatre.org

Kurt Beattie, *Artistic Director*

Submission procedure: no unsolicited scripts; synopsis, 10-page dialogue sample and letter of inquiry from Northwest playwrights only. **Types of material:** full-length plays, translations, adaptations, musicals, solo pieces. **Special interests:** current social, political and psychological issues; plays theatrical in imagination and storytelling; multicultural themes; prefer no kitchen-sink realism or "message" plays. **Facilities:** The Allen, 387 seats, arena stage; The Falls, 381 seats, thrust stage; The Bullitt, 150 seats, cabaret. **Best submission time:** Sep-Apr. **Response time:** 6 months letter; 12 months script. **Special programs:** new play development workshops. FirstACT: play commissions and workshops.

ACT II PLAYHOUSE

(Founded 1998)

Box 555, 56 E Butler Ave; Ambler, PA 19002; (215) 654-0200,
      FAX 654-5001; email act2@libertynet.org; website www.act2.org

Steve Blumenthal, *Producing Artistic Director*

Submission procedure: accepts unsolicited scripts. **Types of material:** full-length plays, musicals, solo pieces. **Special interests:** no experimental plays; contemporary works. **Facilities:** Act II Playhouse, 130 seats, black box. **Production considerations:** cast limit of 6, 1 set; low ceiling, limited fly space, approximately 600 square feet. **Best submission time:** year-round. **Response time:** 1 month.

ADIRONDACK THEATRE FESTIVAL

(Founded 1995)

Box 3203; Glens Falls, NY 12801; (518) 798-7479, FAX 793-1334;
      email atf@ATFestival.org; website www.atfestival.org

David Turner, *Producing Director*

Submission procedure: no unsolicited scripts; professional recommendation. **Types of material:** full-length plays, adaptations, musicals, cabaret/revues, solo pieces. **Special interests:** contemporary work. **Facilities:** Charles R. Wood Theater, 280 seats, flexible stage. **Production considerations:** prefers cast limit of 10; no fly space. **Best submission time:** Aug-Jan. **Response time:** 6 months letter; 6 months script.

ADOBE THEATRE COMPANY

(Founded 1991)

138 South Oxford St, #4C; Brooklyn, NY 11217; (718) 398-3698;
      website www.adobe.org

Lisa Timmell, *Literary Manager*

Submission procedure: no unsolicited scripts; synopsis, dialogue sample and letter

of inquiry. **Types of material:** full-length plays, one-acts, adaptations. **Special interests:** comedies that subvert conventional theatrical form and genre. **Facilities:** Ohio Theatre, 75 seats, flexible stage. **Production considerations:** prefers large cast and characters in their thirties. **Best submission time:** Jun–Sep. **Response time:** 4 months letter; 8 months script.

A. D. PLAYERS

(Founded 1967)
2710 West Alabama St; Houston, TX 77098; (713) 526-2721,
    FAX 439-0905; email lee@adplayers.org; website www.adplayers.org
Literary Manager

Submission procedure: no unsolicited scripts; synopsis and dialogue sample. **Types of material:** full-length plays, one-acts, adaptations, plays for young audiences, musicals. **Special interests:** plays for students grades K-8; "plays that uphold family values and support moral decisions that allow for growth of individuals with themselves, others and God"; children's plays which have strong role models; no plays about "witchcraft, demons or ghosts." **Facilities:** Grace Theater, 220 seats, proscenium stage; Rotunda Theater, 148 seats, arena stage. **Production considerations:** for Grace Theater: cast limit of 12, prefers less than 10, no more than 2 sets, maximum height 11' 6"; no fly space. For Rotunda Theater: cast limit of 6, minimal scenery, shows no longer than 90 minutes; no wing space. **Best submission time:** year-round. **Response time:** 10 months. **Special programs:** Theater Arts Academy: includes playwriting classes.

AFRICAN CONTINUUM THEATRE CO. (ACTCO)

(Founded 1996)
3523 12th St NE, 2nd Floor; Washington, DC 20017; (202) 529-5763,
    FAX 529-5782; email info@africancontinuumtheatre.com
Jennifer L. Nelson, *Producing Artistic Director*

Submission procedure: accepts unsolicited scripts; prefers 2-page synopsis and 10-page dialogue sample. **Types of material:** full-length plays, translations, adaptations, musicals. **Special interests:** multicultural work, must be relevant to African-American community. **Facilities:** no permanent facility. **Production considerations:** small cast, single set. **Best submission time:** year-round. **Response time:** 12 months. **Special programs:** Fresh Flavas New Works Program, "designed to give a voice to writers on the fringe of an already marginalized community" through reading series.

ALABAMA SHAKESPEARE FESTIVAL

(Founded 1972)
1 Festival Dr; Montgomery, AL 36117-4605; (334) 271-5300,
    FAX 271-5348; website www.asf.net
Bruce Sevy, *Associate Artistic Director*

Submission procedure: accepts unsolicited scripts for Southern Writers' Project only (see below); agent submission for all other plays. **Types of material:** full-length plays, adaptations, plays for young audiences. **Special interests:** new plays with southern or African-American themes. **Facilities:** Festival Stage, 750 seats, modified thrust stage; Octagon, 225 seats, flexible stage. **Best submission time:** late spring. **Response time:** 12 months. **Special programs:** Southern Writers' Project: develops plays with southern and/or African-American themes; address submissions to Southern Writers' Project.

ALGONKUIN THEATRE COMPANY

(Founded 1993)
1231 Pulaski Blvd; Bellingham, MA 02019; (508) 883-1808;
  email BlackEagle@algonkuin.org; website www.algonkuin.org
Marty BlackEagle-Carl, *Artistic Director*

Submission procedure: no unsolicited scripts; email letter of inquiry only. **Types of material:** full-length plays, one-acts, translations, adaptations. **Special interests:** Native American plays. **Facilities:** Algonkuin Theatre, 150 seats, black box. **Production Considerations:** unit set. **Best submission time:** summer. **Response time:** 1 day email; 1 month script. **Special programs:** Shakespeare-in-the-Park: Shakespearean-type play every summer; *deadline:* summer prior to production.

ALLEY THEATRE

(Founded 1947)
615 Texas Ave; Houston, TX 77002; (713) 228-9341;
  website www.alleytheatre.org
Gregory Boyd, *Artistic Director*

Submission procedure: no unsolicited scripts; professional recommendation. **Types of material:** full-length plays, translations, adaptations, musicals. **Facilities:** Hubbard Stage, 824 seats, thrust stage; Neuhaus Stage, 310 seats, arena/thrust stage. **Best submission time:** year-round. **Response time:** 8 months.

ALLIANCE THEATRE COMPANY

(Founded 1968)
1280 Peachtree St NE; Atlanta, GA 30309; FAX (404) 733-4625;
  website www.alliancetheatre.org
Literary Department

Submission procedure: no unsolicited scripts; synopsis, maximum 10-page dialogue sample and letter of inquiry with SASE for response. **Types of material:** full-length plays, one-acts, plays for young audiences, musicals. **Special interests:** work that speaks to a culturally diverse community; plays with compelling stories and engaging characters told in adventurous ways. **Facilities:** Alliance Stage, 800 seats, proscenium stage; Hertz Stage, 200 seats, flexible stage. **Best submission time:** Mar-Sep. **Response time:** 2 months letter; 6 months script.

ALLIED THEATRE GROUP/STAGE WEST

(Founded 1979)

1300 Gendy St; Fort Worth, TX 76107-4056; (817) 735-9995,
FAX 926-8650; email stgwest@ix.netcom.com;
website www.stagewest.org

Jim Covault, *Artistic Director*

Submission procedure: no unsolicited scripts; synopsis and letter of inquiry. **Types of material:** full-length plays, translations, adaptations. **Special interests:** plays by Texas and Southwest playwrights; Hispanic plays; contemporary issues; Texas and Southwest themes. **Facilities:** Scott Theatre, 580 seats, thrust stage; Sanders Theatre, 100 seats, flexible stage. **Production considerations:** prefers cast limit of 9. **Best submission time:** Jan-Mar. **Response time:** 1 month letter; 3 months script.

AMAS MUSICAL THEATRE, INC.

(Founded 1968)

450 West 42nd St, Suite 2J; New York, NY 10036; (212) 563-2565,
FAX 268-5501; email amas@amasmusical.org;
website www.amasmusical.org

Donna Trinkoff, *Producing Director*

Submission procedure: accepts unsolicited scripts. **Types of material:** musicals, cabaret/revues. **Special interests:** multicultural casts and themes. **Facilities:** no permanent facility; company performs in various proscenium or black box venues with 74-99 seats. **Production considerations:** cast limit of 10. **Best submission time:** summer, winter. **Response time:** 6 months. **Special programs:** Amas Mainstage Productions: 1-2 scripts a year receive 4-week showcase production; Amas Workshop: 1-2 scripts a year receive 2 weeks of rehearsal culminating in public staged reading; Amas Six O'Clock Musical Theatre Lab: 6-8 scripts a year receive minimal rehearsal culminating in public concert reading; writer must supply cast and musical director; Amas provides theatre and publicity.

AMERICAN CONSERVATORY THEATER

(Founded 1965)

30 Grant Ave, 6th Floor; San Francisco, CA 94108-5800;
FAX (415) 433-2711; website www.act-sf.org

Johanna Pfaelzer, *Associate Artistic Director*

Submission procedure: no unsolicited scripts; agents may send synopsis, maximum 10-page dialogue sample and letter of inquiry. **Types of material:** full-length plays, translations, adaptations. **Facilities:** Geary Theater, 1000 seats, proscenium stage. **Best submission time:** year-round. **Response time:** 12 months.

AMERICAN FOLKLORE THEATRE (AFT)

(Founded 1990)
Box 273; Fish Creek, WI 54212; (920) 854–6117, FAX 854–9106;
email aft@folkloretheatre.com; website www.folkloretheatre.com
M. Kaye Christman, *Managing Director*

Submission procedure: no unsolicited scripts; synopsis and letter of inquiry with SASE for response. **Types of material:** full-length plays, one-acts, adaptations, plays for young audiences, musicals. **Special interests:** musicals appropriate for families. **Facilities:** summer: Peninsula State Park Theatre, 800 seats, modified proscenium stage; fall: various town halls, 125-200 seats. **Production considerations:** summer show: cast limit of 10, fall show: cast limit of 4; minimal set. **Best submission time:** year-round. **Response time:** 2 months letter; 3-6 months script. **Special programs:** workshops of new work; potential stipend and/or commission for development; Fred Alley Musical Theatre Award.

AMERICAN MUSIC THEATER FESTIVAL/ PRINCE MUSIC THEATER

(Founded 1984)
100 South Broad St, Suite 650; Philadelphia, PA 19110; (215) 972-1000,
FAX 972-1020; website www.princemusictheater.org

Submission procedure: no unsolicited scripts; synopsis, cassette and letter of inquiry. **Types of material:** music-theatre works including musical comedy, music drama, opera, experimental works, solo pieces. **Facilities:** Prince Music Theater, 450 seats, proscenium stage. **Best submission time:** year-round. **Response time:** 8 months.

AMERICAN REPERTORY THEATRE

(Founded 1979)
64 Brattle St; Cambridge, MA 02138; (617) 495-2668;
website www.amrep.org
Scott Zigler, *Artistic Coordinator, New Play Development*

Submission procedure: no unsolicited scripts; agent submission. **Types of material:** full-length plays, translations, adaptations, musicals, cabaret/revues. **Special interests:** prefers "nonrealistic material that lends itself to extremely theatrical staging." **Facilities:** Loeb Drama Center, 556 seats, flexible stage; Zero Arrow Street Theatre, 300 seats, flexible stage (opening Jan 2005); Church Street Theatre, 200 seats, black box. **Best submission time:** Sep-Jan. **Response time:** 6 months.

AMERICAN STAGE

(Founded 1977)
Box 1560; St. Petersburg, FL 33731; (727) 823-1600,
FAX 821-2444; website www.americanstage.org

Submission procedure: no unsolicited scripts; professional recommendation.

Types of material: full-length plays, adaptations, plays for young audiences. **Facilities:** American Stage, 148 seats, thrust stage. **Production considerations:** cast limit of 8, 1 set. **Best submission time:** year-round. **Response time:** 12 months. **Special programs:** New Visions: play reading series; Shakespeare in the Park series.

AMERICAN THEATER COMPANY

(Founded 1985)
1909 West Byron St; Chicago, IL 60613; (773) 929-6009,
FAX 929-5171; email info@actweb.org; website www.atcweb.org
Damon Kiely, *Artistic Director*

Submission procedure: no unsolicited scripts; synopsis, 10-page sample and letter of inquiry with SASP for response. **Types of material:** full-length plays, translations, adaptations, musicals. **Special interests:** prefers playwright familiar with theatre's mission statement and history (see website); distinctly American, language-oriented plays that utilize heightened theatrical reality; musicals; substantive comedies; social and political themes. **Facilities:** American Theater Company, 109 seats, modified thrust stage. **Production considerations:** prefers cast limit of 15; modest technical demands. **Best submission time:** year-round. **Response time:** 4 months letter; 12 months script.

AMERICAN THEATRE OF ACTORS, INC.

(Founded 1976)
314 West 54th St; New York, NY 10019; (212) 581-3044
James Jennings, *Artistic Director*

Submission procedure: accepts unsolicited scripts. **Types of material:** full-length plays, one-acts. **Special interests:** realistic plays dealing with contemporary social issues. **Facilities:** Chernuchin Theatre, 140 seats, proscenium stage; Sargent Theatre, 65 seats, proscenium stage; Beckmann Theatre, 35 seats, arena stage. **Production considerations:** cast limit of 8; minimal sets. **Best submission time:** year-round. **Response time:** 2 weeks.

THE AQUILA THEATRE COMPANY

(Founded 1991)
58 West 10th St; New York, NY 10011; (212) 992-9642;
email aquilausa6@aol.com; website www.aquilatheatre.com
Jennie Connery, *Production Coordinator*

Submission procedure: no unsolicited scripts; professional recommendation. **Types of material:** full-length plays, one-acts, translations, adaptations, plays for young audiences, movement-based works. **Facilities:** no permanent facility. **Best submission time:** year-round. **Response time:** 3 months.

ARDEN THEATRE COMPANY
(Founded 1988)
40 North 2nd St; Philadelphia, PA 19106; (215) 922-8900,
FAX 922-7011; email dsmeal@ardentheatre.org;
website www.ardentheatre.org
Dennis Smeal, *Literary Manager*

Submission procedure: no unsolicited scripts; 20-page dialogue sample, synopsis, character breakdown, play's developmental history, bio and letter of inquiry by email; agent submissions only should be sent to Amy Dugas Brown, Associate Artistic Director. **Types of material:** full-length plays, translations, adaptations, musicals. **Special interests:** new adaptations of literary works. **Facilities:** Haas Stage/mainstage, 400 seats, flexible stage; Arcadia Stage/studio theatre, 175 seats, flexible stage. **Best submission time:** year-round. **Response time:** 3 months letter; 6 months script.

ARENA STAGE
(Founded 1950)
1101 6th St SW; Washington, DC 20024; (202) 554-9066,
FAX 488-4056
Literary Manager

Submission procedure: no unsolicited scripts; 1-page synopsis, 10-page dialogue sample and bio. **Types of material:** full-length plays, translations, adaptations, musicals. **Special interests:** plays of North and South America, with emphasis on living writers; American themes, history, culture and literary traditions. **Facilities:** Fichandler Stage, 827 seats, arena stage; The Kreeger Theater, 514 seats, modified thrust stage; The Old Vat Room, 110 seats, cabaret stage. **Best submission time:** year-round. **Response time:** 1 week letter; 5 months script. **Special programs:** Downstairs series: new play development initiative; scripts selected through theatre's normal submission procedure.

ARIZONA THEATRE COMPANY
(Founded 1966)
Box 1631; Tucson, AZ 85702-1631; (520) 884-8210
Jennifer Bazzell, *Literary Department*

Submission procedure: no unsolicited scripts; synopsis, 10-page dialogue sample, production history, resume and letter of inquiry. **Types of material:** full-length plays, translations, adaptations, musicals. **Facilities:** Herberger Theater Center (in Phoenix), 800 seats, proscenium stage; Temple of Music and Art (in Tucson), 600 seats, proscenium stage. **Best submission time:** spring–summer. **Response time:** 1 month letter; 6 months script. **Special programs:** National Latino Playwriting Award (see Prizes).

ARKANSAS ART CENTER CHILDREN'S THEATRE

(Founded 1979)

Box 2137; Little Rock, AR 72202; (501) 372-4000;
    email banderson@arkarts.com; website www.arkarts.com

Bradley Anderson, *Artistic Director*

Submission procedure: no unsolicited scripts; professional recommendation. **Types of material:** full-length plays, one-acts, adaptations, plays for young audiences, musicals. **Facilities:** Arkansas Art Center, 348 seats, proscenium stage; studio, 150 seats, flexible stage. **Best submission time:** Nov–Dec. **Response time:** 4 months.

ARKANSAS REPERTORY THEATRE

(Founded 1976)

Box 110; Little Rock, AR 72203-0110; (501) 378-0445,
    FAX 378-0012

Brad Mooy, *Literary Manager*

Submission procedure: no unsolicited scripts; synopsis and letter of inquiry. **Types of material:** full-length plays, musicals, cabaret/revues, solo pieces. **Facilities:** Arkansas Repertory Theatre, 354 seats, proscenium stage; Second Stage, 99 seats, black box. **Production considerations:** prefers small cast. **Best submission time:** year-round. **Response time:** 3 months letter; 6 months script. **Special programs:** New Play Reading Series

ARTISTS REPERTORY THEATRE

(Founded 1981)

1516 Southwest Alder St; Portland, OR 97205; (503) 241-9807,
    FAX 241-8268; email allen@artistsrep.org; website www.artistsrep.org

Allen Nause, *Artistic Director*

Submission procedure: no unsolicited scripts; synopsis and letter of inquiry. **Types of material:** full-length plays, adaptations. **Facilities:** Reiersgaard Theatre, 170 seats, black box. **Production considerations:** cast limit of 13. **Best submission time:** year-round. **Response time:** 1 month letter; 6 months script. **Special programs:** Play Lab: staged reading series.

ART STATION

(Founded 1986)

Box 1998; Stone Mountain, GA 30086; (770) 469-1105,
    FAX 469-0355; email jon@artstation.org;
    website www.artstation.org

Jon Goldstein, *Literary Manager*

Submission procedure: accepts unsolicited scripts; prefers synopsis and dialogue sample. **Types of material:** full-length plays, adaptations, musicals, solo pieces. **Special interests:** works not produced professionally; plays by southern playwrights, or which describe the southern experience. **Facilities:** ART Station

Theatre, 108 seats, proscenium/thrust stage. **Production considerations:** cast limit of 6, single set; no fly space. **Best submission time:** Jun–Dec. **Response time:** 8 months. **Special programs:** ART Station Playwrights Project: year-round playwrights group meets bimonthly to critique and develop new works; presents monthly staged readings.

ARVADA CENTER FOR THE ARTS & HUMANITIES
(Founded 1976)
6901 Wadsworth Blvd; Arvada, CO 80003; (720) 898-7285,
   FAX 898-7217; website www.arvadacenter.org
Kathy Kuehn, *Performing Arts Director*

Submission procedure: no unsolicited scripts; synopsis and letter of inquiry. **Types of material:** plays for young audiences only. **Special interests:** plays for preschool-grade 6. **Facilities:** Arvada Center Amphitheater, 1200 seats, proscenium stage; Arvada Center Main Stage, 498 seats, thrust stage. **Production considerations:** cast limit of 6-9, minimal set. **Best submission time:** Sep–Mar. **Response time:** 5 months letter; 8 months script.

ASIAN AMERICAN THEATER COMPANY
(Founded 1973)
690 5th St, Suite 211; San Francisco, CA 94107; (415) 543-5738,
   FAX 543-5638; email info@asianamericantheater.org;
   website www.asianamericantheater.org
Sean Lim, *Managing Artistic Director*

Submission procedure: accepts unsolicited scripts with synopsis, character breakdown, resume and letter of inquiry. **Types of material:** full-length plays, adaptations, comedy sketches. **Special interests:** innovative new voices reflecting America's Asian heritage; satire based on race and ethnicity; modern Asian-American kitchen-sink drama; romantic comedies. **Facilities:** no permanent facility. **Best submission time:** year-round. **Response time:** 6 months.

ASOLO THEATRE COMPANY
(Founded 1960)
5555 North Tamiami Trail; Sarasota, FL 34243-2141; (941) 351-9010,
   FAX 351-5796; email bruce_rodgers@asolo.org;
   website www.asolo.org
Bruce E. Rodgers, *Associate Artistic Director*

Submission procedure: no unsolicited scripts; 1-page synopsis and letter of inquiry with SASE for response. **Types of material:** full-length plays, translations, adaptations, solo pieces. **Facilities:** The Mertz Theatre, 499 seats, proscenium stage; The Cook Theatre, 161 seats, proscenium stage. **Best submission time:** Jun–Aug. **Response time:** 2 months letter; 6 months script.

ATLANTIC THEATER COMPANY

(Founded 1984)

336 West 20th St; New York, NY 10011; (212) 645-8015,

FAX 645-8755; website www.atlantictheater.org

Christian Parker, *Director of New Play Development*

Submission procedure: no unsolicited scripts; agent submission. **Types of material:** full-length plays, adaptations, musicals. **Facilities:** Atlantic Theater Mainstage, 180 seats, proscenium stage; Black Box, 70 seats, proscenium stage. **Production considerations:** small cast musicals. **Best submission time:** year-round. **Response time:** 6 months. **Special programs:** Atlantic 453: year-round play readings, workshops and productions in Black Box.

ATTIC THEATRE AND FILM CENTER

(Founded 1987)

5429 West Washington Blvd; Los Angeles, CA 90016; (323) 525-0600;

email AtticTheatre@aol.com; website www.AtticTheatre.org

James Carey, *Producing Artistic Director*

Submission procedure: no unsolicited scripts; synopsis, dialogue sample and letter of inquiry with SASE for response. **Types of material:** full-length plays, one-acts. **Facilities:** Attic Theatre and Film Center, 49 seats, flexible stage. **Production considerations:** simple sets; no fly or wing space. **Best submission time:** year-round. **Response time:** 3 months letter; 6 months script. **Special programs:** developmental workshops; reading series; Attic Theatre Ensemble's One-Act Marathon (see Prizes).

AURORA THEATRE COMPANY

(Founded 1992)

2081 Addison St; Berkeley, CA 94704; (510) 843-4042,

FAX 843-4826; website www.auroratheatre.org

Literary Manager

Submission procedure: no unsolicited scripts; synopsis and letter of inquiry. **Types of material:** full-length plays, adaptations. **Special interests:** plays emphasizing language and ideas. **Facilities:** Aurora Theatre, 150 seats, arena stage. **Production considerations:** cast limit of 8; minimal production demands. **Best submission time:** year-round. **Response time:** 6 months letter; 6 months script.

AURORA THEATRE, INC.

(Founded 1999)

3087 B Main St; Duluth, GA 30096; (770) 476-7926;

email info@auroratheatre.com; website www.auroratheatre.com

Anthony Rodriguez, *Producing Artistic Director*

Submission procedure: accepts unsolicited scripts with bio; include cassette or CD with script containing at least 1 song for musicals. **Types of material:** full-length plays, musicals. **Special interests:** Hispanic plays in English or Spanish; plays appealing to all ages. **Facilities:** mainstage, 200 seats, thrust stage. **Production**

consideration: prefers small cast, simple set; no fly space. **Best submission time:** year-round. **Response time:** 3 months.

BAILIWICK REPERTORY

(Founded 1982)
Bailiwick Arts Center; 1229 West Belmont; Chicago, IL 60657-3205;
    (773) 883-1090; email bailiwickr@aol.com; website www.bailiwick.org
Bo List, *Associate Artistic Director*

Submission procedure: varies with each program; submission guidelines available on web. **Types of material:** full-length plays, translations, adaptations, musicals, solo pieces. **Special interests:** theatrically inventive and/or politically intriguing works; work appropriate for Deaf Bailiwick Artists, especially work by deaf or hard-of-hearing writers. **Facilities:** mainstage, 150 seats, flexible/thrust stage; cabaret/studio, 100 seats, flexible stage. **Best submission time:** year-round. **Response time:** 8-12 months. **Special programs:** Pride Performance Series: year-round exploration of works of interest to lesbian and gay communities, culminating in summer festival. Director's Festival: annual directors' showcase of one-act plays, 10-50 minutes long. Workshop Series: workshops and readings of plays, performance pieces and musicals.

BARKSDALE THEATRE

(Founded 1953)
1601 Willow Lawn Dr, Suite 301E; Richmond, VA 23230; (804) 282-9440,
    FAX 288-6470; website www.barksdalerichmond.org
Bruce Miller, *Artistic Director*

Submission procedure: no unsolicited scripts; synopsis and letter of inquiry. **Types of material:** full-length plays. **Facilities:** mainstage, 207 seats, thrust stage. **Production considerations:** small cast; no fly or wing space. **Best submission time:** year-round. **Response time:** 6 months letter; 12 months script.

BARRINGTON STAGE COMPANY

(Founded 1995)
Box 1205; Sheffield, MA 01257; (413) 528-8806, FAX 528-8807;
    email bsc@berkshire.net; website www.barringtonstageco.org
Literary Manager

Submission procedure: no unsolicited scripts; 1-page synopsis, 10-page dialogue sample and letter of inquiry; include cassette or CD for musicals. **Types of material:** full-length plays, translations, adaptations, musicals, cabaret/revues, solo pieces. **Facilities:** Consolati Performing Arts Center, 460 seats, proscenium stage; Stage II, 100 seats, thrust stage. **Production considerations:** cast limit of 4-8 for plays, cast limit of 15-16 for musicals; modest set requirements. **Best submission time:** fall. **Response time:** 1 month letter; 6 months script. **Special programs:** The Musical Theatre Genesis Project program for developing new musicals: selected script receives public reading, possible honorarium contingent on funding; *deadline:* 1 Feb 2005.

THE BARROW GROUP

(Founded 1986)

312 West 36th St, #4W; New York, NY 10018; (212) 760-2615,
FAX 760-2962; email barrowgroup@barrowgroup.org;
website www.barrowgroup.org

K. Lorrell Manning, *Literary Manager*

Submission Procedure: no unsolicited scripts; synopsis and letter of inquiry. **Types of material:** full-length plays, one-acts, translations, adaptations. **Facilities:** loft, 99 seats, black box; studio, 35 seats, flexible stage. **Best submission time:** year-round. **Response time:** 1 month letter; 4 months script. **Special programs:** Short Stuff: short play festival (1 Jan-1 Mar).

BARTER THEATRE

(Founded 1933)

Box 867; Abingdon, VA 24212-0867; (276) 628-2281,
FAX 619-3335; email barter@naxs.com;
website www.bartertheatre.com

Richard Rose, *Producing Artistic Director*

Submission procedure: no unsolicited scripts; synopsis, dialogue sample and letter of inquiry; include cassette for musicals. **Types of material:** full-length plays, translations, adaptations, plays for young audiences, musicals. **Special interests:** social issues and current events; works that expand theatrical form; nonurban-oriented material. **Facilities:** Barter Theatre, 508 seats, proscenium stage; Barter's Stage II, 140 seats, flexible stage. **Production considerations:** cast limit of 4-10. **Best submission time:** Mar, Sep. **Response time:** 9 months letter; 12 months script. **Special programs:** Barter's Early Stages: script development program; Appalachian Festival of Plays & Playwrights.

BAY STREET THEATRE

(Founded 1991)

Box 810; Sag Harbor, NY 11963; (631) 725-0818, FAX 725-0906;
website www.baystreet.org

Mia Emlen Grosjean, *Literary Manager*

Submission procedure: no unsolicited scripts; agent submission. **Types of material:** full-length plays, musicals, solo pieces. **Special interests:** plays that challenge as well as entertain; plays that "address the heart of our community and champion the human spirit." **Facilities:** mainstage, 299 seats, thrust stage. **Production considerations:** cast limit of 8-9, prefers unit set, small-scale musicals only; no fly or wing space. **Best submission time:** year-round. **Response time:** 6 months. **Special programs:** play reading series: readings of 2 new plays each fall and spring; playwright receives $50 honorarium and travel from New York City; scripts for special programs selected through theatre's normal submission procedure.

BERKELEY REPERTORY THEATRE

(Founded 1968)

2025 Addison St; Berkeley, CA 94702; (510) 647-2900, FAX 647-2910;
email ngalland@berkeleyrep.org; website www.berkeleyrep.org

Nicole Galland, *Literary Manager/Dramaturg*

Submission procedure: accepts unsolicited scripts from Bay Area playwrights only; professional recommendation or agent submission for all others. **Types of material:** full-length plays, translations, adaptations. **Facilities:** Roda Theatre, 600 seats, proscenium stage; Mark Taper Stage, 400 seats, thrust stage. **Best submission time:** year-round. **Response time:** 6 months.

BERKSHIRE THEATRE FESTIVAL

(Founded 1928)

Box 797; Stockbridge, MA 01262; (413) 298-5536, FAX 298-3368;
email admin@berkshiretheatre.org; website www.berkshiretheatre.org

Kate Maguire, *Executive Director*

Submission procedure: no unsolicited scripts; agent submission. **Types of material:** full-length plays, musicals, solo pieces. **Facilities:** Playhouse, 450 seats, proscenium stage; Unicorn Theatre, 122 seats, thrust stage. **Production considerations:** small orchestra for musicals. **Best submission time:** Oct-Dec. **Response time:** 12 months.

BILINGUAL FOUNDATION OF THE ARTS

(Founded 1973)

421 North Ave 19; Los Angeles, CA 90031; (323) 225-4044,
FAX 225-1250

Margarita Galban, *Artistic Director*

Submission procedure: accepts unsolicited scripts. **Types of material:** full-length plays, translations, adaptations, plays for young audiences. **Special interests:** plays by Hispanic playwrights or with Hispanic themes only. **Facilities:** BFA Theatre, 99 seats, thrust stage; uses other venues in Los Angeles for some mainstage productions. **Production considerations:** cast limit of 10, simple set. **Best submission time:** year-round. **Response time:** 3-6 months.

BLOOMSBURG THEATRE ENSEMBLE

(Founded 1978)

226 Center St; Bloomsburg, PA 17815; (570) 784-5530,
FAX 784-4912; website www.bte.org

Play Selection Chair

Submission procedure: no unsolicited scripts; synopsis, dialogue sample, professional recommendation and letter of inquiry. **Types of material:** full-length plays, translations, adaptations. **Special interests:** new translations of classics; rural themes; plays suitable for small acting ensemble. **Facilities:** Alvina Krause Theatre, 350 seats, proscenium stage. **Production considerations:** small to mid-sized cast, 1 set or unit set. **Best submission time:** summer. **Response time:** 3 months letter; 6 months script.

BOARSHEAD THEATER

(Founded 1966)

425 South Grand Ave; Lansing, MI 48933; (517) 484-7800, FAX 484-2564

Geoffrey Sherman, *Artistic Director*

Submission procedure: no unsolicited scripts; synopsis, character breakdown, 6-10-page dialogue sample and letter of inquiry with SASP for response. **Types of material:** full-length plays, plays for young audiences. **Special interests:** one-act plays for young audiences only; social issues; comedies; plays that make use of theatrical conventions or create new ones. **Facilities:** Center for the Arts, 249 seats, thrust stage. **Production considerations:** cast limit of 4-6 for children's shows. **Best submission time:** year-round. **Response time:** 1 month letter; 6 months script. **Special programs:** staged readings of 5 new plays a year.

BORDERLANDS THEATER

(Founded 1986)

Box 2791; Tucson, AZ 85702; (520) 882-8607, FAX 884-4264;
    email bltheater@aol.com

Submission procedure: no unsolicited scripts; synopsis and letter of inquiry. **Types of material:** full-length plays, translations, adaptations. **Special interests:** cultural diversity; race relations; "border" issues, including concerns of the geographical border region as well as the metaphorical borders of gender, class and race. **Facilities:** no permanent facility. **Production considerations:** cast limit of 12; minimal set. **Best submission time:** year-round. **Response time:** 1 month letter; 6 months script.

BOSTON THEATRE WORKS

(Founded 1998)

325 Columbus Ave, Suite 11; Boston, MA 02116; (617) 728-4321,
    FAX 262-8633; email litmanager@bostontheatreworks.com;
    website www.bostontheatreworks.com

Literary Office

Submission procedure: no unsolicited scripts; synopsis, 10-page dialogue sample and letter of inquiry. **Types of material:** full-length plays, one-acts, translations, adaptations, musicals, solo pieces. **Special interests:** non-traditional, socially relevant, ethnically diverse plays. **Facilities:** mainstage, 176 seats, proscenium stage; second stage, 80 seats, flexible stage. **Best submission time:** Sep-Jan. **Response time:** 6 months letter; 9 months script. **Special programs:** BTW Unbound : annual festival of new works; 4-6 plays receive public reading followed by audience discussion, primarily interested in plays that push the boundaries of traditional narrative form; send SASE for guidelines; *deadline:* 1 Jan 2005.

BRAT PRODUCTIONS
(Founded 1998)
340 North 12th St, Suite 417; Philadelphia, PA 19107; (215) 413-0975,
FAX 413-0976; email info@bratproductions.org;
website www.bratproductions.org

Submission procedure: no unsolicited scripts; synopsis, dialogue sample and letter of inquiry. **Types of material:** full-length plays, translations, adaptations, musicals, solo pieces. **Special interests:** "material that connects with audiences in new and unique ways." **Facilities:** no permanent facility. **Production considerations:** cast limit of 5, prefers unit set. **Best submission time:** summer. **Response time:** 1 month letter; 6 months script.

BRAVA! FOR WOMEN IN THE ARTS
(Founded 1986)
2781 24th St; San Francisco, CA 94110; (415) 641-7657,
FAX 641-7684; email info@brava.org; website www.brava.org
Literary Manager

Submission procedure: no unsolicited scripts; synopsis, dialogue sample and letter of inquiry. **Types of material:** full-length plays, one-acts, plays for young audiences. **Special interests:** premieres by women of color; lesbian playwrights. **Facilities:** Brava Theater Center, 371 seats, thrust stage; second theater, 100 seats, flexible black box. **Best submission time:** year-round. **Response time:** 6 months letter; 8 months script. **Special programs:** year-round playwriting and performance classes for young artists. Adult playwriting workshops. S.F. Running Crew: technical theatre training program for youth.

BRISTOL RIVERSIDE THEATRE
(Founded 1986)
Box 1250; Bristol, PA 19007; (215) 785-6664, FAX 785-2762;
email brtboss@aol.com; website www.brtstage.org
Maribeth Maksymowich, *Artistic Administrator*

Submission procedure: accepts unsolicited scripts. **Types of material:** full-length plays, one-acts, translations, adaptations, musicals, solo pieces. **Special interests:** cutting-edge works; plays that experiment with form; translations; musicals. **Facilities:** Bristol Riverside Theatre, 302 seats, flexible stage. **Production considerations:** cast limit of 10 for plays, 18 for musicals, 9 for orchestra; prefers smaller cast and orchestra; minimal production demands. **Best submission time:** spring. **Response time:** 18 months. **Special programs:** year-round reading series.

THE B STREET THEATRE

(Founded 1991)

2711 B St; Sacramento, CA 95816; (916) 443-5391, FAX 443-0874;
email rhellesen@bstreettheatre.org; website www.bstreettheatre.org
Buck Busfield, *Artistic Director*

Submission procedure: no unsolicited scripts; agent submission. **Types of material:** full-length plays. **Special interests:** contemporary comedies and dramas. **Facilities:** The B Street Theatre, 150 seats, black box. **Production considerations:** cast limit of 6, modest production demands; no fly space. **Best submission time:** year-round. **Response time:** 6 months.

BURNING COAL THEATRE COMPANY

(Founded 1995)

Box 90904; Raleigh, NC 27675-0904; website www.burningcoal.org
Joseph Megel, *Director of New Play Development*

Submission procedure: accepts unsolicited scripts with SASE for response. **Types of material:** full-length plays. **Special interests:** literate, politically interesting and socially challenging works; preference given to North Carolina playwrights; works 90 minutes or shorter only. **Facilities:** Rialto Theater, 350 seats, proscenium stage. **Best submission time:** 1 Jan-1 May. **Response time:** 1 month letter; 6 months script.

CALIFORNIA THEATRE CENTER

(Founded 1976)

Box 2007; Sunnyvale, CA 94087; (408) 245-2979, FAX 245-0235;
email ctc@ctcinc.org; website www.ctcinc.org
Will Huddleston, *Resident Director*

Submission procedure: accepts unsolicited scripts; prefers synopsis and letter of inquiry. **Types of material:** plays for young audiences. **Special interests:** classics adapted for young audiences; adaptations of literature, historical material. **Facilities:** company primarily tours to large proscenium-stage theatres; Sunnyvale Performing Arts Center (home theatre), 200 seats, proscenium stage. **Production considerations:** cast limit of 8 for professional touring productions, minimum cast of 15 for conservatory productions, modest production demands. **Best submission time:** year-round. **Response time:** 1 month letter; 4-6 months script.

CAMELOT THEATRE

(Formerly Actors' Theatre)
(Founded 1983)

Box 780; Talent, OR 97540; (541) 535-5250; website www.attalent.org
Creighton D. Barnes, *President*

Submission procedure: no unsolicited scripts; synopsis, dialogue sample and letter of inquiry. **Types of material:** full-length plays, one-acts, translations, adaptations. **Facilities:** Actors' Theatre, 108 seats, thrust stage. **Best submission time:** year-round. **Response time:** 3 months letter; 4 months script.

THE CAPE COD THEATRE PROJECT

(Founded 1994)

259 West 4th St, #19; New York, NY 10014; (508) 457-4242;
email pjmckey@adelphia.net; website www.capecodtheatreproject.org

Andrew Polk, *Artistic Director*

Submission procedure: accepts unsolicited scripts; prefers professional recommendation or agent submission. **Types of material:** full-length plays, musicals, solo pieces. **Special interests:** contemporary American plays. **Facilities:** Falmouth Academy, 160 seats, proscenium stage. **Production considerations:** minimal staging. **Best submission time:** Aug–Feb. **Response time:** 2 months.

CAPITAL REPERTORY THEATRE

(Founded 1981)

111 North Pearl St; Albany, NY 12207; (518) 462-4531, ext 219,
FAX 465-0213

Margaret Mancinelli-Cahill, *Producing Artistic Director*

Submission procedure: no unsolicited scripts; agent submission. **Types of material:** full-length plays, translations, adaptations, musicals. **Special interests:** ethnically diverse works. **Facilities:** Capital Repertory Theatre, 299 seats, thrust stage. **Production considerations:** prefers small cast. **Best submission time:** late spring. **Response time:** 9 months.

CELEBRATION THEATRE

(Founded 1982)

7985 Santa Monica Blvd, Suite 109-1; West Hollywood, CA 90046;
(323) 957-1884, FAX 957-1826; email celebrationthtr@earthlink.net;
website www.celebrationtheatre.com

Literary Manager

Submission procedure: accepts unsolicited scripts; prefers letter of inquiry with SASE for response. **Types of material:** full-length plays, one-acts, adaptations, musicals, cabaret/revues. **Special interests:** plays not previously produced on the West Coast with gay and lesbian themes. **Facilities:** Celebration Theatre, 65 seats, thrust stage. **Production considerations:** cast limit of 12, single set. **Best submission time:** year-round. **Response time:** 6 months.

CENTER STAGE

(Founded 1963)

700 North Calvert St; Baltimore, MD 21202-3686; (410) 685-3200,
FAX 539-3912; email madeleine@centerstage.org

Madeleine Oldham, *Literary Manager*

Submission procedure: no unsolicited scripts; synopsis, dialogue sample and letter of inquiry. **Types of material:** full-length plays, translations, adaptations, musicals, solo pieces. **Special interests:** plays with no previous mainstage production; plays about the African-American experience. **Facilities:** Pearlstone Theater, 541 seats, modified thrust stage; Head Theater, 300 seats, flexible stage. **Best submission time:** year-round. **Response time:** 7 weeks letter; 6 months script.

CENTRE STAGE–SOUTH CAROLINA!

(Founded 1983)

Box 8451; Greenville, SC 29604-8451; (864) 233-6733,
> FAX 233-3901; email information@centrestage.org;
> website www.centrestage.org

Douglas P. McCoy, *Executive Artistic Director*

Submission procedure: accepts unsolicited scripts. **Types of material:** full-length plays. **Special interests:** works not previously produced. **Facilities:** mainstage, 292 seats, thrust stage. **Production considerations:** single set, no fly space, limited wing space. **Best submission time:** year-round. **Response time:** 2 months. **Special programs:** Readers' Theatre: regularly scheduled rehearsed readings presented for public followed by audience discussion. New Playwrights Festival: 6 plays presented annually with winner receiving production in next season; *dates:* Aug.

THE CENTER THEATER COMPANY

(Formerly Tampa Bay Performing Arts Center)

(Founded 1987)

1010 North W. C. MacInnes Place; Tampa, FL 33602;
> (813) 222-1000, FAX 222-1057; website www.tbpac.org

Karla Hartley, *Artistic Associate*

Submission procedure: accepts unsolicited scripts. **Types of material:** full-length plays. **Special interests:** plays by women writers. **Facilities:** Carol Morsani Hall, 2500 seats, proscenium stage; Ferguson Hall, 1000 seats, proscenium stage; Jaeb, 300 seats, proscenium stage; Shimberg Playhouse, 150 seats, black box. **Production considerations:** small cast, 1 set. **Best submission time:** summer. **Response time:** 2 months.

CHARLESTON STAGE

(Founded 1977)

Box 356; Charleston, SC 29402; (843) 577-5967, FAX 577-5422;
> email cstage@charlestonstage.com; website www.charlestonstage.com

Julian Wiles, *Producing Artistic Director*

Submission procedure: no unsolicited scripts; professional recommendation with SASE for response. **Types of material:** full-length plays. **Facilities:** The Historic Dock Street Theatre, 450 seats, proscenium stage. **Production considerations:** prefers small cast. **Best submission time:** year-round. **Response time:** 2 months.

CHERRY LANE THEATRE

(Founded 1997)
38 Commerce St; New York, NY 10014; (212) 989-2020,
FAX 989-2867; email company@cherrylanetheatre.org;
website www.cherrylanetheatre.org
Dave Batan, *Operations Manager*

Submission procedure: no unsolicited scripts; submissions should be sent to nominating committee (see website) and will be considered for Mentor Project only. **Types of material:** full-length plays. **Facilities:** Cherry Lane Theatre, 178 seats, proscenium stage; Studio Theatre, 60 seats, black box. **Best submission time:** Mar-Jun. **Response time:** Oct. **Special programs:** Mentor Project: 3 writers work with master playwright for a season. Celebrating Women Playwrights and Celebrating Black Playwrights, plays chosen from Mentor Project submissions. Some semifinalists from Mentor Project will be considered for Tongues Play Reading Series.

THE CHILDREN'S THEATRE COMPANY

(Founded 1965)
2400 Third Ave S; Minneapolis, MN 55404-3597; (612) 874-0500,
FAX 874-8119
Elissa Adams, *Director of New Play Development*

Submission procedure: no unsolicited scripts; agent submission. **Types of material:** plays for young audiences including full-length plays, adaptations, musicals. **Special interests:** work samples from writers with no previous experience writing for children's theatre who have interest in the field. **Facilities:** Children's Theatre Company, 745 seats, proscenium stage. **Best submission time:** Jul-Feb. **Response time:** 6 months. **Special programs:** Threshold: 1-4 works for young audiences commissioned each year for development and production.

CHILDSPLAY

(Founded 1977)
Box 517; Tempe, AZ 85280; (402) 350-8101, FAX 350-8584
David Saar, *Artistic Director*

Submission procedure: no unsolicited scripts; synopsis, 10-page dialogue sample and letter of inquiry. **Types of material:** plays for young audiences including full-length plays, adaptations, musicals, performance art. **Special interests:** nontraditional plays; material that entertains and challenges both performers and audiences; 2nd and 3rd productions of unpublished work. **Facilities:** Herberger Theater Center Stage, 800 seats, proscenium stage; Scottsdale Center for the Arts, 800 seats, proscenium stage; Stage West, 350 seats, proscenium stage; Tempe Performing Arts Center, 175 seats, black box; also performs in Tucson (no permanent space). **Production considerations:** some van-sized touring productions. **Best submission time:** Jun-Oct. **Response time:** 1 month letter; 3 months script. **Special programs:** commissioning program.

CIDER MILL PLAYHOUSE

(Founded 1976)

Box 482; 2 South Nanticoke Ave; Endicott, NY 13760; (607) 748-7363

Mark Bader, *Dramaturg*

Submission procedure: no unsolicited scripts; agent submission with SASE for response. **Types of material:** full-length plays, translations, adaptations. **Facilities:** Cider Mill Playhouse, 287 seats, thrust stage. **Production considerations:** prefers small cast, single or unit set; no fly space. **Best submission time:** Sep-Dec. **Response time:** 6 months.

CINCINNATI PLAYHOUSE IN THE PARK

(Founded 1960)

Box 6537; Cincinnati, OH 45206-0537; (513) 345-2242;

website www.cincyplay.com

Edward Stern, *Producing Artistic Director*

Submission procedure: no unsolicited scripts; synopsis, 10-page dialogue sample, character breakdown, resume, list of previous productions and letter of inquiry; include CD or cassette for musicals. **Types of material:** full-length plays, translations, adaptations, musicals. **Special Interests:** previously unproduced works that take linguistic and/or stylistic risks. **Facilities:** Robert S. Marx Theatre, 626 seats, thrust stage; Thompson Shelterhouse, 225 seats, thrust stage. **Best submission time:** year-round. **Response time:** 3 months letter; 6 months script.

CINCINNATI SHAKESPEARE FESTIVAL

(Founded 1993)

717-719 Race St; Cincinnati, OH 45202; (513) 381-2289, FAX 381-2298;

email csfed@cincyshakes.com; website www.cincyshakes.com

Brian Isaac Phillips, *Artistic Director*

Submission procedure: no unsolicited scripts; synopsis, first 20 pages of dialogue and letter of inquiry. **Types of material:** full-length plays, translations, adaptations, solo pieces. **Special interests:** language plays, heightened text. **Facilities:** Cincinnati Shakespeare Festival Theater, 180 seats, thrust stage. **Production considerations:** minimal production demands. **Best submission time:** spring-summer. **Response time:** 2 months letter; 6 months script. **Special programs:** CSF Studio (see Development).

CITY GARAGE

(Founded 1987)

Box 2016; Santa Monica, CA 90406; (310) 319-9939, FAX 396-1040;

email citygarage@earthlink.net; website www.citygarage.org

Paul Rubenstein, *Literary Manager*

Submission procedure: no unsolicited scripts; synopsis and letter of inquiry. **Types of material:** full-length plays, translations, adaptations. **Special interests:** nonrealistic experimental work only; no family dramas, personal or confessional plays. **Facilities:** City Garage, 48 seats, thrust stage. **Production considerations:**

single set. **Best submission time:** year-round. **Response time:** 2 weeks letter; 6 weeks script.

CITY THEATRE

(Founded 1996)
444 Brickell Ave, Suite 229; Miami, FL 33131; (305) 755-9401,
FAX 755-9404; email info@citytheatre.com;
website www.citytheatre.com
Stephanie Norman, *Producing Artistic Director*

Submission procedure: accepts unsolicited scripts. **Types of material:** one-acts; include cassette for musicals. **Special interests:** plays that represent a diverse mix of subject matters, styles and genres including comedies, dramas, farces, monologues and musicals; bilingual plays, especially Spanish/English, encouraged. **Facilities:** Broward Center/Amaturo, 580 seats, proscenium stage; Ring Theatre, 300 seats, prosceium/thrust; various school and community venues, 30-200 seats. **Production considerations:** cast limit of 8, plays performed by multicultural ensemble ages 20-60; prefers simple sets. **Best submission time:** year-round; scripts received by 1 Jul 2005 considered for 2006-07 season. **Response time:** varies; plays for summer announced Apr-May.

CITY THEATRE COMPANY

(Founded 1974)
1300 Bingham St; Pittsburgh, PA 15203; (412) 431-4400,
FAX 431-5535; email caquiline@citytheatrecompany.org;
website www.citytheatrecompany.org
Carlyn Aquiline, *Literary Manager/Dramaturg*

Submission procedure: no unsolicited scripts; synopsis, 15-20-page dialogue sample, character breakdown, resume, development/production history and letter of inquiry with SASE for response; include cassette or CD for musicals. **Types of material:** full-length plays, translations, adaptations, musicals, solo pieces. **Special interests:** plays of substance and ideas; unconventional approach to form, content and/or use of language; plays by underrepresented voices. **Facilities:** Mainstage, 272 seats, flexible stage; Hamburg Studio, 110 seats, thrust stage. **Production considerations:** cast limit of 10, prefers 6 or fewer. **Best submission time:** year-round. **Response time:** 2 months letter; 10 months script. **Special Programs:** City Theatre Young Playwrights: contest with productions for 7th-12th graders in Western Pennsylvania (see website). MOMENTUM-New Plays at Different Stages: annual new play festival of readings, workshops and productions.

CLARENCE BROWN THEATRE COMPANY

(Founded 1974)
206 McClung Tower; Knoxville, TN 37996; (865) 974–6011,
FAX 974–4867; email cbt@utk.edu;
website www.clarencebrowntheatre.org
Blake Robison, *Producing Artistic Director*

Submission procedure: no unsolicited scripts; synopsis, 1–2 page dialogue sample, character breakdown and letter of inquiry. **Types of material:** full-length plays. **Special interests:** contemporary American plays. **Facilities:** Clarence Brown Theatre, 576 seats, proscenium stage; Carousel Theatre, 250 seats, arena stage. **Best submission time:** year-round. **Response time:** 1 month letter; 1 month script.

THE CLEVELAND PLAY HOUSE

(Founded 1916)
8500 Euclid Ave; Cleveland, OH 44106–0189; (216) 795–7000,
FAX 795–7007
Seth Gordon, *Director of New Play Development*

Submission procedure: no unsolicited scripts; synopsis, 10–page dialogue sample, resume and letter of inquiry with SASE for response. **Types of material:** full-length plays, adaptations, musicals. **Facilities:** Kenyon C. Bolton Theatre, 548 seats, proscenium stage; Francis E. Drury Theatre, 504 seats, proscenium stage; Baxter Stage, 300 seats, thrust stage. **Best submission time:** year-round. **Response time:** 2 months letter; 6 months script. **Special programs:** The Next Stage Festival of New Plays (see Development).

CLEVELAND PUBLIC THEATRE

(Founded 1981)
6415 Detroit Ave; Cleveland, OH 44102–3011; (216) 631–2727,
FAX 631–2575; email literary@cptonline.org; website www.cptonline.org
Randy Rollison, *Producing Artistic Director*

Submission procedure: no unsolicited scripts; synopsis, 5–10 page dialogue sample, production history (if any) and letter of inquiry. **Types of material:** full-length plays, one-acts, solo pieces. **Special interests:** experimental, poetic, politically, intellectually and spiritually challenging works; voices not heard in the mainstream (people of color, women, gays and lesbians, seniors, youth under 18; no standard commercial fare or "anything you might see on TV." **Facilities:** Gordon Square Theatre, 220 seats, flexible proscenium; Cleveland Public Theatre, 150–175 seats, flexible proscenium. **Best submission time:** year-round. **Response time:** 2 months letter; 9 months script. **Special programs:** New Plays Festival: biennial 4-week developmental workshops culminating in stage readings; scripts selected through theatre's normal submission procedure; $1000 Frank and Janet Levin Award of Excellence for best new play in festival; *deadline:* Nov 2004; exact date TBA.

COCONUT GROVE PLAYHOUSE

(Founded 1956)

3500 Main Highway; Miami, FL 33133; (305) 442–2662, FAX 444–6437

Arnold Mittelman, *Producing Artistic Director*

Submission procedure: no unsolicited scripts; synopsis and letter of inquiry. **Types of material:** full-length plays, translations, musicals, cabaret/revues. **Special interests:** dramas, musicals. **Facilities:** mainstage, 1100 seats, proscenium stage; Encore Room, 150 seats, cabaret. **Best submission time:** year-round. **Response time:** 3 months letter; 3 months script.

THE COLONY THEATRE COMPANY

(Founded 1975)

555 North Third St; Burbank, CA 91502; (818) 558–7000, FAX 558–7110; email wayneliebman@colonytheatre.org; website www.colonytheatre.org

Wayne Liebman, *Literary Manager*

Submission procedure: no unsolicited scripts; agent submission with 1-page synopsis. **Types of material:** full-length plays, adaptations. **Facilities:** Burbank Center Stage, 276 seats, thrust stage. **Production considerations:** cast limit of 3-12. **Best submission time:** Feb–Nov. **Response time:** 3 months letter; 12 months script.

COLUMBUS CHILDREN'S THEATRE

(Founded 1963)

372 West Nationwide Blvd; Columbus, OH 43215–2310;
(614) 224–6672, FAX 224–8844; email BGShows@aol.com;
website www.colschildrenstheatre.org

William Goldsmith, *Artistic Director*

Submission procedure: accepts unsolicited scripts. **Types of material:** one-acts, plays for young audiences. **Special interests:** social-issue one-acts suitable for touring to schools. **Facilities:** Columbus Children's Theatre, 170 seats, black box/thrust. **Production considerations:** cast limit of 4 for touring productions; prefers unit sets for mainstage season. **Best submission time:** Sep–Nov. **Response time:** 4 months.

COMMONWEAL THEATRE COMPANY

(Founded 1989)

Box 15; Lanesboro, MN 55949; (507) 467–2905, FAX 467–2468;
email info@commonwealtheatre.org;
website www.commonwealtheatre.org

Hal Cropp, *Core Artist*

Submission procedure: no unsolicited scripts; professional recommendation with work sample. **Types of material:** full-length plays, translations, adaptations. **Facilities:** St. Mane Theatre, 126 seats, proscenium stage. **Production**

considerations: prefers cast limit of 9, 1 set; no wing space. **Best submission time:** Aug–Nov. **Response time:** 1 month. **Special programs:** Commonweal New Play Workshop: 4 playwrights contracted to work for 4 weeks each, culminating in public reading, 2 scripts then chosen for additional 1-week workshop, 1 play chosen for full production in subsequent season; plays chosen from theatre's regular submission procedure; playwright receives housing during workshop.

COMPANY OF FOOLS

(Founded 1992)

Box 329; Hailey, ID 83333; (208) 788–6520, FAX 788–1053;
email Denise@companyoffools.org; website www.companyoffools.org
Denise Simone, *Associate Artistic Director*

Submission procedure: no unsolicited scripts; synopsis and letter of inquiry. **Types of material:** full-length plays, one-acts, translations, adaptations, plays for young audiences. **Special interests:** plays with focus on American themes; stories of "the human heart in conflict with itself." **Facilities:** Liberty, 240 seats, proscenium/thrust stage. **Production considerations:** cast limit of 13. **Best submission time:** year-round. **Response time:** 3 months letter; 4 months script.

CONEY ISLAND, USA

(Founded 1980)

1208 Surf Ave; Coney Island, NY 11224; (719) 372–5159, FAX 372–5101;
email dzigun@coneyisland.com; website www.coneyisland.com
Dick D. Zigun, *Artistic Director*

Submission procedure: no unsolicited scripts; synopsis, resume, reviews of prior work and letter of inquiry. **Types of material:** company books already existing productions of plays and performance art. **Special interests:** new and old vaudeville; pop music; pop culture; Americana bizarro. **Facilities:** Sideshows by the Seashore, 99 seats, arena stage; Coney Island Museum, 74 seats, cabaret stage; also open-air performances on streets. **Best submission time:** year-round. **Response time:** 1 month letter; 6 months script.

CONTEMPORARY AMERICAN THEATRE COMPANY

(Founded 1984)

77 South High St; Columbus, OH 43215; (614) 461–1382, FAX 460–7216;
email rgordon@catco.org; website www.catco.org
Robin Gordon, *Artistic Administrator*

Submission procedure: accepts unsolicited scripts; prefers letter of inquiry. **Types of material:** full-length plays, one-acts, adaptations, solo pieces. **Special interests:** mysteries, comedies. **Facilities:** Capitol Theatre, 903 seats, proscenium stage; Studio One, 243 seats, proscenium stage; Studio Two, 147 seats, thrust stage. **Production considerations:** prefers cast limit of 8. **Best submission time:** year-round. **Response time:** 6 months. **Special programs:** The Shorts Festival: biennial festival of 10–15-minute plays with common setting; *deadline:* Dec 2005; *notification:* exact date TBA; *dates:* Apr 2006.

CONTEMPORARY AMERICAN THEATER FESTIVAL

(Founded 1991)
Box 429; Shepherdstown, WV 25443; (304) 876-3473,
FAX 876-5443; website www.catf.org
Ed Herendeen, *Producing Director*

Submission procedure: no unsolicited scripts; synopsis and letter of inquiry. **Types of material:** full-length plays. **Special interests:** new American plays; contemporary issues. **Facilities:** Frank Center Stage, 400 seats, proscenium stage; Studio Theater, 130 seats, black box. **Best submission time:** fall. **Response time:** 3 months letter; 6 months script.

CORNERSTONE THEATER COMPANY

(Founded 1986)
708 Traction Ave; Los Angeles, CA 90013; (213) 613-1700,
FAX 613-1714; email mvaldez@cornerstonetheater.org
Mark Valdez, *Associate Artistic Director*

Submission procedure: no unsolicited scripts; letter of inquiry only. **Types of material:** full-length plays, adaptations, musicals. **Special interests:** company primarily interested in collaborating with playwrights to develop new works or contemporary adaptations of classics, focusing on specific communities. **Facilities:** no permanent facility. **Best submission time:** year-round. **Response time:** 2 months.

THE COTERIE THEATRE

(Founded 1979)
2450 Grand Ave; Kansas City, MO 64108-2520; (816) 474-6785,
FAX 474-7112; email jefchurch@aol.com;
website www.thecoterie.com
Jeff Church, *Producing Artistic Director*

Submission procedure: no unsolicited scripts; synopsis, resume and letter of inquiry with SASE for response. **Types of material:** works for young and family audiences only, including adaptations, musicals and solo pieces. **Special interests:** ground-breaking works only; plays with culturally diverse casts or themes; social issues; adaptations of classic or contemporary literature; musicals. **Facilities:** The Coterie Theatre, 240 seats, flexible stage. **Production considerations:** cast limit of 12, prefers 5-7; no fly or wing space. **Best submission time:** year-round. **Response time:** 8 months letter; 8 months script.

COURT THEATRE

(Founded 1955)
5535 South Ellis Ave; Chicago, IL 60637; (773) 702-0434,
FAX 834-1897

Submission procedure: no unsolicited scripts; synopsis, dialogue sample and letter

of inquiry with email address for response. **Types of material:** translations and adaptations of classic texts only. **Special interests:** infrequently produced or "undiscovered" material. **Facilities:** Abelson Auditorium, 253 seats, thrust stage. **Production considerations:** limited fly space. **Best submission time:** summer. **Response time:** 6 weeks letter; 6 months script.

CUMBERLAND COUNTY PLAYHOUSE

(Founded 1965)

Box 830; Crossville, TN 38557; (931) 484-4324, FAX 484-6299

Jim Crabtree, *Producing Director*

Submission procedure: no unsolicited scripts; synopsis and letter of inquiry. **Types of material:** full-length plays, adaptations, plays for young audiences, musicals. **Special interests:** works for family audiences; works with southern or rural themes; works about Tennessee history or culture. **Facilities:** Cumberland County Playhouse, 490 seats, proscenium stage; Theater-in-the-Woods, 200 seats, outdoor arena; Adventure Theater, 180-220 seats, flexible black box. **Best submission time:** Aug–Dec. **Response time:** 2 weeks letter; 12 months script.

CURIOUS THEATRE COMPANY

(Founded 1997)

1080 Acoma St; Denver, CO 80204; (303) 623-2349, FAX 592-7953;
        email laura@curiousatacoma.com; website www.curiousatacoma.com

Laura Tesman, *Literary Manager*

Submission procedure: no unsolicited scripts; 1-page synopsis, 10-page dialogue sample, resume, developmental history of submitted script and letter of inquiry. **Types of material:** full-length plays, translations, adaptations, solo pieces. **Special interests:** plays with cultural and/or political emphasis; plays with challenging design elements. **Facilities:** Acoma Center, 199 seats, thrust stage. **Production considerations:** cast limit of 8; no fly space. **Best submission time:** year-round. **Response time:** 6 months. **Special programs:** informal developmental workshops; new play reading series; commissioning program.

DAD'S GARAGE THEATRE CO.

(Founded 1995)

280 Elizabeth St, Suite C101; Atlanta, GA 30307; (404) 523-3141,
        FAX 688-6644; email sean@dadsgarage.com;
        website www.dadsgarage.com

Sean Daniels, *Artistic Director*

Submission procedure: accepts unsolicited scripts. **Types of material:** full-length plays, translations, adaptations, musicals, solo pieces. **Special interests:** non-traditional plays, comedy. **Facilities:** Dad's Garage, 160 seats, proscenium stage; Top Shelf, 40 seats, flexible stage. **Best submission time:** year-round. **Response time:** 3 months letter; 3 months script.

DALLAS CHILDREN'S THEATER

(Founded 1984)
The Rosewood Center for Family Arts; 5938 Skillman; Dallas, TX 75231;
website www.dct.org
Artie Olaisen, *Artistic Associate*

Submission procedure: no unsolicited scripts; synopsis, character/set breakdown and letter of inquiry. **Types of material:** full-length plays, adaptations, plays for young audiences. **Special interests:** works for family audiences; adaptations of classics; historical plays; socially relevant works. **Facilities:** El Centro Theater, 500 seats, proscenium stage; Baker Theater, 400 seats, proscenium stage. **Best submission time:** year-round. **Response time:** 3 months letter; 6 months script.

DALLAS THEATER CENTER

(Founded 1959)
3636 Turtle Creek Blvd; Dallas, TX 75219-5598; (214) 526-8210,
FAX 521-7666
Claudia Zelevansky, *Associate Director*

Submission procedure: no unsolicited scripts; professional recommendation. **Types of material:** full-length plays, adaptations, translations, solo pieces. **Special interests:** plays that explore language or form; material relating to the African-American or Hispanic experience. **Facilities:** Arts District Theater, 530 seats, flexible stage; Kalita Humphreys Theater, 466 seats, thrust stage. **Best submission time:** year-round. **Response time:** 12 months.

DELAWARE THEATRE COMPANY

(Founded 1978)
200 Water St; Wilmington, DE 19801-5030; (302) 594-1104,
FAX 594-1107
John Grassilli, *Resident Director*

Submission procedure: no unsolicited scripts; synopsis and letter of inquiry from DE, MD and PA playwrights only. **Types of material:** full-length plays, translations, adaptations. **Facilities:** Delaware Theatre Company, 390 seats, thrust stage. **Production considerations:** cast limit of 10. **Best submission time:** Feb–May. **Response time:** 1 month letter; 3 months script.

THE DELL'ARTE COMPANY

(Founded 1971)
Box 816; Blue Lake, CA 95525; (707) 668-5663, FAX 668-5665;
email dellarte@aol.com; website www.dellarte.com
Michael Fields, *Producing Artistic Director*

Submission procedure: no unsolicited scripts; synopsis and letter of inquiry. **Types of material:** full-length plays, adaptations, plays for young audiences. **Special interests:** physical theatre; new adaptations of classics; physical plays for young audiences. **Facilities:** 400 seats, outdoor amphitheatre; Dell'Arte Players, 100 seats, flexible stage. **Production considerations:** company of 3-4 actors; production demands adaptable to touring. **Best submission time:** Jan-Mar. **Response time:** 3 weeks letter; 6 weeks script.

DENVER CENTER THEATRE COMPANY
(Founded 1979)
1050 13th St; Denver, CO 80204; website www.denvercenter.org
Nagle Jackson, *Director of New Play Development*

Submission procedure: no unsolicited scripts; agent submission. **Types of material:** full-length plays. **Special interests:** work not produced professionally. **Facilities:** The Stage, 642 seats, thrust stage; The Space, 450 seats, arena stage; The Ricketson, 250 seats, proscenium stage; The Source, 200 seats, thrust stage. **Best submission time:** year-round. **Response time:** 6 weeks letter; 6 months script. **Special programs:** WorkingStages: fully rehearsed workshop productions.

DETROIT REPERTORY THEATRE
(Founded 1957)
13103 Woodrow Wilson St; Detroit, MI 48238-3686;
    (313) 868-1347, FAX 868-1705; email DetRepTH@aol.com;
    website www.detroitreptheatre.com
Barbara Busby, *Literary Manager*

Submission procedure: accepts unsolicited scripts. **Types of material:** full-length plays. **Special interests:** issue-oriented plays. **Facilities:** Detroit Repertory Theatre, 194 seats, proscenium stage. **Production considerations:** prefers cast limit of 7. **Best submission time:** Sep-Feb. **Response time:** 6 months.

DOBAMA THEATRE
(Founded 1960)
1846 Coventry Rd; Cleveland Heights, OH 44118; (216) 932-6838,
    FAX 932-3259; website www.dobama.org

Submission procedure: accepts unsolicited scripts from OH playwrights only; others send synopsis, sample pages and letter of inquiry. **Types of material:** full-length plays, solo pieces. **Special interests:** plays with opportunities for ethnically diverse casting; plays that make statement about contemporary life. **Facilities:** Dobama Theatre, 200 seats, thrust stage. **Production considerations:** prefers cast limit of 9, limited production demands; no fly space. **Best submission time:** year-round. **Response time:** 9 months letter; 12 months script. **Special programs:** 1 world premiere: production of 1 new play included in mainstage season each year; preference given to members of Cleveland Play House Playwrights' Unit. Marilyn Bianchi Kids' Playwriting Festival: annual short-play competition open to students attending Cuyahoga County schools, grades 1-12; winners receive savings bonds, publication and/or full production; write for application starting Sep 2004 or visit website for downloadable form; *deadline:* Jan-Feb 2005; exact date TBA.

DORSET THEATRE FESTIVAL

(Founded 1976)

Box 510; Dorset, VT 05251–0510; (802) 867–2223, FAX 867–0144;
 email theatre@sover.net; website www.dorsettheatrefestival.org

William John Aupperlee, *Artistic Director*

Submission procedure: no unsolicited scripts; synopsis, 10-page dialogue sample, character/set breakdown and letter of inquiry with SASP for response; include production history of readings in New York City–New England area if available. **Types of material:** full-length plays. **Special interests:** plays with broad commercial appeal. **Facilities:** Dorset Playhouse, 295 seats, proscenium stage. **Production considerations:** cast limit of 8, prefers 1 set or unit set. **Best submission time:** Sep–Dec. **Response time:** 3 months letter; 12 months script. **Special programs:** Dorset Colony for Writers (see Colonies).

DOUBLE EDGE THEATRE

(Founded 1982)

948 Conway Rd, Ashfield, MA 01330; (413) 628–0277,
 FAX 628–0026; email office@doubleedgetheatre.org;
 website www.doubleedgetheatre.org

Carlos Uriona, *Associate Director*

Submission procedure: no unsolicited scripts; accepts video of original performance only. **Types of material:** solo pieces, performance art. **Special interests:** artists who create their own work, "art theatre." **Facilities:** DET Performance Space, 100 seats, flexible stage; DET Pavillion, 75 seats, flexible stage. **Best submission time:** year-round. **Response time:** 6 months. **Special programs:** internships: 3–12-month program in which artists create original performance work at DET, housing and rehearsal space provided. Training Intensives: 2–5-week intensive work periods with groups of national and international artists. University Programs: touring performances and 2-day–5-week residencies creating original performance work in university settings.

EAST WEST PLAYERS

(Founded 1965)

120 North Judge John Aiso St; Los Angeles, CA 90012; (213) 625–7000,
 FAX 625–7111; email info@eastwestplayers.org;
 website www.eastwestplayers.org

Judy Soo Hoo, *Literary Manager*

Submission procedure: accepts unsolicited scripts with SASE for response. **Types of material:** full-length plays, translations, adaptations, plays for young audiences, musicals. **Special interests:** plays by or about Asian-Pacific Americans. **Facilities:** The David Henry Hwang Theatre at Union Center for the Arts, 265 seats, proscenium stage. **Production considerations:** minimal production demands. **Best submission time:** year-round. **Response time:** 9 months. (See David Henry Hwang Writers Institute in Development.)

ECCENTRIC THEATRE COMPANY

(Founded 1992)

413 D St; Anchorage, AK 99501; (907) 274-2599, FAX 277-4698;
    email cyrano@ak.net; website www.cyranos.org

Sandy Harper, *Producer*

Submission procedure: no unsolicited scripts; professional recommendation. **Types of material:** full-length plays, one-acts, adaptations, solo pieces. **Facilities:** Cyrano's Off Center Playhouse, 86 seats, black box. **Best submission time:** year-round. **Response time:** 8 months.

EGYPTIAN THEATRE COMPANY

(Founded 1981)

Box 3119; Park City, UT 84060; (435) 645-0671, FAX 649-0446;
    email dana@egyptiantheatrecompany.org;
    website www.egyptiantheatrecompany.org

Dana Keiter, *Artistic Director*

Submission procedure: no unsolicited scripts; professional recommendation. **Types of material:** full-length plays, translations, adaptations, plays for young audiences, musicals, cabaret/revues, solo pieces. **Facilities:** Egyptian Theatre, 266 seats, proscenium stage. **Best submission time:** year-round. **Response time:** 3-6 months.

1812 PRODUCTIONS

(Founded 1997)

525 South 4th St, Suite 479; Philadelphia, PA 19147; (215) 592-9560,
    FAX 592-9580; email info@1812productions.org;
    website www.1812productions.org

Jennifer Childs, *Artistic Director*

Submission procedure: accepts unsolicited scripts. **Types of material:** full-length plays, translations, adaptations, musicals, cabaret/revues, solo performance. **Special interests:** comedies only. **Facilities:** Adrienne Theatre, 106 seats, proscenium stage. **Best submission time:** summer. **Response time:** 3 months.

EL CENTRO SU TEATRO

(Founded 1971)

4725 High St; Denver, CO 80216; (303) 296-0219, FAX 296-4614;
    email elcentro@suteatro.org; website www.suteatro.org

Tony Garcia, *Artistic Director*

Submission procedure: accepts unsolicited scripts. **Types of material:** full-length plays, one-acts, translations, adaptations, plays for young audiences. **Special interests:** bilingual and/or Spanish-language plays; plays dealing with the Chicano/Latino cultural aesthetic and political experience. **Facilities:** mainstage, 107 seats, black box. **Production considerations:** cast limit of 6-8; minimal production requirements. **Best submission time:** Oct–Jan. **Response time:** 6 months.

THE EMELIN THEATRE FOR THE PERFORMING ARTS

(Founded 1972)
153 Library Lane; Mamaroneck, NY 10543; (914) 698–3045,
FAX 698–1404; email emelin98@aol.com;
website www.emelin.org
John Raymond, *Managing Director*

Submission procedure: no unsolicited scripts; professional recommendation only. **Types of material:** full-length plays, cabaret/revues. **Facilities:** The Emelin Theatre, 275 seats, proscenium stage. **Production considerations:** small cast; no fly space. **Best submission time:** year-round. **Response time:** 6 months.

THE EMPTY SPACE THEATRE

(Founded 1970)
3509 Fremont Ave N; Seattle, WA 98103–8813; (206) 547–7633,
FAX 547–7635; website www.emptyspace.org
Adam Greenfield, *Associate Artistic Director/Literary Manager*

Submission procedure: no unsolicited scripts; synopsis, 10-page dialogue sample and letter of inquiry with SASP for response. **Types of material:** full-length plays, translations, adaptations, musicals, solo pieces. **Special interests:** "plays unique to the event of live theatre." **Facilities:** The Empty Space Theatre at the Fremont Palace, 150 seats, endstage. **Production considerations:** prefers small casts. **Best submission time:** year-round. **Response time:** 5 months. **Special programs:** Play Readings: reading series with plays selected through theatre's regular submission procedure.

THE ENSEMBLE THEATRE

(Founded 1977)
3535 Main St; Houston, TX 77002–9529; (713) 520–0055,
FAX 520–1269
Marsha Jackson Randolph, *Producing Artistic Director*

Submission procedure: accepts unsolicited scripts with professional recommendation and SASE; synopsis, sample scene, resume and letter of inquiry with SASE for all others; include cassette or CD for musicals. **Types of material:** full-length plays, adaptations, plays for young audiences, musicals. **Special interests:** plays portraying the African or African-American experience; imaginative plays written, performed or for young audiences; plays suitable for touring by 5-person ensemble; contemporary plays or adaptations. **Facilities:** Performance Stage, 400 seats, flexible stage; Hawkins Stage, 199 seats, proscenium stage; Lawson Arena Stage, 80 seats, black box. **Production considerations:** cast limit of 7, no more than 2 sets; limited wing space. **Best submission time:** Oct. **Response time:** 5 months. **Special programs:** George Hawkins Playwrighting Contest (see Prizes).

ENSEMBLE THEATRE COMPANY

(Founded 1979)

Box 2307; Santa Barbara, CA 93120; (805) 965-6252,
   FAX 965-5322; email production@ensembletheatre.com;
   website www.ensembletheatre.com

Robert Grande-Weiss, *Artistic Director*

Submission procedure: no unsolicited scripts; synopsis and letter of inquiry; professional recommendation and agent submission. **Types of material:** full-length plays, one-acts, translations, adaptations, plays for young audiences. **Facilities:** Alhecama Theatre, 140 seats, proscenium/thrust stage. **Production considerations:** cast limit of 2-8; unit set. **Best submission time:** Dec-Feb. **Response time:** 1 month letter; 6 weeks script. **Special programs:** Story Book Theatre: 2 plays for elementary school age audiences presented in fall and spring. Starting Point Series: new plays given readings each spring.

ENSEMBLE THEATRE OF CINCINNATI

(Founded 1986)

1127 Vine St; Cincinnati, OH 45202; (513) 421-3555,
   FAX 562-4104

D. Lynn Meyers, *Producing Artistic Director*

Submission procedure: no unsolicited scripts; synopsis, dialogue sample, resume and letter of inquiry. **Types of material:** full-length plays, adaptations, plays for young audiences. **Facilities:** Ensemble Theatre of Cincinnati, 191 seats, thrust stage. **Production considerations:** cast limit of 6, simple set. **Best submission time:** Sep. **Response time:** 1 month letter; 4 months script.

EXPRESS CHILDREN'S THEATRE

(Founded 1991)

Box 980817; Houston, TX 77098; (713) 759-1314, FAX 802-9902;
   email expresstheatre@ev1.net; website www.expresstheatre.com

Pat Silver, *Executive Director*

Submission procedure: accepts unsolicited scripts; prefers synopsis and letter of inquiry. **Types of material:** plays for young audiences. **Special interests:** 40-minute plays; multicultural plays; bilingual plays. **Facilities:** no permanent facility; touring company. **Production considerations:** cast limit of 3-4; portable minimal set. **Best submission time:** year-round. **Response time:** 2 weeks letter; 8 weeks script. **Special programs:** commissioning program; after-school education program.

FAMOUS DOOR THEATRE

(Founded 1987)

Box 57029, Chicago, IL 60657; (773) 404-8283, FAX 404-8292;
   email theatre@famousdoortheatre.org;
   website www.famousdoortheatre.org

Marc Grapey, *Artistic Director*

Submission procedure: no unsolicited scripts; synopsis, 10-15-page dialogue sample, resume and letter of inquiry. **Types of material:** full-length plays, translations, adaptations. **Facilities:** Theatre Building North Theatre, 150 seats, thrust stage. **Best submission time:** Nov-Mar. **Response time:** 1 month letter; 3 months script.

THE 5TH AVENUE THEATRE

(Founded 1980)

1308 5th Ave; Seattle, WA 98101; (206) 625-1418, FAX 292-9610;
   email admin@5thavenuetheatre.org; website www.5thavenuetheatre.org

Bill Berry, *Associate Artistic Director*

Submission procedure: accepts unsolicited scripts. **Types of material:** musicals. **Facilities:** 5th Avenue Theatre, 2115 seats, proscenium stage. **Best submission time:** year-round. **Response time:** 6 months. **Special programs:** Adventure Musical Theatre: on-going program that commissions original musicals performed for K-6 students; commissions range from $1000-4000.

FIRSTFLIGHTS

(Founded 2003)

Department of Theatre Arts; 1231 University of Oregon; Eugene, OR 97403;
   (541) 346-4171, FAX 346-1978; email flights@uoregon.edu;
   website theatre.uoregon.edu/FirstFlights/

Jeffrey D. Mason, *Head*

Submission procedure: accepts unsolicited scripts. **Types of material:** full-length plays, translations, adaptations. **Facilities:** Robinson Theatre, 385 seats, proscenium stage; Arena Theatre, 100-150 seats, flexible stage. **Best submission time:** Oct-Apr. **Response time:** 6 months.

FIRST STAGE CHILDREN'S THEATER

(Founded 1987)

929 North Water St; Milwaukee, WI 53202; (414) 273-2314,
   FAX 273-5595; email rgoodman@firststage.org;
   website www.firststage.org

Rob Goodman, *Managing Director*

Submission procedure: no unsolicited scripts; synopsis, resume and letter of inquiry. **Types of material:** works for young audiences, including translations, adaptations and musicals. **Facilities:** Marcus Center for the Performing Arts's Todd

Wehr Theater, 500 seats, thrust stage. **Best submission time:** spring–summer. **Response time:** 1 month letter; 3 months script.

FLEA THEATER

(Founded 1997)
41 White St; New York, NY 10013; (212) 226-0051,
    email garyw@theflea.org; website www.theflea.org
Gary Winter, *Literary Manager*

Submission procedure: no unsolicited scripts; agent submission. **Types of material:** full-length plays. **Special interests:** political themes; language-driven plays. **Facilities:** mainstage, 70-99 seats, flexible stage; downstairs, 40 seats, fixed stage. **Production considerations:** resident acting company composed primarily of 20-30-year-old actors. **Best submission time:** May–Sep. **Response time:** 12 months. **Special programs:** Pataphysics: workshops for writers led by master playwrights.

FLORIDA REPERTORY THEATRE

(Founded 1998)
Drawer 2483; Fort Myers, FL 33902-2483; (941) 332-4665, FAX 332-1808;
    email flrepertory@aol.com; website www.floridarep.org
Robert Cacioppo, *Producing Artistic Director*

Submission procedure: no unsolicited scripts; professional recommendation or agent submission. **Types of material:** full-length plays, translations, adaptations, plays for young audiences, musicals, cabaret/revues. **Facilities:** Arcade Theatre, 393 seats, proscenium stage; Black Box, 80 seats, black box. **Production considerations:** cast limit of 10; single or unit set; no fly space. **Best submission time:** Apr–May. **Response time:** 12 months.

FLORIDA STAGE

(Founded 1987)
262 South Ocean Blvd; Manalapan, FL 33462; (561) 585-3404,
    FAX 588-4708; email info@floridastage.org;
    website www.floridastage.org
Louis Tyrrell, *Producing Director*

Submission procedure: no unsolicited scripts; agent submission. **Types of material:** full-length plays, plays for young audiences. **Special interests:** contemporary issues and ideas. **Facilities:** Florida Stage, 250 seats, thrust stage. **Production considerations:** cast limit of 2-6, 1 set. **Best submission time:** year-round. **Response time:** 3-4 months. **Special programs:** reading series.

FLORIDA STUDIO THEATRE

(Founded 1973)
1241 North Palm Ave; Sarasota, FL 34236; (941) 366–9017
James Ashford, *Casting & Literary Coordinator*

Submission procedure: no unsolicited scripts; synopsis, 5-page dialogue sample and letter of inquiry with SASE for response. **Types of material:** full-length plays, translations, adaptations, musicals, cabaret/revues, solo pieces. **Facilities:** Florida Studio Theatre, 173 seats, proscenium stage; Gompertz Theatre, 154 seats, proscenium; FST Cabaret Club, 109 seats, cabaret space. **Best submission time:** Aug–Apr. **Response time:** 2 weeks letter; 6 months script. **Special programs:** Sarasota Festival of New Plays: 3-tier festival includes Young Playwrights Festival: workshop productions of plays by playwrights grades 2–12; *deadline:* 1 Apr 2005; *dates:* May 2005. Richard and Betty Burdick New Play Festival: workshop productions of 3 new plays; playwright receives stipend, travel, housing; scripts selected through theatre's normal submission procedure; *dates:* May 2005.

THE FOOTHILL THEATRE COMPANY

(Founded 1977)
Box 1812; Nevada City, CA 95959; (530) 265–9320, FAX 265–9325;
    email gary@foothilltheatre.org
Gary Wright, *Literary Manager*

Submission procedure: accepts unsolicited scripts. **Types of material:** full-length plays. **Special interests:** no 10-minute plays. **Facilities:** The Nevada Theatre, 243 seats, proscenium stage; also rents small spaces with 50–100 seats. **Production considerations:** cast limit of 7, very limited fly and wing space. **Best submission time:** year-round. **Response time:** 12 months. **Special programs:** New Voices of the Wild West: annual spring series that produces staged readings of 4 plays dealing with issues pertaining to rural American West; accepts submissions year-round.

FORD'S THEATRE

(Founded 1968)
511 Tenth St NW; Washington, DC 20004; (202) 638–2941, FAX 737–3017
Paul Tetreault, *Producing Director*

Submission procedure: no unsolicited scripts; synopsis, sample pages and letter of inquiry. **Types of material:** full-length plays, musicals. **Special interests:** small-scale musicals and works celebrating the African-American experience. **Facilities:** Ford's Theatre, 699 seats, proscenium/thrust stage. **Production considerations:** cast limit of 15. **Best submission time:** spring–summer. **Response time:** 3 months letter; 12 months script.

THE FOUNTAIN THEATRE
(Founded 1990)
5060 Fountain Ave; Los Angeles, CA 90029; (323) 663-2235,
    FAX 663-1629
Simon Levy, *Producing Director/Dramaturg*

Submission procedure: no unsolicited scripts; professional recommendation. **Types of material:** full-length plays, translations, adaptations. **Special interests:** lyrical dramas; social and political dramas; works with dance; adaptations of American literature. **Facilities:** Fountain Theatre Mainstage, 78 seats, thrust stage. **Production considerations:** cast limit of 12, 1 set; no fly space, low ceiling. **Best submission time:** year-round. **Response time:** 3 months letter; 6 months script.

FREEDOM REPERTORY THEATRE
(Founded 1966)
1346 North Broad St; Philadelphia, PA 19121; (215) 765-2793,
    FAX 765-4191; website www.freedomtheatre.org
Literary Department

Submission procedure: no unsolicited scripts; professional recommendation or agent submission. **Types of material:** full-length plays, musicals. **Special interests:** contemporary plays with African-American themes. **Facilities:** John E. Allen Theatre, 299 seats, proscenium stage; Freedom Black Box Theatre, 120 seats, flexible stage. **Best submission time:** year-round. **Response time:** 3 months.

FREE STREET PROGRAMS
(Founded 1969)
1419 West Blackhawk St; Chicago, IL 60622; (773) 772-7248,
    FAX 772-7248; email gogogo@freestreet.org
Rodney Terwilliger, *Executive Director*

Submission procedure: no unsolicited scripts; letter from writer with "a concept for the creation of a new performance with youth"; prefers email inquiries. **Types of material:** work developed by company. **Special interests:** "creating with youth to enhance literacy and experiment with play structure, content and shape." **Facilities:** no permanent facility, national/international touring company of youth (Teen Street). **Production considerations:** limited technical support, youth production crew. **Best submission time:** year-round. **Response time:** 1 week. **Special programs:** PANG (Performing Arts for a New Generation): producing company of youth curates fringe, edgy performances; performers and music groups send letter of inquiry to PANG.

GABLESTAGE
(Founded 1979)
1200 Anastasia Ave; Coral Gables, FL 33134; (305) 446-1116,
FAX 445-8645; email jadler@gablestage.org;
website www.gablestage.org
Joseph Adler, *Producing Artistic Director*

Submission procedure: no unsolicited scripts; synopsis with SASE for response. **Types of material:** full-length plays. **Facilities:** GableStage, 150 seats, proscenium stage. **Best submission time:** year-round. **Response time:** 3 months letter; 6 months script.

GALA HISPANIC THEATRE
(Founded 1976)
Box 43209; Washington, DC 20010; (202) 234-7174, FAX 332-1247;
email info@galatheatre.org; website www.galatheatre.org
Hugo J. Medrano, *Producing/Artistic Director*

Submission procedure: no unsolicited scripts; synopsis/description of play and letter of inquiry. **Types of material:** full-length plays, solo pieces. **Special interests:** plays by Spanish, Latino or Hispanic-American writers in Spanish or English only; prefers Spanish-language works with accompanying English translation; works that reflect sociocultural realities of Hispanics in Latin America, the Caribbean or Spain, as well as the Hispanic-American experience. **Facilities:** GALA Hispanic Theatre, 200 seats, proscenium stage. **Production considerations:** cast limit of 6-8. **Best submission time:** Apr-May. **Response time:** 1 month letter; 12 months script (script will not be returned). **Special programs:** poetry onstage.

GEFFEN PLAYHOUSE
(Founded 1995)
10886 LeConte Ave; Los Angeles, CA 90024; (310) 208-6500,
FAX 208-0341
Amy Levinson Millán, *Literary Manager/Dramaturg*

Submission procedure: no unsolicited scripts; agent submission. **Types of material:** full-length plays, adaptations, musicals. **Facilities:** Geffen Playhouse, 498 seats, proscenium stage. **Best submission time:** year-round. **Response time:** 6 months.

GEORGE STREET PLAYHOUSE
(Founded 1974)
9 Livingston Ave; New Brunswick, NJ 08901-1903; (732) 846-2895,
FAX 247-9151; website www.georgestplayhouse.org
Literary Manager

Submission procedure: no unsolicited scripts; synopsis, 10-page dialogue sample, character/set breakdown and letter of inquiry with SASE for response. **Types of**

material: full-length plays, one-acts. **Special interests:** social issue one-acts suitable for touring to schools (not seeking any other kind of one-acts); comedies and dramas that present a fresh perspective on our society; "work that tells a compelling, personal, human story while entertaining, challenging and stretching the imagination." **Facilities:** mainstage, 367 seats, proscenium/thrust stage. **Production considerations:** prefers cast limit of 7. **Best submission time:** year-round. **Response time:** 14 months.

GERMINAL STAGE DENVER

(Founded 1974)
2450 West 44th Ave; Denver, CO 80211; (303) 455-7108;
  email gsden@privatei.com; website www.germinalstage.com
Ed Baierlein, *Director/Manager*

Submission procedure: no unsolicited scripts; synopsis, 5-page dialogue sample and letter of inquiry with SASP for response; no email submissions. **Types of material:** full-length plays, translations, adaptations. **Special interests:** adaptations that use both dialogue and narration. **Facilities:** Germinal Stage Denver, 100 seats, thrust stage. **Production considerations:** cast limit of 10; minimal production requirements. **Best submission time:** year-round. **Response time:** 2 weeks letter; 6 months script.

GEVA THEATRE CENTER

(Founded 1972)
75 Woodbury Blvd; Rochester, NY 14607-1717; (585) 232-1366
Marge Betley, *Literary Manager/Resident Dramaturg*

Submission procedure: no unsolicited scripts; synopsis, dialogue sample, production history, resume and letter of inquiry. **Types of material:** full-length plays, translations, adaptations. **Facilities:** Elaine P. Wilson Theatre, 552 seats, modified thrust stage; Ronald and Donna Fielding Nextstage, 180 seats, modified proscenium. **Best submission time:** year-round. **Response time:** 1 month letter; 6 months script. **Special programs:** American Voices New Play Reading Series; Hibernatus Interruptus, A Winter Festival of New Plays: customized workshops of 3 plays; Regional Playwrights and Young Writers Festival.

GOODMAN THEATRE

(Founded 1925)
170 North Dearborn St; Chicago, IL 60601; (312) 443-3811,
  FAX 443-7448; website www.goodmantheatre.org
Rick DesRochers, *Literary Director*

Submission procedure: no unsolicited scripts; synopsis, professional recommendation and letter of inquiry. **Types of material:** full-length plays, translations, musicals. **Facilities:** Albert Ivar Goodman Theatre, 830 seats, proscenium stage; Owen Bruner Goodman Theatre, 200-400 seats, flexible stage. **Best submission time:** year-round. **Response time:** 3 months letter; 8 months script.

GOODSPEED MUSICALS

(Founded 1963)

Box A; East Haddam, CT 06423; (860) 873-8664, FAX 873-2329;
    email info@goodspeed.org; website www.goodspeed.org

Lawrence Thelen, *Literary Manager*

Submission procedure: no unsolicited scripts; letter of inquiry. **Types of material:** original musicals only. **Facilities:** Goodspeed Opera House, 400 seats, proscenium stage; The Norma Terris Theatre, 200 seats, proscenium stage. **Best submission time:** Jan-Feb. **Response time:** 2 months letter; 8 months script.

GREAT LAKES THEATER FESTIVAL

(Founded 1961)

1501 Euclid Ave, Suite 300; Cleveland, OH 44115; (216) 241-5490,
    FAX 241-6315; website www.greatlakestheater.org

Artistic Department

Submission procedure: no unsolicited scripts; professional recommendation. **Types of material:** full-length plays, translations, adaptations. **Special interests:** translations and adaptations of classic plays, new works with specific relevance to the classic repertoire. **Facilities:** Ohio Theatre, 1000 seats, proscenium stage. **Best submission time:** year-round. **Response time:** 3 months.

GREENBRIER VALLEY THEATRE

(Founded 1966)

113 East Washington St; Lewisburg, WV 24901; FAX (304) 645-3818;
    email cathey@gvtheatre.org; website www.gvtheatre.org

Cathey Sawyer, *Artistic Director*

Submission procedure: no unsolicited scripts; synopsis and letter of inquiry. **Types of material:** full-length plays, one-acts, plays for young audiences, musicals. **Special interests:** regional plays. **Facilities:** Hollowell Theatre, 150-200 seats, black box; Studio, 25-35 seats, flexible stage. **Production considerations:** cast limit of 10 for plays; small or unit set preferred. **Best submission time:** late fall. **Response time:** 1 month letter; 6 months script.

GREENWAY ARTS ALLIANCE

(Founded 1992)

544 North Fairfax Ave; Los Angeles, CA 90036; (323) 655-7679,
    FAX 655-7906; email wwgaa@aol.com; website www.greenwayarts.org

Whitney Weston, *Co-Artistic Director*

Submission procedure: no unsolicited scripts; synopsis emailed or faxed. **Types of material:** full-length plays, one-acts, translations, adaptations. **Special interests:** large casts; current political themes. **Facilities:** Greenway Court Theatre, 99 seats, flexible stage. **Best submission time:** year-round. **Response time:** 3 months letter; 2 months script.

GRETNA THEATRE
(Founded 1926)
Box 578; Mt. Gretna, PA 17064; (717) 964-3322, FAX 964-2189

Submission procedure: no unsolicited scripts; synopsis, 5-page dialogue sample, character list with descriptions, production history and letter of inquiry; include CD or cassette for musicals. **Types of material:** full-length plays, musicals. **Special interests:** plays suitable for summer audiences; musicals; prefers comedies. **Facilities:** Mt. Gretna Playhouse, 700 seats, proscenium stage. **Production considerations:** open-air facility; 14' ceiling over stage. **Best submission time:** Aug-Apr. **Response time:** 1 month letter; 3 months script.

THE GROWING STAGE THEATRE
(Founded 1982)
Box 36; Netcong, NJ 07857; (973) 347-4946, FAX 691-7069;
    email info@growingstage.com; website www.growingstage.com
Stephen L. Fredericks, *Executive Director*

Submission procedure: accepts unsolicited scripts with production history and bio; include SASE for response. **Types of material:** plays for young audiences including full-length plays, translations, adaptations, musicals. **Special interests:** "intelligent theatre for the entire family." **Facilities:** Palace Theatre, 299 seats, proscenium stage. **Production considerations:** touring shows that require casts of no more than 3; mainstage work more flexible. **Best submission time:** Jun-Aug. **Response time:** 4 months.

THE GUTHRIE THEATER
(Founded 1963)
725 Vineland Place; Minneapolis, MN 55403; (612) 347-1175,
    FAX 347-1188; email amyw@guthrietheater.org;
    website www.guthrietheater.org
Amy Wegener, *Literary Manager*

Submission procedure: no unsolicited scripts; agent submission. **Types of material:** full-length plays, translations, adaptations. **Special interests:** intelligent, imaginative, highly theatrical works of depth and significance; rich language, humor, and complex ideas; political themes and contemporary issues. **Facilities:** Guthrie Theater, 1309 seats, thrust stage; Guthrie Lab, 350 seats, flexible stage. **Best submission time:** year-round. **Response time:** 6 months.

HANGAR THEATRE

(Founded 1974)

Box 205; Ithaca, NY 14851; (607) 273-8588, FAX 273-4516;
website www.hangartheatre.org

Kevin Moriarty, *Artistic Director*

Submission procedure: no unsolicited scripts; synopsis, first 10 pages of dialogue. **Types of material:** full-length plays, one-acts, musicals. **Facilities:** Mainstage, 359 seats, thrust stage. **Best submission time:** Sep–Dec. **Response time:** 9 months. **Special programs:** commissioning program for plays for young audiences. Lab Company Playwrighting Residencies for one-acts. Developmental readings and workshops. Annual New Play Festival in Jul.

HARWICH JUNIOR THEATRE

(Founded 1950)

Box 168; West Harwich, MA 02671; (508) 432-2002, ext 12, FAX 432-0726;
email hjt@capecod.net; website www.hjtcapecod.org

Nina K. Schuessler

Submission procedure: no unsolicited scripts; synopsis and dialogue sample. **Types of material:** full-length plays, one-acts, translations, adaptations, plays for young audiences, musicals, cabaret/revues, solo performance. **Special interests:** intergenerational casts; plays for family audiences or with young adult themes. **Facilities:** Harwich Junior Theatre, 186 seats, thrust stage; Theatre In Corner, 60 seats, open space. **Production considerations:** no fly space; prefers conceptual designs over literal settings. **Best submission time:** early fall. **Response time:** 6 months letter; 6 months script.

THE HAVEN PROJECT

(Founded 1995)

821 Northwest Flanders, #305; Portland, OR 97209; (503) 872-9635,
FAX 872-9652; email info@havenproject.org;
website www.havenproject.org

Gretchen Corbett, *Artistic Director*

Submission procedure: no unsolicited scripts; synopsis and letter of inquiry with SASE for response. **Types of material:** full-length plays, one-acts, plays for young audiences, musicals. **Facilities:** various theatres in Portland area. **Production considerations:** prefers cast of 2-10. **Best submission time:** year-round. **Response time:** 1 month letter; 6 months script.

HEDGEROW THEATRE

(Founded 1923)

146 West Rose Valley Rd; Wallingford, PA 19086; (610) 565-4211,
FAX 565-1672; email hedgerowtheatre@comcast.net;
website www.hedgerowtheatre.org

Walt Vail, *Literary Manager*

Submission procedure: no unsolicited scripts; synopsis and letter of inquiry. **Types of material:** full-length plays. **Special interests:** new plays by DE, NJ and PA playwrights; mysteries; comedies. **Facilities:** mainstage, 144 seats, proscenium stage. **Production considerations:** minimal production demands; small stage. **Best submission time:** year-round. **Response time:** 2 months letter; 4 months script.

THE HENLOPEN THEATER PROJECT

(Founded 1987)

Box 606; Rehoboth Beach, DE 19971; (302) 226-4103, FAX 226-4104;
email stars@ce.net; website www.henlopentheatreproject.com

Submission procedure: no unsolicited scripts; dialogue sample and letter of inquiry. **Types of material:** full-length plays, one-acts, adaptations, plays for young audiences, musicals, cabaret/revues, solo pieces. **Special interests:** playwrights of color encouraged. **Facilities:** Little Theatre, 250 seats, proscenium stage. **Production considerations:** cast limit of 6, minimal technical demands. **Best submission time:** Sep. **Response time:** 2 months letter; 3 months script.

HIP POCKET THEATRE

(Founded 1977)

Box 136758; Fort Worth, TX 76136; (817) 246-9775, FAX 246-5651;
email mdmolemo@aol.com; website www.hippocket.org

Johnny Simons, *Artistic Director*

Submission procedure: no unsolicited scripts; synopsis and dialogue sample; include cassette for musicals. **Types of material:** full-length plays, translations, adaptations, plays for young audiences, musicals, solo pieces, multimedia works. **Special interests:** well-crafted stories with poetic, mythic slant that incorporate ritual and ensemble; works utilizing masks, puppetry, music, dance, mime and strong visual elements. **Facilities:** outdoor amphitheatre. **Production considerations:** simple sets. **Best submission time:** Oct-Feb. **Response time:** 6 weeks.

THE HIPPODROME STATE THEATRE

(Founded 1973)

25 Southeast Second Place; Gainesville, FL 32601-6596;
(352) 373-5968, FAX 371-9130; website hipp.gator.net

Tamerin Dygert, *Dramaturg*

Submission procedure: no unsolicited scripts; agent submission. **Types of material:** full-length plays, one-acts. **Special interests:** short plays. **Facilities:** Mainstage Theatre, 266 seats, thrust stage; Second Stage, 87 seats, flexible stage.

Production considerations: cast limit of 6, unit set. **Best submission time:** Jul-Oct. **Response time:** 5 months. **Special programs:** informal play reading series: possibility of production on Second Stage or in site-specific gallery and bar spaces; scripts selected through theatre's normal submission procedure.

HONOLULU THEATRE FOR YOUTH
(Founded 1955)
2846 Ualena St; Honolulu, HI 96819-1910; (808) 839-9885,
 FAX 839-7018; email mark@htyweb.org;
 website www.htyweb.org
Mark Lutwak, *Artistic Director*

Submission procedure: no unsolicited scripts; synopsis, resume and letter of inquiry. **Types of material:** plays for young audiences. **Special interests:** plays with contemporary themes for audiences from pre-school through high school; small-cast adaptations of classics; new works based on Pacific Rim cultures; plays with compelling language that are imaginative and socially relevant to young people in Hawaii. **Facilities:** Richardson Theatre, 800 seats, proscenium stage; Leeward Community College Theatre, 650 seats, proscenium stage; McCoy Pavilion, 300 seats, flexible stage; Tenney Theatre, 300 seats, proscenium stage; shows also tour to school theatres, gymnasiums and cafeterias. **Production considerations:** cast limit of 7. **Best submission time:** year-round. **Response time:** 1 month letter; 5 months script.

HORIZON THEATRE COMPANY
(Founded 1983)
Box 5376; Atlanta, GA 31107; (404) 523-1477, FAX 584-8815;
 email horizonco@mindspring.com; website www.horizontheatre.com
Addae Moon, *Literary Manager*

Submission procedure: no unsolicited scripts except for Festival (see below); synopsis, resume and letter of inquiry. **Types of material:** full-length plays, translations, adaptations, musicals. **Special interests:** contemporary issues; plays by women and African-Americans; southern urban themes; comedies. **Facilities:** Horizon Theatre, 175 seats, modified thrust stage. **Production considerations:** plays cast from ensemble of up to 12 actors. **Best submission time:** year-round. **Response time:** 6 months letter; 12 months script. **Special programs:** Teen Ensemble: one-acts about teen issues to be performed by teens. Senior Citizens Ensemble: one-acts about senior citizen issues to be performed by senior citizens. New South Festival: annual festival of readings, workshops and full productions of plays by playwrights speaking from, for and about the South; *deadline:* 15 Mar 2005; *notification:* 15 May 2005; *dates:* Jun-Jul 2005.

HUDSON THEATRE

(Founded 1991)

6539 Santa Monica Blvd; Hollywood, CA 90038; (323) 856–4252,
FAX 856–4316

Elizabeth Reilly, *Artistic Director*

Submission procedure: no unsolicited scripts; synopsis and letter of inquiry. **Types of material:** full-length plays, one-acts, musicals, solo pieces. **Facilities:** mainstage, 99 seats, modified thrust stage; Backstage Theatre, 99 seats, proscenium stage; Avenue Theatre, 99 seats, runway; Guild Theatre, 43 seats, proscenium stage. **Best submission time:** year-round. **Response time:** 6 months letter; 12 months script.

THE HUMAN RACE THEATRE COMPANY

(Founded 1986)

126 North Main St, Suite 300; Dayton, OH 45402–1710;
(937) 461–3823, FAX 461–7223; email hrtheatre@aol.com;
website www.humanracetheatre.org

Tony Dallas, *Playwright in Residence*

Submission procedure: no unsolicited scripts; professional recommendation. **Types of material:** full-length plays, one-acts, adaptations, plays for young audiences. **Special interests:** OH playwrights; adaptations and original works for junior and senior high school audiences; contemporary issues. **Facilities:** The Loft, 219 seats, thrust stage. **Production considerations:** small cast, plays for young audiences tour to schools; no fly space. **Best submission time:** Dec–Feb. **Response time:** 6 months.

HUNTINGTON THEATRE COMPANY

(Founded 1981)

264 Huntington Ave; Boston MA 02115–4606; (617) 266–7900,
FAX 353–8300; website www.huntingtontheatre.org

Ilana Brownstein, *Literary Manager*

Submission procedure: accepts unsolicited scripts from Boston-area playwrights only; agent submission for others; include SASE for response. **Types of material:** full-length plays, translations, adaptations, musicals, solo pieces; include CD for musicals. **Facilities:** Boston University Theatre, 890 seats, proscenium stage; Virginia Wimberly Theatre, 360 seats, proscenium stage; Nancy and Edward Roberts Studio Theatre, 200 seats, flexible stage. **Best submission time:** year-round. **Response time:** 12 months.

HYDE PARK THEATRE

(Founded 1992)
511 West 43rd St; Austin, TX 78751; (512) 479-7530,
FAX 479-7531; email inbox@hydeparktheatre.org;
website www.hydeparktheatre.org
Ken Webster, *Artistic Director*
Peck Phillips, *Literary Manager*

Submission procedure: no unsolicited scripts; synopsis and letter of inquiry. **Types of material:** full-length plays, translations, adaptations, solo pieces. **Facilities:** Hyde Park Theatre, 90 seats, flexible stage. **Best submission time:** year-round. **Response time:** 3 months letter; 6 months script. **Special programs:** Hyde Park Theatre Play Development Reading Series: quarterly reading series for developing new work.

HYPOTHETICAL THEATRE CO., INC.

(Founded 1992)
344 East 14th St; New York, NY 10003; (212) 780-0800, ext 254,
FAX 780-0859; email hypothetical@bigfoot.com
Literary Manager

Submission procedure: no unsolicited scripts; agent submission. **Types of material:** full-length plays. **Special interests:** contemporary, ground-breaking plays. **Facilities:** Hypothetical Theatre, 99 seats, proscenium stage. **Best submission time:** year-round. **Response time:** 6 months.

ILLINOIS THEATRE CENTER

(Founded 1976)
Box 397; Park Forest, IL 60466; (708) 481-3510, FAX 481-3693;
email ilthctr@bigplanet.com; website www.ilthctr.org
Literary Manager

Submission procedure: no unsolicited scripts; synopsis and letter of inquiry with SASE for response. **Types of material:** full-length plays, musicals. **Facilities:** Illinois Theatre Center, 180 seats, proscenium/thrust stage. **Production considerations:** cast limit of 9 for plays, 14 for musicals. **Best submission time:** year-round. **Response time:** 1 month letter; 2 months script.

ILLUSION THEATER

(Founded 1974)
528 Hennepin Ave, Suite 704; Minneapolis, MN 55403;
(612) 339-4944, FAX 337-8042; email info@illusiontheater.org
Michael Robins, *Executive Producing Director*

Submission procedure: no unsolicited scripts; professional recommendation. **Types of material:** full-length plays, one-acts, translations, adaptations, musicals, solo pieces. **Special interests:** writers to collaborate on new works with company. **Facilities:** Illusion Theater, 250 seats, semi-thrust stage. **Best submission time:**

Sep-Jan. **Response time:** 18 months. **Special programs:** Fresh Ink Series: 5-6 plays presented with minimal set and costumes for 1 weekend; post-performance discussion with audience; scripts selected through theatre's normal submission procedure.

IMAGINATION STAGE

(Formerly BAPA's Imagination Stage)
(Founded 1992)
4908 Auburn Ave; Bethesda, MD 20814; (301) 961-6060,
   FAX 718-9526; email jstanford@imaginationstage.org;
   website www.imaginationstage.org
Janet Stanford, *Artistic Director*

Submission procedure: no unsolicited scripts; dialogue sample and letter of inquiry. **Types of material:** plays for young audiences, musicals. **Special interests:** 60-90-minute plays, "innovative treatment of children's classics," culturally diverse material. **Facilities:** Imagination Stage, 400 seats, thrust stage. **Production considerations:** cast size 4-10. **Best submission time:** year-round. **Response time:** 2 months letter; script varies.

INDIANA REPERTORY THEATRE

(Founded 1972)
140 West Washington St; Indianapolis, IN 46204-3465;
   (317) 635-5277, FAX 236-0767
Literary Manager

Submission procedure: no unsolicited scripts; synopsis and letter of inquiry with SASE for response. **Types of material:** full-length plays, translations, adaptations, solo pieces. **Special interests:** adaptations of classic literature; plays that explore cultural/ethnic issues "with a Midwestern voice." **Facilities:** mainstage, 600 seats, modified proscenium stage; Upperstage, 300 seats, modified thrust stage. **Production considerations:** cast limit of 8. **Best submission time:** year-round (season chosen by Jan each year). **Response time:** 4 months letter; 6 months script. **Special programs:** Discovery Series: presentation of plays for family audiences with focus on youth and culturally/ethnically diverse plays with emphasis on history and literature; scripts selected through theatre's normal submission procedure.

INTAR HISPANIC AMERICAN ARTS CENTER

(Founded 1966)
Box 756; New York, NY 10108; (212) 695-6134, ext 11, FAX 268-0102
Lorenzo Mans, *Artistic Associate*

Submission procedure: accepts unsolicited scripts. **Types of material:** full-length plays. **Special interests:** new plays by Hispanic-American writers and translations and adaptations of Hispanic works only. **Facilities:** INTAR 53, 74 seats, black box. **Production considerations:** small cast, modest production values. **Best submission time:** year-round (season chosen late summer-early fall). **Response**

time: 3 months. **Special programs:** NewWorks Lab: workshop productions; reading series.

INTERACT THEATRE COMPANY
(Founded 1988)
2030 Sansom St; Philadelphia, PA 19103; (215) 568–8077,
    FAX 568–8095; email interact@interacttheatre.org;
    website www.interacttheatre.org
Larry Loebell, *Dramaturg*

Submission procedure: no unsolicited scripts; synopsis, bio and letter of inquiry with SASE for response. **Types of material:** full-length plays. **Special interests:** contemporary plays that theatrically explore issues of cultural and social significance; no "kitchen-sink dramas, relationship plays or light romantic comedies." **Facilities:** The Adrienne, 106 seats, proscenium stage. **Production considerations:** cast limit of 10. **Best submission time:** year-round. **Response time:** 3 months letter; 12 months script.

INTERNATIONAL CITY THEATRE
(Founded 1986)
One World Trade Center, Suite 300; Box 32069; Long Beach, CA 90832;
    (562) 495–4595, FAX 436–7895; email shashinict@earthlink.net;
    website www.ictlongbeach.com
Shashin Desai, *Artistic Director/Producer*

Submission procedure: no unsolicited scripts; professional recommendation. **Types of material:** full-length plays, translations, adaptations, plays for young audiences, musicals, cabaret/revues, solo pieces. **Facilities:** ICT Center Theater, 349 seats, thrust stage. **Production considerations:** cast limit of 3-8, single or unit set; no fly space. **Best submission time:** year-round. **Response time:** 6 months.

INTIMAN THEATRE
(Founded 1972)
Box 19760; Seattle, WA 98109; (206) 269–1901, FAX 269–1928;
    website www.intiman.org
Literary Manager

Submission procedure: no unsolicited scripts; professional recommendation. **Types of material:** full-length plays, translations, adaptations. **Special interests:** plays of complex ideas; unique use of form; language-oriented plays; no domestic realism. **Facilities:** Intiman Playhouse, 480 seats, modified thrust stage. **Best submission time:** Nov–Mar. **Response time:** 8 months.

IRISH CLASSICAL THEATRE COMPANY
(Founded 1990)
625 Main St; Buffalo, NY 14203; (716) 853-1380, FAX 853-0592;
  email pezz@irishclassical.com; website www.irishclassicaltheatre.com
Fortunato Pezzimenti, *Associate Artistic Director*

Submission procedure: no unsolicited scripts; professional recommendation. **Types of material:** full-length plays, one-acts, translations, adaptations, musicals, cabaret/revues, solo pieces. **Special interests:** plays by Irish or Irish-American writers, plays with Irish or Irish-American themes. **Facilities:** Andrews Theatre, 200 seats, arena stage. **Production considerations:** unit set, fluid set changes; limited storage space. **Best submission time:** May-Jun. **Response time:** 1 month letter; 3 months script.

IRONDALE ENSEMBLE PROJECT
(Founded 1983)
Box 150604; Brooklyn, NY 11215; (718) 488-9233, FAX 488-9185;
  email irondalert@aol.com; website www.irondale.org
Jim Niesen, *Artistic Director*

Submission procedure: no unsolicited scripts; letter of inquiry from playwright interested in developing work with ensemble through ongoing workshop process. **Types of material:** full-length plays, adaptations, musicals. **Special interests:** works with political or social relevance. **Facilities:** no permanent facility. **Production considerations:** cast limit of 8-9. **Best submission time:** Apr-Sep. **Response time:** 10 weeks.

JEWISH ENSEMBLE THEATRE
(Founded 1989)
6600 West Maple Rd; West Bloomfield, MI 48322-3002;
  (248) 788-2900, FAX 788-5160; email jetplay@aol.com;
  website www.comnet.org/jet
Evelyn Orbach, *Artistic Director*

Submission procedure: accepts unsolicited scripts. **Types of material:** full-length plays, plays for young audiences. **Special interests:** works on Jewish themes and/or by Jewish writers; work not previously produced professionally. **Facilities:** Aaron DeRoy Theatre, 193 seats, thrust stage. **Production considerations:** no fly space. **Best submission time:** late spring-summer. **Response time:** 6 months. **Special programs:** Festival of New Plays in Staged Readings: 4 plays given readings, possibly leading to mainstage production; scripts selected through theatre's normal submission procedure.

JUNGLE THEATER
(Founded 1990)
2951 South Lyndale Ave; Minneapolis, MN 55408; (612) 822–4002,
FAX 822–9408; email info@jungletheater.com;
website www.jungletheater.com
Buffy Sedlachek, *Literary Manager*

Submission procedure: no unsolicited scripts; synopsis, 10-page dialogue sample, resume and letter of inquiry. **Types of material:** full-length plays. **Facilities:** The Jungle Theater, 149 seats, proscenium stage. **Best submission time:** Jan-May. **Response time:** 2 months letter; 5 months script. **Special programs:** Emerging Playwrights Reading Series: public readings of new plays by early-career playwrights; travel, housing and stipend provided; scripts selected through theatre's normal submission procedure; *deadline:* 30 Jun 2005.

THE KAVINOKY THEATRE
(Founded 1981)
320 Porter Ave; Buffalo, NY 14221; (716) 829–7652, FAX 829–7790;
email kavinokytheatre@dyc.yellowcat.edu;
website www.kavinokytheatre.com
David Lamb, *Artistic Director*

Submission procedure: no unsolicited scripts; professional recommendation. **Types of material:** full-length plays, adaptations, musicals. **Facilities:** Kavinoky Theatre, 260 seats, proscenium/thrust stage. **Production considerations:** prefers cast limit of 7; no fly and limited wing space. **Best submission time:** Jun-Aug. **Response time:** 1 month.

KENTUCKY REPERTORY THEATRE AT HORSE CAVE
(Formerly Horse Cave Theatre)
(Founded 1977)
Box 215; Horse Cave, KY 42749; (270) 786–1200, FAX 786–5298;
email rbrock@kentuckyrep.org; website www.kentuckyrep.org
Robert Brock, *Artistic Director*

Submission procedure: no unsolicited scripts; professional recommendation. **Types of material:** full-length plays. **Special interests:** KY-based plays by KY playwrights. **Facilities:** Kentucky Repertory Theatre at Horse Cave, 346 seats, thrust stage. **Production considerations:** cast limit of 10, 1 set. **Best submission time:** Oct-Apr. **Response time:** varies.

KITCHEN DOG THEATER COMPANY

(Founded 1990)
3120 McKinney Ave; Dallas, TX 75204; (214) 953-2258,
FAX 953-1873; email admin@kitchendogtheater.org;
website www.kitchendogtheater.org
Dan Day, *Artistic Director*

Submission procedure: accepts unsolicited scripts. **Types of material:** full-length plays, translations, adaptations, solo pieces. **Special interests:** plays by TX and Southwest playwrights. **Facilities:** The McKinney Avenue Contemporary, 100-150 seats, thrust stage; Second Space, 75-100 seats, black box. **Production considerations:** cast limit of 5, moderate production demands, moderate set. **Best submission time:** year-round. **Response time:** 8 months. **Special programs:** New Works Festival: annual presentation of new plays, including one full production, staged readings, mini workshops and artist residencies; submit script with SASP for response; *deadline:* 15 Mar 2005; *notification:* 15 Apr 2005; *dates:* Jun–Jul 2005.

KUMU KAHUA THEATRE

(Founded 1971)
46 Merchant St; Honolulu, HI 96813; (808) 536-4222, FAX 536-4226
Harry Wong III, *Artistic Director*

Submission procedure: accepts unsolicited scripts with SASE for response. **Types of material:** full-length plays, one-acts, adaptations. **Special interests:** plays set in Hawaii or dealing with the Hawaiian experience. **Facilities:** Kumu Kahua Theatre, 100 seats, black box. **Best submission time:** year-round. **Response time:** 4 months. **Special programs:** Kumu Kahua Theatre/UHM Theatre Department Playwriting Contest: includes the Hawai'i Prize, Pacific Rim Prize and Resident Prize (see Prizes).

LA JOLLA PLAYHOUSE

(Founded 1947)
Box 12039; La Jolla, CA 92039; (858) 550-1070, FAX 550-1075;
website www.lajollaplayhouse.com
Literary Manager

Submission procedure: no unsolicited scripts; 1-page synopsis, 10-page dialogue sample with letter of inquiry and SASE for response. **Types of material:** full-length plays, translations, adaptations, musicals, solo pieces. **Special interests:** world-premiere works only; innovative form and language, emphasis on ideas and theatricality. **Facilities:** Mandell Weiss Center for the Performing Arts, 500 seats, proscenium stage; Potiker Theatre, 450 seats, convertible black box; Weiss Forum, 400 seats, thrust stage. **Best submission time:** Jun–Nov. **Response time:** 1 month letter; 10 months script.

LA MAMA EXPERIMENTAL THEATRE CLUB
(Founded 1961)
74A East 4th St; New York, NY 10003; (212) 254-6468, FAX 254-7597;
email lamama@lamama.org; website www.lamama.org
Ellen Stewart, *Artistic Director*

Submission procedure: no unsolicited scripts; professional recommendation. **Types of material:** full-length plays, one-acts, musicals, performance art. **Special interests:** culturally diverse works with music, movement and media. **Facilities:** Annex Theater, 299 seats, flexible stage; The Club Theater, 99 seats, black box; First Floor Theater, 99 seats, black box. **Best submission time:** year-round. **Response time:** 6 months. **Special programs:** concert play reading series curated by George Ferencz; poetry series curated by William Electric Black; theatrical workshops and premiere productions involving collaboration among artists of varying geographic and ethnic origins that promote intercultural understanding and artistic exchange. La MaMa Umbria: summer artist's residency program outside Spoleto in Umbria, Italy; contact theatre for more information.

LAMB'S PLAYERS THEATRE
(Founded 1971)
Box 182229; Coronado, CA 92178; (619) 437-6050, FAX 437-6053
Literary Department

Submission procedure: no unsolicited scripts; synopsis, maximum 10-page dialogue sample and letter of inquiry; include cassette for musicals. **Types of material:** full-length plays, one-acts, plays for young audiences, musicals, cabaret/revues. **Facilities:** Harder Stage, 350 seats, thrust stage; Lyceum, 200 seats, flexible stage. **Best submission time:** year-round. **Response time:** 6 weeks letter; 6 months script.

L. A. THEATRE WORKS
(Founded 1974)
681 Venice Blvd; Venice, CA 90291; (310) 827-0808, FAX 827-4949;
email latworks@aol.com
Susan Raab, *Associate Producer*

Submission procedure: no unsolicited scripts; agent submission. **Types of material:** full-length plays, adaptations. **Facilities:** Skirball Cultural Center, 330 seats, auditorium. **Best submission time:** year-round. **Response time:** 6 months.

LIFELINE THEATRE
(Founded 1982)
6912 North Glenwood Ave; Chicago, IL 60626; (773) 262-3790,
FAX 761-4582; website www.lifelinetheatre.com
Dorothy Milne, *Artistic Director*

Submission procedure: no unsolicited scripts; synopsis and letter of inquiry. **Types of material:** adaptations. **Facilities:** Lifeline Theatre, 100 seats, proscenium stage.

Best submission time: year-round. **Response time:** 1 month letter; 6 months script.

LINCOLN CENTER THEATER

(Founded 1966)

150 West 65th St; New York, NY 10023; (212) 362-7600;
    website www.lct.org

Anne Cattaneo, *Dramaturg*

Submission procedure: no unsolicited scripts; agent submission. **Types of material:** full-length plays, one-acts, translations, adaptations, musicals. **Facilities:** Vivian Beaumont, 1000 seats, thrust stage; Mitzi E. Newhouse, 300 seats, thrust stage. **Best submission time:** year-round. **Response time:** 4 months.

LIVE BAIT THEATRICAL COMPANY

(Founded 1987)

3914 North Clark; Chicago, IL 60613; (773) 871-1212, FAX 871-3191;
    email info@livebaittheater.org; website www.livebaittheater.org

Managing Director

Submission procedure: no unsolicited scripts; synopsis and letter of inquiry from Chicago-area playwrights only; no other submissions accepted. **Types of material:** full-length plays, translations, adaptations, solo pieces. **Special interests:** nonrealistic plays; performance poetry; performance art; multimedia works; works that emphasize visual aspects of staging. **Facilities:** Live Bait Theater, 70 seats, black box. **Production considerations:** prefers cast limit of 9, 1 set; no fly or wing space. **Best submission time:** year-round. **Response time:** 6 weeks letter; 6 months script.

LONG WHARF THEATRE

(Founded 1965)

222 Sargent Dr; New Haven, CT 06511; (203) 787-4284, FAX 776-2287

Carrie Ryan, *Dramaturg/Literary Manager*

Submission procedure: no unsolicited scripts; synopsis, 10-page dialogue sample, resume and letter of inquiry with SASE for response. **Types of material:** full-length plays, translations, adaptations. **Special interests:** dramatic plays and comedies about human relationships, social concerns, ethical and moral dilemmas. **Facilities:** Newton Schenck Stage, 484 seats, thrust stage; Stage II, 199 seats, proscenium stage. **Best submission time:** year-round. **Response time:** 3 months letter; 12 months script.

LOST NATION THEATER

(Founded 1977)

39 Main St–City Hall; Montpelier, VT 05602; (802) 229-0492, FAX 223-9608;
    email info@lostnationtheater.org; website www.lostnationtheater.org

Mr. Kim Bent, *Co-Producing Artistic Director*

Submission procedure: no unsolicited scripts; synopsis, dialogue sample, resume

and letter of inquiry. **Types of material:** full-length plays, translations, adaptati
plays for young audiences. **Special interests:** no "spectacles"; plays with music
acceptable, but not musicals. **Facilities:** City Hall Auditorium, 100 seats, black box.
Production considerations: cast limit of 10; unit set; no fly space. **Best
submission time:** Nov. **Response time:** 1 month letter; 3 months script. **Special
programs:** New Works Showcase: summer new play reading series on mainstage or
cabaret stage in theatre lobby, 1-2 rehearsals before reading in front of audience
with post-reading feedback/discussion session; indicate interest in having reading
only.

THE LYRIC STAGE COMPANY OF BOSTON
(Founded 1974)
140 Clarendon St; Boston, MA 02116; website www.lyricstage.com
Spiro Veloudos, *Artistic Director*

Submission procedure: no unsolicited scripts; 1-page synopsis, dialogue sample,
character breakdown, set description and letter of inquiry; include cassette or CD for
musicals. **Types of material:** full-length plays, musicals. **Special interests:** MA
writers; women and minority writers; small-cast comedies and musicals; Boston
themes. **Facilities:** mainstage, 236 seats, thrust stage. **Production considerations:**
cast limit of 6 for plays, 9 for musicals, limited backstage space; prefers unit set.
Best submission time: Jun-Jul. **Response time:** 2 months letter; 6 months script.
Special programs: script development to production; commissioning program for
MA writers.

MADISON REPERTORY THEATRE
(Founded 1969)
122 State St, Suite 201; Madison, WI 53703-2500; (608) 256-0029,
    FAX 256-7433; email postmaster@madisonrep.org;
    website www.madisonrep.org
Richard Corley, *Associate Artistic Director*

Submission procedure: no unsolicited scripts; agent submission. **Types of material:**
full-length plays, translations, adaptations, musicals. **Facilities:** Isthmus Playhouse,
330 seats, thrust stage. **Production considerations:** cast limit of 15; no fly space.
Best submission time: Jun-Aug. **Response time:** 6 months. **Special programs:** Fall
Festival of the Future: annual new play festival of readings and workshops for plays
in development.

MAGIC THEATRE
(Founded 1967)
Fort Mason Center, Bldg D; San Francisco, CA 94123; (415) 441-8001,
    FAX 771-5505; website www.magictheatre.org
Mark Routhier, *Literary Manager*

Submission procedure: no unsolicited scripts; synopsis, 10-20-pages dialogue
sample, resume and letter of inquiry. **Types of material:** full-length plays. **Special**

American premieres; new plays with "a sense of urgency, ...it." **Facilities:** Magic Theatre Southside, 160 seats, proscenium ... e Northside, 160 seats, thrust stage. **Best submission time:** Sep-... me: 6 weeks letter; 8 months script.

:T THEATER
/75)

254u . s Blvd; Houston, TX 77005–3225; (713) 524–3622,
FAX 524–3977; email rudden@mainstreettheater.com;
website www.mainstreettheater.com
Rebecca Greene Udden, *Artistic Director*

Submission procedure: no unsolicited scripts; synopsis, dialogue sample and letter of inquiry. **Types of material:** full-length plays, one-acts, translations, adaptations, plays for young audiences, musicals. **Special interests:** plays by women; plays dealing with multicultural issues. **Facilities:** MST-Chelsea Market, 196 seats, thrust stage; MST-Times Blvd, 92 seats, thrust stage. **Production considerations:** cast limit of 12. **Best submission time:** year-round. **Response time:** 1 month letter; 6 months script.

MANHATTAN ENSEMBLE THEATER
(Founded 1999)
55 Mercer St; New York, NY 10013; (212) 925–1900, FAX 925–1947;
email info@met.com; website www.met.com
Elizabeth Bojsza, *Literary Manager*

Submission procedure: no unsolicited scripts; professional recommendation. **Types of material:** adaptations. **Special interests:** adaptations of 20th-century literature, biographies, film and lesser-known plays. **Facilities:** Manhattan Ensemble Theater, 139 seats, proscenium stage. **Production considerations:** cast limit of 10. **Best submission time:** year-round. **Response time:** 3 months.

MANHATTAN THEATRE CLUB
(Founded 1972)
311 West 43rd St, 8th Floor; New York, NY 10036; (212) 399–3000,
FAX 399–4329; website www.manhattantheatreclub.com
Paige Evans, *Director of Artistic Development*
Clifford Lee Johnson III, *Director of Musical Development*

Submission procedure: no unsolicited scripts; agent submission. **Types of material:** full-length plays, musicals. **Facilities:** Biltmore Theatre, 650 seats, proscenium stage; Stage I at City Center, 299 seats, proscenium stage; Stage II, 150 seats, thrust stage. **Production considerations:** prefers cast limit of 8, 1 set or unit set. **Best submission time:** year-round. **Response time:** 6 months. **Special programs:** readings and workshop productions of new musicals; 6@6: Rehearsed Readings of New Work reading series: in-house readings of new plays.

MARIN THEATRE COMPANY

(Founded 1967)

397 Miller Ave; Mill Valley, CA 94941; (415) 388-5200, FAX 388-0768;
email info@marintheatre.org; website www.marintheatre.org
Lee Sankowich, *Artistic Director*

Submission procedure: no unsolicited scripts; agent submission. **Types of material:** full-length plays, translations, adaptations, plays for young audiences. **Facilities:** Marin Theatre, 250 seats, proscenium stage; 2nd theatre, 109 seats, black box. **Best submission time:** Jun–Aug. **Response time:** 6 months.

MARK TAPER FORUM/KIRK DOUGLAS THEATRE

(Founded 1967)

601 West Temple St; Los Angeles, CA 90012; (213) 972-8033;
website www.taperahmanson.com
Pier Carlo Talenti, *Literary Manager*

Submission procedure: no unsolicited scripts; synopsis, 5–10-page dialogue sample and letter of inquiry with SASE for response. **Types of material:** full-length plays, translations, adaptations, plays for young audiences, musicals, solo pieces, performance art. **Facilities:** Mark Taper Forum, 742 seats, thrust stage; Kirk Douglas Theatre, 320 seats, proscenium stage. **Best submission time:** year-round. **Response time:** 10 weeks letter; 10 weeks script. **Special programs:** Performing for Los Angeles Youth (P.L.A.Y.): 55-minute plays that tour Southern CA schools; maximum 6 actors; suitable for grades K–8 or 9–12; scripts selected through theatre's normal submission procedure. Mark Taper Forum/Kirk Douglas Theatre Developmental Programs (see Development).

MA-YI THEATER COMPANY

(Founded 1989)

520 8th Ave, Suite 309; New York, NY 10018; (212) 971-4862;
email info@ma-yitheatre.org; website www.ma-yitheatre.org
Ralph Peña, *Artistic Director*

Submission procedure: no unsolicited scripts; synopsis and letter of inquiry. **Types of material:** full-length plays, one-acts, plays for young audiences, musicals, solo pieces. **Special interests:** works by Asian-American and non-Asian playwrights. **Facilities:** no permanent facility. **Best submission time:** Nov–Feb. **Response time:** 2 months letter; 6 months script.

MCCARTER THEATRE CENTER

(Founded 1972)

91 University Place; Princeton, NJ 08540; (609) 683-9100, FAX 497-0369;
email literary@mccarter.org; website www.mccarter.org
Carrie Hughes, *Literary Manager*

Submission procedure: no unsolicited scripts; professional recommendation. **Types of material:** full-length plays, musicals. **Facilities:** Matthews Theatre, 1077 seats, proscenium stage; Berlind Theatre, 380 seats, proscenium stage. **Best submission time:** Sep–May. **Response time:** 3 months.

MCC THEATER
(Founded 1986)
145 West 28th St, 8th Floor; New York, NY 10001; (212) 727-7722,
    FAX 727-7780
Stephen Willems, *Literary Manager*

Submission procedure: no unsolicited scripts; synopsis, 10-page dialogue sample and letter of inquiry with SASE or SASP for response. **Types of material:** full-length plays, one-acts, translations, adaptations, musicals. **Facilities:** MCC Theater, 99 seats, black box. **Production considerations:** cast limit of 10. **Best submission time:** year-round. **Response time:** 2 weeks letter; 2 months script.

MEADOW BROOK THEATRE
(Founded 1967)
Oakland University; Wilson Hall; Rochester, MI 48309; (248) 370-3310,
    FAX 370-3108; email JM@MBTheatre.com
David L. Regal, *Artistic Director*

Submission procedure: no unsolicited scripts; professional recommendation. **Types of material:** full-length plays, adaptations. **Special interests:** plays with Michigan location or subject matter. **Facilities:** Meadow Brook Theatre, 584 seats, proscenium stage. **Production considerations:** no fly space. **Best submission time:** Sep–May. **Response time:** 2 months (if interested).

MELTING POT THEATRE COMPANY
(Founded 1997)
2444 Broadway, Suite 231; New York, NY 10024; (212) 330-7211,
    FAX 874-6054; email larry@meltingpottheatre.com;
    website www.meltingpottheatre.com
Larry Hirschhorn, *Founding Artistic Director*

Submission procedure: accepts unsolicited scripts. **Types of material:** full-length plays, plays for young audiences, musicals. **Special interests:** plays about American history, biography, multiculturalism. **Facilities:** no permanent facility. **Production considerations:** cast limit of 10; moderate technical requirements. **Best submission time:** year-round. **Response time:** 3 months.

MERRIMACK REPERTORY THEATRE
(Founded 1979)
132 Warren St; Lowell, MA 01852; (978) 654-7550, FAX 654-7575;
    website www.merrimackrep.org
Charles Towers, *Artistic Director*

Submission procedure: no unsolicited scripts; agent submission. **Types of**

material: full-length plays, translations, adaptations. **Special interests:** plays that reflect the contemporary American experience. **Facilities:** Liberty Hall, 320 seats, proscenium/thrust stage. **Production considerations:** moderate cast size. **Best submission time:** year-round. **Response time:** 10 months.

MERRY-GO-ROUND PLAYHOUSE
(Founded 1958)
Box 506; Auburn, NY 13021; (315) 255-1305, FAX 252-3815;
email mgrplays@dreamscape.com; website www.merry-go-round.com
Youth Theatre Script Submissions

Submission procedure: accepts unsolicited scripts. **Types of material:** plays for young audiences including one-acts, translations, adaptations, musicals. **Special interests:** participatory plays for young audiences, plays for grades K-12; prefers familiarity with NY State learning standards and curriculum. **Facilities:** no permanent facility; touring company. **Production considerations:** cast limit of 4. **Best submission time:** Jan-Feb. **Response time:** 2 months.

METROSTAGE
(Founded 1984)
1201 North Royal St; Alexandria, VA 22314; (703) 548-9044,
FAX 548-9089; website www.metrostage.org
Carolyn Griffin, *Producing Artistic Director*

Submission procedure: no unsolicited scripts; synopsis, first 10 pages of dialogue, list of productions/readings and letter of inquiry. **Types of material:** full-length plays. **Facilities:** MetroStage, 130 seats, thrust stage. **Production considerations:** cast limit of 8, prefers 4; prefers 1 set. **Best submission time:** year-round. **Response time:** 1 month letter; 1 month script. **Special programs:** First Stage: staged reading series Oct-May.

METRO THEATER COMPANY
(Founded 1973)
8308 Olive Blvd; St. Louis, MO 63132-2814; (314) 997-6777,
FAX 997-1811; website www.metrotheatercompany.org
Carol North, *Artistic Director*

Submission procedure: no unsolicited scripts; professional recommendation. **Types of material:** plays for young audiences. **Special interests:** no works longer than 60 minutes; plays with music that are not dramatically limited by traditional concepts of "children's theatre." **Facilities:** no permanent facility; touring company. **Production considerations:** works cast from ensemble of 5, sets suitable for touring. **Best submission time:** year-round. **Response time:** 3 months. **Special programs:** new play readings, commissioning program; interested writers send letter of inquiry with recommendations from theatres who have produced writer's work.

MILWAUKEE CHAMBER THEATRE

(Founded 1975)

158 North Broadway; Milwaukee, WI 53202; (414) 276-8842,
FAX 277-4477; email mail@chamber-theatre.com

Montgomery Davis, *Artistic Director*

Submission procedure: no unsolicited scripts; professional recommendation. **Types of material:** full-length plays, translations, adaptations. **Special interests:** strong, well-crafted plays. **Facilities:** Broadway Theatre Center: Cabot Theatre, 358 seats, proscenium stage; studio, 96 seats, black box. **Production considerations:** 1 set or unit set. **Best submission time:** summer. **Response time:** 4 months.

MILWAUKEE REPERTORY THEATER

(Founded 1954)

108 East Wells St; Milwaukee, WI 53202; (414) 224-1761, FAX 224-9097;
email pkosidowski@milwaukeerep.com; website www.milwaukeerep.com

Paul Kosidowski, *Literary Director*

Submission procedure: no unsolicited scripts; professional recommendation or agent submission. **Types of material:** full-length plays, translations, adaptations, cabaret/revues. **Facilities:** Quadracci Powerhouse Theatre, 720 seats, thrust stage; Stiemke Theatre, 200 seats, flexible stage; Stackner Cabaret, 100 seats, cabaret stage. **Production considerations:** works for cabaret must not exceed 90 minutes in length. **Best submission time:** year-round. **Response time:** 4 months.

MILWAUKEE SHAKESPEARE COMPANY

(Founded 2000)

225 East Saint Paul Ave, #205; Milwaukee, WI 53202; (414) 298-9930,
FAX 298-9961; email milwshakespeare@aol.com;
website www.milwaukeeshakespeare.com

Paula Suozzi, *Artistic Director*

Submission procedure: no unsolicited scripts; synopsis and letter of inquiry. **Types of material:** full-length plays, one-acts, translations, adaptations. **Special interests:** new works with classical themes. **Facilities:** UWM Mainstage, 349 seats, thrust stage; UWM Studio, 99 seats, black box. **Best submission time:** May–Jun. **Response time:** 3 weeks letter; 6 months script.

THE MIRACLE THEATRE GROUP

(Founded 1985)

425 Southeast Sixth Ave; Portland, OR 97214; (503) 236-7253,
FAX 236-4174; email mainstage@milagro.org;
website www.milagro.org

Olga Sanchez, *Artistic Director of Miracle Mainstage*

Submission procedure: accepts unsolicited scripts. **Types of material:** full-length plays, translations, adaptations. **Special interests:** Hispanic playwrights, plays that deal with the Hispanic experience. **Facilities:** El Centro Milagro, 120 seats, thrust stage. **Production considerations:** cast limit of 10, unit set; no fly space. **Best submission time:** year-round. **Response time:** 5 months.

MISSOURI REPERTORY THEATRE
(Founded 1964)
4949 Cherry St; Kansas City, MO 64110-2263; (816) 235-2727,
FAX 235-6562; email theatre@umkc.edu;
website www.missourireptheatre.org
Peter Altman, *Producing Artistic Director*

Submission procedure: no unsolicited scripts; agent submission. **Types of material:** full-length plays, translations, adaptations. **Facilities:** Spencer Theatre, 645 seats, modified thrust stage.

MIXED BLOOD THEATRE COMPANY
(Founded 1975)
1501 South Fourth St; Minneapolis, MN 55454; (612) 338-0937;
email czar@mixedblood.com
Dave Kunz, *Script Czar*

Submission procedure: no unsolicited scripts; 1-page synopsis and letter of inquiry. **Types of material:** full-length plays, musicals, cabaret/revues. **Special interests:** political, issue-oriented comedies; contemporary plays set in U.S.; world theatre pieces; plays by and about people with disabilities. **Facilities:** Main Stage, 200 seats, flexible stage. **Best submission time:** Aug-Jan. **Response time:** varies; will only respond if interested.

THE MONTANA REPERTORY THEATRE
(Founded 1968)
Department of Drama and Dance; University of Montana;
Missoula, MT 59812-8136; (406) 243-6809, FAX 243-5726;
email montana.rep@mso.umt.edu
Greg Johnson, *Artistic Director*

Submission procedure: no unsolicited scripts; synopsis, resume and letter of inquiry. **Types of material:** full-length plays, one-acts, musicals. **Special interests:** plays by and about Native Americans. **Facilities:** no permanent facility; touring company. **Best submission time:** summer. **Response time:** 3 months letter; 6 months script.

MOVING ARTS

(Founded 1992)

514 South Spring St; Los Angeles, CA 90013; (213) 622-8906,
FAX 622-8946; email treynichols@movingarts.org;
website www.movingarts.org

Trey Nichols, *Literary Director*

Submission procedure: no unsolicited scripts; synopsis, dialogue sample, resume and letter of inquiry with SASE for response. **Types of material:** full-length plays, translations, adaptations. **Special interests:** work not previously produced in Los Angeles area. **Facilities:** Los Angeles Theatre Center, 60 seats, black box. **Production considerations:** modest production demands; limited wing and fly space. **Best submission time:** year-round. **Response time:** 3 months letter; 9 months script. **Special Programs:** Premiere One-Act Festival: annual fall festival of one-acts chosen from one-act competition. (See Premiere One-Act Competition in Prizes.)

MU PERFORMING ARTS

(Formerly Theater Mu)

(Founded 1992)

2700 Northeast Winter St, Suite 1A; Minneapolis, MN 55413;
(612) 824-4804, FAX 824-3396; email info@theatermu.org;
website www.theatermu.org

Rick Shiomi, *Artistic Director*

Submission procedure: accepts unsolicited scripts. **Types of material:** full-length plays, one-acts, adaptations, plays for young audiences. **Special interests:** Asian-American plays; plays combining traditional Asian performance with western theatre styles; short plays suitable for touring to schools. **Facilities:** no permanent facility; company performs in various proscenium venues with approximately 150 seats. **Production considerations:** cast limit of 10, simple sets. **Best submission time:** year-round. **Response time:** 2 months letter; 3 months script. **Special programs:** annual weekend staged reading series; touring and outreach programs.

NACL THEATRE (NORTH AMERICAN CULTURAL LABORATORY)

(Founded 1997)

Box 2201 Times Square Station; New York, NY 10108; (718) 398-4586,
FAX 398-2794; email nacl@nacl.org; website www.nacl.org

Brad Krumholz, *Director*

Submission procedure: no unsolicited scripts; professional recommendation. **Types of material:** full-length plays, one-acts, translations, adaptations. **Special interests:** experimental, multidisciplinary performance works. **Facilities:** NaCl Catskills, 150 seats, flexible stage. **Production considerations:** cast limit of 4-8; minimal set requirements. **Best submission time:** year-round. **Response time:** 10 weeks. **Special programs:** The Catskill Festival of New Theatre annual festival of new work; write for application and guidelines.

NATIONAL THEATRE OF THE DEAF

(Founded 1967)
139 North Main St; West Hartford, CT 06107; (860) 236-4193,
FAX 236-4163; email info@ntd.org; website www.ntd.org
Paul L. Winters, *Executive Director*

Submission procedure: no unsolicited scripts; synopsis, character breakdown, sample pages and letter of inquiry with SASE for response. **Types of material:** full-length plays, adaptations, plays for young audiences. **Special interests:** work not produced professionally; deaf issues; culturally diverse plays. **Facilities:** no permanent facility; touring company. **Production considerations:** cast limit of 10; production must tour. **Best submission time:** year-round. **Response time:** 1 month letter; 6 months script.

NEBRASKA THEATRE CARAVAN

(Founded 1976)
6915 Cass St; Omaha, NE 68132; (402) 553-4890, FAX 553-6288;
    email caravan@omahaplayhouse.com
Jerry O'Connor, *Producing Director*

Submission procedure: no unsolicited scripts; synopsis and letter of inquiry. **Types of material:** adaptations, plays for young audiences, musicals. **Special interests:** work suitable for elementary, intermediate and high school audiences only. **Facilities:** no permanent facility; touring company. **Production considerations:** cast limit of 6, cast limit of 5-7 for musicals; 1 set. **Best submission time:** Sep-Dec. **Response time:** 1 month letter; 3 months script.

NEVADA THEATRE COMPANY

(Founded 1997)
2928 Lake East Dr; Las Vegas, NV 89117; (702) 873-0191,
    FAX 877-6051; email nvtheatreco@aol.com
Deanna Duplechain, *Artistic Director*

Submission procedure: no unsolicited scripts; professional recommendation. **Types of material:** plays for young audiences. **Special interests:** irreverent, innovative storytelling low on production values and high on actor-driven theatricality. **Facilities:** mainstage, 80 seats, black box. **Production considerations:** cast limit of 4. **Best submission time:** year-round. **Response time:** 4 months. **Special programs:** BOOKS ALIVE!: touring program performs original scripts based on books and/or history; 50-minute maximum, cast limit of 4; scripts chosen through theatre's normal submission process.

THE NEW CONSERVATORY THEATRE CENTER

(Founded 1981)

25 Van Ness, Lower Lobby; San Francisco, CA 94102; (415) 861–4914,
FAX 861–6988; email email@nctcsf.org; website www.nctcsf.org
Ed Decker, *Artistic/Executive Director*

Submission procedure: no unsolicited scripts; synopsis and letter of inquiry. **Types of material:** full-length plays, plays for young audiences, musicals. **Special interests:** gay plays for adult audiences. **Facilities:** Decker Theatre, 132 seats, proscenium stage; Walker Theatre, 75 seats, black box; City Theatre, 55 seats, black box. **Best submission time:** year-round. **Response time:** 3 months letter; 6 months script.

NEW FEDERAL THEATRE

(Founded 1970)

292 Henry St; New York, NY 10002; (212) 353–1176, FAX 353–1088;
email newfederal@aol.com; website www.newfederaltheatre.org
Woodie King, Jr., *Producing Director*

Submission procedure: no unsolicited scripts; professional recommendation. **Types of material:** full-length plays. **Special interests:** social and political issues; family and community themes related to minorities and women. **Facilities:** Henry Street Settlement: Harry De Jur Playhouse, 300 seats, proscenium stage; Experimental Theatre, 143 seats, black box; Recital Hall, 100 seats, thrust stage. **Production considerations:** small cast, no more than 2 sets. **Best submission time:** year-round. **Response time:** 5 months.

NEW GEORGES

(Founded 1992)

109 West 27th St, Suite 9A; New York, NY 10001; (646) 336–8077,
FAX 336–8051; email info@newgeorges.org;
website www.newgeorges.org
Emily DeVoti, *Literary Manager*

Submission procedure: accepts unsolicited scripts. **Types of material:** full-length plays. **Special interests:** plays by women only; works with "vigorous use of language and heightened perspectives on reality." **Facilities:** no permanent facility. **Best submission time:** year-round. **Response time:** 3 months letter; 9 months script.

NEW GROUND THEATRE

(Founded 2001)

1821 Sunset Dr; Bettendorf, IA 52722; (563) 326–7529,
FAX 359–7576; email litdept@newgroundtheatre.org;
website www.newgroundtheatre.org
Chris Jansen, *Artistic Director*

Submission procedure: accepts unsolicited scripts. **Types of material:** full-length plays, one-acts, musicals. **Special interests:** plays by Midwestern playwrights. **Facilities:** Becherer Hall, 350 seats, proscenium stage. **Production considerations:** prefers cast limit of 6, 1 set or flexible staging; no fly space **Best submission time:** Apr–Jun. **Response time:** 6 months.

THE NEW GROUP
(Founded 1991)
410 West 42nd St; New York, NY 10036; email info@thenewgroup.org;
   website www.thenewgroup.org
Ian Morgan, *Associate Artistic Director*

Submission procedure: no unsolicited scripts; 10–20-page dialogue sample, resume and letter of inquiry with SASE for response. **Types of material:** full-length plays. **Special interests:** works not previously produced in New York City; "challenging, risk-taking plays that explore character and emotion in a contemporary context." **Facilities:** various 99–199 seat theatres. **Best submission time:** year-round. **Response time:** 9 months. **Special programs:** New Group Associates Program: regular meetings and reading series for playwrights; writers admitted based on quality of submitted script.

NEW JERSEY REPERTORY COMPANY
(Founded 1997)
179 Broadway; Long Branch, NJ 07740; (732) 229–3166, FAX 229–3167;
   email info@njrep.org; website www.njrep.org
SuzAnne Barabas, *Artistic Director*

Submission procedure: accepts unsolicited scripts with synopsis and character breakdown. **Types of material:** full-length plays, one-acts, musicals. **Special interests:** work not produced professionally; social, humanistic themes. **Facilities:** Main Stage, 72 seats, black box; Second Stage, 50 seats, flexible stage. **Production considerations:** cast limit of 5, unit or simple set. **Best submission time:** year-round. **Response time:** 12 months. **Special programs:** Script-in-Hand: year-round reading series for more than 20 plays; of these, up to 6 selected for Main Stage production.

THE NEW JOMANDI PRODUCTIONS, INC.
(Formerly Jomandi Productions)
(Founded 1978)
City Hall East; 675 Ponce de Leon Ave, 8th Floor; Atlanta, GA 30308;
   (404) 876–6346, FAX 872–5764; email iroyall@jomandi.com;
   website www.jomandi.com
Inda C. Royall, *Communications Director*

Submission procedure: accepts unsolicited scripts with synopsis, dialogue sample, resume and letter of inquiry. **Types of material:** full-length plays, adaptations, plays for young audiences, musicals, solo pieces. **Special interests:** historical or contemporary portrayals of the African-American experience; adaptations of African-

American literature. **Facilities:** 14th Street Playhouse, 370 seats, proscenium/thrust stage. **Production considerations:** prefers small cast, prefers unit set. **Best submission time:** spring–summer. **Response time:** 12 months (if interested).

NEW REPERTORY THEATRE
(Founded 1985)
Box 610418; Newton Highlands, MA 02461; (617) 928-9831;
    email adamzahler@newrep.org; website www.newrep.org
Rick Lombardo, *Producing Artistic Director*

Submission procedure: no unsolicited scripts; synopsis, dialogue sample and letter of inquiry. **Types of material:** full-length plays, translations, adaptations. **Special interests:** plays of ideas that center around pressing issues of our time; multicultural themes; intimate, interpersonal themes. **Facilities:** New Repertory Theatre, 155 seats, thrust stage. **Production considerations:** cast limit of 7. **Best submission time:** May–Aug. **Response time:** 2 months letter; 6 months script.

NEW STAGE THEATRE
(Founded 1966)
1100 Carlisle; Jackson, MS 39202; (601) 948-3533, FAX 948-3538;
    email newstage@netdoor.com;
    website www.newstagetheatre.com

Submission procedure: no unsolicited scripts; synopsis and letter of inquiry. **Types of material:** full-length plays, one-acts, solo pieces. **Facilities:** Meyer Crystal Auditorium, 364 seats, proscenium stage. **Production considerations:** cast limit of 8. **Best submission time:** summer–fall. **Response time:** 1 month letter; 3 months script. **Special programs:** Eudora Welty New Play Series.

NEW THEATRE
(Founded 1986)
4120 Laguna St; Coral Gables, FL 33146; (305) 443-5373,
    FAX 443-1642; email admin@new-theatre.org;
    website www.new-theatre.org
Rafael De Acha, *Artistic Director*

Submission procedure: no unsolicited scripts; synopsis, resume and letter of inquiry. **Types of material:** full-length plays, translations, adaptations. **Special interests:** prefers theatrical, language-driven plays. **Facilities:** New Theatre, 120 seats, endstage. **Production considerations:** cast limit of 7. **Best submission time:** year-round. **Response time:** 3 months letter; 6 months script.

NEW YORK STAGE AND FILM

(Founded 1984)

315 West 36th St, Suite 1006; New York, NY 10018; (212) 736-4240,
FAX 736-4241; email info@newyorkstageandfilm.org

Elizabeth Timperman, *Managing Producer*

Submission procedure: no unsolicited scripts; synopsis, resume and letter of inquiry. **Types of material:** full-length plays. **Facilities:** Powerhouse Theatre, 135 seats, black box; Coal Bin, 135 seats, black box. **Best submission time:** 1 Sep–31 Oct only. **Response time:** 2 months letter; 3 months script.

NEW YORK STATE THEATRE INSTITUTE

(Founded 1974)

37 First St; Troy, NY 12180; (518) 274-3200, FAX 274-3815;
email pbs@capital.net; website www.nysti.org

Patricia Di Benedetto Snyder, *Producing Artistic Director*

Submission procedure: no unsolicited scripts; synopsis, cast/scene breakdown and letter of inquiry. **Types of material:** full-length plays, adaptations, musicals. **Special interests:** works for family audiences only. **Facilities:** Schacht Fine Arts Center, 800 seats, proscenium stage. **Best submission time:** Mar–Sep. **Response time:** 2 months letter; 6 months script. **Special programs:** developmental workshops: playwrights receive staged reading or workshop production, negotiable remuneration, travel and housing.

NEW YORK THEATRE WORKSHOP

(Founded 1979)

83 East 4th St; New York, NY 10003; (212) 780-9037;
website www.nytw.org

Tony Amicarella, *Director of Project Development/Dramaturgy*

Submission procedure: no unsolicited scripts; synopsis, 10-page dialogue sample, resume and letter of inquiry. **Types of material:** full-length plays, one-acts, translations, musicals, solo pieces. **Special interests:** exploration of political and historical events and institutions that shape contemporary life. **Facilities:** 79 East 4th Street Theatre, 180 seats, proscenium stage; East 4th Street Theatre, 70 seats, proscenium stage. **Best submission time:** year-round. **Response time:** 3 months letter; 8 months script. **Special programs:** Mondays @ 3: in-house readings. Larson Lab: in-house developmental workshops for musicals. Summer Residencies Out-Of-Town: application by invitation only. New York Theatre Workshop Playwriting Fellowship for emerging writers of color based in New York (see Fellowships and Grants).

NEXT ACT THEATRE

(Founded 1990)

Box 394; Milwaukee, WI 53201; (414) 278–7780, FAX 278–5930

David Cecsarini, *Artistic Director/Producer*

Submission procedure: no unsolicited scripts; agent submission of synopsis, cast list, production requirements and letter of inquiry. **Types of material:** full-length plays, adaptations, solo pieces. **Facilities:** Studio Space, 99 seats, thrust stage. **Production considerations:** small cast size, minimal production demands. **Best submission time:** spring. **Response time:** 1 month letter; 6 months script.

A NOISE WITHIN

(Founded 1991)

234 South Brand Blvd; Glendale, CA 91204; (818) 240–0910, FAX 240–0826

Geoff Elliot, *Artistic Director*

Submission procedure: accepts unsolicited scripts. **Types of material:** translations, adaptations. **Special interests:** translations and adaptations of classical material only. **Facilities:** A Noise Within, 145 seats, thrust stage. **Best submission time:** fall. **Response time:** 8 months.

NORTH COAST REPERTORY THEATRE

(Founded 1982)

987D Lomas Santa Fe Dr; Solana Beach, CA 92075; (858) 481–2155,
    FAX 481–0530; email NCRT@northcoastrep.org;
    website www.northcoastrep.org

David Ellenstein, *Artistic Director*

Submission procedure: no unsolicited scripts; synopsis, bio and letter of inquiry. **Types of material:** full-length plays, translations, adaptations, plays for young audiences, musicals, cabaret/revues. **Facilities:** NCRT, 194 seats, thrust stage. **Production considerations:** small cast size; limited space. **Best submission time:** year-round. **Response time:** 6 months letter; 6 months script.

THE NORTHEAST THEATRE (TNT)

(Founded 1992)

One College Green; La Plume, PA 18440; (570) 945–5141 ext 2222;
    email contact@thenortheasttheatre.org;
    website www.thenortheasttheatre.org

Literary Manager

Submission procedure: no unsolicited scripts; synopsis and letter of inquiry. **Types of material:** full-length plays, solo pieces. **Facilities:** The Northeast Theatre, 99–150 seats, flexible stage. **Production considerations:** prefers cast limit of 6; minimal production demands. **Best submission time:** May–Aug. **Response time:** 3 months letter; 3 months script. **Special programs:** staged reading series.

NORTHERN STAGE

(Founded 1992)
Box 4287; White River Junction, VT 05001; (802) 291-9009,
FAX 291-9156; email info@northernstage.org;
website www.northernstage.org
Robert Jay Cronin, *Associate Artistic Director*

Submission procedure: accepts unsolicited scripts. **Types of material:** full-length plays, one-acts, musicals. **Special interests:** New England playwrights. **Facilities:** Briggs Opera House, 245 seats, thrust stage. **Production considerations:** minimal production requirements. **Best submission time:** year-round. **Response time:** 8 months.

NORTHLIGHT THEATRE

(Founded 1975)
9501 North Skokie Blvd; Skokie, IL 60076; (847) 679-9501,
FAX 679-1879; website www.northlight.org
Rosanna Forrest, *Dramaturg/Literary Manager*

Submission procedure: no unsolicited scripts; synopsis, 10-page dialogue sample, cast list and letter of inquiry with SASE for response. **Types of material:** full-length plays, chamber musicals. **Special interests:** the public world and public issues; plays of ideas; works that are passionate and/or hilarious; heightened realism, but nothing overtly experimental or absurdist. **Facilities:** Center East Theatre, 850 seats, proscenium stage; Northlight Theatre, 345 seats, thrust stage. **Production considerations:** prefers cast limit of 2-6, 1 unit or flexible set. **Best submission time:** year-round. **Response time:** 1 month letter; 8 months script.

NORTH SHORE MUSIC THEATRE

(Founded 1955)
62 Dunham Rd; Beverly, MA 01915; (978) 232-7203, FAX 921-7874;
website www.nsmt.org
John LaRock, *Associate Producer*

Submission procedure: no unsolicited scripts; synopsis and letter of inquiry with SASE for response; include cassette or CD for musicals. **Types of material:** musicals, musicals for young audiences. **Special interests:** musicals only. **Facilities:** Main Stage, 1800 seats, arena stage; Workshop, 100 seats, flexible stage. **Production considerations:** prefers cast limit of 12. **Best submission time:** year-round. **Response time:** 1 month letter; 6 months script. **Special programs:** New Works Development Program: spring, fall and summer (with annual summer festival) workshop productions of new works with authors in residence; theatre pays (rate varies) and houses writers; contact theatre for information.

ODYSSEY THEATRE ENSEMBLE
(Founded 1969)
2055 South Sepulveda Blvd; Los Angeles, CA 90025; (310) 477-2055
Sally Essex-Lopresti, *Director of Literary Programs*

Submission procedure: no unsolicited scripts; synopsis, 8-10-page dialogue sample, play's production history (if any), resume and letter of inquiry with SASE for response; include cassette for musicals. **Types of material:** full-length plays, translations, adaptations, musicals. **Special interests:** culturally diverse works; works with innovative form or provocative subject matter; works exploring the enduring questions of human existence and the possibilities of the live theatre experience; works with political or sociological impact. **Facilities:** Odyssey 1, 99 seats, flexible stage; Odyssey 2, 99 seats, thrust stage; Odyssey 3, 99 seats, endstage. **Production considerations:** plays must be 90 minutes or longer. **Best submission time:** year-round. **Response time:** 1 month letter; 6 months script.

OLDCASTLE THEATRE COMPANY
(Founded 1972)
Box 1555; Bennington, VT 05201-1555; (802) 447-1267,
    FAX 442-3704
Eric Peterson, *Producing Artistic Director*

Submission procedure: accepts unsolicited scripts. **Types of material:** full-length plays, musicals. **Facilities:** Bennington Center for the Arts, 300 seats, modified proscenium stage. **Best submission time:** winter. **Response time:** 6 months.

THE OLD GLOBE
(Formerly The Globe Theatres)
(Founded 1935)
Box 2171; San Diego, CA 92112-2171; (619) 231-1941
Diane Sinor, *Dramaturgy Associate*

Submission procedure: no unsolicited scripts; synopsis and letter of inquiry with SASE for response. **Types of material:** full-length plays, translations, adaptations. **Special interests:** well-crafted, strongly theatrical material. **Facilities:** Lowell Davies Festival Stage, 620 seats, outdoor stage; Old Globe Theatre, 581 seats, modified thrust stage; Cassius Carter Centre Stage, 225 seats, arena stage. **Production considerations:** prefers cast limit of 8. **Best submission time:** year-round. **Response time:** 3 months letter; 10 months script.

OLNEY THEATRE CENTER FOR THE ARTS
(Founded 1937)
2001 Olney-Sandy Spring Rd; Olney, MD 20832; (301) 924-4485,
    FAX 924-2654
Jim Petosa, *Artistic Director*

Submission procedure: no unsolicited scripts; professional recommendation. **Types of material:** full-length plays, translations, adaptations, solo pieces. **Facilities:** mainstage, 500 seats, proscenium stage; The Lab Theatre, 200 seats, flexible stage. **Production considerations:** cast limit of 8. **Best submission time:** year-round. **Response time:** 6 months.

OMAHA THEATER COMPANY FOR YOUNG PEOPLE
(Founded 1949)
2001 Farnam St; Omaha, NE 68102; (402) 345-4852, FAX 344-7255
James Larson, *Artistic Director*

Submission procedure: no unsolicited scripts; professional recommendation. **Types of material:** plays for young audiences. **Special interests:** 60-minute plays only; plays based on children's literature and contemporary issues. **Facilities:** Omaha Theater Company, 932 seats, proscenium stage; second stage, 175 seats, black box. **Production considerations:** cast limit of 10; prefers unit set. **Best submission time:** year-round. **Response time:** 6 months.

OPEN CIRCLE THEATER
(Founded 1992)
429 Boren Ave N; Seattle, WA 98109; (206) 382-4250;
    website www.octheater.com
Ron Sandahl, *Artistic Director*

Submission procedure: no unsolicited scripts; synopsis, 10-page dialogue sample, resume and letter of inquiry; local professional recommendation. **Types of material:** full-length plays, adaptations, musicals. **Special interests:** "new works and adaptations that speak to the human condition through fantasy and mythic storytelling"; plays suitable for site-specific staging; plays incorporating new music and dance or movement; language-oriented plays; no naturalism. **Facilities:** Open Circle Theater, 70 seats, flexible stage. **Best submission time:** year-round. **Response time:** 3 months letter; 6 months script.

THE OPEN EYE THEATER
(Founded 1972)
Box 959; Margaretville, NY 12455; (845) 586-1660, FAX 586-1660;
    email openeye@catskill.net; website www.theopeneye.org
Amie Brockway, *Producing Artistic Director*

Submission procedure: no unsolicited scripts; synopsis and letter of inquiry with self-addressed envelope (no postage) for response. **Types of material:** full-length plays, one-acts, translations, adaptations, plays for young audiences. **Special interests:** plays for young and multigenerational audiences; culturally diverse themes; plays with music; ensemble plays; plays 10 minutes or longer; Catskill Mountain-area writers. **Facilities:** 960 Main Street, 99 seats, modified proscenium stage. **Production considerations:** minimal set. **Best submission time:** Oct-Apr. **Response time:** 1 week letter (if interested); 6 months script. **Special programs:** New Play Works: new-play developmental program of readings and workshop productions.

OPENSTAGE THEATRE & COMPANY

(Founded 1973)

Box 617; Fort Collins, CO 80522; (970) 484–5237, FAX 482–4858;
email jessicav@openstagetheatre.org;
website www.openstagetheatre.org

Jessica V. Freestone, *Producing Artistic Director*

Submission procedure: accepts unsolicited scripts; prefers resume and letter of inquiry. **Types of material:** full-length plays, one-acts, translations, adaptations, solo pieces. **Facilities:** second-stage, 25–75 seats, black box. **Production considerations:** minimal technical capabilities; limited space. **Best submission time:** year-round. **Response time:** 1 month letter; 6 months script.

OREGON SHAKESPEARE FESTIVAL

(Founded 1935)

Box 158; Ashland, OR 97520; (541) 482–2111, FAX 482–0446;
email literary@ostashland.org

Lue Morgan Douthit, *Director of Literary Development/Dramaturgy*

Submission procedure: no unsolicited scripts; letter or email of inquiry. **Types of material:** full-length plays. **Special interests:** plays of ideas; language-oriented plays; women and minority writers encouraged. **Facilities:** Elizabethan Theatre, 1194 seats, outdoor Elizabethan stage; Angus Bowmer Theatre, 600 seats, thrust stage; New Theatre, 250–350 seats, flexible stage. **Best submission time:** year-round. **Response time:** 6 months. **Special programs:** reading series; commissioning programs.

PAN ASIAN REPERTORY THEATRE

(Founded 1977)

520 Eighth Ave; New York, NY 10018; (212) 868–4030, FAX 868–4033;
email panasian@aol.com; website www.panasianrep.org

Tisa Chang, *Artistic/Producing Director*

Submission procedure: no unsolicited scripts; synopsis and letter of inquiry. **Types of material:** full-length plays, translations, adaptations, musicals. **Special interests:** Asian or Asian-American themes only. **Facilities:** West End Theatre (in the church of St. Paul and St. Andrew), 99 seats, proscenium stage. **Production considerations:** prefers cast limit of 7. **Best submission time:** summer. **Response time:** 6 months letter; 9 months script. **Special programs:** staged readings and workshops.

PANGEA WORLD THEATER

(Founded 1995)

711 West Lake St, Suite 102; Minneapolis, MN 55408; (612) 822–0015,
FAX 821–1070; email pangea@pangeaworldtheater.org;
website www.pangeaworldtheater.org

Meena Natarajan, *Executive & Literary Director*

Submission procedure: no unsolicited scripts; letter of inquiry. **Types of material:**

full-length plays, translations, adaptations, solo pieces. **Special interests:** adaptations of international literature; multiethnic works. **Facilities:** no permanent facility. **Best submission time:** year-round. **Response time:** 6 months.

THE PASADENA PLAYHOUSE
(Founded 1917)
39 South El Molino Ave; Pasadena, CA 91101; (626) 792–8672,
  FAX 792–7343; email patroninfo@pasadenaplayhouse.org;
  website www.pasadenaplayhouse.org
Jayson Raitt, *Production Associate*

Submission procedure: no unsolicited scripts; agent submission. **Types of material:** full-length plays, musicals. **Facilities:** The Pasadena Playhouse, 686 seats, proscenium stage. **Production considerations:** cast limit of 2–7, 1 set or unit set, modest musical requirements. **Best submission time:** year-round. **Response time:** 12 months.

PASSAGE THEATRE
(Founded 1985)
Box 967; Trenton, NJ 08605; (609) 392–0766, FAX 392–0318;
  email info@passagetheatre.org; website www.passagetheatre.org
Nancy Vitale, *Literary Manager*

Submission procedure: no unsolicited scripts; professional recommendation. **Types of material:** full-length plays, solo pieces. **Special interests:** African-American or Jewish-themed works encouraged. **Facilities:** Mill Hill Playhouse, 120 seats, thrust stage. **Production considerations:** small cast; very little wing space, no fly space. **Best submission time:** summer. **Response time:** 3 months.

PCPA THEATERFEST
(Founded 1964)
Box 1700; Santa Maria, CA 93456–1700; (805) 928–7731,
  FAX 928–7506; email jfarr@pcpa.org; website www.pcpa.org
Jeanette D. Farr, *Literary Coordinator*

Submission procedure: no unsolicited scripts; synopsis and letter of inquiry. **Types of material:** full-length plays, translations, adaptations, musicals. **Facilities:** Festival Theater, 708 seats, thrust stage; Marian Theatre, 448 seats, thrust stage; Severson Theater, 180 seats, black box. **Best submission time:** year-round. **Response time:** 3 months letter; 6 months script. **Special programs:** InterPlay: The Stage Between Reading Series.

THE PEARL THEATRE COMPANY, INC.

(Founded 1982)

80 Saint Marks Pl; New York, NY 10003; (212) 505–3404,
    FAX 505–3404; website www.pearltheatre.org

Shepard Sobel, *Artistic Director*

Submission procedure: no unsolicited scripts; letter of inquiry. **Types of material:** translations. **Special interests:** translations (not adaptations) of classical plays. **Facilities:** Theatre 80, 160 seats, proscenium stage. **Best submission time:** year-round. **Response time:** 2 weeks letter; 3 months script.

PEGASUS PLAYERS

(Founded 1978)

1145 West Wilson; Chicago, IL 60640; (773) 878–9761,
    FAX 271–8057; email pegasusp@megsinet.net

Alex Levy, *Literary Manager*

Submission procedure: no unsolicited scripts; synopsis and letter of inquiry. **Types of material:** full-length plays, translations, adaptations, musicals, solo pieces. **Facilities:** The O'Rourke Center for the Performing Arts, 250 seats, proscenium stage. **Best submission time:** year-round. **Response time:** 1 month letter; 6 months script. **Special programs:** Chicago Young Playwrights Festival: annual Jan festival of plays by Chicago-area high school students; write for information.

PENDRAGON THEATRE

(Founded 1980)

15 Brandy Brook Ave; Saranac Lake, NY 12983; (518) 891–1854,
    FAX 891–7012; email pdragon@northnet.org;
    website www.pendragontheatre.com

Molly Pietz, *Literary Manager*

Submission procedure: no unsolicited scripts; synopsis, dialogue sample and letter of inquiry with SASP for response. **Types of material:** full-length plays, plays for young audiences. **Special interests:** plays suitable for performance by 11–16-year-olds. **Facilities:** Pendragon Theatre, 132 seats, black box. **Production considerations:** cast limit of 8; simple set. **Best submission time:** year-round. **Response time:** 1 month letter; 3 months script.

THE PENUMBRA THEATRE COMPANY

(Founded 1976)

The Martin Luther King Bldg; 270 North Kent St;
    St. Paul, MN 55102–1794; (651) 224–4601, FAX 224–7074

Lou Bellamy, *Artistic Director*

Submission procedure: accepts unsolicited scripts with resume. **Types of material:** full-length plays, one-acts, translations, adaptations, plays for young audiences, musicals. **Special interests:** works that address the African-American experience and the African diaspora. **Facilities:** Hallie Q. Brown Theatre, 260 seats, proscenium/thrust stage. **Best submission time:** year-round. **Response time:** 9

months. **Special programs:** Summer Institute Youth Program: *dates:* mid Jun–mid Jul.

THE PEOPLE'S LIGHT AND THEATRE COMPANY

(Founded 1974)

39 Conestoga Rd; Malvern, PA 19355-1798; (610) 647-1900;

  email cortese@peopleslight.org; website www.peopleslight.org

Alda Cortese, *Literary Manager*

Submission procedure: no unsolicited scripts; synopsis, 10-page dialogue sample, cast list and letter of inquiry. **Types of material:** full-length plays, translations, adaptations. **Special interests:** intelligent, original scripts for a family audience. **Facilities:** People's Light and Theatre, 350 seats, flexible stage; Steinbright Stage, 99–150 seats, flexible stage. **Production considerations:** 1 set or unit set. **Best submission time:** year-round. **Response time:** 2 weeks letter; 10 months script.

PERFORMANCE NETWORK THEATRE

(Founded 1981)

120 East Huron; Ann Arbor, MI 48104; (734) 663-0696,

  FAX 663-7367; email info@performancenetwork.org;

  website www.performancenetwork.org

Carla Milarch, *Artistic Director*

Submission procedure: no unsolicited scripts; synopsis, 10-page dialogue sample and SASP. **Types of material:** full-length plays, musicals. **Facilities:** Performance Network, 139 seats, black box/thrust. **Production considerations:** prefers cast limit of 10; no fly space. **Best submission time:** year-round. **Response time:** 6 months.

PERSEVERANCE THEATRE

(Founded 1979)

914 3rd St; Douglas, AK 99824; (907) 364-2421, FAX 364-2603;

  email info@perseverancetheatre.org;

  website www.perseverancetheatre.org

Submission procedure: no unsolicited scripts; synopsis, dialogue sample and letter of inquiry from AK playwrights only. **Types of material:** full-length plays, one-acts, solo pieces, musicals. **Special interests:** AK playwrights; gay/lesbian playwrights and themes; women playwrights; Native American playwrights and themes; political/social issues; musicals. **Facilities:** mainstage, 150 seats, thrust stage; Phoenix, 50–75 seats, flexible stage. **Best submission time:** year-round. **Response time:** 1 month letter; 3 months script. **Special programs:** Spring Playreading Festival: annual spring presentation of diverse new work from across AK and the country. Native Playreading and Performance Festival: annual Nov presentation of Native American work.

PHILADELPHIA THEATRE COMPANY

(Founded 1974)

230 South 15th St, 4th Floor; Philadelphia, PA 19102; (215) 985-1400,
FAX 985-5800; website www.phillytheatreco.com

Michele Volansky, *Dramaturg*

Submission procedure: no unsolicited scripts; agent submission. **Types of material:** full-length plays. **Special interests:** new American plays; social/humanistic themes; no mysteries or plays for young audiences. **Facilities:** Plays and Players Theater, 324 seats, proscenium stage. **Best submission time:** year-round. **Response time:** 6 months. **Special programs:** STAGES: program of staged readings, possibly leading to mainstage production; scripts selected through theatre's normal submission procedure.

PHOENIX ARTS ASSOCIATION THEATRE

(Founded 1985)

138 Carl St; San Francisco, CA 94117-3930; (415) 759-7696,
FAX 664-5001; email Lbaf23@aol.com

Linda Ayres-Frederick, *Executive Artistic Producing Director*

Submission procedure: no unsolicited scripts; synopsis and letter of inquiry. **Types of material:** full-length plays, one-acts, translations, adaptations, cabarets/revues, solo pieces. **Special interests:** plays about women, especially those dealing with mature women's issues; plays about contemporary and historical figures; plays in French and English. **Facilities:** Phoenix Theatre, 49-65 seats, thrust stage. **Production considerations:** cast limit of 7; maximum 2 sets, 1 set or unit set preferred; limited fly space. **Best submission time:** year-round. **Response time:** 6 weeks letter; 6 months script. **Special programs:** West Coast Playwrights Alliance.

PHOENIX THEATRE

(Founded 1920)

100 East McDowell Rd; Phoenix, AZ 85004; (602) 258-1974,
FAX 253-3626; website www.phoenixtheatre.net

Michael Barnard, *Artistic Director*

Submission procedure: no unsolicited scripts; synopsis, production history (if any) and letter of inquiry with SASE for response. **Types of material:** plays for young audiences, musicals, cabaret/revues. **Special interests:** plays with strong narratives suitable for a general audience. **Facilities:** mainstage, 373 seats, proscenium stage; Cookie Company, 150 seats, arena stage. **Best submission time:** Jun-Aug. **Response time:** 6 months letter; 6 months script.

THE PHOENIX THEATRE

(Founded 1983)
749 North Park Ave; Indianapolis, IN 46202; (317) 635-7529,
FAX 635-0010; email info@phoenixtheatre.org;
website www.phoenixtheatre.org
Bryan Fonseca, *Producing Director*

Submission procedure: no unsolicited scripts; agent submission. **Types of material:** full-length plays, one-acts. **Facilities:** mainstage, 150 seats, proscenium stage; Underground, 75 seats, black box. **Best submission time:** Jan-Feb. **Response time:** 1 week letter; 3 months script. **Special programs:** The Festival of Emerging American Theatre (FEAT) Competition (direct solicitation to playwright only).

PILLSBURY HOUSE THEATRE

(Founded 1992)
3501 Chicago Ave S; Minneapolis, MN 55407; (612) 825-0459
Literary Manager

Submission procedure: no unsolicited scripts; synopsis and letter of inquiry. **Types of material:** full-length plays, translations, adaptations. **Facilities:** Pillsbury House Theatre, 100 seats, proscenium stage. **Best submission time:** year-round. **Response time:** 5 months letter; 6 months script.

PIONEER THEATRE COMPANY

(Founded 1962)
University of Utah, 300 South, 1400 East, Room 205;
Salt Lake City, UT 84112-0660; (801) 581-6356, FAX 581-5472
Charles Morey, *Artistic Director*

Submission procedure: no unsolicited scripts; synopsis and letter of inquiry. **Types of material:** full-length plays, translations, adaptations, musicals. **Facilities:** Simmons Pioneer Memorial Theatre, 912 seats, proscenium stage. **Best submission time:** fall. **Response time:** 1 month letter; 6 months script.

PITTSBURGH PUBLIC THEATER

(Founded 1975)
621 Penn Ave; Pittsburgh, PA 15222-3204; (412) 316-8200,
FAX 316-8216; website www.ppt.org
Kyle Brenton, *Resident Dramaturg*

Submission procedure: no unsolicited scripts; synopsis, dialogue sample and letter of inquiry with SASE for response. **Types of material:** full-length plays, translations, adaptations. **Facilities:** O'Reilly Theater, 650 seats, thrust stage. **Best submission time:** May-Sep. **Response time:** 2 months letter; 6 months script.

PLAYHOUSE ON THE SQUARE

(Founded 1968)

51 South Cooper St; Memphis, TN 38104; (901) 725-0776, FAX 272-7530

Jackie Nichols, *Executive Producer*

Submission procedure: accepts unsolicited scripts. **Types of material:** full-length plays, musicals. **Facilities:** Playhouse on the Square, 250 seats, proscenium stage; Circuit Playhouse, 136 seats, proscenium stage. **Best submission time:** year-round. **Response time:** 5 months. **Special programs:** Playhouse on the Square New Play Competition (see Prizes).

PLAYMAKERS REPERTORY COMPANY

(Founded 1976)

CB #3235, Center for Dramatic Art; Country Club Rd;

Chapel Hill, NC 27599-3235; (919) 962-2484, FAX 962-4069

David Hammond, *Artistic Director*

Submission procedure: no unsolicited scripts; agent submission. **Types of material:** full-length plays, translations, adaptations. **Facilities:** Paul Green Theatre, 498 seats, thrust stage. **Best submission time:** Aug-May. **Response time:** 6 months.

PLAYWRIGHTS HORIZONS

(Founded 1971)

416 West 42nd St; New York, NY 10036-6896; (212) 564-1235,

FAX 594-0296; website www.playwrightshorizons.org

Lisa Timmel, *Literary Manager*

Andrea Watson-Canning, *Musical Theatre Department*

Submission procedure: accepts unsolicited scripts with bio and cover letter; for musicals, send script and cassette or CD (no synopses). **Types of material:** full-length plays, musicals. **Special interests:** works by American writers only; works with strong sense of language that take theatrical risks; no adaptations, historical dramas, translations, solo pieces or one-acts. **Facilities:** mainstage, 198 seats, proscenium stage; studio theater, 98 seats, black box. **Best submission time:** year-round. **Response time:** 2 months letter; 8 months script.

PLAYWRIGHTS THEATRE OF NEW JERSEY

(Founded 1986)

Box 1295; Madison, NJ 07940; (973) 514-1787 ext 18, FAX 514-2060;

email phays@ptnj.org; website www.ptnj.org

Peter Hays, *Literary Manager*

Submission procedure: no unsolicited scripts; synopsis, 10-page dialogue sample, development history, bio, list of previous productions and letter of inquiry. **Types of material:** full-length plays, one-acts. **Special interests:** new American plays of substance and passion (comedies and dramas) that raise challenging questions about ourselves and our communities. **Facilities:** Playwrights Theatre of New Jersey, 99 seats, proscenium stage. **Production considerations:** prefers cast limit of 8; 1 set or unit set; no fly space. **Best submission time:** 1 May–30 Jun. **Response time:** 8 months letter; 12 months script.

PORCHLIGHT MUSIC THEATRE CHICAGO

(Founded 1995)
1919 West Oakdale; Chicago, IL 60657; (773) 325–9884;
    email porchlighttheatre@yahoo.com;
    website www.porchlighttheatre.com
L. Walter Stearns, *Artistic Director*

Submission procedure: accepts unsolicited scripts with cassette or CD. **Types of material:** full-length and one-act musicals. **Facilities:** Theatre Building Chicago, 148 seats, black box. **Production considerations:** cast limit of 16. **Best submission time:** year-round. **Response time:** 6 months.

PORTLAND CENTER STAGE

(Founded 1988)
1111 Southwest Broadway; Portland, OR 97205; (503) 248–6309,
    FAX 796–6509; website www.pcs.org
Mead Hunter, *Literary Director*

Submission procedure: no unsolicited scripts; 10-page dialogue sample, resume and letter of inquiry. **Types of material:** full-length plays. **Facilities:** Newmark Theatre, Portland Center for the Performing Arts, 860 seats, proscenium stage; Winningstad Theatre, 274 seats, thrust stage. **Production considerations:** prefers cast limit of 12. **Best submission time:** year-round. **Response time:** 3 months letter; 6 months script. **Special programs:** Just Add Water/West Festival: best submission time Nov–Feb; visit website for submission guidelines.

PORTLAND STAGE COMPANY

(Founded 1970)
Box 1458; Portland, ME 04104; (207) 774–1043, FAX 774–0576;
    email literary@portlandstage.com; website www.portlandstage.com
Literary Manager

Submission procedure: no unsolicited scripts; synopsis, 10-page dialogue sample and cast breakdown. **Types of material:** full-length plays. **Facilities:** Portland Stage Company, 286 seats, proscenium stage. **Best submission time:** May–Nov. **Response time:** 3 months letter; 6 months script. **Special programs:** The Little Festival of the Unexpected: script development process in spring with playwrights in residence for one week of rehearsals and staged readings; scripts selected through theatre's normal submission procedure (see Development).

PRIMARY STAGES

(Founded 1983)

131 West 45th St; New York, NY 10036; (212) 840-9705, FAX 840-9725

Andrew Leynse, *Artistic Director*

Submission procedure: no unsolicited scripts; synopsis, 10-page dialogue sample, description of play style, resume and letter of inquiry with SASE for response; include CD for musicals. **Types of material:** full-length plays, musicals. **Special interests:** plays not previously produced in New York City only; highly theatrical works by American playwrights for American or New York City premiere; plays by women and minorities; no strict realism or standard film and television fare. **Facilities:** Primary Stages Theatre, 99 seats, proscenium stage; Phil Bosakowski Theatre, 65 seats, proscenium stage. **Production considerations:** cast limit of 6; unit set or simple set changes; no fly or wing space. **Best submission time:** Sep-Jun. **Response time:** 4 months letter; 12 months script.

THE PUBLIC THEATER

(Founded 1954)

The Joseph Papp Public Theater; 425 Lafayette St; New York, NY 10003;
    (212) 539-8530, FAX 539-8505; website www.publictheater.org

Michael Kenyon, *Literary Manager*

Submission procedure: no unsolicited scripts; synopsis, 10-page sample scene and letter of inquiry; include cassette of 3-5 songs for musicals and operas. **Types of material:** full-length plays, translations, adaptations, musicals, operas, solo pieces. **Facilities:** Newman Theater, 299 seats, proscenium stage; Anspacher Theater, 275 seats, thrust stage; Martinson Hall, 200 seats, proscenium stage; LuEsther Hall, 150 seats, flexible stage; Shiva Theater, 100 seats, flexible stage. **Best submission time:** year-round. **Response time:** 1 month letter; 6 months script.

PULSE ENSEMBLE THEATRE

(Founded 1989)

266 West 37th St, 22nd Floor; New York, NY 10018; (212) 695-1596;
    email brian@pulseensembletheatre.org;
    website www.pulseensembletheatre.org

Brian Richardson, *Company Manager*

Submission procedure: no unsolicited scripts; synopsis, dialogue sample, character breakdown, resume and letter of inquiry; include cassette or CD for musicals. **Types of material:** full-length plays, one-acts, musicals, solo pieces. **Special interests:** plays with science themes or social relevance. **Facilities:** mainstage, 55 seats, black box; studio, 40 seats, flexible stage. **Production considerations:** no fly space. **Best submission time:** year-round. **Response time:** 6 months letter; 6 months script.

THE PURPLE ROSE THEATRE COMPANY

(Founded 1991)

Box 220; Chelsea, MI 48118; (734) 433-7782, FAX 475-0802;
email purplerose@earthlink.net;
website www.purplerosetheatre.org

Anthony Caselli, *Associate Artistic Director*

Submission procedure: no unsolicited scripts; synopsis, 10-page dialogue sample, character breakdown and letter of inquiry. **Types of material:** full-length plays. **Special interests:** plays that speak to a middle-American audience. **Facilities:** mainstage, 168 seats, thrust stage. **Production considerations:** cast limit of 10; no fly or wing space. **Best submission time:** year-round. **Response time:** 2 months letter; 9 months script.

QUEENS THEATRE IN THE PARK

(Founded 1993)

Box 520069; Flushing, NY 11352; (718) 760-0686, FAX 760-1972;
email Urbinati@aol.com; website www.queenstheatre.org

Rob Urbinati, *Director of New Play Development*

Submission procedure: accepts unsolicited scripts. **Types of material:** full-length plays, one-acts, translations, adaptations, plays for young audiences, musicals, solo pieces. **Facilities:** Claire Shulman Playhouse, 464 seats, proscenium stage; Studio Theatre, 99 seats, black box. **Production considerations:** prefers cast limit of 10. **Best submission time:** year-round. **Response time:** 6 months. **Special programs:** Immigrant Voices Project: year-round project that seeks new plays reflecting the diverse demographics of the borough of Queens for play reading series, developmental workshops and full productions. Plays A Mother Would Love Series: year-round project that seeks new, mainstream comedies, musicals and thrillers with small casts (8 actors or fewer) for play reading series, developmental workshops and full productions.

RED BARN THEATRE

(Founded 1981)

Box 707; Key West, FL 33040; (305) 293-3035, FAX 293-3035;
email mmcdon3444@aol.com

Mimi McDonald, *Managing Director*

Submission procedure: no unsolicited scripts; synopsis and letter of inquiry with professional recommendation. **Types of material:** full-length plays, musicals, cabaret/revues. **Facilities:** Red Barn Theatre, 88 seats, proscenium stage. **Production considerations:** cast limit of 8, small band for musicals; no fly space, limited wing space. **Best submission time:** Mar-Jul. **Response time:** 6 months letter (if interested); 6 months script.

REPERTORIO ESPAÑOL

(Founded 1968)

138 East 27th St; New York, NY 10016; email info@repertorio.org;
website www.repertorio.org

Robert Weber Federico, *Artistic Associate Producer*

Submission procedure: no unsolicited scripts; synopsis and letter of inquiry. **Types of material:** full-length plays, adaptations, plays for young audiences. **Special interests:** plays dealing with Hispanic themes; comedies. **Facilities:** Gramercy Arts Theatre, 130 seats, proscenium stage. **Production considerations:** small cast. **Best submission time:** summer. **Response time:** 6 months. **Special programs:** Met Life Foundation Nuestras Voces National Playwriting Competition; download guidelines from web. (See listing in Prizes.)

THE REPERTORY THEATRE OF ST. LOUIS

(Founded 1966)

130 Edgar Rd; Box 191730; St. Louis, MO 63119; (314) 968-7340;
email sgregg@repstl.org

Susan Gregg, *Associate Artistic Director*

Submission procedure: no unsolicited scripts; synopsis, character breakdown, technical requirements and letter of inquiry, preferably by email. **Types of material:** full-length plays. **Special interests:** nonnaturalistic plays; contemporary social and political issues. **Facilities:** Main Stage, 750 seats, thrust stage; Studio Theatre, 130 seats, black box. **Production considerations:** small cast; modest production demands. **Best submission time:** year-round. **Response time:** 4 months letter; 24 months script.

RIVERLIGHT AND COMPANY

(Founded 1981)

75 Wendell St; Battle Creek, MI 49017-3821; (269) 962-2453,
FAX 441-2707; email jkline_hobbs@glfn.org
website www.willard.lib.mi.us/npa/rilight/index.html

J. Kline Hobbs, *Project Director*

Submission procedure: no unsolicited scripts; letter of inquiry. **Types of material:** full-length plays, adaptations, plays for young audiences, musicals, solo pieces. **Special interests:** plays for grades 7-12; American history, literature and social issues. **Facilities:** Binda Theatre, 375 seats, proscenium stage; Discovery Theatre, 175 seats, thrust stage; company tours to high school auditoriums. **Production considerations:** cast limit of 5, variable performance spaces. **Best submission time:** year-round. **Response time:** 2 weeks letter; 1 month script.

RIVERSIDE THEATRE

(Founded 1985)

3250 Riverside Park Dr; Vero Beach, FL 32963; (772) 231-5860;
email backstage@riversidetheatre.com;
website www.riversidetheatre.com

New Play Department

Submission procedure: no unsolicited scripts; synopsis and letter of inquiry. **Types of material:** full-length plays, translations, adaptations, plays for young audiences, musicals. **Facilities:** Riverside Theatre, 615 seats, proscenium stage; Ann Morton Theatre, 300 seats, flexible stage. **Production considerations:** cast limit of 10. **Best submission time:** spring. **Response time:** 3 months letter; 5 months script.

RIVERSIDE THEATRE

(Founded 1981)

213 North Gilbert St; Iowa City, IA 52245; (319) 338-7672,
FAX 887-1362; email artistic@riversidetheatre.org;
website www.riversidetheatre.org

Ron Clark and Jody Hovland, *Co-Artistic Directors*

Submission procedure: no unsolicited scripts; synopsis and letter of inquiry. **Types of material:** full-length plays, translations, adaptations, cabaret/revues. **Facilities:** Riverside Theatre, 118 seats, flexible stage. **Production considerations:** small cast, simple set. **Best submission time:** year-round. **Response time:** 1 month letter (if interested); 5 months script.

ROADSIDE THEATER

(Founded 1975)

91 Madison Ave; Whitesburg, KY 41858; (606) 633-0108, FAX 633-1009;
email roadside@appalshop.org; website www.appalshop.org/rst

Dudley Cocke, *Director*

Submission procedure: no unsolicited scripts; synopsis, dialogue sample and letter of inquiry. **Types of material:** full-length plays. **Special interests:** plays about the Appalachian region only. **Facilities:** Appalshop Theater, 150 seats, thrust stage. **Production considerations:** small cast, simple sets suitable for touring. **Best submission time:** year-round. **Response time:** 3 weeks letter; 2 months script. **Special programs:** reading and workshop series. Playwright residencies initiated by theatre; playwright may not apply.

ROUND HOUSE THEATRE

(Founded 1978)

Box 30688; Bethesda, MD 20824; (240) 644-1099, FAX 644-1090;
email productionstaff@roundhousetheatre.org;
website www.roundhousetheatre.org

Production Department

Submission procedure: no unsolicited scripts; synopsis, 10-page dialogue sample, cast breakdown, technical requirements, resume and SASE for response. **Types of material:** full-length plays, translations, adaptations, plays for young audiences, musicals, solo pieces. **Special interests:** solo pieces; contemporary issues; new translations of lesser-known classics; experimental works. **Facilities:** Round House Theatre, 400 seats, modified thrust stage; second stage, 150 seats, black box. **Production considerations:** prefers cast limit of 8. **Best submission time:** year-round. **Response time:** 2 months letter; minimum 12 months script. **Special programs:** New Works Play Reading Series: reading series of new, unproduced plays and musicals by regional (DC, MD, VA, WV) playwrights; scripts are selected through theatre's normal submission procedure; send submissions to Nick Olcott, New Works Coordinator; *deadline:* ongoing.

ROXY REGIONAL THEATRE

(Founded 1983)

100 Franklin St; Clarksville, TN 37040; (931) 645-7699;
email roxytheatre@midsouth.net; website www.roxyregionaltheatre.org

Tom Thayer, *Managing Director*

Submission procedure: accepts unsolicited scripts; include cassette for musicals. **Types of material:** full-length plays, adaptations, plays for young audiences, musicals. **Facilities:** Roxy Regional, 170 seats, proscenium stage; The Other Space, 50 seats, black box. **Production considerations:** prefers small cast. **Best submission time:** Jan-Feb. **Response time:** varies.

SACRAMENTO THEATRE COMPANY

(Founded 1942)

1419 H St; Sacramento, CA 95814; (916) 446-7501, FAX 446-4066;
website www.sactheatre.org

Peggy Shannon, *Artistic Director*

Submission procedure: no unsolicited scripts; agent submission. **Types of material:** full-length plays, adaptations, cabaret/revues. **Special interests:** contemporary social and political issues; "craftsmanship, theatricality, vital language." **Facilities:** Mainstage, 300 seats, proscenium stage; Stage II, 90 seats, black box. **Production considerations:** cast limit of 10. **Best submission time:** Jun-Dec. **Response time:** 6 months.

THE SALT LAKE ACTING COMPANY

(Founded 1970)
168 West 500 N; Salt Lake City, UT 84103; (801) 363-0526, FAX 532-8513
David Mong, *Literary Manager*

Submission procedure: no unsolicited scripts; professional recommendation with bio and letter of inquiry with SASE for response. **Types of material:** full-length plays, translations, adaptations, musicals. **Special interests:** western American writers "who understand the unique synergistic effect that playwright, actor and audience enjoy when a work is produced for the stage." **Facilities:** Upstairs, 150 seats, thrust stage. **Best submission time:** year-round. **Response time:** 6 months. **Special programs:** reading series four times annually.

SANCTUARY: PLAYWRIGHTS THEATRE

(Founded 1997)
616 East 19th St; Brooklyn, NY 11230; (718) 859-6625, FAX 421-4178;
        email jude@pipeline.com; website sanctuarytheatre.home.pipeline.com
Bob Jude Ferrante, *Co-Artistic Director*

Submission procedure: accepts unsolicited scripts with resume and list of current projects with letter of inquiry and SASE for response. **Types of material:** full-length plays. **Special interests:** accepts playwrights with at least one professional production only; prefers plays with "unusual structure, radical core ideas, epic form, work that's off the map or otherwise seen as impractical"; no "kitchen sink" or "TV sitcom-style" plays; no "worthy social issue earnestly told in realistic mien" plays. **Facilities:** no permanent facility. **Production considerations:** playwright controls resources of company for duration of project. **Best submission time:** year-round. **Response time:** 6 months.

SAN DIEGO REPERTORY THEATRE

(Founded 1976)
79 Horton Plaza; San Diego, CA 92101; (619) 231-3586, FAX 235-0939
Artistic Department

Submission procedure: no unsolicited scripts; synopsis and letter of inquiry. **Types of material:** full-length plays, translations, adaptations, musicals, literary cabaret, mixed-media events. **Special interests:** multiethnic and intercultural work; hard-hitting social and political work; offbeat hip musicals; dramatic work with unusual incorporation of music; women's issues; sharp-edged comedy; poetic visions. **Facilities:** Lyceum Stage, 570 seats, modified thrust stage; Lyceum Space, 270 seats, flexible stage. **Production considerations:** no fly space in Lyceum Space. **Best submission time:** Apr-Aug. **Response time:** 3 months letter; 12 months script. **Special programs:** readings and workshop productions.

SAN JOSE REPERTORY THEATRE

(Founded 1980)

101 Paseo de San Antonio; San Jose, CA 95113; (408) 367-7206,

FAX 367-7237; website www.sjrep.com

Literary Department

Submission procedure: no unsolicited scripts; professional recommendation. **Types of material:** full-length plays, translations, adaptations, musicals, solo pieces. **Special interests:** plays by and about traditionally under-represented voices. **Facilities:** San Jose Repertory Theatre, 525 seats, proscenium stage. **Best submission time:** Aug–Nov. **Response time:** 6 months.

SANTA MONICA PLAYHOUSE

(Founded 1962)

1211 4th St; Santa Monica, CA 90401-1391; (310) 394-9779,

FAX 393-5573; website www.santamonicaplayhouse.com

Chris DeCarlo and Evelyn Rudie, *Co–Artistic Directors*

Submission procedure: no unsolicited scripts; synopsis and letter of inquiry. **Types of material:** full-length plays, one-acts, translations, adaptations, plays for young audiences, musicals. **Facilities:** The Main Stage, 88 seats, arena/thrust stage; The Other Space, 70 seats, black box. **Production considerations:** cast limit of 8; simple production demands. **Best submission time:** year-round. **Response time:** 6 months letter; 9 months script.

SEACOAST REPERTORY THEATRE

(Founded 1986)

125 Bow St; Portsmouth, NH 03801; (603) 433-4793,

FAX 431-7818; email info@seacoastrep.org;

website www.seacoastrep.org

Roy M. Rogosin, *Producing Artistic Director*

Submission procedure: no unsolicited scripts; agent submission (1-page synopsis only; include cassette for musicals). **Types of material:** full-length plays, plays for young audiences, musicals. **Special interests:** new American plays; small-scale musicals; plays for young audiences. **Facilities:** Seacoast Repertory Theatre, 230 seats, thrust stage. **Best submission time:** year-round. **Response time:** 6 months.

SEASIDE MUSIC THEATER

(Founded 1977)

Box 2835; Daytona Beach, FL 32120; (386) 252-3394, FAX 252-8991;

website www.seasidemusictheater.org

Lester Malizia, *Artistic Director*

Submission procedure: no unsolicited scripts; synopsis, cassette or CD of music and letter of inquiry. **Types of material:** musicals for young and adult audiences, cabaret/revues. **Facilities:** Winter Theater, 576 seats, proscenium stage; Summer Theater, 500 seats, proscenium stage; Theater for Children, 576 seats, proscenium stage. **Production considerations:** cast limit of 10 for Winter Theater, 30 for Summer Theater, 10 for Theater for Children; small musical combo for Theater for Children and Winter Theater, 25-member orchestra for Summer Theater; no wing or orchestra space in Winter Theater, no fly space except in Summer Theater. **Best submission time:** Sep-Nov. **Response time:** 3 months letter; 6 months script.

SEATTLE CHILDREN'S THEATRE
(Founded 1975)
201 Thomas St; Seattle, WA 98109; (206) 443-0807, FAX 443-0442;
email kevinm@sct.org; website www.sct.org
Kevin Maifeld, *Managing Director*

Submission procedure: accepts unsolicited scripts for Drama School Summer season only; professional recommendation for mainstage. **Types of material:** full-length plays for family audiences, translations, adaptations, musicals, solo pieces. **Special interests:** sophisticated works for young audiences that also appeal to adults. **Facilities:** Charlotte Martin Theatre, 485 seats, proscenium stage; Eve Alvord Theatre, 280 seats, modified proscenium. **Best submission time:** year-round. **Response time:** 8 months. **Special programs:** Drama School Summer season: one-act plays, 30-60 minutes long for student performance, must have roles for 12-18 actors, ages 8-19; submit script with SASE for response to Don Fleming, Education Associate.

SECOND STAGE THEATRE
(Founded 1979)
307 West 43rd St; New York, NY 10036; (212) 787-8302, FAX 397-7066;
email CBURNEY@secondstagetheatre.com;
website www.secondstagetheatre.com
Christopher Burney, *Associate Artistic Director*

Submission procedure: no unsolicited scripts; synopsis, 5-10-page dialogue sample, resume, production history and letter of inquiry. **Types of material:** full-length plays, adaptations, musicals. **Special interests:** new and previously produced American plays; "heightened" realism; sociopolitical issues; plays by women and minority writers. **Facilities:** Midtown Theatre, 296 seats, proscenium stage; McGinn/Cazale Theatre, 108 seats, endstage. **Best submission time:** year-round. **Response time:** 1 month letter; 6 months script. **Special programs:** annual series of readings of new and previously produced plays.

SEEM-TO-BE-PLAYERS
(Founded 1973)
Lawrence Arts Center; 940 New Hampshire St; Lawrence, KS 66044;
(785) 843-2787, FAX 843-6629; email raverill@sunflower.com;
website www.lawrenceartscenter.com
Ric Averill, *Artistic Director*

Submission procedure: accepts unsolicited scripts. **Types of material:** plays for young audiences only. **Special interests:** no adaptations. **Facilities:** Lawrence Arts Center, 300 seats, proscenium stage; Liberty Hall, 100 seats, proscenium stage; Performance Lab, 100 seats, black box. **Production considerations:** cast limit of 6; plays for youth to perform, cast limit of 30. **Best submission time:** Mar–May. **Response time:** 6 weeks letter, 3 months script.

SERENDIPITY THEATRE COMPANY

(Founded 1999)

2936 North Southport Ave; Chicago, IL 60657; (773) 296-0165,
   FAX 296-0163; email laronika@serendipitytheatre.org;
   website www.serendipitytheatre.org

LaRonika Thomas, *Literary Manager*

Submission procedure: no unsolicited scripts; sample scene and synopsis with letter of inquiry. **Types of material:** full-length plays, one-acts, adaptations. **Special interests:** "work that provides a forum for social dialogue"; work by early-career or lesser-known playwrights. **Facilities:** no permanent facility. **Production considerations:** modest production demands. **Best submission time:** year-round. **Response time:** 6 months letter, 6 months script.

SEVEN ANGELS THEATRE

(Founded 1991)

Box 3358; Waterbury, CT 06705; (203) 591-8223, FAX 757-1807;
   website www.sevenangelstheatre.org

Semina De Laurentis, *Artistic Director*

Submission procedure: no unsolicited scripts; professional recommendation. **Types of material:** full-length plays, musicals. **Facilities:** Seven Angels Theatre, 350 seats, proscenium stage. **Production considerations:** cast limit of 10; prefers unit set; no fly space. **Best submission time:** year-round. **Response time:** 12 months script (if interested).

SHADOWBOX CABARET

(Founded 1994)

1 Levee Way, Suite 4101; Newport, KY 41071; (859) 957-7625,
   FAX 957-0032; email sschneider@shadowboxcabaret.com;
   website www.shadowboxcabaret.com

Sam Schneider, *Dramaturg*

Submission procedure: accepts unsolicited scripts. **Types of material:** one-acts, solo pieces. **Special interests:** comedic plays only; 10–20 minute works for actors ages 15–50 ideal. **Facilities:** ShadowBox South, 180 seats, black box; ShadowBox East, 180 seats, black box; 2co's Cabaret, 90 seats, black box. **Production considerations:** cast limit of 5; limited set and staging requirements. **Best submission time:** year-round. **Response time:** 10 months.

SHADOWLIGHT PRODUCTIONS
(Founded 1994)
22 Chattanooga St; San Francisco, CA 94114; (415) 648–4461,
FAX 641–9734; email info@shadowlight.com;
website www.shadowlight.com
Kate Sheehan, *Managing Director*

Submission procedure: no unsolicited scripts; agent submission or professional recommendation. **Types of material:** full-length plays, one-acts, translations, adaptations, plays for young audiences, musicals, cabaret/revues, solo pieces. **Special interests:** plays suitable for shadow theatre only, utilizing puppets as well as live actors; scripts dealing with mythological or historical figures; adaptations of stories or novels. **Facilities:** no permanent facility. **Production considerations:** cast limit of 15. **Best submission time:** year-round. **Response time:** 1 month.

SHAKESPEARE & COMPANY
(Founded 1978)
70 Kemble St; Lenox, MA 01240; (413) 637–1199, FAX 637–4274;
email mccleary@shakespeare.org; website www.shakespeare.org
Dan McCleary, *Artistic Associate for Submissions*

Submission procedure: no unsolicited scripts; synopsis, 4-page dialogue sample and letter of inquiry. **Types of material:** full-length plays, one-acts. **Special interests:** plays based on or adapted from works by Edith Wharton and other women authors, Henry James, Herman Melville, Nathaniel Hawthorne or other writers with connections to the Berkshires. **Facilities:** Founders' Theatre, 420 seats, Elizabethan stage; Spring Lawn Theatre, 101 seats, salon. **Production considerations:** small casts, minimal set pieces. **Best submission time:** winter-spring. **Response time:** 6 months letter (if interested); 6 months script.

THE SHAKESPEARE FESTIVAL AT TULANE
(Founded 1993)
Department of Theatre and Dance; Tulane University;
New Orleans, LA 70118; (504) 865–5105, FAX 865–5104;
website www.neworleansshakespeare.com
Aimée K. Michel, *Artistic Director*

Submission procedure: no unsolicited scripts; synopsis, dialogue sample, resume and letter of inquiry with SASE for response. **Types of material:** full-length plays, one-acts, adaptations. **Special interests:** Louisiana playwrights only. **Facilities:** Lupin theatre, 150 seats, black box; Lagniappe Stage, 100 seats, black box. **Production considerations:** 1 set preferred; no fly space. **Best submission time:** Aug-Nov only. **Response time:** 2 months letter; 3 months script.

THE SHAKESPEARE THEATRE

(Founded 1986)

516 8th St; Washington, DC 20003-2834; (202) 547-3230,
FAX 547-0226; email smazzola@shakespearedc.org;
website www.shakespearedc.org

Steven Scott Mazzola, *Assistant to the Artistic Director*

Submission procedure: no unsolicited scripts; professional recommendation. **Types of material:** translations, adaptations. **Special interests:** translations and adaptations of classics only. **Facilities:** The Shakespeare Theatre, 449 seats, proscenium stage. **Best submission time:** summer. **Response time:** 4 months.

SHOTGUN PLAYERS

(Founded 1992)

1901 Ashby Ave; Berkeley, CA 94703; (510) 704-8210,
email info@shotgunplayers.org; website www.shotgunplayers.org

Patrick Dooley, *Artistic Director*

Submission procedure: no unsolicited scripts; synopsis, dialogue sample and letter of inquiry. **Types of material:** full-length plays, one-acts. **Special interests:** experimental work that pushes the boundaries of traditional storytelling. **Facilities:** The Ashby Stage, 150 seats, proscenium stage. **Production considerations:** prefers cast limit of 6; unit set. **Best submission time:** May–Aug. **Response time:** 6 months letter; 6 months script.

SIGNATURE THEATRE

(Founded 1990)

3806 South Four Mile Run Dr; Arlington, VA 22206; (703) 820-9771

Marcia Gardner, *Literary Manager*

Submission procedure: no unsolicited scripts; agent submission. **Types of material:** full-length plays, adaptations, musicals. **Special interests:** work not produced professionally only; social issues; comedies. **Facilities:** Signature Theatre, 146 seats, black box. **Production considerations:** prefers cast limit of 10; no fly space. **Best submission time:** Feb–Jul. **Response time:** 4 months. **Special programs:** Stages: staged readings of new plays-in-process.

SKYLIGHT OPERA THEATRE

(Founded 1959)

158 North Broadway; Milwaukee, WI 53202; (414) 291-7811,
FAX 291-7815; email dianac@skylightopera.com;
website www.skylightopera.com

Diana Carl, *Company Manager*

Submission procedure: no unsolicited scripts; synopsis and letter of inquiry; include cassette or CD for musicals. **Types of material:** musicals, cabaret/revues. **Special interests:** small-scaled musicals and operas. **Facilities:** Cabot Theatre, 358 seats, proscenium stage. **Production considerations:** cast limit of 22, orchestra limit 18; prefers smaller casts. **Best submission time:** summer. **Response time:** 2 months letter; 12 months script.

SLEDGEHAMMER THEATRE

(Founded 1986)

964 5th Ave, Suite 224; San Diego, CA 92101; (619) 544-1484,

FAX 544-1485; email jhayatshahi@sledgehammer.org;

website www.sledgehammer.org

Janet Hayatshahi, *Development Associate*

Submission procedure: no unsolicited scripts; synopsis, dialogue sample and letter of inquiry with SASE for response. **Types of material:** full-length plays, translations, adaptations. **Special interests:** scripts that break and challenge style, tradition and form. **Facilities:** St. Cecilia's Playhouse, 150 seats, proscenium stage. **Production considerations:** prefers cast limit of 10; unit set. **Best submission time:** year-round. **Response time:** 6 months letter; 6 months script.

SOHO REPERTORY THEATRE

(Founded 1975)

86 Franklin St. 4th Floor; New York, NY 10013; (212) 941-8632,

FAX 941-7148; website www.sohorep.org

Daniel Aukin, *Artistic Director*

Submission procedure: accepts unsolicited scripts for Writer/Director Lab only (see below); direct solicitation to playwright or agent for all other plays. **Types of material:** full-length plays, one-acts, solo pieces. **Facilities:** Soho Rep, 70 seats, black box. **Special programs:** Writer'Director Lab: 6 writers, paired with directors, spend 6 months developing new play, culminating in reading series; see website for application; *deadline:* May 2005 (exact date TBA); *notification:* Sep 2005.

SOUTH COAST REPERTORY

(Founded 1964)

Box 2197; Costa Mesa, CA 92628-2197; (714) 708-5500;

website www.scr.org

Jennifer Kiger, *Literary Manager*

Submission procedure: no unsolicited scripts; synopsis, dialogue sample and letter of inquiry. **Types of material:** full-length plays, translations, adaptations, musicals. **Facilities:** Segerstrom Stage, 507 seats, modified thrust stage; Julianne Argyros Stage, 336 seats, proscenium stage; Nicholas studio, 94 seats, black box. **Best submission time:** year-round. **Response time:** 3 weeks letter; 4 months script. **Special programs:** COLAB (Collaboration Laboratory) New Play Program: developmental program culminating in readings, staged readings, workshop productions and full productions; playwright receives grant, commission and/or royalties depending on nature of project. Pacific Playwrights Festival: annual 3-week developmental program for playwrights writing in English culminating in staged readings, workshop productions and full productions performed for the public and theatre colleagues; plays are chosen through theatre's normal submission procedure and by invitation; not-for-profit theatres are also welcome to submit work; *dates:* May 2005.

SPOKANE INTERPLAYERS ENSEMBLE
(Founded 1981)
Box 1961; Spokane, WA 99210; (509) 624-5902, FAX 624-9348;
    email info@interplayers.com; website www.interplayers.com
Robin Stanton, *Producing Artistic Director*

Submission procedure: no unsolicited scripts; synopsis, dialogue sample, cast list, set requirements, production history, reviews (if any) and letter of inquiry. **Types of material:** full-length plays. **Facilities:** Spokane Interplayers Ensemble, 253 seats, thrust stage. **Production considerations:** prefers cast limit of 8; 1 set. **Best submission time:** year-round. **Response time:** 3 months letter (if interested); 6 months script.

SPRINGER OPERA HOUSE
(Founded 1871)
103 10th St; Columbus, GA 31901; (706) 324-5714, FAX 324-4461;
    email p_pierce@springeroperahouse.org;
    website www.springeroperahouse.org
Paul Pierce, *Producing Artistic Director*

Submission procedure: no unsolicited scripts; synopsis and letter of inquiry only. **Types of material:** full-length plays, plays for young audiences, musicals, cabaret/revues. **Special interests:** musicals, comedies. **Facilities:** mainstage, 700 seats, proscenium stage; studio II, 170 seats, flexible stage. **Production considerations:** small cast, unit set. **Best submission time:** Nov-Feb. **Response time:** 2 months letter; 6 months script.

STAGE ONE: THE LOUISVILLE CHILDREN'S THEATRE
(Founded 1946)
501 West Main; Louisville, KY 40202-2957; (502) 589-5946,
    FAX 588-5910; email stageone@stageone.org;
    website www.stageone.org
J. Daniel Herring, *Artistic Director*

Submission procedure: no unsolicited scripts; synopsis and letter of inquiry. **Types of material:** plays for young audiences. **Special interests:** plays about young people in the real world; good, honest treatments of familiar titles. **Facilities:** Moritz von Bomard Theater, 610 seats, thrust stage; Louisville Gardens, 300 seats, arena stage; Todd Hall, 300 seats, flexible stage. **Production considerations:** prefers cast limit of 12; some productions tour. **Best submission time:** Oct-Dec. **Response time:** 3 months.

STAGES REPERTORY THEATRE

(Founded 1978)
3201 Allen Prkwy, #101; Houston, TX 77019-1897; (713) 527-0220,
FAX 527-8669; website www.stagestheatre.com
Rob Bundy, *Artistic Director*
Submission procedure: accepts unsolicited scripts. **Types of material:** full-length plays, plays for young audiences. **Special interests:** nonrealistic, edgy works. **Facilities:** Stages Repertory Theatre, 231 seats, arena stage; Stages Repertory Theatre, 171 seats, thrust stage. **Production considerations:** prefers cast limit of 6; maximum 1 hour running time for children's shows. **Best submission time:** year-round. **Response time:** 9 months.

STAGES THEATRE CENTER

(Founded 1982)
1540 North McCadden Place; Hollywood, CA 90028; (323) 463-5356,
FAX 463-3904; email ask@stageshollywood.com;
website www.stageshollywood.com
Paul Verdier, *Artistic Director*
Submission procedure: accepts unsolicited scripts. **Types of material:** full-length plays, one-acts, translations, adaptations, plays for young audiences. **Special interests:** plays by foreign writers both in original language and in translation; theatre regularly produces plays in Spanish, French and English but can also find actors fluent in other languages; challenging, experimental work; non-text, movement-based work. **Facilities:** Ampitheatre, 99 seats, outdoor flexible stage; mainstage, 49 seats, proscenium stage; Lab, 25 seats, classroom. **Best submission time:** year-round. **Response time:** 12 months.

STAGES THEATRE COMPANY

(Founded 1984)
1111 Mainstreet; Hopkins, MN 55343; (952) 979-1121, FAX 979-1124;
email email@stagestheatre.org; website www.stagestheatre.org
Steve Barberio, *Producing Director*
Submission procedure: accepts unsolicited scripts with synopsis, character breakdown, resume and letter of inquiry. **Types of material:** plays for young audiences. **Facilities:** mainstage, 723 seats, proscenium stage; FAIR, 300 seats, proscenium stage; studio, 150 seats, black box. **Best submission time:** year-round. **Response time:** 3 months.

STAGEWORKS HUDSON

(Founded 1993)

133 Warren St; Hudson, NY 12534-3118; (518) 828-7843;
FAX 828-4026; email contact@stageworkstheater.org;
website www.stageworkstheater.org

Laura Margolis, *Executive Artistic Director*

Submission procedure: no unsolicted scripts; synopsis and letter of inquiry. **Types of material:** full-length plays, translations, adaptations, musicals, solo pieces. **Facilities:** Max and Lillian Katzman Theater, 100 seats, proscenium/thrust stage. **Production considerations:** cast limit of 10, 1 set or unit set; no fly space. **Best submission time:** year-round. **Response time:** 8 months. **Special programs:** Play by Play: annual festival of new short plays; participation by invitation only.

STAMFORD THEATRE WORKS

(Founded 1988)

95 Atlantic St; Stamford, CT 06901; (203) 359-4414, FAX 356-1846

Steve Karp, *Producing Director*

Submission procedure: no unsolicited scripts; professional recommendation. **Types of material:** full-length plays, translations, adaptations, musicals. **Special interests:** plays that are contemporary, innovative and thought-provoking; socially and culturally relevant; challenging and entertaining. **Facilities:** Center Stage, 150 seats, modified thrust stage. **Production considerations:** prefers small cast; unit set. **Best submission time:** year-round. **Response time:** 2 months letter; 6 months script. **Special programs:** Windows on the Works: developmental workshop for 3 new plays; each play receives rehearsals, staged readings and audience discussions; scripts selected through theatre's normal submission procedure; *dates:* Feb–Mar.

STATE THEATER COMPANY

(Founded 1982)

719 Congress Ave; Austin, TX 78701; (512) 692-0509, FAX 472-7199;
email mpolgar@austintheatrealliance.org;
website www.austintheatrealliance.org

Michelle Polgar, *Associate Artistic Director*

Submission procedure: no unsolicited scripts; agent submission. **Types of material:** full-length plays, adaptations, solo pieces. **Special interests:** work not produced professionally; TX plays. **Facilities:** State Theater, 320 seats, proscenium stage. **Best submission time:** 1 Jan–1 Apr. **Response time:** 6 months.

STEPPENWOLF THEATRE COMPANY
(Founded 1976)
758 West North Ave, 4th floor; Chicago, IL 60610; (312) 335-1888,
FAX 335-0808; email theatre@steppenwolf.org;
website www.steppenwolf.org
Edward Sobel, *Director of New Play Development*

Submission procedure: no unsolicited scripts; synopsis, 10-page dialogue sample, short bio or resume and letter of inquiry. **Types of material:** full-length plays. **Special interests:** ensemble pieces with dynamic acting roles. **Facilities:** Downstairs, 510 seats, proscenium stage; Upstairs, 150-300 seats, flexible stage. Garage, 80 seats, flexible stage. **Best submission time:** year-round. **Response time:** 3 months letter; 9 months script.

ST. LOUIS BLACK REPERTORY COMPANY
(Founded 1976)
634 North Grand Blvd, Suite 10-F; St. Louis, MO 63103; (314) 534-3807,
FAX 534-8456; email ronhimes@stlouisblackrep.com
Ronald J. Himes, *Producing Director*

Submission procedure: no unsolicited scripts; synopsis, 3-5-page dialogue sample, resume and letter of inquiry. **Types of material:** full-length plays, plays for young audiences, musicals. **Special interests:** works by African-American and Third World playwrights. **Facilities:** Grandel Theatre, 470 seats, thrust stage. **Best submission time:** Jun-Aug. **Response time:** 2 months letter; 2 months script. **Special programs:** touring company presenting works for young audiences.

STONEHAM THEATRE
(Founded 2000)
395 Main St; Stoneham, MA 02180; (781) 279-2200, FAX 279-3216;
email troy@stonehamtheatre.org; website www.stonehamtheatre.org
Troy Siebels, *Producing Director*

Submission procedure: no unsolicited scripts; synopsis, 10-page dialogue sample and letter of inquiry. **Types of material:** full-length plays, musicals, cabaret/revues. **Facilities:** mainstage, 350 seats, proscenium stage. **Production considerations:** cast limit of 8 for plays; minimal orchestration, unit set for musicals. **Best submission time:** year-round. **Response time:** 2 months letter; 2 months script.

STRAY DOG THEATRE
(Founded 2003)
4378 Forest Park Ave; Saint Louis, MO 63108; (314) 531-5923,
FAX 531-5923; email straydogtheatre@aol.com;
website www.straydogtheatre.org
Gary F. Bell, *Artistic Director*

Submission procedure: no unsolicited scripts; synopsis, 20-page dialogue sample, resume and letter of inquiry with SASE for response; include cassette for musicals. **Types of material:** full-length plays, one-acts, translations, adaptations, musicals. **Facilities:** mainstage, 175 seats, proscenium stage; black box, 80 seats, black box. **Production considerations:** prefers cast limit of 15; no fly space. **Best submission time:** year-round. **Response time:** 2 months letter; 6 months script.

STUDIO ARENA THEATRE
(Founded 1965)
710 Main St; Buffalo, NY 14202-1990; website www.studioarena.org
Gavin Cameron-Webb, *Artistic Director*

Submission procedure: no unsolicited scripts; agent submission with 1-page synopsis and character breakdown. **Types of material:** full-length plays, translations, adaptations. **Special interests:** plays of local interest; plays of a theatrical nature; American history and culture; ethnic cultures, including plays about minorities. **Facilities:** Studio Arena Theatre, 637 seats, thrust stage. **Production considerations:** cast limit of 6; no fly system and limited wing space. **Best submission time:** year-round. **Response time:** 6 months.

SYNCHRONICITY PERFORMANCE GROUP
(Founded 1997)
Box 6012; Atlanta, GA 31107; (404) 325-5168, FAX 325-5168;
email synchrotheatre@mindspring.com;
website www.synchrotheatre.com
Rachel May, Hope Mirlis and Michele Pearce, *Co-Producing Artistic Directors*

Submission procedure: no unsolicited scripts; synopsis, dialogue sample, resume and letter of inquiry with SASE for response. **Types of material:** full-length plays, translations, plays for young audiences, cabaret/revues. **Special interests:** plays by or about women; social issues. **Facilities:** Alliance Hertz Stage, 200 seats, black box; 7 Stages, 70 seats, black box. **Production considerations:** prefers cast limit of 12; no fly space. **Best submission time:** Jan-Jun. **Response time:** 1 month letter; 3 months script.

SYRACUSE STAGE
(Founded 1973)
820 East Genesee St; Syracuse, NY 13210-1508; (315) 443-4008,
FAX 443-9846; website www.syracusestage.org
Literary Department

Submission procedure: no unsolicited scripts; synopsis, 10-page dialogue sample, character description and letter of inquiry with SASE for response. **Types of material:** full-length plays. **Special interests:** no translations, adaptations or musicals. **Facilities:** John D. Archbold Theatre, 499 seats, proscenium stage. **Production considerations:** prefers small cast. **Best submission time:** year-round. **Response time:** 6 months.

TADA! YOUTH THEATER

(Founded 1984)

15 West 28th St, 3rd Floor; New York, NY 10001; (212) 252-1619,

FAX 252-8763; email info@tadatheater.com;

website www.tadatheater.com

Emmanuel Wilson, *Artistic Associate/Literary Manager*

Submission procedure: accepts unsolicited scripts. **Types of material:** one-acts, plays for young audiences, musicals. **Special interests:** work to be performed by children and teenagers. **Facilities:** mainstage, 98 seats, black box. **Production considerations:** modest production demands. **Best submission time:** year-round. **Response time:** 6 months.

TEATRO VISIÓN

(Founded 1984)

1700 Alum Rock Ave, Suite 265; San Jose, CA 95116; (408) 272-9926,

FAX 928-5580; email teatrovision@teatrovision.org;

website www.teatrovision.org

Raul Lozano, *Executive Director*

Submission procedure: no unsolicited scripts; professional recommendation. **Types of material:** full-length plays, one-acts, translations, adaptations, musicals, solo pieces. **Special interests:** new works by and about Chicano-Latino experiences and stories. **Facilities:** Mexican Heritage Plaza, 500 seats, proscenium stage. **Production considerations:** cast limit of 12. **Best submission time:** summer. **Response time:** 1 month letter; 1 month script. **Special programs:** CODICES Program: an annual new works program that works in both commissioning and development format. See website for details.

TAMPA BAY PERFORMING ARTS CENTER

(Founded 1987)

1010 North W. C. MacInnes Place; Tampa, FL 33602;

(813) 222-1000; FAX 222-1057; website www.tbpac.org

Karla Hartley, *Artistic Associate*

Submission procedure: accepts unsolicited scripts. **Types of material:** full-length plays. **Special interests:** plays by women writers. **Facilities:** Carol Morsani Hall, 2500 seats, proscenium stage; Ferguson Hall, 1000 seats, proscenium stage; Jaeb, 300 seats, proscenium stage; Shimberg Playhouse, 150 seats, black box. **Production considerations:** small cast, 1 set. **Best submission time:** summer. **Response time:** 2 months.

TECTONIC THEATER PROJECT
(Founded 1992)
204 West 84th St; New York, NY 10024; (212) 579-6111, FAX 579-6112;
email lnewman@tectonictheaterproject.org; website
www.tectonictheaterproject.org
Laura Newman, *Company Administrator*

Submission procedure: no unsolicited scripts; 10-page dialogue sample, synopsis, character breakdown, resume and letter of inquiry. **Types of material:** full-length plays, one-acts, translations, adaptations, musicals. **Facilities:** no permanent facility. **Best submission time:** year-round. **Response time:** 8 months.

TENNESSEE REPERTORY THEATRE
(Founded 1985)
Box 198768; Nashville, TN 37219; (615) 782-4000, FAX 782-4001;
website www.tnrep.org
Stephen Greil, *President*

Submission procedure: accepts unsolicited scripts with SASE for response; include synopsis and CD or cassette for musicals. **Types of material:** full-length plays, musicals, cabaret/revues. **Facilities:** War Memorial Auditorium, 1400 seats, proscenium stage; Polk Theatre, 1100 seats, proscenium stage; Johnson Theatre, 88 seats, black box. **Production considerations:** small cast, small orchestra; minimal technical requirements. **Best submission time:** Jun–Sep. **Response time:** 12 months.

TEN THOUSAND THINGS
(Founded 1990)
3153 36th Ave S; Minneapolis, MN 55406; (612) 724-4494, FAX 724-4494;
email tenthousandthings@mail.com;
website www.tenthousandthings.org
Michelle Hensley, *Artistic Director*

Submission procedure: no unsolicited scripts; synopsis, 10-page dialogue sample and letter of inquiry with SASE for response. **Types of material:** full-length plays, translations, adaptations, plays for young audiences, musicals. **Special interests:** "big human stories set in another time and place." **Facilities:** no permanent facilities, touring company. **Best submission time:** summer. **Response time:** 1 month letter; 3 months script.

THALIA SPANISH THEATRE
(Founded 1977)
41-17 Greenpoint Ave; Sunnyside, NY 11104; (718) 729-3880,
FAX 729-3388; email info@thaliatheatre.org;
website www.thaliatheatre.org
Angel Gil Orrios, *Artistic/Executive Director*

Submission procedure: accepts unsolicited scripts. **Types of material:** full-length plays, translations, adaptations. **Special interests:** plays with Hispanic themes. **Facilities:** Thalia Spanish Theatre, 74 seats, proscenium stage. **Best submission time:** year-round. **Response time:** 3 months.

THEATRE ARIEL
(Founded 1990)
Box 0334; Merion, PA 19066; (215) 735–9481;
   email theatreariel@netreach.net
Deborah Baer Mozes, *Artistic Director*

Submission procedure: no unsolicited scripts; synopsis, 10-page dialogue sample, character breakdown, resume and letter of inquiry. **Types of material:** full-length plays, one-acts, adaptations, plays for young audiences. **Special interests:** plays with Jewish themes only. **Facilities:** no permanent facility; touring company. **Production considerations:** cast limit of 5, simple sets, sets must be able to tour. **Best submission time:** May–Oct. **Response time:** 1 month letter; 9 months script. **Special programs:** Theatre Loves Conversation : play reading series of new works held 4 times a year, stipend provided.

THE THEATER @ BOSTON COURT
(Founded 2003)
Box 60187; Pasadena, CA 91116–6187; (626) 683–6883,
   FAX 683–6886; email bryand@bostoncourt.com;
   website www.bostoncourttheatre.com
Bryan Davidson and Tom Jacobson, *Co-Literary Managers*

Submission procedure: no unsolicited scripts; synopsis, first 10 pages of dialogue and letter of inquiry with SASP for response. **Types of material:** full-length plays, translations, adaptations, musicals. **Facilities:** mainstage, 99 seats, thrust stage; Branson, seats vary, black box. **Best submission time:** year-round. **Response time:** 6 weeks letter; 6 months script. **Special programs:** play reading series in fall.

THE THEATER AT MONMOUTH
(Founded 1970)
Box 385; Monmouth, ME 04259–0385; (207) 933–2952,
   FAX 933–2952; email tamoffice@theateratmonmouth.org;
   website www.theateratmonmouth.org
David Greenham, *Producing Director*

Submission procedure: no unsolicited scripts; synopsis and letter of inquiry. **Types of material:** adaptations, plays for young audiences. **Special interests:** large-cast adaptations of classic literature; plays for young audiences. **Facilities:** Cumston Hall, 275 seats, thrust stage. **Production considerations:** simple set. **Best submission time:** Sep. **Response time:** 6 weeks letter; 6 months script.

THEATRE BUILDING CHICAGO

(Founded 1969)

1225 West Belmont; Chicago, IL 60657-3205; (773) 929-7367, ext 222,
FAX 327-1404; email jsparks@theatrebuildingchicago.org

John Sparks, *Artistic Director*

Submission procedure: varies; see submission guidelines on web. **Types of material:** musicals. **Facilities:** 3 theatres, 150 seats each, black box. **Best submission time:** Oct. **Response time:** 2 months letter; 3 months script. **Special programs:** Annual STAGES Festival held every summer; musical writers' workshop; monthly reading series; studio presentation series.

THEATER BY THE BLIND

(Founded 1979)

306 West 18th St; New York, NY 10011; (212) 243-4337, FAX 243-4337;
email gar@nyc.rr.com; website www.tbtb.org

Ike Schambelan, *Artistic Director*

Submission procedure: accepts unsolicited scripts. **Types of material:** full-length plays, one-acts, musicals. **Special interests:** work by and about the blind. **Facilities:** no permanent facility; company performs in various 99-seat venues. **Best submission time:** year-round. **Response time:** 2 months.

THEATER CATALYST

(Founded 1998)

2030 Sansom St; Philadelphia, PA 19103; (215) 563-4330, FAX 563-4843

Jessica Graham, *Producing Artistic Director*

Submission procedure: accepts unsolicited scripts. **Types of material:** full-length plays, one-acts, translations, adaptations, solo pieces. **Special interests:** female playwrights; female casts. **Facilities:** The Playground, 120 seats, thrust stage; 2nd Stage, 60 seats, black box. **Production considerations:** cast limit of 10; limited space. **Best submission time:** year-round. **Response time:** 6 months.

THEATRE DE LA JEUNE LUNE

(Founded 1979)

105 First St N; Minneapolis, MN 55401; (612) 332-3968, FAX 332-0048

Barbara Berlovitz, *Co-Artistic Director*

Submission procedure: no unsolicited scripts; synopsis and letter of inquiry. **Types of material:** full-length plays, translations, adaptations. **Facilities:** Theatre de la Jeune Lune, 500 seats, flexible stage. **Best submission time:** year-round. **Response time:** varies.

THEATER FOR THE NEW CITY

(Founded 1970)

155-57 First Ave; New York, NY 10003-2906; (212) 254-1109,

FAX 979-6570; website www.theaterforthenewcity.net

Crystal Field, *Executive Artistic Director*

Submission procedure: accepts unsolicited scripts with SASE for response. **Types of material:** full-length plays. **Special interests:** plays with no previous mainstage production; experimental American works; plays with poetry, music and dance; social issues. **Facilities:** Joyce and Seward Johnson Theater, 200 seats, flexible stage; Cino theatre, 99 seats, flexible stage; Community Theater, 99 seats, flexible stage; Cabaret theatre, 75 seats, flexible stage. **Best submission time:** summer. **Response time:** 12 months.

THEATRE IV

(Founded 1975)

114 West Broad St; Richmond, VA 23220; (804) 783-1688, FAX 775-2325;

email bmiller@theatreiv.org; website www.theatreiv.org

Bruce Miller, *Artistic Director*

Submission procedure: no unsolicited scripts; synopsis and letter of inquiry. **Types of material:** plays for young audiences only, including full-length plays, translations and adaptations. **Special interests:** scripts adaptable for touring with cast of 3-5. **Facilities:** Empire Theatre, 604 seats, proscenium stage; Little Theatre, 84 seats, flexible space. **Best submission time:** year-round. **Response time:** 2 months letter; 24 months script.

THEATRE IN THE SQUARE

(Founded 1982)

11 Whitlock Ave; Marietta, GA 30064; (770) 422-8369, FAX 424-2637

Jessica West, *Literary Manager*

Submission procedure: no unsolicited scripts; synopsis and letter of inquiry. **Types of material:** full-length plays, translations, plays for young audiences, musicals. **Special interests:** world and southeastern premieres. **Facilities:** mainstage, 225 seats, proscenium stage; Alley Stage, up to 120 seats, thrust stage. **Production considerations:** cast limit of 9 for mainstage, 5 for Alley Stage; unit set; no fly space. **Best submission time:** Jun-Dec. **Response time:** 1 month letter (if interested); 6 months script.

THEATER J

(Founded 1991)

1529 16th St NW; Washington, DC 20036; (202) 777-3229, FAX 518-9421;

email patricia@dcjcc.org; website www.theaterj.org

Ari Roth, *Artistic Director*

Submission procedure: accepts unsolicited scripts with synopsis and SASE for response. **Types of material:** full-length plays, translations, adaptations, musicals, solo pieces. **Special interests:** multicultural, political and Jewish themes. **Facilities:** Cecile Goldman Theater, 236 seats, proscenium stage. **Best submission time:** spring. **Response time:** 6 months.

THEATER OF THE FIRST AMENDMENT

(Founded 1990)

MS 3E6; George Mason University; Fairfax, VA 22030-4444;

(703) 993-1122, FAX 993-2191; email kneshati@gmu.edu

Kristin Johnsen-Neshati, *Dramaturg/Artistic Associate*

Submission procedure: no unsolicited scripts; synopsis, sample pages, resume and letter of inquiry. **Types of material:** full-length plays, translations, adaptations, plays for young audiences. **Special interests:** sophisticated plays for younger audiences; "cultural history made dramatic as opposed to history dramatized; large battles joined; hard questions asked; word and image stretched." **Facilities:** TheaterSpace, 150-200 seats, flexible space. **Production considerations:** roles for younger actors welcome. **Best submission time:** Aug-Jan. **Response time:** 2 weeks letter; 6 months script. **Special programs:** readings, workshops and other development activities.

THE THEATRE OUTLET

(Founded 1988)

Box 715; Allentown, PA 18105-0715; (610) 820-9270, FAX 820-9130;

email theatero@aol.com; website www.theatreoutlet.org

George Miller, *Artistic Director*

Submission procedure: no unsolicited scripts; synopsis and letter of inquiry. **Types of material:** full-length plays, one-acts, translations, adaptations, solo pieces. **Special interests:** historical material relevant to eastern Pennsylvania; plays dealing with the Celtic experience; topical and socially relevant work; work exploring cultural diversity. **Facilities:** mainstage, 100 seats, black box. **Production considerations:** limited fly and wing space. **Best submission time:** summer. **Response time:** 1 month letter; 2 months script. **Special programs:** TO2 Special Events: reading series of new plays and performance art.

THEATRE PREVIEWS AT DUKE

(Founded 1986)

Box 90680; 209 Bivins Building; Durham, NC 27708-0680;

(919) 660-3347, FAX 684-8906; email zannie@duke.edu

Zannie Giraud Voss, *Producing Director*

Submission procedure: no unsolicited scripts; agent submission. **Types of material:** full-length plays, translations, adaptations, musicals. **Facilities:** Reynolds Theatre, 600 seats, proscenium stage; Sheafer Theatre, 110 seats, black box. **Best submission time:** spring. **Response time:** 3 months letter; 2-6 months script.

THEATRE RHINOCEROS

(Founded 1977)
2926 16th St; San Francisco, CA 94103; (415) 552-4100,
FAX 558-9044; website www.therhino.org
John Fisher, *Artistic Director*

Submission procedure: no unsolicited scripts; agent submission. **Types of material:** full-length plays, one-acts, solo pieces. **Special interests:** gay and lesbian works only. **Facilities:** Theatre Rhinoceros, 112 seats, proscenium stage; The Studio at Theatre Rhinoceros, 60 seats, studio. **Best submission time:** year-round. **Response time:** 6 months.

THEATRE THREE

(Founded 1969)
Box 512; Port Jefferson, NY 11777-0512; (631) 928-9202,
FAX 928-9120
Jeffrey Sanzel, *Artistic Director*

Submission procedure: no unsolicited scripts; send SASE for guidelines. **Types of material:** one-acts. **Special interests:** works not previously produced only. **Facilities:** Second Stage, 80-100 seats, black box. **Production considerations:** prefers cast limit of 6; 1 set; minimal production demands. **Best submission time:** year-round. **Response time:** 1 month letter; 6 months script. **Special programs:** Annual Festival of One-Act Plays: fully staged productions; send SASE to theatre for guidelines; *deadline:* 30 Sep 2004; *notification:* 30 Dec 2004; *dates:* Feb-Mar 2005.

THEATRE THREE, INC.

(Founded 1961)
2800 Routh St; Dallas, TX 75201; (214) 871-2933, FAX 871-3139;
email theatre3@airmail.net
Jac Alder, *Executive Producer-Director*

Submission procedure: no unsolicited scripts; agent submission. **Types of material:** full-length plays, musicals. **Facilities:** Theatre Three, 242 seats, arena stage; Theatre Too, 60 seats, black box. **Best submission time:** Sep-Dec. **Response time:** 3 months.

THEATREWORKS

(Founded 1969)
Box 50458; Palo Alto, CA 94303; (650) 463-7120,
FAX 463-1963; email kent@theatreworks.org;
website www.theatreworks.org
Kent Nicholson, *New Works Director*

Submission procedure: no unsolicited scripts; synopsis, dialogue sample and resume; for translations and adaptations, send letter of inquiry with SASP for response. **Types of material:** full-length plays, translations, adaptations, musicals.

Special interests: works offering opportunities for multiethnic casting; no one-acts. **Facilities:** Mountain View Center, 625 seats, proscenium stage; Lucie Stern Theatre, 425 seats, proscenium stage. **Best submission time:** year-round. **Response time:** 2 months letter; 6 months script. **Special programs:** New Works Initiative: developmental reading series for plays, musicals and music-theatre pieces, visit website for guidelines.

THEATREWORKS/USA
(Founded 1961)
151 West 26th St, 7th Floor; New York, NY 10001; (212) 647-1100,
    FAX 924-5377; email malltop@twusa.org;
    website www.theatreworksusa.org
Michael Alltop, *Literary Manager*

Submission procedure: no unsolicited scripts; synopsis, sample scene(s) and songs (include cassette or CD and lyric sheet) and letter of inquiry. **Types of material:** plays and musicals for young audiences grades K-12. **Special interests:** literary adaptations; historical/biographical themes; fairy tales; contemporary issues. **Facilities:** Auditorium at the Equitable Tower, 487 seats, proscenium stage; also tours. **Production considerations:** cast limit of 7 (can play multiple roles); sets suitable for touring. **Best submission time:** Oct-Nov; Mar-Jun. **Response time:** 1 month letter; 6 months script. **Special programs:** Theatreworks/USA Commissioning Program.

THEATRE X
(Founded 1969)
158 North Broadway; Milwaukee, WI 53202; (414) 278-0555;
    email theatrex@sbcglobal.net
Flora Coker, *Managing Director*

Submission procedure: no unsolicited scripts; synopsis with SASE for response. **Types of material:** full-length plays. **Special interests:** contemporary plays; "pseudo-naturalism and self-conscious theatricality involving the ongoing fruits of interdisciplinary collaboration." **Facilities:** Black Box, 99 seats, flexible stage. **Production considerations:** cast limit of 8. **Best submission time:** year-round. **Response time:** 6 months.

THEATRICAL OUTFIT
(Founded 1976)
Box 1555; Atlanta, GA 30301; (404) 577-5257, FAX 577-5259;
    email kate.warner@theatricaloutfit.org;
    website www.theatricaloutfit.org
Kate Warner, *Managing Director/Artistic Associate*

Submission procedure: no unsolicited scripts; 1-page synopsis and letter of inquiry with SASP for response. **Types of material:** full-length plays, adaptations, solo pieces. **Facilities:** Balzer Theater at Herren's, 200 seats, proscenium stage. **Best submission time:** Apr-Jun. **Response time:** 2 months letter; 2 months script.

TOUCHSTONE THEATRE
(Founded 1981)
321 East 4th St; Bethlehem, PA 18015; (610) 867-1689,
FAX 867-0561; email touchstone@nni.com;
website www.touchstone.org
Mark McKenna, *Artistic Director*

Submission procedure: no unsolicited scripts; letter of inquiry. **Types of material:** proposals for works to be created in collaboration with company's ensemble only. **Facilities:** Touchstone Theatre, 74 seats, black box. **Production considerations:** 18' x 21' playing area. **Best submission time:** year-round. **Response time:** 8 months.

TRIANGLE PRODUCTIONS!
(Founded 1989)
3430 Southeast Belmont; Portland, OR 97214; (503) 230-9404,
FAX 230-9303; email trianglepro@juno.com;
website www.tripro.org
Donald L. Horn, *Artistic/Managing Director*

Submission procedure: no unsolicited scripts; letter of inquiry with email address for response. **Types of material:** full-length plays, plays for young audiences, musicals, solo pieces. **Special interests:** comedies; gay and lesbian themes. **Facilities:** World Trade Center, 223 seats, thrust stage; Arena Stage, 120 seats, arena stage; Black Box, 90 seats, thrust stage. **Production considerations:** cast limit of 4; set suitable for touring. **Best submission time:** fall. **Response time:** 1 month letter; 7 months script.

TRIARTS AT THE SHARON PLAYHOUSE
(Founded 1989)
Box 1187; Sharon, CT 06069; (860) 364-7469, FAX 364-8043;
email info@triarts.net; website www.triarts.net
Michael Berkeley, *Artistic Director*

Submission procedure: no unsolicited scripts; synopsis and letter of inquiry; include cassette or CD for musicals. **Types of material:** plays and musicals for young audiences. **Facilities:** The Sharon Playhouse, 370 seats, proscenium stage; Gallery, 120 seats, flexible stage. **Production considerations:** no fly space. **Best submission time:** Jul-Aug. **Response time:** 1-2 months letter; 4-6 months script.

TRINITY REPERTORY COMPANY
(Founded 1964)
201 Washington St; Providence, RI 02903; (401) 521-1100,
FAX 521-0447; website www.trinityrep.com
Craig Watson, *Literary Manager*

Submission procedure: no unsolicited scripts; synopsis, dialogue sample and letter

of inquiry. **Types of material:** full-length plays, translations, adaptations, musicals, solo pieces. **Facilities:** Upstairs Theatre, 500 seats, thrust stage; Downstairs Theatre, 297 seats, thrust stage. **Best submission time:** Sep–May. **Response time:** 2 months letter; 4 months script.

TRUSTUS THEATRE

(Founded 1985)

Box 11721; Columbia, SC 29211–1721; (803) 254–9732, FAX 771–9153; email trustus88@aol.com; website www.trustus.org

Jon Tuttle, *Literary Manager*

Submission procedure: accepts unsolicited scripts. **Types of material:** one-acts. **Special interests:** one-acts 45–75 minutes in length; experimental, hard-hitting, off-the-wall one-act comedies or "dramadies" for open-minded Late-Night series, no topic taboo; full-length plays accepted only for Trustus Playwrights' Festival (see below); no musicals or plays for young audiences. **Facilities:** mainstage, 100 seats, flexible proscenium stage. **Production considerations:** small cast, moderate production demands. **Best submission time:** Aug–Dec. **Response time:** 4 months. **Special programs:** Trustus Playwrights' Festival (see Prizes).

TWO RIVER THEATRE COMPANY

(Founded 1994)

Box 8035; Red Bank, NJ 07702; (732) 345–1400, FAX 345–1414; email info@trtc.org

Jonathan Fox, *Artistic Director*

Submission procedure: no unsolicited scripts; agents may send 10-page dialogue sample, synopsis and SASE for response. **Types of material:** full-length plays, adaptations. **Facilities:** Algonquin Arts Theatre, 500 seats, proscenium stage; Two River Theatre main stage, 300 seats, thrust stage; Marion Huber Theater, 90 seats, black box. **Production considerations:** cast limit of 10. **Best submission time:** year-round. **Response time:** 10 months script.

UNICORN THEATRE

(Founded 1974)

3828 Main St; Kansas City, MO 64111; (816) 531–7529, ext 15, FAX 531–0421; website www.unicorntheatre.org

Herman Wilson, *Literary Assistant*

Submission procedure: accepts unsolicited scripts with synopsis, character breakdown, bio or resume and cover letter with SASE for response. **Types of material:** full-length plays. **Special interests:** contemporary social issues. **Facilities:** Unicorn Theatre, 180 seats, thrust stage. **Best submission time:** year-round. **Response time:** 8 months. **Special programs:** Unicorn Theatre New Play Development (see Prizes).

URBAN STAGES

(Founded 1985)
17 East 47th St; New York, NY 10017; (212) 421-1380;
　　email urbanstage@aol.com; website www.urbanstages.org
Frances Hill, *Artistic Director*

Submission procedure: accepts unsolicited scripts with production history, bio and SASE for response. **Types of material:** full-length plays. **Facilities:** mainstage, 70 seats, proscenium stage. **Best submission time:** Jun-Aug. **Response time:** 6 months. **Special programs:** Emerging Playwright Award: outreach program that tours throughout New York City library systems. (See Prizes.)

VALLEY YOUTH THEATRE

(Founded 1989)
807 North 3rd St; Phoenix, AZ 85004; (602) 253-8188, FAX 253-8282;
　　email Bobb@vyt.com; website www.vyt.com
Bobb Cooper, *Producing Artistic Director*

Submission procedure: no unsolicited scripts; letter of inquiry; include cassette for musicals. **Types of material:** plays for young audiences, musicals. **Special interests:** large-scale musicals for family audiences. **Facilities:** Herberger Theater, 750 seats, proscenium stage; Main Stage, 202 seats, proscenium stage; Performing Arts Center, 80 seats, black box. **Best submission time:** Aug-Dec. **Response time:** 2 weeks letter; 2 months script.

VICTORY GARDENS THEATER

(Founded 1974)
2257 North Lincoln Ave; Chicago, IL 60614; (773) 549-5788,
　　FAX 549-2779
Sandy Shinner, *Associate Artistic Director*

Submission procedure: accepts unsolicited scripts from Chicago-area writers only; others send synopsis, 10-page dialogue sample and letter of inquiry with SASE for response. **Types of material:** full-length plays, adaptations, musicals. **Special interests:** Chicago and Midwest playwrights; plays by women and writers of color. **Facilities:** Mainstage Two, 200 seats, thrust stage; Mainstage One, 195 seats, modified thrust stage; 2 studio theatres, 70 seats each, black box. **Production considerations:** prefers cast limit of 10, simple set; small-cast musicals only. **Best submission time:** Mar-Jun. **Response time:** 2 months letter; 9 months script. **Special programs:** Victory Gardens Playwrights Ensemble: core group of 12 resident writers. Readers Theater: staged readings of works-in-progress by area writers twice a month. Artist Development Workshop: playwriting class offered throughout the year that brings people with and without disabilities together in a creative environment.

THE VICTORY THEATRE CENTER

(Founded 1979)

3326 West Victory Blvd; Burbank, CA 91505; (818) 841–4404,
FAX 841–6328; email thevictory@mindspring.com;
website www.thevictorytheatrecenter.org

Maria Gobetti and Tom Ormeny, *Co-Artistic Directors*

Submission procedure: no unsolicited scripts; synopsis, first 15 pages of dialogue, resume and letter of inquiry. **Types of material:** full-length plays, adaptations. **Special interests:** plays involving relationships; character-driven plays; plays with social and political issues; "well-made, but cutting-edge" plays. **Facilities:** The Big Victory Theatre, 99 seats, arena stage; The Little Victory, 48 seats, arena stage. **Production considerations:** prefers cast limit of 12; maximum 2 simple sets; no fly space. **Best submission time:** year-round. **Response time:** 2 months letter; 3 months script.

VILLAGE THEATRE

(Founded 1979)

303 Front St N; Issaquah, WA 98027; (425) 392–1942, FAX 391–3242;
website www.villagetheatre.org

Brian Yorkey, *Associate Artistic Director*

Submission procedure: accepts unsolicited scripts with character breakdown and vocal ranges; include cassette or CD. **Types of material:** musicals. **Facilities:** Everett Performing Arts Center, 512 seats, proscenium/thrust stage; Francis J. Gaudette, 488 seats, proscenium stage; First Stage, 222 seats, proscenium stage. **Best submission time:** year-round. **Response time:** 6 months. **Special programs:** Village Originals : musical development program culminating in workshop production, possible full production as part of theatre's regular season.

VINEYARD THEATRE

(Founded 1981)

108 East 15th St; New York, NY 10003–9689; (212) 353–3366,
FAX 353–3803

Douglas Aibel, *Artistic Director*

Submission procedure: no unsolicited scripts; synopsis or project description, 10-page dialogue sample, resume and letter of inquiry; include cassette or CD for musicals. **Types of material:** full-length plays, musicals. **Facilities:** Vineyard Dimson Theatre, 129 seats, flexible stage. **Best submission time:** year-round. **Response time:** 12 months letter; 6 months script (will only contact if interested).

VIRGINIA STAGE COMPANY

(Founded 1979)

Box 3770; Norfolk, VA 23514; (757) 627–6988, FAX 628–5958;
website www.vastage.com

Jennifer Woolley, *Assistant to the Directors*

Submission procedure: no unsolicited scripts; synopsis and letter of inquiry. **Types**

of material: full-length plays, musicals. **Special interests:** plays by VA writers; world premieres; works about "twenty-somethings" and youth culture; poetic drama and comedy; hard-hitting, issue-oriented plays. **Facilities:** mainstage, 700 seats, proscenium stage; laboratory theatre, 99 seats, flexible stage. **Best submission time:** year-round. **Response time:** 1 month letter; 6 months script.

VS THEATRE COMPANY

(Founded 2003)

Box 46477; Los Angeles, CA 90046; (310) 210-0469,
    FAX (323) 850-6045, ext 11; email lanhalalana@earthlink.net;
    website www.vstheatre.org
Kimberly-Rose Walter, *Artistic Director*

Submission procedure: accepts unsolicited scripts only with submission form, available online; include SASP for response. **Types of material:** full-length plays, one-acts, translations, adaptations. **Special interests:** world premieres or pieces rarely performed; work with an emphasis on the unique, daring and edgy. **Facilities:** Little Victory Theatre, 48 seats, black box. **Production considerations:** cast limit of 6; no big, elaborate sets. **Best submission time:** year-round. **Response time:** 6 months.

THE WALNUT STREET THEATRE

(Founded 1809)

825 Walnut St; Philadelphia, PA 19107-5107; (215) 574-3550,
    FAX 574-3598; website www.wstonline.org
Beverly Elliott, *Literary Manager*

Submission procedure: no unsolicited scripts; synopsis, cast list, 10-20-page dialogue sample and letter of inquiry with SASE for response from Dramatist Guild members only; include professional-quality cassette or CD for musicals. **Types of material:** full-length plays, musicals. **Special interests:** original, socially relevant musicals with uplifting themes; commercially viable works for Main Stage; meaningful comedies and dramas with some broad social relevance for Studio 3. **Facilities:** Main Stage, 1078 seats, proscenium stage; Studio 3, 79-99 seats, flexible stage. **Production considerations:** cast limit of 4 for Studio 3. **Response time:** 3 months letter; 6 months script.

WATERTOWER THEATRE, INC.

(Founded 1976)

15650 Addison Rd; Addison, TX 75001; (972) 450-6230,
    FAX 450-6244; website www.watertowertheatre.org
Terry Martin, *Artistic Director*

Submission procedure: no unsolicited scripts; synopsis, 10-20-page dialogue sample, resume and letter of inquiry with SASE for response. **Types of material:** full-length plays, musicals. **Special interests:** comedies; plays that make creative use of flexible space. **Facilities:** Addison Conference & Theatre Centre, 100-300 seats, flexible stage. **Best submission time:** Aug–Dec. **Response time:** 4 months letter; 6 months script. **Special programs:** Out of the Loop Festival: readings of previously unproduced full-length plays; submit synopsis, character breakdown and SASE for response.

WEISSBERGER THEATER GROUP
(Founded 1992)
240 West 44th St; New York, NY 10036; (212) 644-3335, FAX 644-3343
Jay Harris, *Producer*

Submission procedure: no unsolicited scripts; synopsis and letter of inquiry. **Types of material:** full-length plays. **Special interests:** topical, issue-oriented plays. **Facilities:** no permanent facility. **Production considerations:** cast limit of 7. **Best submission time:** year-round. **Response time:** 1 month letter; 2 months script.

WELLFLEET HARBOR ACTORS THEATER
(Founded 1985)
Box 797; Wellfleet, MA 02667; (508) 349-3011, FAX 349-3011;
    email source@WHAT.org; website www.WHAT.org
Jeff Zinn, *Producing Artistic Director*

Submission procedure: no unsolicited scripts; professional recommendation. **Types of material:** full-length plays, translations, adaptations, solo pieces. **Facilities:** WHAT mainstage, 90 seats, proscenium stage. **Best submission time:** year-round. **Response time:** 3 months letter; 6 months script.

WEST COAST ENSEMBLE
(Founded 1982)
Box 38728; Los Angeles, CA 90038; (323) 876-9337, FAX 876-8916
Les Hanson, *Artistic Director*

Submission procedure: accepts unsolicited scripts. **Types of material:** full-length plays, one-acts, translations, adaptations, musicals. **Special interests:** plays not previously produced in Southern CA only; musicals; short plays. **Facilities:** mainstage, 85 seats, proscenium stage. **Production considerations:** simple set; no fly space. **Best submission time:** Jun–Dec. **Response time:** 6 months. **Special programs:** staged readings of new plays. West Coast Ensemble Contests (see Prizes).

THE WESTERN STAGE
(Founded 1974)
156 Homestead Ave; Salinas, CA 93901; (831) 755-6990, FAX 755-6954
Jon Patrick Selover, *Artistic Director*

Submission procedure: no unsolicited scripts; synopsis and letter of inquiry; include cassette for musicals; for adaptations of work not in public domain, enclose copy of letter granting rights. **Types of material:** full-length plays, adaptations, plays for young audiences, musicals, cabaret/revues. **Special interests:** adaptations of works of literary significance; large-cast plays and ensemble pieces; plays for young performers; diverse casts; plays featuring strong roles for women. **Facilities:**

Mainstage, 500 seats, proscenium stage; Cabaret, 250 seats, proscenium stage; Studio, 115 seats, arena stage. **Best submission time:** year-round. **Response time:** 6 weeks letter; 3 months script.

WESTPORT COUNTRY PLAYHOUSE

(Founded 1931)
25 Powers Ct; Westport, CT 06880; (203) 227-5137, FAX 221-7482;
    website www.westportplayhouse.org
Anne Keefe, *Associate Artistic Director*

Submission procedure: no unsolicited scripts; professional recommendation. **Types of material:** full-length plays, translations, adaptations, musicals. **Facilities:** Westport Country Playhouse, 580 seats, proscenium stage. **Production considerations:** cast limit of 12. **Best submission time:** Aug-Jan. **Response time:** 8 months.

WILL GEER THEATRICUM BOTANICUM

(Founded 1973)
Box 1222; Topanga, CA 90290; (310) 455-2322, FAX 455-3724;
    email info@theatricum.com; website www.theatricum.com
Ellen Geer, *Artistic Director*

Submission procedure: no unsolicited scripts; synopsis, dialogue sample and letter of inquiry; include cassette for musicals. **Types of material:** full-length plays, musicals. **Special interests:** work suitable for large outdoor playing space. **Facilities:** Will Geer Theatricum Botanicum, 300 seats, outdoor amphitheatre. **Production considerations:** cast limit of 10; simple sets. **Best submission time:** Sep. **Response time:** 1 month letter; 6 months script.

WILLIAMSTOWN THEATRE FESTIVAL

(Founded 1955)
Sep-May: 229 West 42nd St, Suite 801; New York, NY 10036-7299;
    (212) 395-9090, FAX 395-9099
Jun-Aug: Box 517; Williamstown, MA 01267-0517; (413) 458-3200,
    FAX 458-3147; website www.wtfestival.org
Michael Ritchie, *Producer*

Submission procedure: no unsolicited scripts; agent submission. **Types of material:** full-length plays, adaptations, musicals, solo pieces. **Facilities:** Main Stage, 521 seats, proscenium stage; 2nd stage, 96 seats, thrust stage. **Best submission time:** 1 Oct-15 Feb. **Response time:** 12 months. **Special programs:** New Play Staged Readings Series.

WILLOWS THEATRE COMPANY

(Founded 1977)

1425 Gasoline Alley; Concord, CA 94520; (925) 798-1300,
    FAX 676-5726; email willowsth@aol.com;
    website www.willowstheatre.org

Richard H. Elliott, *Artistic Director*

Submission procedure: accepts unsolicited scripts. **Types of material:** full-length plays, adaptations, musicals. **Special interests:** musicals; plays based on figures and events drawn from American history, especially CA history; contemporary comedies. **Facilities:** John Muir Amphitheater, 1200 seats, outdoor stage; Willows Theatre, 210 seats, proscenium stage. **Production considerations:** cast limit of 35. **Best submission time:** 1 Apr-1 Jun only. **Response time:** 12 months. **Special programs:** staged readings and workshop development productions.

THE WILMA THEATER

(Founded 1979)

265 South Broad St; Philadelphia, PA 19107; (215) 893-9456,
    FAX 893-0895; email info@wilmatheater.org;
    website www.wilmatheater.org

Nakissa Etemad, *Dramaturg & Literary Manager*

Submission procedure: no unsolicited scripts; 10-page dialogue sample with professional recommendation and letter of inquiry. **Types of material:** full-length plays, translations, adaptations, musicals. **Special interests:** new translations and adaptations from the international repertoire with emphasis on innovative, bold staging; world premieres; ensemble works; works with poetic dimension; plays with music; multimedia works; social issues. **Facilities:** The Wilma Theater, 300 seats, flexible/proscenium stage. **Production considerations:** prefers cast limit of 10; stage 44' x 46'. **Best submission time:** year-round. **Response time:** 12 months.

WINGS THEATRE COMPANY, INC.

(Founded 1986)

154 Christopher St; New York, NY 10014; (212) 627-2960, FAX 462-0024;
    email jcorrick@wingstheatre.com; website www.wingstheatre.com

Submission procedure: accepts unsolicited scripts. **Types of material:** full-length plays, musicals. **Special interests:** new musicals and gay-themed plays only. **Facilities:** Wings Theatre, 74 seats, proscenium stage. **Best submission time:** year-round. **Response time:** plays received by 1 May receive response in Sep of that year; plays received after 1 May receive response Sep of following year.

WOMEN'S PROJECT & PRODUCTIONS

(Founded 1978)
55 West End Ave; New York, NY 10023; (212) 765-1706, FAX 765-2024;
email info@womensproject.org; website www.womensproject.org
Karen Keagle, *Literary Manager*

Submission procedure: no unsolicited scripts; synopsis, 10-page dialogue sample and letter of inquiry with SASE for response. **Types of material:** full-length plays, musicals. **Special interests:** plays by women only. **Facilities:** Women's Project Theatre, 199 seats, proscenium stage. **Best submission time:** year-round. **Response time:** 3 months letter; 12 months script. **Special programs:** Playwrights Lab and Directors Forum: developmental program including play readings and work-in-progress presentations; participation by invitation only.

WOODSTOCK FRINGE

(Founded 2000)
Box 157; Lake Hill, NY 12448; (845) 679-0167;
email info@woodstockfringe.org; website www.woodstockfringe.org
Wallace Norman, *Producing Artistic Director*

Submission procedure: no unsolicited scripts; synopsis, 10-15-page dialogue sample and letter of inquiry; resume, press/publicity materials and letter of inquiry for performance artists and solo performers only. **Types of material:** full-length plays, one-acts, translations, adaptations, musicals, solo pieces, performance art. **Facilities:** Byrdcliffe Theater in Woodstock, 100 seats, flexible stage. **Production considerations:** modest production requirements. **Best submission time:** Sep–Mar. **Response time:** 3 weeks letter; 6 months script. **Special programs:** annual Woodstock Fringe Festival of Theatre and Song : annual. Woodstock Fringe Playwrights Unit : readings of new plays in New York City.

WOOLLY MAMMOTH THEATRE COMPANY

(Founded 1981)
917 M St NW; Washington, DC 20001; (202) 289-2443;
email mary@woollymammoth.net; website www.woollymammoth.net
Mary Resing, *Literary Manager*

Submission procedure: no unsolicited scripts; professional recommendation. **Types of material:** full-length plays, translations, adaptations, solo pieces. **Special interests:** theatrical and provocative plays which combine elevated language with edgy situations and complex characters. **Facilities:** no permanent facility. **Production considerations:** prefers cast limit of 6. **Best submission time:** Jun. **Response time:** 12 months. **Special programs:** Foreplay: reading series. Playground: writer's group. Playmaking: community playbuilding projects.

WORCESTER FOOTHILLS THEATRE COMPANY

(Founded 1974)

100 Front St, Suite 137; Worcester, MA 01608; (508) 754-3314,
FAX 767-0676

Brad Kenney, *Artistic Director*

Submission procedure: no unsolicited scripts; synopsis and letter of inquiry. **Types of material:** full-length plays, translations, adaptations. **Special interests:** plays for multigenerational audiences. **Facilities:** Worcester Foothills Theatre, 349 seats, proscenium stage. **Production considerations:** prefers cast limit of 10, simple set. **Best submission time:** Sep. **Response time:** 3 months letter; 4 months script.

WRITERS' THEATRE

(Founded 1992)

378 Park Ave; Glencoe, IL 60022; (847) 242-6000, FAX 242-6011;
email info@writerstheatre.org

Shade Murray, *Associate Producer*

Submission procedure: accepts unsolicited scripts with professional recommendation. **Types of material:** full-length plays, translations, adaptations. **Special interests:** highly literary plays by or about great writers and writing. **Facilities:** Glencoe Woman's Club, 108 seats, thrust stage; Books On Vernon, 50 seats, flexible stage. **Production considerations:** intimate spaces; minimal production demands. **Best submission time:** year-round. **Response time:** 3 months.

YALE REPERTORY THEATRE

(Founded 1965)

Box 208244, Yale Station; New Haven, CT 06520-8244; (203) 432-1560,
FAX 432-1070; email catherine.sheehy@yale.edu

Catherine Sheehy, *Resident Dramaturg*

Submission procedure: no unsolicited scripts; synopsis, 10-page dialogue sample and letter of inquiry. **Types of material:** full-length plays, translations, adaptations. **Special interests:** new work; new translations of classics; contemporary foreign plays. **Facilities:** University Theatre, 654 seats, proscenium stage; Yale Repertory Theatre, 487 seats, modified thrust stage. **Best submission time:** year-round. **Response time:** 2 months letter; 3 months script.

THE YORK THEATRE COMPANY

(Founded 1968)

The Theatre at Saint Peter's Church; Citicorp Center; 619 Lexington Ave;
New York, NY 10022-4610; (212) 935-5824, FAX 832-0037

Literary Department

Submission procedure: accepts unsolicited scripts with SASE for response; include music on cassette or CD. **Types of material:** musicals, revues. **Special interests:** small-cast musicals. **Facilities:** The Theatre at Saint Peter's Church, 178 seats, flexible stage. **Best submission time:** year-round. **Response time:** 6 months.

PRIZES

What competitions are included here?

All the playwriting contests we know of that offer prizes of at least $200 or, in the case of awards to playwrights 19 or under, the equivalent in production or publication. Most awards for which the playwright cannot apply—the Joseph Kesselring Award, the Pulitzer Prize—are not listed. Exceptions are made when, as with The Susan Smith Blackburn Prize, the nominating process allows playwrights to encourage nomination of their work by theatre professionals.

How can I give myself the best chance of winning?

Send your script in well before the deadline, when the readers are fresh and enthusiastic, rather than buried by an avalanche of submissions. Assume the deadline is the date your script must be received (not the postmark date, unless otherwise stated). Make sure you don't mistake a notification date for the submission deadline. If a listing specifies "write for guidelines," be sure to follow this instruction. It usually means that we don't have space in our brief listing to give you all the information you need; also, contests may change their rules or their deadlines after this book has been published. Always send an SASE with your submission if you expect your materials to be returned.

Should I enter contests that charge entry fees?

It's true that a number of listings require a fee. Many contest sponsors are unable to secure sufficient funding to cover their costs, which are considerable. We have not included those listings with unusually high fees. Some playwrights will not pay fees as a matter of principle, others consider it part of doing business. It's up to you.

How can I find out about new prizes and updates?

Write or check the web for guidelines to ensure that you have the most recent rules. Also refer to the Membership and Service Organizations, Useful Publications and Online Resources sections in this book for those groups that list current contest news.

A couple of *Sourcebook* reminders:

"Full-length play" means a full-length, original work without a score or libretto. One-acts, musicals, adaptations, translations, plays for young audiences and solo pieces are listed separately.

Sourcebook entries are alphabetized by first word (excluding "the") even if the title starts with a proper name. So, for instance, you'll find the "Harold Morton Landon Translation Award" under H. In the index, you will also find this prize cross-listed under L.

Deadlines: Some deadlines may fall outside the publication period of this book, which is biennial. All deadlines reflect the next upcoming submission deadline for an organization at press time. Deadlines for annual awards may stay the same from year to year, but this is not absolute—always obtain the latest information (an organization's website is the best place to check) before submitting. Also note that some prizes may be given every three or four years, so it is very important to read dates closely.

AMERICAN TRANSLATORS ASSOCIATION AWARDS
225 Reinekers Ln, Suite 590; Alexandria, VA 22314;
FAX (703) 683-6122; email ata@atanet.org
Chair, ATA Honors and Awards

GERMAN LITERARY TRANSLATION PRIZE
Types of material: translations of full-length plays and one-acts. **Frequency:** biennial. **Remuneration:** $1000, up to $500 expenses to attend ATA annual conference. **Guidelines:** translation from German published in U.S. by American publisher during 2 years before deadline as single volume or in collection. **Submission procedure:** no submission by translator; publisher nominates translation and submits 2 copies of book plus 10 consecutive pages of German original, extra jacket and any advertising copy, bio of translator. **Deadline:** 15 May 2005. **Notification:** fall 2005.

LEWIS GALANTIERE LITERARY TRANSLATION PRIZE
Types of material: translations of full-length plays and one-acts. **Frequency:** biennial. **Remuneration:** $1000, up to $500 expenses to attend ATA annual conference. **Guidelines:** translation from any language except German published in U.S. by American publisher during 2 years before deadline as single volume or in collection. **Submission procedure:** no submission by translator; publisher nominates translation and submits 2 copies of book plus 10 consecutive pages of original, extra jacket and any advertising copy, bio of translator. **Deadline:** 15 May 2005. **Notification:** Sep 2005.

ANNA ZORNIO MEMORIAL CHILDREN'S THEATRE PLAYWRITING AWARD
Department of Theatre and Dance; University of New Hampshire;
Paul Creative Arts Center; 30 College Rd;
Durham, NH 03824-3538; (603) 862-3038, FAX 862-0298
Administrative Manager

Types of material: plays and musicals for young audiences. **Frequency:** every 4 years. **Remuneration:** $1000, production by UNH Department of Theatre and Dance in the 2005-2006 season. **Guidelines:** U.S. or Canadian resident; unpublished work not produced professionally and not more than 60 minutes in length; 2 submission limit; prefers single or unit set. **Submission procedure:** script with brief synopsis, character breakdown and statement of design/technical considerations; SASP for acknowledgment of receipt; include cassette for musical; write for guidelines. **Deadline:** 1 Sep 2004. **Notification:** Nov 2004.

THE ANNUAL NATIONWIDE BLANK THEATRE COMPANY YOUNG PLAYWRIGHTS FESTIVAL

1301 Lucile Ave; Los Angeles, CA 90026-1519; (323) 662-7734;
email info@theblank.com; websites www.theblank.com,
www.youngplaywrights.com

Types of material: full-length plays, one-acts, plays for young audiences, musicals, operas, solo pieces. **Frequency:** annual. **Remuneration:** workshop production for approximately 9-12 playwrights; some scripts receive full production. **Guidelines:** playwright 19 years of age or younger as of deadline date; original play of any length on any subject; send SASE in late Jan for guidelines. **Submission procedure:** script with cover sheet containing name, date of birth, home address, phone number and email address; pages must be numbered and unbound; if applicable, also include name of school and/or production history. **Deadline:** 15 Mar 2005. **Notification:** May 2005.

APPALACHIAN FESTIVAL OF PLAYS & PLAYWRIGHTS

Barter Theatre; Box 867; Abingdon, VA 24212-0867;
(276) 619-3316, FAX 619-3335; email apfestival@bartertheatre.com;
website www.bartertheatre.com
Derek Davidson, *Festival Coordinator*

Types of material: full-length plays; one-acts; adaptations; plays for young audiences; musicals. **Frequency:** annual. **Remuneration:** $250; 3-6 plays chosen for staged reading; travel and housing stipend available for rehearsals. **Guidelines:** unproduced scripts on Appalachian themes, locations and/or setting; if playwright is from Appalachian region, play may be on any subject or theme and need not be set in Appalachia; see website for guidelines. **Submission procedure:** script only. **Deadline:** 23 Apr 2005. **Notification:** 3-6 months.

THE ARTS & LETTERS PRIZE IN DRAMA

Georgia College & State University; Campus Box 89;
Milledgeville, GA 31061-0490; (478) 445-1289;
email al@mail.gcsu.edu; website al.gcsu.edu
David Muschell, *Drama Editor*

Types of material: one-acts. **Frequency:** annual. **Remuneration:** $1000, production, publication in *Arts & Letters* journal. **Guidelines:** unpublished one-act. **Submission procedure:** script with separate title page containing name and address of playwright and $15 fee; includes subscription to journal. **Deadline:** 1 Apr 2005. **Notification:** Aug 2005.

ARTSPORT NEW WORKS CONTEST

Playhouse on the Green; 177 State St; Bridgeport, CT 06604;
(203) 333-6211, FAX 696-0045;
email kkatcher@artsport.org; website www.playhouseonthegreen.org
Kate Katcher, *Education Director*

Types of material: full-length plays, bill of related one-acts, plays for young audiences. **Frequency:** annual. **Remuneration:** $250 1st prize, staged reading with possible production in subsequent season, playwright attends rehearsal and performance. **Guidelines:** unproduced, unpublished play or bill of related one-acts; cast limit 6. **Submission procedure:** application, 3 copies of script, $20 fee. **Deadline:** 1 Apr 2005. **Notification:** 15 Jun 2005.

ASF TRANSLATION PRIZE

The American–Scandinavian Foundation; 58 Park Ave;
New York, NY 10016; (212) 879-9779, FAX 686-2115;
email ahenkin@amscan.org
Publishing Office

Types of material: translations. **Frequency:** annual. **Remuneration:** $2000, publication of excerpt in *Scandinavian Review*; $1000 for runner-up. **Guidelines:** unpublished translation from a Scandinavian language into English of work written by a Scandinavian author after 1800; manuscript must be at least 50 pages in length if prose drama, 25 pages if verse drama, and must be conceived as part of a book. **Submission procedure:** 4 copies of translation, 1 of original, permission letter from copyright holder; write for guidelines. **Deadline:** 1 Jun 2005. **Notification:** fall 2005.

ATTIC THEATRE ENSEMBLE'S ONE-ACT MARATHON

Attic Theatre Centre; 5429 West Washington Blvd; Los Angeles, CA 90016;
(323) 525-0600; website www.attictheatre.org
James Carey, *Producing Artistic Director*

Types of material: one-acts. **Frequency:** annual. **Remuneration:** $250 1st prize; $50 2nd prize; 6 finalists receive productions. **Guidelines:** unproduced one-act no longer than 45 minutes in length; no adaptations. **Submission procedure:** send SASE for guidelines and application or download from web. **Deadline:** 30 Sep 2004. **Notification:** Jan 2005. **Dates:** Jun 2005. (See Attic Theatre Ensemble in Production.)

AURAND HARRIS MEMORIAL PLAYWRITING AWARD

New England Theatre Conference Inc.; PMB 502; 198 Tremont St;
Boston, MA 02116; (617) 851-8535;
email mail@netconline.org; website www.netconline.org

Types of material: plays for young audiences. **Frequency:** annual. **Remuneration:** $1000 1st prize; $500 2nd prize. **Guidelines:** resident of CT, MA, ME, NH, RI, VT or member of the New England Theatre Conference (NETC) (see Membership and Service Organizations); unpublished work not produced professionally; 1 submission limit. **Submission procedure:** script, synopsis, character breakdown and statement that play has not been published or professionally produced and is not under consideration for publication or production prior to 1 Sep 2004, $20 fee (fee is waived for NETC members); send SASP for acknowledgment of receipt; script will not be returned; send SASE for guidelines. **Deadline:** 1 May 2005. **Notification:** Sep 2005 (winners only).

BAKER'S PLAYS HIGH SCHOOL PLAYWRITING CONTEST

Box 699222; Quincy, MA 02269-9222; (617) 745-0805, FAX 745-9891;
email editor@bakersplays.com; website www.bakersplays.com

Types of material: full-length plays, one-acts, plays for young audiences, musicals.
Frequency: annual. **Remuneration:** $500 1st prize, publication; $250 2nd prize;
$100 3rd prize. **Guidelines:** high school student sponsored by high school drama or
English teacher; prefers play that has been produced or given public reading.
Submission procedure: script with signature of sponsoring teacher; write for
guidelines. **Deadline:** 31 Jan 2005. **Notification:** May 2005. (See Baker's Plays in
Publication.)

BEVERLY HILLS THEATRE GUILD—CALIFORNIA MUSICAL THEATRE AWARD

Box 148; Beverly Hills, CA 90213; (310) 273-3390;
website www.beverlyhillstheatreguild.org
Toni Webb, *Competition Coordinator*

Types of material: musicals. **Frequency:** annual. **Remuneration:** $3000, possible
staged reading. **Guidelines:** resident of CA and NY only, musical must be written in
English, not previously published, produced, under professional option, or the
winner or any other major competition. **Submission procedure:** application, script,
cassette or CD of music selections; material will not be returned; send SASE for
guidelines and application or download from web. **Deadline:** 15 Oct 2004.
Notification: Feb 2005.

BEVERLY HILLS THEATRE GUILD PLAYWRITING AWARDS

Box 39729; Los Angeles, CA 90039-0729
Dick Dotterer, *Competition Coordinator*

JULIE HARRIS PLAYWRITING AWARDS

Types of material: full-length plays. **Frequency:** annual. **Remuneration:** $3500 1st
place award; $2500 Maxwell and Janet Salter Award; $1500 Dr. Henry and Lilian
Nesburn Award; possible staged reading for all winners. **Guidelines:** U.S. citizen or
legal resident; play must be written in English; 1 submission, not published,
produced, optioned or winner of any other major competition; 75 minutes or more
in length; no adaptations, bills of related one-acts or musicals. **Submission
guidelines:** application and script; script will not be returned; send SASE for
guidelines and application. **Deadline:** 1 Nov 2004; no submission before 1 Aug 2004.
Notification: Jun 2005.

THE MARILYN HALL AWARDS

Types of material: adaptations, translations, plays for young audiences. **Frequency:**
annual. **Remuneration:** $500 1st prize, $300 2nd prize, $200 3rd prize; possible
staged reading for all winners. **Guidelines:** U.S. citizen or legal resident; plays
suitable for grades 6-8 or grades 9-12, must be written in English, not previously
submitted, published, under professional option, or winner of any other major
competition; approximately 45-90 minutes in length; plays may have had 1 non-

professional or educational theatre production; plays with songs (but not traditional musicals) accepted; 2 submission limit. **Submission procedure:** application and script; scripts will not be returned; send SASE for guidelines and application. **Deadline:** postmarked by 28 Feb 2005; no submissions before 15 Jan 2005. **Notification:** Jun 2005.

BIENNIAL PROMISING PLAYWRIGHT AWARD

Colonial Players, Inc; Box 2167; Annapolis, MD 21404;
   website www.cplayers.com
Contest Coordinator

Types of material: full-length plays, adaptations. **Frequency:** biennial. **Remuneration:** $1000, workshop; possible full production. **Guidelines:** resident of CT, DC, DE, GA, MA, MD, NC, NH, NJ, NY, PA, RI, SC, VA or WV; playwright must be available to attend rehearsals; play not produced professionally, suitable for arena stage, between 90-120 minutes in length; 2-set limit, cast limit of 10; only adaptation of material in public domain; no musicals; see website for details. **Submission procedure:** script, summary, sample pages and application form; see website for details. **Deadline:** 1 Dec 2004; no submission before 1 Sep 2004. **Notification:** 15 Jun 2005.

BUNTVILLE CREW

Box 445; Buckley, IL 60918-0445; (217) 394-2772; email buntville@yahoo.fr
Steven Packard, *Artistic Director*

AWARD BLUE

Types of material: one-acts. **Frequency:** annual. **Remuneration:** $200, possible full or workshop production or staged reading. **Guidelines:** IL high-school student enrolled in the recent school year; unpublished, unproduced play no longer than 15 pages in length. **Submission procedure:** script with playwright's name, address, phone number, age and name of school on title page and bio. **Deadline:** postmarked by 31 May 2005. **Notification:** fall 2005.

DAS GOLDKIEL

Types of material: full-length plays. **Frequency:** annual. **Remuneration:** $250, possible full or workshop production or staged reading. **Guidelines:** unpublished, unproduced play; scripts may be in English, French, German or Spanish; no translations or adaptations. **Submission procedure:** script, bio and $8 fee. **Deadline:** postmarked by 31 May 2005. **Notification:** fall 2005.

PRIX HORS PAIR

Types of material: one-acts. **Frequency:** annual. **Remuneration:** $200, possible full or workshop production or staged reading. **Guidelines:** unpublished, unproduced play no longer than 15 pages in length; scripts may be in English, French, German or Spanish; no translations or adaptations. **Submission procedure:** script, bio and $8 fee. **Deadline:** postmarked by 31 May 2005. **Notification:** fall 2005.

CALIFORNIA YOUNG PLAYWRIGHTS CONTEST

Playwrights Project; 450 B St; Suite 1020; San Diego, CA 92101–8093;
(619) 239–8222, FAX 239–8225; email write@playwrightsproject.com;
website www.playwrightsproject.com

Deborah Salzer, *Executive Director*

Types of material: full-length plays, one-acts. **Frequency:** annual. **Remuneration:** 3-5 awards of $100, full production, travel, housing and board; all entrants receive written evaluation of work. **Guidelines:** resident of CA; playwright 19 years of age or younger as of 1 Jun 2005; work at least 10 pages in length; previous submissions ineligible. **Submission procedure:** 2 copies of script with playwright's date of birth on title page and cover letter; script will not be returned. **Deadline:** 1 Jun 2005. **Notification:** Aug 2005.

CHICANO/LATINO LITERARY PRIZE

Department of Spanish & Portuguese; University of California–Irvine;
322 Humanities Hall; Irvine, CA 92697–5275; (949) 824–5443;
email cllp@uci.edu;
website www.hnet.uci.edu/spanishandportuguese/contest.html

Adriana Gallardo, *Prize Coordinator*

Types of material: full-length plays. **Frequency:** every 4 years. **Remuneration:** $1000 1st prize, publication by Arte Público Press, travel to attend award ceremony; $500 2nd prize; $250 3rd prize. **Guidelines:** U.S. citizen or resident; unpublished play written in Spanish or English; 1 submission limit. **Submission procedure:** 3 copies of script, minimum 90 typed, double-spaced pages. **Deadline:** 1 Jun 2006. **Notification:** Oct 2006.

CLAUDER COMPETITION FOR NEW ENGLAND PLAYWRIGHTS

Portland Stage Company; Box 1458; Portland, ME 04104;
(207) 774–1043, FAX 774–0576;
email info@portlandstage.com; website www.portlandstage.com

Literary Manager

Types of material: full-length plays. **Frequency:** biennial. **Remuneration:** $3000 towards royalties for fully staged production/development process at Portland Stage Company's discretion, fully staged production for winner; $500 optional for runners-up. **Guidelines:** New England playwrights only (will consider exception if play is relevant to region, see website); unpublished, unproduced play; cast limit of 8; see website for details. **Submission procedure:** email for application and guidelines. **Deadline:** 1 Apr 2005. **Notification:** Jan 2006.

COE COLLEGE NEW WORKS FOR THE STAGE COMPETITION

Department of Theatre Arts; 1220 First Ave NE; Cedar Rapids, IA 52402;
(319) 399–8624, FAX 399–8557; email swolvert@coe.edu

Susan Wolverton, *Chair, Playwriting Festival*

Types of material: full-length plays. **Frequency:** biennial, contingent on funding.

Remuneration: $325, staged reading, travel, room and board for 1-week residency during spring term. **Guidelines:** unpublished, unproduced play dealing with the theme of Playwriting Festival and Symposia (theme "crossing borders"); festival includes workshops and public discussions; no translations, adaptations or musicals; send SASE for guidelines. **Submission procedure:** script and resume. **Deadline:** 1 Nov 2004. **Notification:** 15 Jan 2005. **Dates:** 28 Mar–1 Apr 2005.

COFFEYVILLE COMMUNITY COLLEGE KANSAS PLAYWRIGHT CONTEST

Coffeyville Community College; 400 West 11th St; Coffeyville, KS 67337;
(620) 251-7700, FAX 251-7098;
email markf@coffeyville.edu; website www.ccc.cc.ks.us
Mark Frank, *Theatre Director*

Types of material: full-length plays, one-acts, translations, adaptations, plays for young audiences, musicals, solo pieces. **Frequency:** annual. **Remuneration:** $200, staged reading, housing provided during performances. **Guidelines:** Kansas plays only; unpublished, unproduced play, moderate cast; see website for specific guidelines. **Submission procedure:** script, 50-word synopsis, character description, reading time, SASE. **Deadline:** 31 Dec 2004. **Notification:** 15 Jan 2005.

THE CUNNINGHAM COMMISSION FOR YOUTH THEATRE

The Theatre School; DePaul University; 2135 North Kenmore;
Chicago, IL 60614-4111; (773) 325-7938, FAX 325-7920;
email lgoetsch@depaul.edu;
website theatreschool.depaul.edu/programs/prize.htm
Lara Goetsch, *Director of Marketing and Public Relations*

Types of material: plays for young audiences. **Frequency:** annual. **Remuneration:** up to $5000, possible production. **Guidelines:** Chicago-area playwright; winner commissioned to write a play for young audiences which "affirms the centrality of religion, broadly defined, and the human quest for meaning, truth and community." **Submission procedure:** 20-page dialogue sample, brief statement about interest in commission and resume; write for guidelines. **Deadline:** 1 Dec 2004. **Notification:** 1 May 2005.

DAYTON PLAYHOUSE FUTUREFEST

1301 East Siebenthaler Ave; Dayton, OH 45414; (937) 333-7469,
FAX 333-2827; website www.daytonplayhouse.com
David Seyer, *Executive Director*

Types of material: full-length plays. **Frequency:** annual. **Remuneration:** $1000 1st prize, Speert Publishing Award and publication by Speert Publishing (see listing in Publication); 5 $100 runners-up; 3 plays receive full productions, 3 plays receive reading during FutureFest weekend the end of July; travel and housing to attend weekend. **Guidelines:** unproduced, unpublished play not under consideration for publication or production prior to FutureFest weekend. **Submission procedure:**

script and resume; send SASE, fax number or visit website for guidelines. **Deadline:** postmarked by 31 Oct 2004. **Notification:** May 2005.

DOROTHY SILVER PLAYWRITING COMPETITION

Jewish Community Center of Cleveland; 3505 Mayfield Rd;
　　Cleveland Heights, OH 44118; (216) 382-4000, ext 274,
　　FAX 382-5401; email kbarnes@clevejcc.org
Deborah Bobrow, *Coordinator*

Types of material: full-length plays. **Frequency:** annual. **Remuneration:** $1000 (including $500 to cover residency expenses), staged reading, possible production. **Guidelines:** unproduced play that provides "fresh and significant" perspective on the range of the Jewish experience. **Submission procedure:** script only. **Deadline:** 1 May 2005. **Notification:** early fall 2005.

DRURY UNIVERSITY ONE-ACT PLAY COMPETITION

900 North Benton Ave; Springfield, MO 65802; (417) 873-7430;
　　email msokol@lib.drury.edu
Mick Sokol, *Assistant Professor of Theatre*

Types of material: one-acts. **Frequency:** biennial. **Remuneration:** $300 1st prize, possible production; winners recommended to The Open Eye Theater (see Production); 2 runners-up receive $150. **Guidelines:** unproduced, unpublished play 20–45 minutes in length; prefers small cast, 1 set; 1 submission limit. **Submission procedure:** script only; send SASE or email for guidelines. **Deadline:** 1 Dec 2004. **Notification:** 1 Apr 2005.

DUBUQUE FINE ARTS PLAYERS NATIONAL
ONE-ACT PLAYWRITING CONTEST

1686 Lawndale Dr; Dubuque, IA 52001-4200; (319) 588-0646;
　　email gary.arms@clarke.edu;
Gary Arms, *Coordinator*

Types of material: one-acts. **Frequency:** annual. **Remuneration:** $600 1st prize; $300 2nd prize; $200 3rd prize; possible production for all 3 plays. **Guidelines:** unproduced, unpublished play maximum 35 pages and 40 minutes in length; one-act adaptations accepted; prefers cast limit of 5, 1 set; no submission limit; only adaptations of material in public domain. **Submission procedure:** entry form, 2 copies of script, 1 paragraph synopsis and $10 fee per submission; optional SASE for critique and optional SASP for acknowledgment of receipt; send SASE for guidelines and application. **Deadline:** 31 Jan 2005; no submission before 1 Nov 2004. **Notification:** 30 Jun 2005.

ECODRAMA PLAYWRIGHT FESTIVAL

Earth Matters On Stage; Humboldt State University; Theatre, Film and Dance;
TA 20; 1 Harist St; Ancata, CA 95521; FAX (775) 521-9206;
email lkf@naturalchoice.net; website www.humboldt.edu/emos
Larry Fried, *Festival Coordinator*

Types of material: full-length plays, one-acts, adaptations, musicals. **Frequency:** biennial. **Remuneration:** $2000, workshop production, travel and housing provided for rehearsals. **Guidelines:** must qualify as ecodrama; see website for extensive and specific guidelines. **Submission procedure:** script. **Deadline:** 1 May 2006. **Notification:** Jul 2006.

EMERGING PLAYWRIGHT AWARD

Urban Stages; 17 East 47th St; New York, NY 10017;
(212) 421-1380, FAX 421-1387; email urbanstage@aol.com;
website www.urbanstages.org
Frances Hill, *Artistic Director*

Types of material: full-length plays. **Frequency:** annual. **Remuneration:** $500, production, multiple staged readings, $25 per reading. **Guidelines:** play unproduced in New York; multicultural, multiethnic plays dealing with social issues in nondidactic manner. **Submission procedure:** script, production history (if any), bio and $5 fee. **Deadline:** ongoing; best submission time Jul-Aug. (See Urban Stages in Production.)

ESSENTIAL THEATRE PLAYWRITING AWARD

Box 1872; Atlanta, GA 30306; (404) 212-0815
Peter Hardy, *Producing Artistic Director*

Types of material: full-length plays. **Frequency:** annual. **Remuneration:** $400, production in Festival of New American Theatre; runners-up given staged readings during festival. **Guidelines:** resident of GA; unproduced play. **Submission procedure:** script with SASE for response. **Deadline:** 15 Apr 2005. **Notification:** 1 Oct 2005. **Dates:** Jan-Feb 2005.

FIREHOUSE THEATRE PROJECT FESTIVAL OF NEW AMERICAN PLAYS

1609 West Broad St; Richmond, VA 23220; (804) 355-2001;
email newplays@firehousetheatre.org;
website www.firehousetheatre.org
Literary Manager

Types of material: full-length plays, solo pieces. **Frequency:** annual. **Remuneration:** $1000 1st place, staged reading, possible production; $500 2nd place; $250 3rd place. **Guidelines:** U.S. resident; unpublished, unproduced play; no translations or adaptations; 1 submission limit. **Submission procedure:** agent submission or script with professional letter of recommendation by director, literary manager or dramaturg; download guidelines from web. **Deadline:** TBA (15 Jun in 2004).

FREMONT CENTRE THEATRE NEW PLAYWRIGHT CONTEST

California Performing Arts Centre (CPAC); 1000 Fremont Ave;
    South Pasadena, CA 91030; (626) 441–5977, FAX 441–5976;
    email fct@fremontcentretheatre.com;
    website www.fremontcentretheatre.com
Lissa Reynolds, *Contest Manager*

Types of material: full-length plays, one-acts, plays for young audiences (suitable for grades 6–12). **Frequency:** annual. **Remuneration:** $350 1st prize; $250 2nd prize; $100 3rd prize; staged reading. **Guidelines:** unpublished plays not produced professionally; all genres and age groups, especially plays based on historical events, persons or moments; maximum 10 characters. **Submission procedure:** script, 1-page synopsis, character breakdown, resume and $15 fee. **Deadline:** 1 Apr 2005. **Notification:** 15 Jun 2005.

GEORGE HAWKINS PLAYWRITING CONTEST

The Ensemble Theatre; 3535 Main St; Houston, TX; (713) 520–0055,
    FAX 520–1269
Marsha Jackson Randolph, *Producing Artistic Director*

Types of material: plays for young audiences, musicals (performed for and by youth ages 7–17). **Frequency:** annual. **Remuneration:** $500 1st prize; staged reading for 1st, 2nd and 3rd place scripts; royalty paid for plays selected as part of Tour Education repertoire. **Guidelines:** original work, not professionally produced, that illuminates the African or African-American experience; prefers work 45–60 minutes in length; touring shows must have cast limit of 5, portable set and props. **Submission procedure:** script, synopsis, resume and SASE for response. **Deadline:** 1 Dec 2004; no submission before 1 Oct 2004. **Notification:** Mar 2005. (See The Ensemble Theatre in Production.)

GEORGE R. KERNODLE PLAYWRITING CONTEST

Department of Drama; 619 Kimpel Hall; University of Arkansas;
    Fayetteville, AR 72701; (501) 575–2953, FAX 575–7602;
    email rdgross@uark.edu
Roger Gross, *Director*

Types of material: one-acts. **Frequency:** annual. **Remuneration:** $300 1st prize; $200 2nd prize; $100 3rd prize; possible staged reading or production. **Guidelines:** no restriction on style or subject matter; unproduced, unpublished play, maximum 60 minutes in length; 3 submission limit. **Submission procedure:** script with statement that play has not received full production, $3 fee per submission and optional SASE or SASP for acknowledgment of receipt; write or email for guidelines. **Deadline:** 1 Jun 2005; no submission before 1 Jan 2005. **Notification:** 1 Nov 2005.

GOSHEN COLLEGE PEACE PLAYWRITING CONTEST

1700 South Main St; Goshen, IN 46526; (219) 535-7393, FAX 535-7660;
email douglc@goshen.edu

Douglas Caskey, *Director of Theatre*

Types of material: one-acts. **Frequency:** biennial. **Remuneration:** $500 1st prize; $100 2nd prize; production, room and board to attend rehearsals and/or production. **Guidelines:** 1 unproduced submission, 20-30 minutes in length, exploring a contemporary peace or justice theme "broadly defined." **Submission procedure:** script, 1-paragraph synopsis and resume. **Deadline:** 31 Dec 2005. **Notification:** 1 May 2006.

HAROLD MORTON LANDON TRANSLATION AWARD

The Academy of American Poets; 588 Broadway, Suite 604;
New York, NY 10012; (212) 274-0343, FAX 274-9427;
email academy@poets.org; website www.poets.org

Ryan Murphy, *Awards Director*

Types of material: translations. **Frequency:** annual. **Remuneration:** $1000. **Guidelines:** U.S. citizen; published translation of verse, including verse drama, from any language into English verse, book must have been published in 2002. **Submission procedure:** 3 copies of book (no manuscripts). **Deadline:** 31 Dec 2004.

HENRICO THEATRE COMPANY ONE-ACT PLAYWRITING COMPETITION

The County of Henrico; Division of Recreation and Parks; Box 27032;
Richmond, VA 23273-7032; (804) 501-5138, FAX 501-5284;
email per22@co.henrico.va.us

Amy A. Perdue, *Cultural Arts Coordinator*

Types of material: one-acts, musicals. **Frequency:** annual. **Remuneration:** $300 1st prize, production; $200 2nd prize, possible production and video. **Guidelines:** unproduced, unpublished work; no controversial themes or "excessive language"; prefers small cast, simple set. **Submission procedure:** 2 copies of script; write for guidelines. **Deadline:** 1 Jul 2005. **Notification:** 31 Dec 2005.

HRC'S ANNUAL PLAYWRITING CONTEST

Hudson River Classics, Inc; Box 940; Hudson, NY 12534;
(518) 828-0175

Jan M. Grice, *President*

Types of material: full-length plays. **Frequency:** annual. **Remuneration:** $500, staged reading. **Guidelines:** Northeast playwright; 60-90-minute unpublished play. **Submission procedure:** script, bio and $5 fee. **Deadline:** 1 May 2005; no submission before 1 Feb 2005. **Notification:** Sep 2005.

JACKIE WHITE MEMORIAL NATIONAL CHILDREN'S PLAYWRITING CONTEST

309 Parkade Blvd; Columbia, MO 65202; (573) 874-5628

Betsy Phillips, *Director*

Types of material: plays and musicals to be performed by young actors. **Frequency:** annual. **Remuneration:** $500, optional production by Columbia Entertainment Company Children's Theatre School; room and board to attend performance; all entrants receive written evaluation. **Guidelines:** unpublished original work, 60-90 minutes in length, with at least 7 speaking characters of all ages, at least 7 developed in some detail, to be played by students ages 10-15. **Submission procedure:** entry form, script, character breakdown, act/scene synopsis, resume and $10 fee; include cassette and score for musical; send SASE for guidelines. **Deadline:** 1 Jun 2005. **Notification:** 30 Aug 2005.

JAMES D. PHELAN AWARD IN LITERATURE

Intersection for the Arts/The San Francisco Foundation ;

446 Valencia St; San Francisco, CA 94103; (415) 626-2787,

FAX 626-1636; email info@theintersection.org

Awards Coordinator

Types of material: full-length plays, one-acts, plays for young audiences. **Frequency:** annual. **Remuneration:** $2000. **Guidelines:** CA-born author 20-35 years of age as of 31 Jan 2005; unpublished play-in-progress. **Submission procedure:** application and script; send SASE for guidelines and application. **Deadline:** 31 Jan 2005; no submission before 15 Nov 2004. **Notification:** 15 Jun 2005.

JANE CHAMBERS PLAYWRITING AWARD

c/o Division of Theatre; Southern Methodist University; Box 750356;

Dallas, TX 75275-0356; email gesmith@mail.smu.edu

Gretchen E. Smith, *Administrator*

Types of material: full-length plays, one-acts, solo pieces, performance-art pieces. **Frequency:** annual. **Remuneration:** $1000, free registration and rehearsed reading at the Association for Theatre in Higher Education Conference in early Aug; student submissions eligible for $250 Student Award and staged reading at the Women and Theatre Conference in Jul. **Guidelines:** work by a woman that reflects a feminist perspective and contains a majority of roles for women; special interest in work by and about women from a diversity of positions in respect to race, class, sexual preference, physical ability, age and geographical region; experimentation with dramatic form encouraged; 1 submission limit; award administered by the Association for Theatre in Higher Education (see Membership and Service Organizations) and Women and Theatre Program. **Submission procedure:** application, 2 copies of script, synopsis and resume; if possible, professional recommendation; optional SASP for acknowledgment of receipt; send SASE for guidelines and application or email administrator. **Deadline:** 15 Feb 2005. **Notification:** 30 Jun 2005.

JEWEL BOX THEATRE PLAYWRIGHTING AWARD
3700 North Walker; Oklahoma City, OK 73118-7099;
(405) 521-1786, FAX 525-6562
Charles Tweed, *Production Director*

Types of material: full-length plays. **Frequency:** annual. **Remuneration:** $500, possible production. **Guidelines:** unproduced ensemble play with emphasis on character rather than spectacle. **Submission procedure:** entry form, 2 copies of script, application and $10 fee; send SASE in Oct for guidelines and forms. **Deadline:** 15 Jan 2005. **Notification:** Apr 2005.

JOHN GASSNER MEMORIAL PLAYWRITING AWARD
New England Theatre Conference Inc.; Box 502; 198 Tremont St;
Boston, MA 02116; (617) 851-8535; email mail@netconline.org;
website www.netconline.org

Types of material: full-length plays. **Frequency:** annual. **Remuneration:** $1000 1st prize; $500 2nd prize; staged reading, possible publication. **Guidelines:** New England resident or NETC member (see Membership and Service Organizations); unpublished play that has not had professional full production and is not under consideration for publication or professional production; 1 submission limit. **Submission procedure:** script with cover page, character breakdown, brief synopsis and statement that play has not been published or professionally produced and is not under consideration; $10 fee, except for NETC members; SASP for acknowledgment of receipt; script will not be returned; see website for guidelines. **Deadline:** 15 Apr 2005. **Notification:** 1 Sep 2005 (winners only).

THE KAUFMAN AND HART PRIZE FOR NEW AMERICAN COMEDY
Arkansas Repertory Theatre; Box 110; Little Rock, AR 72203-0110;
(501) 378-0445
Brad Mooy, *Literary Manager*

Types of material: full-length plays. **Frequency:** biennial. **Remuneration:** $10,000, staged reading and transportation; additional finalists receive $1000 and staged reading. **Guidelines:** U.S. citizen; comedy not previously published or produced; minimum 65 pages, cast limit of 12; no musicals or plays for young audiences; 1 submission limit. **Submission procedure:** agent submission or script with recommendation from theatre professional only. **Deadline:** 1 Feb 2006. **Notification:** Apr 2006. (See Arkansas Repertory Theatre in Production.)

KENNEDY CENTER AMERICAN COLLEGE THEATER FESTIVAL: MICHAEL KANIN PLAYWRITING AWARDS PROGRAM

The John F. Kennedy Center for the Performing Arts;
Washington, DC 20566-0001; (202) 416-8857, FAX 416-8802;
website www.kennedy-center.org/education/actf
Susan Shaffer, *Co-Manager for Administration*
Gregg Henry, *Co-Manager/Artistic Director*

ANCHORAGE PRESS THEATER FOR YOUTH PLAYWRITING AWARD

Types of material: full-length plays, adaptations, musicals. **Frequency:** annual. **Remuneration:** $1000, $1250 fellowship to attend either the New Visions/New Voices Festival (see Development) or the National Youth Theatre, possible publication by Anchorage Press with royalties. **Guidelines:** writer enrolled as full-time student at college or university during year of production or during either of the 2 years preceding the production; play on theme appealing to young people from kindergarten–12th grade produced by a KC/ACTF-participating college or university; download guidelines from web. **Submission procedure:** college or university which has entered production of work in KC/ACTF registers work for awards program. **Deadline:** 1 Dec 2004. **Dates:** 18–24 Apr 2005.

THE DAVID MARK COHEN PLAYWRITING AWARD

Types of material: full-length plays, bills of related one-acts. **Frequency:** annual. **Remuneration:** $1000, up to $500 for travel, script-in-hand reading at annual Aug meeting of Association for Theatre in Higher Education (ATHE) (see Membership and Service Organization), Dramatic Publishing Company (see Publication) contract offer to publish, license and market play. **Guidelines:** unpublished play or bill of related one-acts not produced professionally, produced by a KC/ACTF-participating college or university theatre program; download guidelines from web. **Submission procedure:** college or university which has entered production of play in KC/ACTF registers work for awards program. **Deadline:** 1 Dec 2004. **Dates:** 18–24 Apr 2005.

THE JEAN KENNEDY SMITH PLAYWRITING AWARD

Types of material: full-length plays, adaptations, musicals. **Frequency:** annual. **Remuneration:** $2500 plus Dramatists Guild (see Membership and Service Organizations) membership and fellowship to attend prestigious playwriting program. **Guidelines:** writer enrolled as full-time student at college or university during year of production; play that explores the human experience of living with disabilities produced by a KC/ACTF-participating college or university; download guidelines from web. **Submission procedure:** college or university which has entered production of work in KC/ACTF registers work for awards program. **Deadline:** 1 Dec 2004. **Dates:** 18–24 Apr 2005.

THE JOHN CAUBLE SHORT PLAY AWARDS PROGRAM

Types of material: one-acts, one-act adaptations. **Frequency:** annual. **Remuneration:** $1000 for 3 or fewer playwrights, publication by Samuel French (see Publication), Dramatists Guild (see Membership and Service Organizations) membership. **Guidelines:** writer enrolled as full-time student at college or university during year of production or during either of the 2 years preceding the production; one-act must be produced by a KC/ACTF-participating college or university; simple production demands (minimal setup and strike time); download guidelines from web. **Submission procedure:** college or university which has entered production of work in KC/ACTF registers work for awards program. **Deadline:** 1 Dec 2004. **Dates:** 18–24 Apr 2005.

THE KC/ACTF LATINO PLAYWRITING AWARD

Types of material: full-length plays. **Frequency:** annual. **Remuneration:** $2500, internship to a prestigious playwriting retreat program; contract from Dramatic Publishing Company to publish, license and market winning play, $500 to the theatre department for producing the award-winning play. **Guidelines:** Latino writer enrolled as full-time student at KC/ACTF-participating college or university during year of production or during either of the 2 years preceding the production; download guidelines from web. **Submission procedure:** college or university which has entered production of work in KC/ACTF registers work for awards program. **Deadline:** 1 Dec 2004. **Dates:** 18–24 Apr 2005.

THE KC/ACTF MUSICAL THEATER AWARD

Types of material: musicals. **Frequency:** annual. **Remuneration:** $1000 for lyrics; $1000 for music; $1000 for book to producing college or university. **Guidelines:** at least 50% of writing team must be enrolled as full-time student(s) at college or university during year of production or during either of the 2 years preceding the production; original and copyrighted work produced by a KC/ACTF-participating college or university; download guidelines from web. **Submission procedure:** college or university which has entered production of work in KC/ACTF registers work for awards program. **Deadline:** 1 Dec 2004. **Dates:** 18–24 Apr 2005.

THE KENNEDY CENTER ACTF TEN-MINUTE PLAY FESTIVAL

Types of material: one-acts. **Frequency:** annual. **Remuneration:** $1000 1st prize, best play in each of 8 regions published by Dramatic Publishing Company (see Publication), development work with director, dramaturg and actors, staged reading followed by response session at KC/ACTF annual Apr conference. **Guidelines:** each region determines own submission criteria; download guidelines from web. **Submission procedure:** college or university which has entered production of work in KC/ACTF registers work for awards program; regional submissions from schools with no other entries will pay $20 fee per submission. **Deadline:** Nov 2004. **Notification:** Dec 2004. **Dates:** Jan and Feb 2005 regional festival; Apr 2005 national festival.

THE LORRAINE HANSBERRY PLAYWRITING AWARD

Types of material: full-length plays. **Frequency:** annual. **Remuneration:** $2500 1st prize for playwright, internship at the O'Neill Playwrights Conference (see Development), publication of play by The Dramatic Publishing Company (see Publication), $750 to producing college or university; $1000 2nd prize to playwright, $500 to producing college or university. **Guidelines:** writer enrolled as full-time student at college or university during year of production or during either of the 2 years preceding the production; play dealing with the black experience produced by an KC/ACTF-participating college or university; download guidelines from web. **Submission procedure:** college or university which has entered production of work in KC/ACTF registers work for awards program. **Deadline:** 1 Dec 2004. **Dates:** 18–24 Apr 2005.

THE NATIONAL STUDENT PLAYWRITING AWARD

Types of material: full-length plays, adaptations, musicals. **Frequency:** annual. **Remuneration:** $2500 for playwright, production at Kennedy Center during festival, publication by Samuel French (see Publication) with royalties, fellowship to attend Sundance Theatre Laboratory (see Development), Dramatists Guild (see Membership and Service Organizations) membership, $1000 to producing college or university. **Guidelines:** writer enrolled as full-time student at college or university during year of production or during either of the 2 years preceding the production; work produced by an KC/ACTF-participating college or university; download guidelines from web. **Submission procedure:** college or university which has entered production of work in KC/ACTF registers work for awards program. **Deadline:** 1 Dec 2004. **Dates:** 18–24 Apr 2005.

THE PAULA VOGEL AWARD IN PLAYWRITING

Types of material: full-length plays. **Frequency:** annual. **Remuneration:** $2500, all expenses paid weeklong residency at Manhattan Theatre Source in June 2005 where the work will receive a staged reading; producing department receives $500 for its support of the work; $1000 second prize, $250 to the producing department for its support of the work. **Guidelines:** writer enrolled as full-time student at college or university during year of production or during either of the 2 years preceding the production; work produced by an KC/ACTF-participating college or university; download guidelines from web; award given to play that "celebrates diversity and encourages tolerance while exploring issues of disempowered voices not traditionally considered mainstream." **Submission procedure:** college or university which has entered production of work in KC/ACTF registers work for awards program. **Deadline:** 1 Dec 2004. **Dates:** 18–24 Apr 2005.

KUMU KAHUA THEATRE/UHM DEPARTMENT OF THEATRE & DANCE PLAYWRITING CONTEST
46 Merchant St; Honolulu, HI 96813; (808) 536–4222, FAX 536–4226
Harry Wong III, *Artistic Director, Kumu Kahua Theatre*

HAWAI'I PRIZE

Types of material: full-length plays. **Frequency:** annual. **Remuneration:** $500. **Guidelines:** play set in HI or dealing with some aspect of HI experience; unproduced play; previous entries ineligible. **Submission procedure:** write for entry brochure. **Deadline:** 2 Jan 2005. **Notification:** May 2005.

PACIFIC RIM PRIZE

Types of material: full-length plays. **Frequency:** annual. **Remuneration:** $400.

Guidelines: play set in or dealing with Pacific Islands, Pacific Rim or Pacific Asian-American experience; unproduced play; previous entries ineligible. **Submission procedure:** write for entry brochure. **Deadline:** 2 Jan 2005. **Notification:** May 2005.

RESIDENT PRIZE

Types of material: full-length plays, one-acts. **Frequency:** annual. **Remuneration:** $200. **Guidelines:** resident of HI at time of submission; previous entries ineligible. **Submission procedure:** write for entry brochure. **Deadline:** 2 Jan 2005. **Notification:** May 2005.

LAMIA INK! INTERNATIONAL ONE-PAGE PLAY COMPETITION

Box 202; Prince St Station; New York, NY 10012
(Ms.) Cortland Jessup, *Artistic Director*

Types of material: 1 page plays. **Frequency:** annual. **Remuneration:** $200, reading in New York City and publication in magazine (see Lamia Ink! in Publication) for winner and 11 other best plays; at least $50 2nd prize; $25 3rd prize. **Guidelines:** 3 submission limit; guidelines are extensive, must send SASE. **Submission procedure:** script, SASE for response and $2 fee per submission or $5 for 3 submissions. **Deadline:** 15 Mar 2005. **Notification:** 15 May 2005.

L. ARNOLD WEISSBERGER AWARD

Box 428; Williamstown, MA 01267-0428; Jun–Aug: (413) 458-3200,
FAX 458-3147; Sep–May (New York): (212) 395-9090, FAX 395-9099;
website www.wtfestival.org
Jenny Gersten, *Associate Producer*

Types of material: full-length plays. **Frequency:** annual. **Remuneration:** $10,000; publication by Samuel French (see Publication). **Guidelines:** 1 unpublished script not professionally produced or scheduled for production prior to 31 Dec; award administered by the Williamstown Theatre Festival (see Production and Development). **Submission procedure:** agent submission or script with recommendation from theatre professional only. **Deadline:** postmarked by 15 Jun 2005. **Notification:** Nov 2005.

THE LITTLE THEATRE OF ALEXANDRIA NATIONAL ONE-ACT PLAYWRITING COMPETITION

600 Wolfe St; Alexandria, VA 22314; (703) 683-5778, FAX 683-1378;
email asklta@thelittletheatre.com
Chairman, One-Act Playwriting Competition

Types of material: one-acts. **Frequency:** annual. **Remuneration:** $350 1st prize; $250 2nd prize; $150 3rd prize; possible production. **Guidelines:** unpublished, unproduced work; prefers plays with running times of 20-60 minutes in length, few scenes and 1 set; 2 submission limit. **Submission procedure:** script, synopsis, character breakdown and $20 fee; send SASE for guidelines. **Deadline:** 30 Apr 2005.

LOS ANGELES DESIGNERS' THEATRE

Box 1883; Studio City, CA 91614-0883; (323) 650-9600,
654-2700 (TDD), FAX 654-3210; email ladesigners@juno.com
Richard Niederberg, *Artistic Director*

Types of material: full-length plays, bills of related one-acts, translations, adaptations, plays for young audiences, musicals, solo pieces, operas. **Frequency:** ongoing. **Remuneration:** negotiable commissioning fee, possible travel to attend rehearsals if developmental work is needed. **Guidelines:** commissioning program for work with commercial potential which has not received professional full production, is not under option and is free of commitment to specific director, actors or other personnel; large casts and multiple sets welcome; prefers controversial material. **Submission procedure:** proposal or synopsis and resume; include cassette or CD for musical; materials will not be returned. **Deadline:** ongoing. **Notification:** at least 4 months.

LOVE CREEK SHORT PLAY FESTIVAL

Love Creek Productions; c/o 162 Nesbit St; Weehawken, NJ 07086-6817
Cynthia Granville–Callahan, *Festival Literary Manager*

Types of material: one-acts. **Frequency:** annual. **Remuneration:** minimum of 60 finalists receive mini-showcase production in New York City during year-round festivals; $300 prize for best play of the year, may be shared by multiple winners. **Guidelines:** unpublished play not produced in NYC area within past year, maximum length of 40 minutes, cast of 2 or more, simple sets and costumes; 2 submission limit; strongly prefers women in major roles and predominantly female cast; mini-festivals centered around specific themes; upcoming themes TBA. **Submission procedure:** script with letter giving theatre permission to produce play if chosen and specifying whether Equity showcase is acceptable; send SASE for themes and deadlines. **Deadline:** ongoing. **Dates:** year-round.

THE MARC A. KLEIN PLAYWRITING AWARD

Department of Theater and Dance; Case Western Reserve University;
10900 Euclid Ave; Cleveland, OH 44106-7077; (216) 368-4868,
FAX 368-5184; email ksg@case.edu
Ron Wilson, *Chair, Reading Committee*

Types of material: full-length plays, bills of related one-acts. **Frequency:** annual. **Remuneration:** $1000 ($500 used to cover residency expenses), production. **Guidelines:** student currently enrolled at U.S. college or university; work endorsed by faculty member of university theatre department that has not received professional full production or trade-book publication. **Submission procedure:** application and script. **Deadline:** 1 Dec 2004. **Notification:** 1 Feb 2005.

MAXIM MAZUMDAR NEW PLAY COMPETITION

Alleyway Theatre; 1 Curtain Up Alley; Buffalo, NY 14202-1911;
(716) 852-2600, FAX 852-2266; email email@alleyway.com

Literary Manager

Types of material: full-length plays, one-acts, musicals. **Frequency:** annual. **Remuneration:** $400, production for full-length play or musical; $100 and production for one-act play or musical. **Guidelines:** unproduced full-length work minimum 90 minutes in length with cast limit of 10 and unit set or simple set, or unproduced one-act less than 20 minutes in length with cast limit of 6 and simple set; prefers work with unconventional setting that explores the boundaries of theatricality; 1 submission limit in each category. **Submission procedure:** script, character breakdown and resume; include cassette or CD of complete score for musicals; $5 fee per playwright. **Deadline:** 1 Jul 2005. **Notification:** 1 Oct 2005 for finalists; 1 Nov 2005 for winners.

MCLAREN MEMORIAL COMEDY PLAYWRITING COMPETITION

Midland Community Theatre; 2000 West Wadley Ave;
Midland, TX 79705; (432) 682-2544, FAX 682-6136;
website www.mctmidland.org

Coordinator

Types of material: full-length plays, one-acts, plays for young audiences. **Frequency:** annual. **Remuneration:** $400 for full-length play; $200 for one-act; 3 finalists in each category receive staged reading. **Guidelines:** play not produced professionally; comedies only; visit website for guidelines. **Submission procedure:** script and $10 fee per play. **Deadline:** 31 Jan 2005; no submission before 1 Dec 2004. **Notification:** Jun 2005.

MET LIFE FOUNDATION NUESTRAS VOCES

Repertorio Español; 138 East 27th St; New York, NY 10016;
(212) 889-2850, FAX 686-3732;
email a.astorvargas@repertorio.org; website www.repertorio.org

Allison Astor-Vargas, *Special Projects Manager*

Types of material: full-length plays. **Frequency:** annual. **Remuneration:** $3000 1st prize, production and royalties; $2000 2nd prize; $1000 3rd prize; 2 runners-up receive $500; 2nd and 3rd prizes and top 10 finalists receive staged reading. **Guidelines:** unpublished work not produced professionally; Hispanic themes, characters and subjects; written in Spanish or English; see website for application. **Submission procedure:** application and 2 copies of script. **Deadline:** 1 May 2005. (See Repertorio Español in Production.)

MILDRED AND ALBERT PANOWSKI PLAYWRITING AWARD

Forest A. Roberts Theatre; Northern Michigan University;
Marquette, MI 49855; (906) 227-2553, FAX 227-2567;
website www.nmu.edu/theatre

James A. Panowski, *Director*

Types of material: full-length plays, translations, adaptations, solo pieces. **Frequency:** annual. **Remuneration:** $2000; production; travel, room and board for 1-week residency. **Guidelines:** 1 unpublished, unproduced submission; rewrites of previous entries ineligible. **Submission procedure:** application and script; write for guidelines. **Deadline:** 22 Nov 2004. **Notification:** Apr 2005.

MORTON R. SARETT NATIONAL PLAYWRITING COMPETITION

Department of Theatre; University of Nevada, Las Vegas;
4505 Maryland Pkwy, Box 455036; Las Vegas, NV 89154-5036;
(702) 895-3666; website www.unlv.edu/colleges/Fine_Arts/Theatre/

Coordinator

Types of material: full-length plays, musicals. **Frequency:** biennial. **Remuneration:** $3000, production, travel and housing to attend rehearsals and opening performance. **Guidelines:** unpublished, unproduced play or musical; no adaptations. **Submission procedure:** application, 2 bound copies of script and 50-word synopsis; include score (prefer piano) or cassette/CD for musical; scripts will not be returned; send SASE for guidelines and applications or download from web. **Deadline:** postmarked by 1 Feb 2005; no submission before 1 Nov 2004. **Notification:** Sep 2005.

MOUNTAIN PLAYHOUSE PLAYWRITING CONTEST

Box 205; Jennerstown, PA 15547; (814) 629-9201, ext 303, FAX 629-9201;
email mtplayhouse@floodcity.net; website www.mountainplayhouse.com

Teresa Marafino, *Producer*

Types of material: full-length plays, adaptations. **Frequency:** biennial. **Remuneration:** $3000, staged reading, consideration for full production in theatre's regular season. **Guidelines:** comedies only; cast limit of 8. **Submission procedure:** script only. **Deadline:** 31 Dec 2004. **Notification:** 30 Apr 2005.

MOVING ARTS PREMIERE ONE-ACT COMPETITION

514 South Spring St; Los Angeles, CA 90013; (213) 622-8906,
FAX 622-8946; email treynichols@movingarts.org;
website www.movingarts.org

Trey Nichols, *Literary Director*

Types of material: one-acts. **Frequency:** annual. **Remuneration:** $200, production in annual fall one-act festival. **Guidelines:** play not previously produced in L.A. area; single set, modest technical requirements. **Submission procedure:** script without author's name or address, cover letter, $10 fee per script payable to Moving Arts and SASE for response. **Deadline:** 28 Feb 2005. **Notification:** Jul 2005. (See Moving Arts in Production.)

NANTUCKET SHORT PLAY FESTIVAL AND COMPETITION

Nantucket Theatrical Productions; Box 2177; Nantucket, MA 02584;
(508) 228-5002
Jim Patrick, *Artistic Director*

Types of material: one-acts. **Frequency:** annual. **Remuneration:** $200; 1 or more staged readings for winning play and selected additional plays as part of summer festival. **Guidelines:** unpublished play which has not received Equity production, maximum length of 40 pages, simple production demands. **Submission procedure:** script and $10 fee; send SASE for guidelines. **Deadline:** 1 Jan 2005. **Notification:** 1-2 months. **Dates:** ongoing.

NATF SCRIPT COMPETITION

The National Audio Theatre Festivals; 115 Dikeman St;
Hempstead, NY 11550; (516) 483-8321, FAX 538-7583;
website www.natf.org
Sue Zizza, *Executive Director*

Types of material: radio plays. **Frequency:** annual. **Remuneration:** $800 split between 2-4 winners, workshop production, published in *NATF Scriptbook.* **Guidelines:** radio plays only, maximum 25 minutes in length, "dialogue that demonstrates how sound can color content," strong female roles and multicultural viewpoints; 1 submission limit. **Submission procedure:** 4 copies of script in radio format, cover letter stating authorship and $25 fee; download guidelines from web. **Deadline:** 15 Nov 2004. **Notification:** Apr 2005. (See The National Audio Theatre Festivals in Membership and Service Organizations.)

NATIONAL CHILDREN'S THEATRE FESTIVAL

Actors' Playhouse at the Miracle Theatre; 280 Miracle Mile;
Coral Gables, FL 33134; (305) 444-9293, ext 615,
FAX 444-4181; website www.actorsplayhouse.org
Earl Maulding, *Director of Theatre for Young Audiences*

Types of material: musicals for young audiences. **Frequency:** annual. **Remuneration:** $500 prize, production, travel and housing to attend festival. **Guidelines:** unpublished musical for young people ages 5-12, 45-60 minutes in length, with cast limit of 8 (may play multiple roles) and minimal sets suitable for touring; translations and adaptations eligible only if writer owns copyright to material; special interest in work dealing with social issues including multiculturalism in today's society and bilingual (Spanish/English) musicals. **Submission procedure:** entry form, script and $10 fee; include score and vocal cassette or CD; write for guidelines or download from web. **Deadline:** 1 Jun 2005. **Notification:** Nov 2005. **Dates:** Apr 2006.

NATIONAL LATINO PLAYWRITING AWARD

Arizona Theatre Company; 40 East 14th St; Tucson, AZ 85701;
  (520) 884-8210, ext 5510, FAX 628-9129
Elaine Romero, *Playwright-in-Residence*

Types of material: full-length plays, adaptations. **Frequency:** annual. **Remuneration:** $1000. **Guidelines:** playwright of Latino heritage residing in U.S. or U.S. territories or Mexico; 1 unproduced, unpublished submission written in English, Spanish or both languages, minimum 50 pages. **Submission procedure:** script (with English translation if original in Spanish), 1 page cover letter including development history, synopsis and bio. **Deadline:** 31 Dec 2004. **Notification:** summer 2005.

NATIONAL NEW PLAY AWARD

Department of Theatre Arts; Humboldt State University;
  Arcata, CA 95521; (707) 826-4606, FAX 826-5494;
  email mtk3@axe.humboldt.edu;
  website www.humboldt.edu/~mtk3
Margaret Thomas Kelso, *Associate Professor of Theatre Arts*

Types of material: full-length plays. **Frequency:** triennial. **Remuneration:** 2 awards of $1000, full production, 2-week residency. **Guidelines:** unproduced, unpublished play. **Submission procedure:** script only; 2 submission limit. **Deadline:** 10 Sep 2004. **Notification:** Dec 2004.

NATIONAL TEN-MINUTE PLAY CONTEST

Actors Theatre of Louisville; 316 West Main St;
  Louisville, KY 40202-4218; (502) 584-1265, FAX 584-1265;
  website www.actorstheatre.org
Adrien-Alice Hansel, *Literary Manager*

Types of material: one-acts. **Frequency:** annual. **Remuneration:** $1000 Heideman Award; possible production with royalty. **Guidelines:** U.S. citizen or resident; play maximum 10 pages in length that has not had Equity production; 1 submission limit, previous entries ineligible. **Submission procedure:** script only; script will not be returned; write for guidelines. **Deadline:** postmarked by 1 Dec 2004. **Notification:** winter 2005.

NATIONAL TRANSLATION AWARD

American Literary Translators Association; University of Texas at Dallas;
  Box 830688; Richardson, TX 75083-0688; (972) 883-2093,
  FAX 883-6303; email dickey@utdallas.edu;
  website www.literarytranslators.org
Jessie Dickey, *Secretary*

Types of material: translations. **Frequency:** annual. **Remuneration:** $2500. **Guidelines:** translation from any language into English published in U.S. by American publisher. **Submission procedure:** no submission by translator; publisher nominates translation and submits 4 copies of book with cover letter. **Deadline:** 31 Mar 2005. **Notification:** 10 Sep 2005.

NEW AMERICAN COMEDY (NAC) WORKSHOP

Ukiah Players Theatre; 1041 Low Gap Rd; Ukiah, CA 95482;
(707) 462-1210, FAX 462-1790; email players@pacific.net
Kate Magruder, *Community Cultural Development Director*

Types of material: full-length plays. **Frequency:** biennial. **Remuneration:** $50 per performance for play selected for full production (6 to 8 performances); $25 each per performance for 2 plays chosen as staged readings; up to $500 travel, housing to attend 1-week workshop and $25 per diem. **Guidelines:** playwright must be available to participate in 1-week developmental workshop; unproduced, unpublished comedy; prefers small cast, simple set; comedies only. **Submission procedure:** application, script with 1-page plot summary, scenic requirements, character breakdown, estimated running time and resume; write for guidelines. **Deadline:** 30 Nov 2005. **Notification:** May 2006. **Dates:** Jun 2006.

NEW HISTORY PLAY CONTEST

Sprenger-Lang Foundation; 1614 20th St NW; Washington DC 20009;
(202) 265-8010, FAX 265-8021; website www.tributeproductions.org
Jonathan Willen, *Associate Producer*

Types of material: full-length plays. **Frequency:** annual. **Remuneration:** $2500 1st place, staged reading, travel and housing to attend rehearsals; $1000 2nd place. **Guidelines:** play not previously produced and not under option; theme of play must "elucidate a significant event, moment or era in pre-1965 U.S. history"; maximum 120 pages, cast limit of 10; special interest in plays with multicultural themes; prior readings, workshops or school productions will not disqualify script but must be disclosed. **Submission procedure:** script and 1-paragraph synopsis. **Deadline:** postmarked by 31 Dec 2004. **Notification:** 31 Mar 2005.

NEW PROFESSIONAL THEATRE WRITERS FESTIVAL

229 West 42nd St, #501; New York, NY 10036; email newprof@aol.com
website www.newprofessionaltheatre.com
Literary Manager

Types of material: full-length plays, musicals. **Frequency:** annual. **Remuneration:** $2000, 2-week residency with dramaturg, staged reading, business seminar, possible production. **Guidelines:** African-American writer. **Submission procedure:** script, resume and SASP for acknowledgment of receipt; include cassette for musical. **Deadline:** 1 Jun 2005. **Notification:** Sep 2005.

NEW ROCKY MOUNTAIN VOICES 2005

Westcliffe Center for the Performing Arts; Box 790; Westcliffe, CO 81252;
(719) 783-3004, FAX (949) 499-3614; email wcpa@ris.net;
website www.westcliffecenter.org
Anne Kimbell Relph, *President*

Types of material: one-acts, plays for young audiences. **Frequency:** annual. **Remuneration:** $200 1st place, workshop production by Westcliffe Center Players, housing provided for performances; $200 2nd place; 3 honorable mentions. **Guidelines:** playwright must live or attend school in CO or NM; one-acts only; cast limit of 6-8; 1 set; multigenerational cast preferred. **Submission procedure:** 4 copies of script, one-page synopsis and bio; SASE if script is to be returned; $5 fee. **Deadline:** 1 Apr 2005. **Notification:** 30 Jun 2005.

NEW YORK CITY 15 MINUTE PLAY FESTIVAL

Turnip Theatre Company; c/o AGT; 145 West 46th St; New York, NY 10036;
(212) 869-9808, FAX 869-9807; email liz@americanglobe.org
Liz Keefe, *Managing Director*

Types of material: one-acts. **Frequency:** annual. **Remuneration:** $100-300 for festival winner, production; $25 royalty for all plays presented. **Guidelines:** one-acts maximum 15 pages; prefer work not produced in New York City; 1 submission limit. **Submission procedure:** send SASE or email for guidelines before submitting. **Deadline:** 15 Dec 2004. **Notification:** mid-Feb 2005. **Dates:** Apr 2005.

OGLEBAY INSTITUTE TOWNGATE THEATRE CONTESTS

Stifel Fine Arts Center; 1330 National Rd; Wheeling, WV 26003;
(304) 242-7700, FAX 242-7767
Performing Arts Department

PLAYWRITING CONTEST

Types of material: full-length plays. **Frequency:** annual. **Remuneration:** $300, production, partial travel to attend performances. **Guidelines:** unpublished, unproduced play, simple set. **Submission procedure:** script and resume. **Deadline:** 30 Dec 2004. **Notification:** 1 May 2005.

PLAYWRITING CONTEST FOR COLLEGE STUDENTS

Types of material: full-length plays. **Frequency:** annual. **Remuneration:** $100, production. **Guidelines:** unpublished, unproduced play, simple set. **Submission procedure:** script only. **Deadline:** 15 Mar 2005. **Notification:** 1 Jun 2005.

ONASSIS INTERNATIONAL THEATRE COMPETITION

Alexander S. Onassis Public Benefit Foundation; 7 Eschinou St;
Athens, Greece 105 58; 302-10-371-3000, FAX 371-3013;
website www./onassis.gr/english/competition_prizes/theatre.html
Barbara Charmis, Administrative Secretary

Types of material: full-length plays, translations. **Frequency:** every 4 years.

Remuneration: 150,000 EURO (about $180,000) 1st place; 100,000 EURO (about $120,000) 2nd prize; 75,000 EURO (about $90,000) 3rd prize; possible staged reading and production in Athens; possible publication. **Guidelines:** playwright must have had 1 play produced; unpublished play that has not been produced; no adaptations, musicals, operettas, poetry or performance art; see website for guidelines. **Submission procedure:** 3 copies of script (1 with author information and 2 without) and bio; see web for guidelines. **Deadline:** 2007 (30 Jun in 2003).

PEN-BOOK-OF-THE-MONTH CLUB TRANSLATION PRIZE

PEN American Center; 568 Broadway; New York, NY 10012;
(212) 334-1660, FAX 334-2181; email motika@pen.org
Stephen Motika, *Coordinator*

Types of material: translations. **Frequency:** annual. **Remuneration:** $3000. **Guidelines:** book-length translation from any language into English published in U.S. during current calendar year. **Submission procedure:** 3 copies of book. **Deadline:** 15 Dec 2004. **Notification:** spring 2005.

PEN CENTER USA WEST LITERARY AWARDS

672 South Lafayette Park Pl, Suite 42; Los Angeles, CA 90057;
(213) 365-8500, FAX 365-9616; email pen@penusa.org;
website www.penusa.org

Types of material: full-length plays, screenplays, teleplays. **Frequency:** annual. **Remuneration:** $1000 award in each of several categories, including drama, screenwriting and television writing. **Guidelines:** writer residing west of Mississippi River; only full-length (original or adapted) screenplays and teleplays, script first produced during 2004 calendar year. **Submission procedure:** 4 copies of script, playbill or press materials verifying eligibility and cover letter giving title of work, author's name and state of residence, name of producer and production dates and $35 fee. **Deadline:** 11 Feb 2005.

PEN/LAURA PELS FOUNDATION AWARD FOR DRAMA

PEN American Center; 568 Broadway; New York, NY 10012-3225;
(212) 334-1660, FAX 334-2181; email motika@pen.org
Stephen Motika, *Coordinator*

Types of material: full-length plays. **Frequency:** annual. **Remuneration:** $5000. **Guidelines:** mid-career American playwright who has had at least 2 full-length plays professionally produced in theatres 299 seats or larger. **Submission procedure:** playwright must be nominated by professional colleague through letter of support accompanied by list of candidate's produced work. **Deadline:** 14 Jan 2005. **Notification:** spring 2005.

PERISHABLE THEATRE WOMEN'S PLAYWRITING FESTIVAL

Box 23132; Providence, RI 02903; (401) 331–2695, FAX 331–7811;
email wpf@perishable.org; website www.perishable.org
Rebecca A. Wolff, *Festival Coordinator*

Types of material: one-acts. **Frequency:** annual. **Remuneration:** 3 awards of $500, production, publication in anthology. **Guidelines:** woman playwright; unproduced one-act, no more than 40 minutes in length; 2 submission limit. **Submission procedure:** 2 copies of script, resume and $5 fee. **Deadline:** 15 Oct 2004. **Notification:** spring 2005.

PETERSON EMERGING PLAYWRIGHT COMPETITION

Theatre Arts Department, Catawba College; 2300 West Innes St;
Salisbury, NC 28144–2488; (704) 637–4481, FAX 637–4207;
email lfkesler@catawba.edu
Linda F. Kesler, *Staff, Theatre Arts Department*

Types of material: full-length plays, musicals. **Frequency:** annual. **Remuneration:** $2000, full production, transportation, room and board to attend rehearsals and performances. **Guidelines:** unpublished, unproduced full-length work by emerging playwright; 2 one-acts with common theme accepted. **Submission procedure:** script and bio; send SASP for acknowledgment of receipt; no email submissions accepted. **Deadline:** 1 Dec 2004. **Notification:** 15 Mar 2005.

THE PINTER REVIEW PRIZE FOR DRAMA

The University of Tampa Press; 401 West Kennedy Blvd;
Tampa, FL 33606; (813) 253–6266; email utpress@ut.edu;
website pinter.ut.edu
Richard Mathews, *Director, University of Tampa Press*

Types of material: full-length plays, bill of related one-acts. **Frequency:** annual. **Remuneration:** $1000, public reading, publication with University of Tampa Press with royalties. **Guidelines:** full-length play or 2 or more short plays; portion of script may have been previously published, provided this is clearly noted. **Submission procedure:** unbound script with 2 title pages (one with author information and one without), 1-page synopsis, SASE for notification and $20 fee. **Deadline:** 31 Dec 2004. **Notification:** 31 Mar 2005.

PLAYHOUSE ON THE SQUARE NEW PLAY COMPETITION

51 South Cooper St; Memphis, TN 38104; (901) 725–0776, 726–4498
Jackie Nichols, *Executive Director*

Types of material: full-length plays, musicals. **Frequency:** annual. **Remuneration:** $500, production. **Guidelines:** unproduced play, small cast; full arrangement for piano for musical; prefers southern playwrights. **Submission procedure:** script only. **Deadline:** 1 Apr 2005.

PLAYS FOR THE 21ST CENTURY

The Playwrights Theater; 6732 Orangewood Dr; Dallas, TX 75220; (469) 374-9639; email alberto_rubio@sbcglobal.net; website www.playwrightstheater.org

Types of material: full-length plays, bill of related one-acts. **Frequency:** annual. **Remuneration:** $1500 1st prize; $500 2nd and 3rd prizes; 1st prize may receive production or reading, funding permitting. **Guidelines:** play not produced professionally or published at time of submission. **Submission procedure:** application, script, $20 fee; download application and submission procedure from web. **Deadline:** 31 Dec 2004; no submission before 1 Sept 2004.

THE PLAYWRIGHTS COLLECTIVE

Brookfield Theatre for the Arts; 12A Ta'Agan Pt Rd; Danbury, CT 06811; (203) 744-6259; email wendellmacneal@msn.com; Wendell R. MacNeal, *Project Coordinator*

Types of material: full-length plays. **Frequency:** annual. **Remuneration:** $400, staged reading; board provided for performaces. **Guidelines:** play not produced professionally; cast limit of 8-10. **Submission procedure:** script and $10 fee. **Deadline:** ongoing.

PLAYWRIGHTS FIRST AWARD

c/o The National Arts Club; 15 Gramercy Park S; New York, NY 10003; (212) 744-1312

Types of material: full-length plays. **Frequency:** annual. **Remuneration:** $1000 for best play; reading for selected plays. **Guidelines:** 1 unproduced play; no translations, adaptations, musicals or cowritten work. **Submission procedure:** script and resume; script will not be returned. **Deadline:** 15 Oct 2004. **Notification:** May 2005.

REGENT UNIVERSITY THEATRE ONE-ACT PLAY COMPETITION

1000 Regent University Dr; Virginia Beach, VA 23464; (757) 226-4223, FAX 226-4279; email theatre@regent.edu; website www.regent.edu/theatre/oneactcomp.htm
Gillette Elvgren, *Chair, Theatre Arts Program*

Types of material: one-acts. **Frequency:** annual. **Remuneration:** $250 1st prize; full production for 1st, 2nd and 3rd place scripts. **Guidelines:** unpublished, unproduced one-act; no adaptations or translations; prefers small cast, simple set. **Submission procedure:** script with author's name, address, phone number and email on cover page only, cast list, and 1-paragraph synopsis. **Deadline:** 1 Sep 2004. **Notification:** 15 Oct 2004.

REVA SHINER FULL-LENGTH PLAY CONTEST

Bloomington Playwrights Project; 312 South Washington St;
    Bloomington, IN 47401; (812) 334-1188;
    email bppwrite@newplays.org; website www.newplays.org
Richard Perez, *Artistic Director*

Types of material: full-length plays, musicals. **Frequency:** annual. **Remuneration:** $500, staged reading and full production. **Guidelines:** unpublished, unproduced work 75-150 minutes in length, suitable for production in small 65-seat theatre; innovative work, small-scale musicals, simple set; write for guidelines or download from web. **Submission procedure:** script, cover letter and $5 fee; include cassette for musical; scripts will not be returned. **Deadline:** 15 Jan 2005. **Notification:** Jun 2005.

REVERIE PRODUCTIONS NEXT GENERATION PLAYWRITING CONTEST

Reverie Productions; 520 8th Ave, Suite 317;
    New York, NY 10018; (212) 244 7803, FAX 244 7813;
    email info@ReverieProductions.org; website www.ReverieProductions.org

Types of material: full-length plays, one-acts, radio plays. **Frequency:** annual. **Remuneration:** $300 for full-length, $200 for one-act, production, partial travel to attend performances. **Guidelines:** unproduced in New York City area, no theme is required, but Reverie tends to produce plays that deal with social issues, see website for details. **Submission procedure:** script and $15 entry fee for full-length plays, $10 for one-acts. **Deadline:** 15 Dec 2004. **Notification:** 5 May 2005.

ROBERT J. PICKERING AWARD FOR PLAYWRITING EXCELLENCE

Coldwater Community Theater; 89 Division St; Coldwater, MI 49036;
    (517) 278-2389, FAX 279-8095
J. Richard Colbeck, *Award Chairman*

Types of material: full-length plays, one-acts, adaptations, plays for young audiences, musicals. **Frequency:** annual. **Remuneration:** $300 1st place, full production; $100 2nd place; $50 3rd place. **Guidelines:** unproduced play. **Submission procedure:** script. **Deadline:** 31 Dec 2004. **Notification:** 28 Feb 2005.

THE RUBY LLOYD APSEY AWARD

University of Alabama at Birmingham Theatre Department;
    101 Bell Building; 700 13th St; Birmingham, AL 35294-3340;
    (205) 934-3236, FAX 934-8076; email mpowers@uab.edu;
    website theatre.hum.uab.edu
Marc Powers, *Department Chair*

Types of material: full-length plays, bills of related one-acts, translations. **Frequency:** biennial. **Remuneration:** $1000, staged reading, possible full production; travel and housing if play is produced. **Guidelines:** plays confronting racial or ethnic issues, especially those calling for ethnically diverse or multiracial casting. **Submission procedure:** script and character/scene breakdown. **Deadline:** postmarked by 1 Dec 2004. **Notification:** 8 Apr 2005.

SANTA CRUZ ACTORS' THEATRE FULL-LENGTH PLAY CONTEST

1001 Center St, Suite 12; Santa Cruz, CA 95060; (831) 425-1003,
FAX 425-7529; email actors@sbcglobal.net; website www.sccat.org
John Howie Patterson, *Managing Director*

Types of material: full-length plays. **Frequency:** annual. **Remuneration:** $200, staged reading, possible full production. **Guidelines:** resident of CA, OR or WA; unpublished play not produced professionally. **Submission procedure:** script and $15 fee; download guidelines from web. **Deadline:** 1 Oct 2004. **Notification:** Jan 2005.

SANTA FE PERFORMING ARTS
NEW PLAYWRIGHTS COMPETITION

Box 22372; Santa Fe, NM 87502; (505) 582-7992, FAX 982-7993
Wayne Sabato, *Executive Artistic Director*

Types of material: full-length plays, one-acts. **Frequency:** annual. **Remuneration:** $1000, full production. **Guidelines:** American playwright; play not previously produced. **Submission procedure:** brief synopsis and character breakdown only. **Deadline:** 1 Sep 2004. **Notification:** Spring 2005.

THE SCHOLASTIC WRITING AWARDS

555 Broadway; New York, NY 10012; (212) 343-6892,
FAX 389-3939; website www.scholastic.com/artandwriting

Types of material: one-acts, screenplays, teleplays, radio plays. **Frequency:** annual. **Remuneration:** $5000 scholarship toward college tuition for author of each of 5 best senior portfolios; cash prizes totaling $175,000 awarded to several top students in each category, including dramatic writing. **Guidelines:** 2 categories: for high school seniors only, portfolios of 3-8 pieces (fiction, poetry, drama, etc.); for students grades 7-12, individual pieces in various categories, including drama (stage, film, television and radio scripts), unpublished script not more than 30 minutes in length; write for further information after 1 Oct 2004. **Submission procedure:** application and script. **Deadline:** varies from state to state; many in mid-Jan 2005; exact date TBA. **Notification:** May 2005.

SHORT GRAIN CONTEST

Grain Magazine; Box 67; Saskatoon, SK S7K 3K1; Canada;
(306) 244-2828, FAX 244-0255; email grainmag@sasktel.net;
website www.grainmagazine.ca
Bobbi Clackson-Walker, *Business Administrator*

Types of material: monologues. **Frequency:** annual. **Remuneration:** 3 prizes of $500. **Guidelines:** unpublished, unproduced monologue not submitted elsewhere; 500-word maximum. **Submission procedure:** U.S. and international entries: entry form and $25 fee plus $4 U.S. postage for subscription mailing cost; Canadian entries: entry form and $25 fee for first 2 entries ($5 fee for each additional entry); fee includes 1-year subscription; write or email for guidelines. **Deadline:** 31 Jan 2005. **Notification:** 30 Apr 2005.

SHUBERT FENDRICH MEMORIAL PLAYWRITING CONTEST

Pioneer Drama Service; Box 4267; Englewood, CO 80155–4267;
   (303) 779–4035, FAX 779–4315; email editors@pioneerdrama.com;
   website www.pioneerdrama.com
Lori Conary, *Editor*

Types of material: full-length plays, one-acts, translations, adaptations, plays for young audiences, musicals. **Frequency:** annual. **Remuneration:** publication with $1000 advance on royalties (10% book royalty, 50% performance royalty); all entries considered for publication. **Guidelines:** produced, unpublished work not more than 90 minutes in length, subject matter and language appropriate for schools and community theatres; prefers work with majority of female roles, minimal set requirements. **Submission procedure:** script with proof of production (e.g., program, reviews); include score or cassette for musical; send SASE for guidelines. **Deadline:** 1 Mar 2005 (scripts received after deadline will be considered for 2006 contest). **Notification:** 1 Jun 2005.

SIENA COLLEGE INTERNATIONAL PLAYWRIGHTS COMPETITION

Department of Creative Arts; Siena College; 515 Loudon Rd;
   Loudonville, NY 12211–1462; (518) 783–2381, FAX 783–2381;
   email maciag@siena.edu; website www.siena.edu/theatre
Gary Maciag, *Director of Theatre*

Types of material: full-length plays. **Frequency:** biennial. **Remuneration:** $2000, production, maximum $2000 to cover residency expenses. **Guidelines:** playwright available for 6-week residency in Jan/Feb 2007; play that has not had previous workshop or full production; prefers play suitable for college audience and featuring characters suitable for college-age performers; prefers small cast and unit set or minimal set change. **Submission procedure:** application and script; send SASE for application and guidelines after 1 Nov 2005. **Deadline:** 30 Jun 2006; no submission before 1 Feb 2006. **Notification:** 30 Sep 2006.

SKETCHBOOK FESTIVAL

Collaboraction; 437 North Wolcott, Suite 201; Chicago, IL 60622;
   (312) 226–9633, FAX 226–6107; email sketchbook@collaboraction.org;
   website www.collaboraction.org
Jay Reed, *Managing Director*

Types of material: one-acts. **Frequency:** annual. **Remuneration:** $500 1st prize, full production; up to 16 finalists also receive full production. **Guidelines:** plays not previously produced, maximum 7 minutes in length; no submission limit.

Submission procedure: application, script and $5 fee if mailed; prefers online submissions. **Deadline:** 1 Jan 2005. **Dates:** Jun 2005.

SOURCE THEATRE COMPANY 2005 LITERARY PRIZE

1835 14th St NW; Washington, DC 20009; (202) 462-1073;
website www.sourcetheatre.com
Keith Parker, *Literary Manager*

Types of material: full-length plays, one-acts, musicals, solo pieces. **Frequency:** annual. **Remuneration:** $250, staged reading, possible production in 25th Annual Washington Theatre Festival (14 Jul-14 Aug 2005). **Guidelines:** work not produced professionally. **Submission procedure:** script, synopsis, resume and $10 fee; 1 submission limit; send SASE for response; materials will not be returned. **Deadline:** postmarked by 15 Jan 2005. **Notification:** 15 May 2005.

SOUTHEASTERN THEATRE CONFERENCE NEW PLAY PROJECT

Box 9868; Greensboro, NC 27429-0868; (336) 272-3645;
email setc@mindspring.com

Types of material: full-length plays, bill of related one-acts. **Frequency:** annual. **Remuneration:** $1000, staged reading at SETC Annual Convention, travel, room and board to attend convention. **Guidelines:** resident of state in SETC region (AL, FL, GA, KY, MS, NC, SC, TN, VA, WV); unproduced work; collection of one-acts bound in 1 cover; limit of 1 full-length submission or collection of one-acts. **Submission procedure:** application and script. **Deadline:** 1 Jun 2005. **Notification:** Nov 2005.

SOUTHERN PLAYWRIGHTS COMPETITION

228 Stone Center; Jacksonville State University; Jacksonville, AL 36265;
(256) 782-5414, FAX 782-5441; email swhitton@jsucc.jsu.edu;
website www.jsu.edu/depart/english/southpla.htm
Steven J. Whitton, *Coordinator*

Types of material: full-length plays, solo pieces. **Frequency:** annual. **Remuneration:** $1000, production, housing to attend rehearsals. **Guidelines:** native or resident of AL, AR, FL, GA, KY, LA, MS, NC, SC, TN, TX, VA or WV; 1 unpublished, original submission that deals with the southern experience and has not received Equity production. **Submission procedure:** entry form, script and synopsis; write for guidelines after Sep 2004. **Deadline:** 15 Feb 2005. **Notification:** 1 May 2005.

THE STANLEY DRAMA AWARD

Wagner College Theatre; 1 Campus Rd; Staten Island, NY 10301;
(718) 390-3157, FAX 390-3323
Kevin Kane and Felicia J. Ruff, *Administrators*

Types of material: full-length plays, one-acts, plays for young audiences, musicals. **Frequency:** annual. **Remuneration:** $2000. **Guidelines:** unpublished, unproduced play or collection of one-acts; 1 submission limit. **Submission procedure:**

application, script, CD or cassette for musicals, $20 application fee; send SASE for guidelines and application. **Deadline:** 1 Oct 2004. **Notification:** Apr 2005.

SUMMERFIELD G. ROBERTS AWARD

The Sons of the Republic of Texas; 1717 8th St; Bay City, TX 77414;
(979) 245-6644, FAX 244-3819; email srttexas@srttexas.org;
website www.srttexas.org
Janet Hickl

Types of material: full-length plays. **Frequency:** annual. **Remuneration:** $2500. **Guidelines:** play about living in Texas, completed during calendar year preceding deadline; see website for details. **Submission procedure:** 5 copies of script; scripts will not be returned. **Deadline:** 15 Jan 2005. **Notification:** Apr 2005.

THE SUSAN SMITH BLACKBURN PRIZE

3239 Avalon Pl; Houston, TX 77019; (713) 308-2842,
FAX 654-8184; website www.blackburnprize.org
Emilie S. Kilgore, *Founder and Co-President*

Types of material: full-length plays. **Frequency:** annual. **Remuneration:** $10,000 1st prize plus signed Willem de Kooning print, made especially for Blackburn Prize; $2000 special commendation at the discretion of the judges; $1000 to each of 8-11 other finalists. **Guidelines:** woman playwright of any nationality writing in English; unproduced play or play produced within one year of deadline; previous winners are not eligible. **Submission procedure:** no submission by playwright; professional artistic directors of specified theatres are invited to nominate play and submit 2 copies of script; playwright may bring script to attention of eligible nominator; send 60¢-postage SASE for guidelines, brochure and list of theatres eligible to nominate or see website. **Deadline:** 20 Sep 2004. **Notification:** Jan 2005 for finalists; Feb 2005 for winner.

SWTA NEW PLAY CONTEST

Southwest Theatre Association, Inc; c/o Theatre Arts Cameron University;
2800 Gore Blvd; Lawton, OK 73505-6377; (580) 581-2427
David Fennema, *New Plays Committee Chair*

Types of material: full-length plays, one-acts. **Frequency:** annual. **Remuneration:** $200, reading at annual SWTA conference in Nov, possible excerpt publication in SWTA journal, *Theatre Southwest*, 1-year membership in SWTA. **Guidelines:** U.S. resident; unproduced, unpublished play; no plays for young audiences; 1 submission limit. **Submission procedure:** script, 1-page synopsis, 1-page bio and $10 fee (check payable to SWTA). **Deadline:** 15 Mar 2005. **Notification:** Sep 2005. **Dates:** Nov 2005.

TADA!'S ONE-ACT PLAYWRITING CONTEST

TADA!; 15 West 28th St, 3rd Floor; New York, NY 10001; (212) 252-1619; email playcontest@tadatheater.com; website www.tadatheater.com
Emmanuel Wilson, *Artistic Associate and Literary Manager*

Types of material: one-act plays. **Frequency:** annual. **Remuneration:** $100, staged reading at TADA!; attendance at rehearsal and performance. **Guidelines:** plays must be submitted in 1 of 2 categories: "Young Writers" for playwrights 18 and under, or "General Submission" for playwrights 19 and over; cast and intended audience must be primarily teens; plays with animals and non-human characters discouraged; no musicals; see web for guidelines and to download application form. **Submission procedure:** application, bio, 3 copies of unbound play, character breakdown and set and costume description. **Deadline:** 5 Jan 2005. **Notification:** Mar 2005.

TENNESSEE WILLIAMS/NEW ORLEANS LITERARY FESTIVAL ONE-ACT PLAY COMPETITION

c/o Creative Writing Workshop; University of New Orleans;
New Orleans, LA 70148; (504) 581-1144, FAX 529-2430;
email info@tennesseewilliams.net;
website www.tennesseewilliams.net

Types of material: one-acts. **Frequency:** annual. **Remuneration:** $1000, staged reading in spring 2005 festival, production in spring 2006 festival; publication in a literary journal. **Guidelines:** unpublished play, not more than 60 minutes in length and not produced professionally. **Submission procedure:** application, script and $15 fee (check payable to Tennessee Williams Festival); script will not be returned; write for guidelines and application before submitting work. **Deadline:** 1 Dec 2004; no submission before 1 Sep 2004. **Dates:** 23-27 Mar 2005.

THEATRE CONSPIRACY ANNUAL NEW PLAY CONTEST

10091 McGregor Blvd; Ft. Myers, FL 33919; (941) 936-3239;
website www.theatreconspiracy.org
Bill Taylor, *Artistic Director*

Types of material: full-length plays. **Frequency:** annual. **Remuneration:** $600, production. **Guidelines:** play not previously produced, cast limit of 8, simple production demands. **Submission procedure:** script, 1-page synopsis, character breakdown, technical requirements, bio and $5 fee. **Deadline:** 30 Nov 2004. **Notification:** Apr 2005. **Dates:** late May-early Jun 2005.

THEATREFEST REGIONAL PLAYWRITING FESTIVAL

Montclair State University; Upper Montclair, NJ 07043;
(973) 655-7071, FAX 655-5335; website www.montclair.edu/theatrefest
John Wooten, *Artistic Director*

Types of material: full-length plays. **Frequency:** annual. **Remuneration:** $1500 John Golden Prize, full production, housing; $500 and equity workshop to 1st runner-up; $500 to 2nd runner-up. **Guidelines:** resident of CT, NJ or NY;

unproduced, unpublished work exploring contemporary issues, cast limit of 8. **Submission procedure:** send SASE for guidelines. **Deadline:** 21 Jan 2005. **Notification:** 15 Mar 2005.

THEATRE OXFORD'S 10 MINUTE PLAY CONTEST

1739 University Ave, PMB 290; Oxford, MS 38655; (662) 513-0159,
    FAX 234-9266; email pmassey@nautiluspublishing.com;
    website www.10minuteplays.com
Neil White, *Contest Director*

Types of material: one-acts. **Frequency:** annual. **Remuneration:** $250 1st prize, full production; 5 finalists receive staged reading. **Guidelines:** play not previously produced, maximum 10 pages in length; no translations or adaptations. **Submission procedure:** script and $10 fee; enclose SASP for acknowledgement of receipt; script will not be returned. **Deadline:** 15 Mar 2005. **Notification:** 30 Apr 2005.

THEODORE WARD PRIZE FOR AFRICAN-AMERICAN PLAYWRIGHTS

Columbia College Chicago Theater/Music Center; 72 East 11th St;
    Chicago, IL 60605; (312) 344-6136, FAX 344-8077;
    email chigochuck@aol.com
Chuck Smith, *Facilitator*

Types of material: full-length plays, translations, adaptations, solo pieces. **Frequency:** annual. **Remuneration:** $2000 1st prize, production, travel and housing to attend rehearsals; $500 2nd prize, staged reading; 3rd prize, staged reading at Goodman Theatre (see Production). **Guidelines:** African-American U.S. resident; 1 full-length submission not produced professionally; translations and adaptations only of material in public domain. **Submission procedure:** script, short synopsis, production history and brief resume; write for guidelines. **Deadline:** 1 Jul 2005; no submission before 1 Apr 2005. **Notification:** Nov 2005.

THREE GENRES DRAMA CONTEST

c/o Stephen Minot; 2225 Mount Vernon Ave; Riverside, CA 92507;
    (909) 369-3938; email s.minot@juno.com
Stephen Minot, *Editor*

Types of material: one-acts. **Frequency:** every four years. **Remuneration:** $500 1st prize; $350 2nd prize; 1st and 2nd prize include publication and 2 complimentary copies of book. **Guidelines:** play must be 10–15 minutes in length, play illustrating "techniques of drama" for publication in college-level textbook; no monologues or musicals. **Submission procedure:** script only. **Deadline:** postmarked by 1 Feb 2005. **Notification:** 2 months.

TOWSON UNIVERSITY PRIZE FOR LITERATURE

Towson, MD 21252; (410) 704-2871
Chair, English

Types of material: book or book-length manuscript; all literary genres eligible, including plays. **Frequency:** annual. **Remuneration:** $2000. **Guidelines:** resident of

MD for 3 years at time prize awarded; work published within 3 years prior to submission or scheduled for publication within the year. **Submission procedure:** publisher or playwright submits application and 5 copies of work; write for guidelines. **Deadline:** 15 Jun 2005. **Notification:** 1 Dec 2005.

TRUSTUS PLAYWRIGHTS' FESTIVAL

Trustus Theatre; Box 11721; Columbia, SC 29211-1721; (803) 254-9732, FAX 771-9153; email Trustus88@aol.com; website www.trustus.org

Jon Tuttle, *Literary Manager*

Types of material: full-length plays. **Frequency:** annual. **Remuneration:** $250, staged reading, 1-year development period followed by additional $500 and full production with travel and housing to attend opening. **Guidelines:** play not produced professionally, cast limit of 8; prefers challenging, innovative dramas and comedies; no musicals or plays for young audiences. **Submission procedure:** application, synopsis and resume; send SASE for guidelines and application. **Deadline:** 1 Feb 2005; no submission before 1 Dec 2004. **Notification:** 1 Jun 2005.

UNICORN THEATRE NEW PLAY DEVELOPMENT

3828 Main St; Kansas City, MO 64111; (816) 531-7529, ext 15, FAX 531-0421

Herman Wilson, *Literary Assistant*

Types of material: full-length plays. **Frequency:** annual. **Remuneration:** $1000, production, possible travel and residency. **Guidelines:** unpublished play not produced professionally; contemporary (post-1950) themes and settings only; special interest in social issues; cast limit of 10; no musicals. **Submission procedure:** synopsis, at least 10 pages of dialogue, character breakdown, resume, cover letter and SASE for response; scripts will not be returned. **Deadline:** ongoing. **Notification:** 4 weeks; 4-8 months if script is requested.

UNIVERSITY OF LOUISVILLE GRAWEMEYER AWARD
FOR MUSIC COMPOSITION

Grawemeyer Music Award Committee; School of Music; University of Louisville; Louisville, KY 40292; (502) 852-6907, FAX 852-0520; email grawemeyermusic@louisville.edu; website www.grawemeyer.org/music/index/html

Types of material: music-theatre works, operas. **Frequency:** annual. **Remuneration:** $200,000 (paid in 5 annual installments of $40,000). **Guidelines:** works premiered between 1999-2004; entry must be sponsored by professional music organization or individual. **Submission procedure:** application, score, cassette, supporting materials and $40 fee submitted jointly by composer and sponsor; write for guidelines. **Deadline:** 24 Jan 2005. **Dates:** spring 2006 for presentation of award.

VERMONT PLAYWRIGHTS AWARD

The Valley Players; Box 441; Waitsfield, VT 05673-0441;
(802) 496-3751; website www.valleyplayers.com

Jennifer Howard, *Coordinator*

Types of material: full-length plays. **Frequency:** annual. **Remuneration:** $1000, probable production. **Guidelines:** resident of ME, NH or VT; unproduced, unpublished play, suitable for community group, that has not won playwriting competition, moderate production demands. **Submission procedure:** entry form and 2 copies of script; send SASE for guidelines. **Deadline:** 1 Feb 2005.

VSA ARTS PLAYWRIGHT DISCOVERY AWARD

1300 Connecticut Ave NW, Suite 700; Washington, DC 20036;
(800) 933-8721, (202) 737-0645 (TTY), FAX 737-0725;
email info@vsarts.org; website www.vsarts.org

Types of material: one-acts. **Frequency:** annual. **Remuneration:** scholarship money; travel, room and board to attend staged reading or production at John F. Kennedy Center for the Performing Arts in Washington, DC. **Guidelines:** U.S. citizen in grades 6-12; unproduced, unpublished play for family audience that deals with experience of living with a disability, less than 40 pages in length; previous submission ineligible; 1 submission limit. **Submission procedure:** application, 2 copies of script; scripts will not be returned; write for guidelines and application or download from web. **Deadline:** 15 Apr 2005.

WEST COAST ENSEMBLE CONTESTS

Box 38728; Los Angeles, CA 90038; (323) 876-9337, FAX 876-8916

Les Hanson, *Artistic Director*

WEST COAST ENSEMBLE FULL-LENGTH PLAY COMPETITION

Types of material: full-length plays. **Frequency:** annual. **Remuneration:** $500, production, royalty on any performances beyond 8-week run. **Guidelines:** 1 submission not produced in southern CA; cast limit of 12. **Submission procedure:** script with SASE or SASP for acknowledgment of receipt. **Deadline:** 31 Dec 2004. **Notification:** Jul 2005.

WEST COAST ENSEMBLE MUSICAL STAIRS

Types of material: music-theatre works. **Frequency:** annual. **Remuneration:** $500, production, royalty on any performances beyond 8-week run. **Guidelines:** 1 unpublished musical submission not produced in Southern CA; all genres and styles eligible, including pop, rock, country and western, etc., cast limit of 12. **Submission procedure:** script, cassette or CD of music (include score and lead sheets if available). **Deadline:** 30 Jun 2005. **Notification:** Jan 2006.

WICHITA STATE UNIVERSITY PLAYWRITING CONTEST

University Theatre; Wichita State University; 1845 Fairmount;
Wichita, KS 67260-0153; (316) 978-3368, FAX 978-3202;
email steve.peters@wichita.edu
Steven J. Peters, *Contest Director*

Types of material: full-length plays, bills of related one-acts. **Frequency:** annual. **Remuneration:** production, expenses for playwright to attend production. **Guidelines:** unpublished, unproduced work at least 90 minutes in length by student currently enrolled at U.S. college or university; no musicals or plays for young audiences. **Submission procedure:** script with unbound cover sheet containing author's name, address and phone number (no author's name on script); send SASP for acknowlegment of receipt; write for guidelines. **Deadline:** 15 Feb 2005. **Notification:** 15 Apr 2005.

WRITE A PLAY! NYC CONTEST

Young Playwrights Inc; 306 West 38th St, Suite 300; New York, NY 10018;
(212) 594-5440; email writeaplay@aol.com;
website youngplaywrights.org
Sheri M. Goldhirsch, *Artistic Director*

Types of material: full-length plays, one-acts, monologues (submissions from elementary school students only). **Frequency:** annual. **Remuneration:** varies. **Guidelines:** New York City students in grades K-12; writers 18 years of age or younger automatically entered in Young Playwrights Festival National Playwriting Contest (see listing this section); plays accepted in three categories: elementary school (K-5), junior high school (6-8) and high school (9-12). **Submission procedure:** script with playwright's name, date of birth, home address, phone number, school and grade on title page; write or email for guidelines. **Deadline:** 1 Apr 2005. **Notification:** 1 Jun 2005.

WRITER'S DIGEST WRITING COMPETITION

4700 East Galbraith Rd; Cincinnati, OH 45236;
(513) 531-2222; email competitions@fwpubs.com;
website www.writersdigest.com
Competition Coordinator

Types of material: full-length plays, screenplays, teleplays. **Frequency:** annual. **Remuneration:** $2500 Grand Prize, travel expenses paid to New York City to meet with editors and agents or to 2005 Maui Writer's Conference; $1000 1st prize; $500 2nd prize; $250 3rd prize (1st, 2nd and 3rd prize winners receive $100 worth of Writer's Digest books); $100 4th prize, current edition of *Writer's Market* and 1-year subscription to *Writer's Digest* magazine; $50 5th prize, current edition of *Writer's Market* and 1-year subscription to *Writer's Digest* magazine. **Guidelines:** unpublished, unproduced work, not accepted by publisher or producer at time of submission; previous entries ineligible. **Submission procedure:** entry form, 1-page synopsis, first 15 pages of script, indication of projected market for work and $10 fee; send SASE for guidelines. **Deadline:** 15 May 2005. **Notification:** fall 2005.

YEAR-END-SERIES (Y.E.S.) NEW PLAY FESTIVAL

Department of Theatre; Northern Kentucky University;
  Highland Heights, KY 41099; (859) 572-6303, FAX 572-6057;
  email forman@nku.edu
Sandra Forman, *Project Director*

Types of material: full-length plays, adaptations, musicals. **Frequency:** biennial. **Remuneration:** 3 awards of $500, production, travel and expenses to attend rehearsals and performance. **Guidelines:** unproduced work in which majority of roles can be handled by students; small orchestra for musicals; 1 submission limit. **Submission procedure:** application and script. **Deadline:** 31 Oct 2004. **Notification:** Jan 2005. **Dates:** 14–24 Apr 2005.

YOUNG CONNECTICUT PLAYWRIGHTS FESTIVAL

Maxwell Anderson Playwrights Series; Box 671; West Redding, CT 06896;
  (203) 270-2951
Bruce Post, *Dramaturg*

Types of material: full-length plays, one-acts, musicals, translations, adaptations, plays for young audiences, solo pieces. **Frequency:** annual. **Remuneration:** staged reading in May festival, certificate. **Guidelines:** CT resident ages 12–19 only; script maximum 60 pages in length. **Submission procedure:** script with playwright's name, date of birth, home address, phone number and name of school on title page; send SASE for guidelines. **Deadline:** 27 Mar 2005. **Notification:** May 2005. **Dates:** May 2005.

YOUNG PLAYWRIGHTS FESTIVAL NATIONAL PLAYWRITING CONTEST

Young Playwrights Inc; 306 West 38th St, Suite 300;
  New York, NY 10018; (212) 594-5440;
  email writeaplay@aol.com; website youngplaywrights.org
Sheri M. Goldhirsch, *Artistic Director*

Types of material: full-length plays, one-acts. **Frequency:** annual. **Remuneration:** staged reading, travel and residency, consideration for full production, 1-year Dramatists Guild membership (see Membership and Service Organizations). **Guidelines:** playwright 18 years of age or younger as of 1 Dec 2004; submissions from playwrights of all backgrounds encouraged. **Submission procedure:** script with playwright's name, date of birth, home address, phone number and email on title page; write for guidelines. **Deadline:** 1 Dec 2004.

PUBLICATION

What is listed in this section?

Those who are primarily or exclusively play publishers, and literary magazines and small presses, all who accept work of unpublished writers.

How can I determine the best places to submit my play?

Think of these publishers as highly individual people looking for very particular kinds of material, which means you should find out as much as possible about their operations before submitting scripts. One of the best sources is the Council of Literary Magazines and Presses (154 Christopher St, Suite 3C; New York, NY 10014-9110; 212-741-9110; email: info@clmp.org; website: www.clmp.org), and their *Directory of Literary Magazines and Presses* (21st edition available now; $19.95 plus $4.00 shipping and handling), a descriptive listing of hundreds of magazines, including many which publish plays. Other leads may be found in *The International Directory of Little Magazines and Small Presses: 2003–2004* (Dustbooks; Box 100; Paradise, CA 95967; 530-877-6110, orders 800-477-6110; email: publisher@dustbooks.com; website: www.dustbooks.com; $35.95 paper, $55.00 cloth, plus $7.00 shipping and handling, $9.00 for priority mail). You should also write to individual publishers listed here and ask for style sheets, catalogs, sample copies, etc. Don't forget that when publishers say they accept unsolicited scripts, they *always* require you to enclose an SASE for return of the manuscript.

ALASKA QUARTERLY REVIEW

University of Alaska, Anchorage; 3211 Providence Dr;
Anchorage, AK 99508; (907) 786-6916, FAX 786-6916;
email ayaqr@uaa.alaska.edu; website www.uaa.alaska.edu/aqr
Ronald Spatz, *Editor*

Types of material: short full-length plays, one-acts, translations. **Remuneration:** 1 complimentary copy; 1 year subscription; payment when grant money is available. **Guidelines:** semiannual literary magazine publishing up to 2 short plays a year in addition to fiction, poetry and nonfiction; interested in new voices; traditional and experimental work. **Submission procedure:** accepts unsolicited scripts. **Response time:** 1 month.

ANCHORAGE PRESS PLAYS

Box 2901; Louisville, KY 40201; (502) 583-2288, FAX 583-2281;
email applays@bellsouth.net; website www.applays.com
Marilee Hebert Miller, *Publisher*

Types of material: works for young audiences, including full-length plays, one-acts, translations, adaptations and musicals. **Remuneration:** negotiated royalty. **Guidelines:** specialty house publishing works for young audiences only; only works produced a minimum of 3 times considered. **Submission procedure:** accepts unsolicited scripts with proof of production. **Response time:** 6 months.

ARTE PÚBLICO PRESS

University of Houston; 452 Cullen Performance Hall;
Houston, TX 77204-2004; (713) 743-2841, FAX 743-2847;
email artrec@mail.uh.edu; website www.artepublicopress.uh.edu
Nicolás Kanellos, *Publisher*

Types of material: full-length plays, one-acts, adaptations, plays for young audiences, musicals. **Remuneration:** negotiated royalty; complimentary copies. **Guidelines:** unpublished works in English or Spanish by Hispanic writers only. **Submission procedure:** accepts unsolicited scripts. **Response time:** 6 months.

ASIAN PACIFIC AMERICAN JOURNAL

The Asian American Writers' Workshop; 16 West 32nd St, Suite 10A;
New York, NY 10001; (212) 494-0061, FAX 494-0062;
email publications@aaww.org; website www.aaww.org
Hanya Yanagihara, *Editor*

Types of material: one-acts. **Remuneration:** 2 complimentary copies. **Guidelines:** semiannual literary journal publishing work by and/or of interest to Asian-Americans; plays maximum 4000 words. **Submission procedure:** accepts unsolicited scripts; send 4 copies of script. **Response time:** 8 months.

BAKER'S PLAYS

Box 699222; Quincy, MA 02269-9222; (617) 745-0805,
FAX 745-9891; email editor@bakersplays.com;
website www.bakersplays.com
Editor

Types of material: full-length plays, one-acts, plays for young audiences, musicals, chancel dramas. **Remuneration:** negotiated book and production royalty. **Guidelines:** prefers produced plays; prefers plays suitable for high school, community and regional theatres; "Plays from Young Authors" division features plays by high school playwrights. **Submission procedure:** accepts unsolicited scripts with resume; include press clippings if play has been produced; include SASE with priority postage for return of script. **Response time:** 8 months. **Special programs:** Baker's Plays High School Playwriting Contest (see Prizes).

BROADWAY PLAY PUBLISHING, INC.

56 East 81st St; New York, NY 10028-0202; (212) 772-8334,
FAX 772-8358; email BroadwayPl@aol.com;
website www.broadwayplaypubl.com

Types of material: full-length plays. **Remuneration:** 10% book royalty, 80% amateur royalty, 90% stock royalty; 10 complimentary copies. **Guidelines:** major interest is in produced, original, innovative work by American playwrights; no historical or autobiographical plays. **Submission procedure:** no unsolicited scripts; letter of inquiry. **Response time:** 2 months letter; 4 months script.

BROOKLYN PUBLISHERS

1841 Cord St; Odessa, TX 79762; (432) 550-5532, FAX 368-0340;
email brookpublishing@aol.com; website www.brookpub.com
David Burton, *Editor*

Types of material: full-length plays, one-acts, adaptations, plays for young audiences, solo pieces, monologues, sketches. **Remuneration:** purchase and royalties; 10 complimentary copies. **Guidelines:** plays for the teen market; works suitable for performers in grades 6-12; special interest in comedies, mysteries. **Submission procedure:** accepts unsolicited scripts. **Response time:** 2 months.

CALLALOO

Department of English; Texas A&M University; 4227 Tamu;
College Station, TX 77843-4227; (979) 458-3108, FAX 458-3275;
email callaloo@tamu.edu; website callaloo.tamu.edu
Charles H. Rowell, *Editor*

Types of material: one-acts (including translations), excerpts of full-length plays. **Remuneration:** complimentary copies and offprints. **Guidelines:** quarterly journal of African-American and African arts and letters published by Johns Hopkins University Press. **Submission procedure:** accepts unsolicited scripts; send 3 copies of script with SASE for response. **Response time:** 6 months.

THE CAPILANO REVIEW

2055 Purcell Way; North Vancouver, BC V7J 3H5; (604) 984-1712;
email trc@capcollege.bc.ca; website www.capcollege.bc.ca/dept/TCR
Carol Hamshaw, *Managing Editor*

Types of material: one-acts, solo pieces, screenplays. **Remuneration:** $50 per page, maximum $200; 2 complimentary copies. **Guidelines:** triannual literary and visual arts journal; publishes 1–2 plays a year; special interest in short, experimental theatre pieces with an "excellent use of language"; unpublished works, maximum 20 pages in length. **Submission procedure:** accepts unsolicited scripts; enclose SASE with Canadian postage or international reply coupons. **Response time:** 4 months.

CONFRONTATION MAGAZINE

English Department; C.W. Post College of Long Island University;
Brookville, NY 11548; (516) 299-2720, FAX 299-2735;
email martin.tucker@liu.edu;
website www.cwpost.liu.edu/cwis/cwp/culture/
Martin Tucker, *Editor*

Types of material: one-acts. **Remuneration:** $25–75; 1 complimentary copy. **Guidelines:** general magazine for "literate" audience; unpublished plays no more than 40 pages in length. **Submission procedure:** accepts unsolicited scripts; no email submissions. **Response time:** 10 weeks.

CONTEMPORARY DRAMA SERVICE

Meriwether Publishing, Ltd; 885 Elkton Dr;
Colorado Springs, CO 80907; (719) 594-4422, FAX 594-9916
Arthur and Theodore Zapel, *Associate Editors*

Types of material: one-acts, adaptations, plays for young audiences, musicals. **Remuneration:** book royalties or payment for amateur and professional performance rights. **Guidelines:** publishes works suitable for teenage, high school and college market, as well as collections of monologues and practical books on theatre arts; prefers comedies. **Submission procedure:** send letter of inquiry and $2 for sample catalog and guidelines. **Response time:** 1 month.

THE DRAMATIC PUBLISHING COMPANY

311 Washington St; Box 129; Woodstock, IL 60098; (815) 338-7170,
FAX 338-8981; email plays@dramaticpublishing.com;
website www.dramaticpublishing.com
Linda Habjan, *Editor*

Types of material: full-length plays, one-acts, translations, adaptations, plays for young audiences, musicals. **Remuneration:** standard royalty; 10 complimentary copies (33% discount on additional copies). **Guidelines:** works for professional, stock and amateur markets; prefers produced plays. **Submission procedure:** accepts unsolicited scripts. **Response time:** 8 months.

DRAMATICS MAGAZINE

Educational Theatre Association; 2343 Auburn Ave;
Cincinnati, OH 45219-2815; (513) 421-3900, FAX 421-7077;
email dcorathers@edta.org; website www.edta.org
Don Corathers, *Editor*

Types of material: full-length plays, one-acts and solo pieces for young performers. **Remuneration:** payment for 1-time serial rights; complimentary copies. **Guidelines:** educational theatre magazine; plays suitable for high school production; prefers produced plays; special interest in plays no longer than 10 minutes. **Submission procedure:** accepts unsolicited scripts. **Response time:** 5 months. (See Educational Theatre Association in Membership and Service Organizations.)

DRAMATISTS PLAY SERVICE, INC.

440 Park Avenue South; New York, NY 10016; (212) 683-8960,
FAX 213-1539; email postmaster@dramatists.com;
website www.dramatists.com
Stephen Sultan, *President*

Types of material: full-length plays, musicals. **Remuneration:** possible advance against royalties; 10% book royalty, 80% amateur royalty, 90% stock royalty; 10 complimentary copies (40% discount on additional copies). **Guidelines:** works for stock and amateur market; prefers works produced in New York City. **Submission procedure:** no unsolicited scripts; 1-page synopsis and letter of inquiry. **Response time:** 6 months letter; 6 months script.

EARTH'S DAUGHTERS

Box 41, Central Park Station; Buffalo, NY 14215;
website www.earthsdaughters.org

Types of material: full-length plays, one-acts, translations, adaptations, plays for young audiences, solo pieces. **Remuneration:** 2 complimentary copies. **Guidelines:** triannual feminist literary and art periodical with focus on experience and creative expression of women; publishes play excerpts with occasional issue devoted to complete text of play. **Submission procedure:** accepts unsolicited scripts. **Response time:** 2 months.

ELDRIDGE PUBLISHING COMPANY

Box 14367; Tallahassee, FL 32317; (800) HI-STAGE;
email editorial@histage.com; website www.histage.com
Nancy S. Vorhis, *Editor*

Types of material: full-length plays, one-acts, musicals. **Remuneration:** outright purchase of religious material only; all other works, 10% book royalty, 50% amateur and educational royalty; complimentary copies (50% discount on additional copies). **Guidelines:** publishes 50-75 plays and musicals a year for school, church and community theatre; comedies, mysteries or serious drama. **Submission procedure:**

accepts unsolicited scripts; if possible, include CD for musicals. **Response time:** 2 months.

ENCORE PERFORMANCE PUBLISHING

2181 West California Ave, Suite 250; Salt Lake City, UT 84104;
(801) 485-5012
Michael C. Perry, *President*

Types of material: full-length plays, one-acts, translations, adaptations, plays for young audiences, musicals, solo pieces. **Remuneration:** 10% book royalty, 50% performance royalty; 10 complimentary copies (discount on additional copies). **Guidelines:** publishes 10-30 plays and musicals a year; works must have had a minimum of 2 amateur or professional productions; special interest in works with strong family or Judeo-Christian message and in Christmas, Halloween and other holiday plays. **Submission procedure:** no unsolicited scripts; synopsis, production information and letter of inquiry; best submission time May–Aug. **Response time:** 1 month letter; 3 months script.

FREELANCE PRESS

Box 548; Dover, MA 02030; (508) 785-8250, FAX 785-8291;
website www.freelancepress.org
Narcissa Campion, *Managing Editor*

Types of material: musicals. **Remuneration:** 10% book royalty, 70% performance royalty. **Guidelines:** unpublished issue-oriented musicals and musical adaptations of classics; approximately 1 hour long; suitable for performing by young people only; large casts with flexible male/female roles. **Submission procedure:** accepts unsolicited scripts. **Response time:** 3 months.

GREEN INTEGER

6022 Wilshire Blvd, Suite 200A; Los Angeles, CA 90036; (323) 857-1115;
info@greeninteger.com; website www.greeninteger.com
Douglas Messerli, *Publisher*

Types of material: full-length plays, translations. **Remuneration:** royalty; 10 complimentary copies. **Guidelines:** press publishing average of 10 single-play volumes a year; unpublished plays; special interest in translations. **Submission procedure:** no unsolicited scripts; send letter of inquiry. **Response time:** 1 month.

HEUER PUBLISHING LLC

Box 248; Cedar Rapids, IA 52406; (319) 368-8008, FAX 364-1771;
website www.hitplays.com
Geri Albrecht, *Editor in Chief*

Types of material: works for young audiences, including full-length plays, one-acts and musicals. **Remuneration:** outright purchase or performance royalty; complimentary copies. **Guidelines:** performing arts works suitable for middle school, high school, college and community theatres only; plays appropriate for family audiences. **Submission procedure:** accepts unsolicited scripts. **Response time:** 2 months.

I. E. CLARK PUBLICATIONS

Box 246; Schulenburg, TX 78956-0246; (979) 743-3232,
  FAX 743-4765; email ieclark@cvtv.net; website www.ieclark.com
Editorial Department

Types of material: full-length plays, one-acts, translations, adaptations, plays for young audiences, musicals. **Remuneration:** book and performance royalties. **Guidelines:** publishes for worldwide professional, amateur and educational markets; prefers produced works. **Submission procedure:** accepts unsolicited scripts; cassette or videotape must accompany musical; include proof of production with reviews and photos for produced works; send $3 for catalog; send SASE for submission guidelines. **Response time:** 6 months.

KALLIOPE, A JOURNAL OF WOMEN'S LITERATURE & ART

Florida Community College; 3939 Roosevelt Blvd;
  Jacksonville, FL 32205; website www.fccj.org/kalliope
Mary Sue Koeppel, *Editor*

Types of material: one-acts, solo pieces. **Remuneration:** 2 complimentary copies or free 1-year subscription. **Guidelines:** biannual journal of women's literature and art publishing short fiction, poetry, artwork, photography, interviews, reviews and an average of 1 play a year; unpublished plays, maximum 20 pages in length, by women only; "no trite themes or erotica." **Submission procedure:** accepts unsolicited scripts. **Response time:** 3-6 months.

THE KENYON REVIEW

104 College Dr; Gambier, OH 43022-9623; (740) 427-5208,
  FAX 427-5417; email kenyonreview@kenyon.edu;
  website www.kenyonreview.org
David H. Lynn, *Editor*

Types of material: one-acts, solo pieces, excerpts from full-length plays. **Remuneration:** cash payment; 2 complimentary copies. **Guidelines:** literary journal publishing an average of 2 plays a year; unproduced, unpublished works maximum 30 pages in length. **Submission procedure:** accepts unsolicited scripts with letter of inquiry. **Response time:** 4 months.

LAMIA INK!

Box 202; Prince St Station; New York, NY 10012
(Ms.) Cortland Jessup, *Artistic Director*

Types of material: very short monologues and performance pieces, 1-page plays for contest (see below). **Remuneration:** 4 complimentary copies. **Guidelines:** annual "art rag" magazine; experimental theatre pieces maximum 5 pages in length, prefers 2-3-page pieces; special interest in Japanese, Pacific Rim and Native American writers, and poets' theatre, performance poems, theatre manifestos and essays. **Submission procedure:** accepts unsolicited scripts with SASE for response. **Response time:** 3 weeks minimum. **Special programs:** Lamia Ink! International One-Page Play Competition (see Prizes).

LILLENAS DRAMA RESOURCES

Lillenas Publishing Company; Box 419527; Kansas City, MO 64141;
(800) 877-0700, FAX (816) 412-8390;
email drama@lillenas.com; website www.lillenasdrama.com
Kimberly R. Messer, *Manager/Editor*

Types of material: full-length plays, one-acts, collections of sketches, playlets, children's recitations. **Remuneration:** outright purchase or royalty. **Guidelines:** unpublished "creatively conceived and practically producible scripts and outlines that provide church and school with an opportunity to glorify God and his creation in drama"; downloadable scripts available via website. **Submission procedure:** accepts unsolicited scripts; send SASE for guidelines and current need letter. **Response time:** 3 months.

NEW PLAYS

Box 5074; Charlottesville, VA 22905; (434) 979-2777,
FAX 984-2230; email patwhitton@aol.com;
website www.newplaysforchildren.com
Patricia Whitton Forrest, *Publisher*

Types of material: plays for young audiences. **Remuneration:** 10% book royalty, 50% performance royalty. **Guidelines:** innovative material not duplicated by other sources of plays for young audiences; produced plays directed by someone other than author; download guidelines from web. **Submission procedure:** accepts unsolicited scripts. **Response time:** 2 months minimum.

PAJ: A JOURNAL OF PERFORMANCE AND ART

Box 260; Village Station; New York, NY 10014-0260;
(212) 243-3885, FAX 243-3885; email pajpub@aol.com;
website mitpress.mit.edu/paj
Bonnie Marranca and Gautam Dasgupta, *Co-Publishers and Editors*

Types of material: one-acts, translations, solo pieces. **Remuneration:** payment varies. **Guidelines:** publishes plays and critical essays on international performance, drama, video, music, film and photography; special interest in translations; prefers plays less than 40 pages in length. **Submission procedure:** no unsolicited scripts; synopsis and letter of inquiry. **Response time:** 2 months letter; 2 months script.

PIONEER DRAMA SERVICE

Box 4267; Englewood, CO 80155-4267; (303) 779-4035,
FAX 779-4315; email editors@pioneerdrama.com;
website www.pioneerdrama.com
Lori Conary, *Submissions Editor*

Types of material: full-length plays, one-acts, plays for young audiences, musicals. **Remuneration:** royalty. **Guidelines:** produced work suitable for educational theatre, including melodramas and Christmas plays; prefers large, ensemble casts with majority of female roles or flexible casting. **Submission procedure:** accepts unsolicited scripts; prefers synopsis and letter of inquiry. **Response time:** 2 weeks letter; 4 months script. **Special programs:** Shubert Fendrich Memorial Playwriting Contest (see Prizes).

PLAYERS PRESS

Box 1132; Studio City, CA 91614-0132; (818) 789-4980
Robert W. Gordon, *Senior Editor*

Types of material: full-length plays, one-acts, translations, adaptations, plays for young audiences, musicals, solo pieces, monologues, scenes, teleplays, screenplays. **Remuneration:** cash option and/or outright purchase or royalty; complimentary copies (20% discount on additional copies). **Guidelines:** theatre press publishing technical and reference books and scripts; produced works for professional, amateur and educational markets. **Submission procedure:** accepts unsolicited scripts with proof of production, resume and 2 business-size SASEs; prefers synopsis, proof of production, resume and letter of inquiry with SASE for response. **Response time:** 6 weeks letter; 6 months script.

PLAYSCRIPTS, INC.

Box 237060; New York, NY 10023; (866) 639-7529;
email questions@playscripts.com; website www.playscripts.com

Types of material: full-length plays, one-acts. **Remuneration:** negotiated royalty from licensed amateur and professional performances and book sales. **Guidelines:** unpublished plays; limit of 2 submissions per author; no musicals. **Submission procedure:** electronic submissions preferred; see full guidelines on web. **Response time:** varies.

PLAYS, THE DRAMA MAGAZINE FOR YOUNG PEOPLE

Sterling Partners, Inc; Box 600160; Newton, MA 02460; (617) 630-9100;
website www.playsmag.com
Elizabeth Preston, *Editor*

Types of material: one-act plays for young audiences, including adaptations of material in the public domain. **Remuneration:** $75-175 depending on length of play. **Guidelines:** publishes 70 plays a year; prefers work 20-30 minutes in length for junior and senior high school, 15-20 minutes for middle grades, 8-15 minutes for lower grades; no religious plays; magazine acquires all rights. **Submission**

procedure: accepts unsolicited original scripts; letter of inquiry for adaptations; prefers format used in magazine; send SASE for guidelines or download from web. **Response time:** 2 weeks letter; 1 month script.

POEMS & PLAYS

English Department; Middle Tennessee State University;
    Murfreesboro, TN 37132; (615) 898-2712, FAX 898-5098;
    email gbrewew@mtsu.edu;
    website www.mtsu.edu/~english/poemplay.html
Gaylord Brewer, *Editor*

Types of material: one-acts. **Remuneration:** 1 complimentary copy. **Guidelines:** annual magazine of poetry and short plays published every March, includes an average of 2-3 plays in each issue; unpublished works; prefers produced works not more than 10-15 pages in length. **Submission procedure:** accepts unsolicited scripts 1 Oct-31 Dec only. **Response time:** 2 months. **Special programs:** Tennessee Chapbook Prize: annual award for either a one-act play or collection of short plays or poetry, maximum manuscript length 24-30 pages in length; winning script published as interior chapbook in magazine; playwright receives 50 complimentary copies; submit script, SASE and $10 fee; *deadline:* 31 Dec 2004; no submissions before 1 Oct 2004.

PRISM INTERNATIONAL

Creative Writing Program; University of British Columbia;
    Buch E462-1866 Main Mall; Vancouver, BC; Canada V6T 1Z1;
    (604) 822-2514, FAX 822-3616;
    email prism@interchange.ubc.ca; website prism.arts.ubc.ca

Types of material: one-acts (including translations and solo pieces), excerpts from full-length plays. **Remuneration:** $20 per printed page; 1-year subscription. **Guidelines:** quarterly literary magazine; unpublished plays, maximum 40 pages in length; send SASE, see website for guidelines. **Submission procedure:** accepts unsolicited scripts, include copy of original with translations. **Response time:** 6 months.

RESOURCE PUBLICATIONS, INC.

160 East Virginia St, #290; San Jose, CA 95112-5876;
    (408) 286-8505, FAX 287-8748; email Ken@rpinet.com;
    website www.resourcepublications.com
Donna Cole, *Editor*

Types of material: plays 7-15 minutes in length. **Remuneration:** royalty. **Guidelines:** collection of skits suitable for middle school or high school students; no one-acts. **Submission procedure:** accepts unsolicited scripts. **Response time:** 2 months.

ROCKFORD REVIEW

Box 858; Rockford, IL 61105; email daveconnieross@aol.com;
website writersguild1.tripod.com

David Ross, *Editor*

Types of material: one-acts, solo pieces. **Remuneration:** 1 complimentary copy. **Guidelines:** triquarterly journal publishing poetry, fiction, satire, artwork and an average of 4-5 plays a year; one-acts not more than 1300 words; prefers work that provides "new insight into the human dilemma." **Submission procedure:** accepts unsolicited scripts with SASE. **Response time:** 2 months.

SAMUEL FRENCH, INC.

45 West 25th St; New York, NY 10010-2751; (212) 206-8990,
FAX 206-1429; email samuelfrench@earthlink.net;
website www.samuelfrench.com

Lawrence Harbison, *Senior Editor*

Types of material: full-length plays, one-acts, plays for young audiences, musicals. **Remuneration:** 10% book royalty; 10 complimentary copies (40% discount on additional copies); pays production royalties, agency commissions vary. **Guidelines:** "Many of our publications have never been produced in New York; these are generally comprised of light comedies, mysteries, mystery-comedies, a handful of one-acts and plays for young audiences, and plays with a preponderance of female roles; however, do not hesitate to send in your future Pulitzer Prize-winner." **Submission procedure:** accepts unsolicited scripts in standard manuscript format. **Response time:** 2 months minimum.

SINISTER WISDOM

Box 3252; Berkeley, CA 94703; email levinkind@netscape.net;
website www.sinisterwisdom.org

Types of material: one-acts, excerpts from full-length plays. **Remuneration:** 2 complimentary copies. **Guidelines:** lesbian journal of art and literature published 2-3 times a year; works by lesbians reflecting the diversity of lesbians; no heterosexual themes; excerpts maximum 3000 words; send SASE for current themes. **Submission procedure:** accepts unsolicited scripts. **Response time:** 9 months.

SMITH AND KRAUS

Box 127; Lyme, NH 03768; (603) 643-6431, FAX 643-1831;
email sandk@sover.net; website www.smithkraus.com

Marisa Smith, *Publisher*

Types of material: full-length plays, one-acts, translations, adaptations, plays for young audiences, solo pieces, monologues. **Remuneration:** payment or royalty. **Guidelines:** theatre press publishing works of interest to theatrical community, especially to actors, including collections of monologues and an average of 50 full-length plays a year; prefers produced plays. **Submission procedure:** no unsolicited scripts; synopsis and letter of inquiry. **Response time:** 3 weeks letter; 4 months script.

SPEERT PUBLISHING

Box 2281; New York, NY 10009; (212) 979-7656;
email espeert@speertpublishing.com;
website www.speertpublishing.com
Eleanore Speert, *President*

Types of material: full-length plays, one-acts, translations, adaptations, plays for young audiences, solo pieces. **Remuneration:** author establishes fee on per-project basis. **Guidelines:** self-publishing company producing industry-standard acting editions for stock, regional theatre, nonprofessional and professional markets; no musicals. **Submission procedure:** call, email or write for information. **Response time:** 1 week. **Special programs:** supports the Dayton Playhouse FutureFest (see listing in Prizes).

THEATREFORUM

Theatre & Dance Department 0344;
University of California–San Diego; 9500 Gilman Dr;
La Jolla, CA 92093-0344; (858) 534-6598, FAX 534-1080;
email TheatreForum@ucsd.edu; website www.theatreforum.org
Jim Carmody, John Rouse, Adele Edling Shank and Theodore Shank, *Editors*

Types of material: full-length plays, translations, adaptations. **Remuneration:** $200; 10 complimentary copies; discount for additional copies. **Guidelines:** biannual international journal focusing on innovative work, publishing 2 professionally produced, unpublished plays in each issue, plus articles, interviews and photographs. **Submission procedure:** no unsolicited scripts; professional recommendation. **Response time:** 3 months.

THEATER MAGAZINE

Yale School of Drama, Box 208244; New Haven, CT 06520-8244;
(203) 432-1568, FAX 432-8336; email theater.magazine@yale.edu;
website www.yale.edu/drama/publications/theater
Tom Sellar, *Editor*

Types of material: full-length plays, translations, adaptations, solo pieces. **Remuneration:** $150 maximum; complimentary copies. **Guidelines:** triquarterly theatre journal publishing an average of 2 plays in each volume, plus articles and essays; special interest in experimental, innovative work; "no standard psychological realism or TV-script clones." **Submission procedure:** no unsolicited scripts; letter of inquiry only. **Response time:** 6 months.

DEVELOPMENT

What's in this section?

Conferences, festivals, workshops and programs whose primary purpose is to develop plays and playwrights. Also listed are some playwright groups and membership organizations whose main activity is play development. Developmental organizations such as New Dramatists whose many programs cannot be adequately described in the brief format used in this section are listed in Membership and Service Organizations. Some programs listed in Prizes also include a developmental element. Note: some programs provide writers with stipends or living situations, etc. Others require a small fee. Read the "financial arrangement" section carefully.

How can I get into these programs?

Keep applying to those for which you are convinced your work is suited. If you're turned down one year, you may be accepted the next on the strength of your latest piece. Remember: All deadlines reflect the next upcoming submission deadline at press time. Deadlines for annual awards may stay the same from year to year but this is not an absolute—always obtain the latest information (an organization's website it the best place to check) before submitting. And if you're required to submit a script with your application, don't forget your SASE!

ABINGDON THEATRE COMPANY

312 West 36th St; New York, NY 10018; (212) 868-2055, FAX 868-2056; email atcnyc@aol.com; website www.abingdon-nyc.org

Pamela Paul, *Artistic Director*

Open to: playwrights. **Description:** 4 plays receive readings each month; 10 plays receive 12 hours of rehearsal and staged readings; of those, 3-4 plays selected for Stage II production and 2 plays selected for mainstage production; 1 playwright annually receives $1000 Christopher Brian Wolk Award for best script submitted; $2000 Witter Bynner fellowship available for playwright-in-residence. **Financial arrangement:** stipend for production. **Guidelines:** play unproduced in New York; full-length plays only. **Application procedure:** script only. **Deadline:** ongoing for developmental programs; 1 Jun 2005 for Wolk Award. **Notification:** 6 months. **Dates:** year-round.

ABRONS ARTS CENTER THEATER

(at Henry Street Settlement)

466 Grand St; New York, NY 10002-4804; (212) 598-0400, FAX 388-1418

Jonathon Ward, *Director of Theater Program*

Open to: playwrights. **Description:** 1-4 plays developed through staged readings, culminating in workshop production. **Financial arrangement:** remuneration varies. **Guidelines:** New York City playwrights only; prefers multicultural plays and musicals that "foster a stronger sense of community and a confident individuality in a culturally diverse world." **Application procedure:** first act or first 10 pages of script, synopsis, character breakdown, resume or brief bio by email or through the mail with SASE; selected playwrights will be interviewed. **Deadline:** ongoing. **Dates:** year-round.

THE ACADEMY FOR NEW MUSICAL THEATRE

2530 Wilshire Blvd, 3rd Floor; Santa Monica, CA 90403; (818) 502-3309; email jsparksco@aol.com; website www.anmt.org

John Sparks, *Artistic Director*

Open to: composers, librettists, lyricists. **Description:** Sep-Jun workshop; in-house staged readings; skeletal productions (Equity contract); some developmental projects with professional theatre companies and producers; new works for young audiences. **Financial arrangement:** 1st-year workshop members pay dues of $700, which include refundable application fee (see below); in subsequent years, members pay dues of $500. **Application procedure:** application; 1-page resume; cassette of 3 songs or equivalent for composer; lyrics for 3 songs for lyricist; short scene for librettist; nonrefundable $50 fee. **Deadline:** 1 Jul 2005. **Notification:** Aug 2005. **Dates:** Sep 2005-Jun 2005.

ANNUAL BACKDOOR THEATRE NEW PLAY PROJECT

Wichita Falls Backdoor Players, Inc; Box 896; Wichita Falls, TX 76307;
(940) 322-5000, FAX 322-8167; email backdoor1@wf.net;
website www.backdoortheatre.org

Linda Bates, *Managing Director*

Open to: playwrights. **Description:** 1 play each Sep receives 5 weeks of rehearsal and workshop production with a minimum of 6 performances. **Financial arrangement:** $500 honorarium; travel and housing. **Guidelines:** special interest in playwrights from Texas and surrounding region; full-length plays which have not received professional production. **Application procedure:** script, brief synopsis, resume and SASP for acknowledgment of receipt. **Deadline:** 15 Mar 2005. **Notification:** Jul 2005. **Dates:** Sep 2005.

ASCAP MUSICAL THEATRE WORKSHOPS

1 Lincoln Plaza; New York, NY 10023; (212) 621-6234, FAX 621-6558;
website www.ascap.com

Michael A. Kerker, *Director of Musical Theatre*

ASCAP/DISNEY MUSICAL THEATRE WORKSHOP

Open to: composers, librettists, lyricists. **Description:** 10-session workshop in CA under the direction of Stephen Schwartz; works presented to panels of musical theatre professionals. **Financial arrangement:** free. **Guidelines:** write for guidelines or download from web. **Application procedure:** synopsis, resume and cassette or CD of 4 theatrical songs. **Deadline:** mid-Dec 2004; exact date TBA. **Dates:** Jan-Feb 2005.

ASCAP MUSICAL THEATRE WORKSHOP

Open to: composers, lyricists. **Description:** 10-session workshop in NY under the direction of Stephen Schwartz; works presented to panels of musical theatre professionals. **Financial arrangement:** free. **Guidelines:** write for guidelines. **Application procedure:** synopsis, resume and cassette of 4 theatrical songs (no pop songs). **Deadline:** Mar 2005; exact date TBA. **Dates:** Apr-May 2005.

ASHLAND NEW PLAYS FESTIVAL

ArtWork Enterprises, Inc; Box 453; Ashland, OR 97520; (541) 482-4357;
website www.ashlandnewplays.org

Open to: playwrights. **Description:** 4 new works given 12 hours of rehearsal with actors and director, culminating in 2 public readings. **Financial arrangement:** $500 stipend and housing. **Guidelines:** U.S. resident; unproduced full-length play; cast limit of 8; 1-submission limit; author's name and contact information on script cover sheet only; send SASE for application or download from web. **Application procedure:** application, script, 2-paragraph synopsis and 2-paragraph bio. **Deadline:** 15 Jan 2005; no submission before 1 Oct 2004. **Notification:** Aug 2005. **Dates:** 19-23 Oct 2005.

ASIAN AMERICAN THEATER COMPANY
NEWWORKS INCUBATOR PROJECT

690 5th St, Suite 211; San Francisco, CA 94107; (415) 543-5738,
FAX 543-5638; email info@asianamericantheater.org;
website www.asianamericantheater.org

Sean Lim, *Managing Artistic Director*

Open to: playwrights. **Description:** developmental workshop for 16 new plays a year, leading to potential staged reading or production; playwrights work on 6-month time-frame with NewWorks Incubator actors. **Financial arrangement:** free; honorarium contingent on funding. **Guidelines:** plays reflecting a distinct Asian Pacific American theatrical voice. **Application procedure:** script, synopsis and character breakdown. **Deadline:** ongoing. **Notification:** 1-6 months.

BALTIMORE PLAYWRIGHTS FESTIVAL

251 South Ann St; Baltimore, MD 21231; (410) 276-2153;
website www.baltplayfest.org

Mark Scharf, *President*

Open to: playwrights, composers, librettists, lyricists. **Description:** selected plays receive 3-5 developmental readings Sep-Mar; from these, participating theatres choose scripts for full production in summer festival. **Financial arrangement:** $100 honorarium for produced scripts. **Guidelines:** past or current resident of MD; unproduced play or musical; send SASE for guidelines. **Application procedure:** 3 copies of script and letter of inquiry with $5 fee. **Deadline:** 30 Sep 2004. **Notification:** 15 Apr 2005. **Dates:** summer 2005.

BAY AREA PLAYWRIGHTS FESTIVAL

Playwrights Foundation; Box 460357; San Francisco, CA 94146;
(415) 626-0453, ext 110; email info@playwrightsfoundation.org;
website www.playwrightsfoundation.org

Amy Mueller, *Artistic Director*

Open to: playwrights. **Description:** 2-week festival of staged readings with professional actors; each script receives 20 hours rehearsal with director/dramaturg team plus pre-festival weekend retreat for initial collaborative activities. **Financial arrangement:** stipend, travel and housing (if needed). **Guidelines:** unproduced full-length plays and short plays 20-35 minutes in length by Bay Area writers only. **Application procedure:** script and resume; students and playwrights with no professional productions must also include letter of recommendation from professional artist. **Deadline:** 15 Jan 2005 and 2006 for full length; 15 Mar for Bay Area Shorts. **Notification:** early May. **Dates:** late Jul or early Aug.

BMI-LEHMAN ENGEL MUSICAL THEATRE WORKSHOP

Broadcast Music, Inc.; 320 West 57th St; New York, NY 10019;
(212) 830-2508, FAX 262-2824; email jbanks@bmi.com

Jean Banks, *Senior Director, Musical Theatre*

Open to: composers, librettists, lyricists. **Description:** 2-year program of weekly workshop meetings; ongoing advanced group for invited alums of Workshop; showcase presentations to invited members of entertainment industry; members eligible for annual Jerry Harrington Musical Theatre Awards, cash prizes for outstanding achievement in workshop. **Financial arrangement:** free. **Application procedure:** application and work samples. **Deadline:** 1 May 2005 for librettists; 1 Aug 2005 for composers and lyricists. **Notification:** Sep 2005.

BROADWAY TOMORROW

191 Claremont Ave, Suite 53; New York, NY 10027; (212) 531-2447, FAX 531-2447
Elyse Curtis, *Artistic Director*

Open to: composers, librettists, lyricists. **Description:** new musicals presented in concert with writers' involvement. **Financial arrangement:** participant pays $50 annual membership fee. **Guidelines:** resident of NY metropolitan area. **Application procedure:** synopsis, resume, cassette of 3 songs with description of scenes in which they occur, reviews if available and SASE for response. **Deadline:** 31 Aug 2005. **Notification:** 3–6 months. **Dates:** year-round.

THE CHESTERFIELD WRITER'S FILM PROJECT

1158 26th St, Box 544; Santa Monica, CA 90401; (213) 683-3977, FAX (310) 260-6116; website www.chesterfield-co.com

Open to: playwrights, screenwriters. **Description:** up to 5 writers annually chosen for year-long screenwriting workshop; writer creates 2 feature-length screenplays; company intends to produce best of year's work. **Financial arrangement:** $20,000 stipend. **Guidelines:** current and former writing-program students encouraged to apply; write or call for information. **Application procedure:** 2 copies of application, writing samples, SASP and $39.50 fee. **Deadline:** Jun 2005; exact date TBA.

CORNERSTONE DRAMATURGY AND DEVELOPMENT PROJECT

Penumbra Theatre Company; 270 North Kent St;
St. Paul, MN 55102-1794; (651) 224-4601, FAX 224-7074
Lou Bellamy, *Artistic Director*

Open to: playwrights. **Description:** 1 playwright a year offered mainstage production with possible 3-4-week residency; 1 playwright offered 4-week workshop-residency culminating in staged reading. **Financial arrangement:** varies according to needs of project. **Guidelines:** full-length play dealing with the African-American and/or Pan-African experience which has not received professional full production; one-acts considered. **Application procedure:** script and resume; write for guidelines. **Deadline:** ongoing.

CREATIVE EVOLUTION
21–70 Crescent St, #A1; Astoria, NY 11105; (212) 502–0807;
   email cevolution@mindspring.com; website
home.mindspring.com/~cevolution/
Michelle Colletti, *Co–Artistic Director*

Open to: playwrights, composers, librettists, lyricists, solo performers, screenwriters. **Description:** ongoing series of readings with one annual production. **Financial arrangement:** free; with stipend for production. **Guidelines:** women only. **Application procedure:** see website for upcoming deadlines and requirements. **Deadline:** ongoing. **Dates:** year-round.

CSF STUDIO
Cincinnati Shakespeare Festival; 717–719 Race St;
   Cincinnati, OH 45202; (513) 381–2289, FAX 381–2298;
   email csfed@cincyshakes.com; website www.cincyshakes.com
Brian Isaac Phillips, *Artistic Director*

Open to: playwrights, translators. **Description:** 3 plays each given 1 week of development, culminating in public staged reading or workshop. **Financial arrangement:** $500 stipend, travel and housing. **Guidelines:** prefer language-focused works-in-progress. **Application procedure:** first 20 pages of script, synopsis and letter of inquiry including current projects and new project ideas. **Deadline:** ongoing; best submission time is spring/summer. **Notification:** 6 months. **Dates:** ongoing. (See Cincinnati Shakespeare Festival in Production.)

DAVID HENRY HWANG WRITERS INSTITUTE
East West Players; 120 North Judge John Aiso St; Los Angeles, CA 90012;
   (213) 625–7000, FAX 625–7111; email info@eastwestplayers.org;
   website www.eastwestplayers.org
Judy Soo Hoo, *Literary Manager*

Open to: playwrights, screenwriters. **Description:** 2 15-session playwriting workshops and 1 12-session screenwriting workshop held each year culminating in public staged readings. **Financial arrangement:** $350 fee for playwriting workshop, $350 fee for screenwriting workshop; 1 scholarship available. **Application procedure:** application, 5–page writing sample, bio, statement of intent describing expectations and goals for workshop and appropriate fee; send SASE for application or download from web. **Deadline:** visit website. (See East West Players in Production.)

DRAMA LEAGUE DIRECTORS PROJECT—NEW DIRECTORS–NEW WORKS SERIES
The Drama League of New York; 520 8th Ave, Suite 320;
   New York, NY 10018; (212) 244–9494, FAX 244–9191;
   email directorsproject@dramaleague.org; website www.dramaleague.org

Open to: collaborative teams composed of director and playwright, translator, composer, librettist or lyricist. **Description:** 3 projects each summer receive up to 4 weeks of rehearsal space in New York City; writer or composer applies as part of collaborative team with director; development ranges from exploratory rehearsals to workshop production according to needs of collaborative team. **Financial arrangement:** maximum $1000 stipend depending on needs of project. **Guidelines:** application submitted by director only. **Application procedure:** download application and guidelines from web. **Deadline:** 1 Feb 2005. **Notification:** 15 May 2005.

ENVISION RETREAT AND LABORATORY

Voice & Vision; 520 8th Ave, #308; New York, NY 10018; (212) 268-3717, FAX 268-5462; email vandv@vandv.org; website www.vandv.org
Jean Wagner, *Artistic Director*

Open to: playwrights, translators, librettists, lyricists, performance artists. **Description:** 6 female writers spend 2 weeks at Bard College working on projects in various stages of development, with opportunities for informal presentations of works-in-progress; 2-3 chosen for further development through ENVISION Lab, located in New York City. **Financial arrangement:** stipend, free room, board, rehearsal space, transportation and most meals. **Guidelines:** women writers only; projects chosen to reflect a broad range of aesthetic and cultural perspectives. **Application procedure:** script, 1-page project description, 3 professional references, resumes of participants, list of special needs and $15 application fee; provide video if applicable. **Deadline:** 1 Apr 2005. **Notification:** 15 Jun 2005. **Dates:** summer 2005.

FESTIVAL OF AMERICAN PLAYWRIGHTS OF COLOR

City College Theatre Arts; 50 Phelan Ave; San Francisco, CA 94112; (415) 239-3100, ext 3, FAX 452-5110
A. Fajilan, *Faculty*

Open to: playwrights. **Description:** up to 10 plays given 4 weeks of rehearsal with student actors and directors culminating in workshop or full production. **Financial arrangement:** $25-100 stipend. **Guidelines:** playwright of color; plays or monologues no longer than 20 minutes only. **Application procedure:** script and resume; scripts will not be returned. **Deadline:** 1 Jun 2005; no submission before 1 Apr 2005. **Notification:** 1 Aug 2005 (accepted playwrights only). **Dates:** fall 2005.

FIRESIDE FESTIVAL OF NEW WORK

Performance Network Theatre; 120 East Huron; Ann Arbor, MI 48104; (734) 663-0696, FAX 663-7367; email carla@performancenetwork.org; website www.performancenetwork.org
Daniel C. Walker, *Artistic Director*

Open to: playwrights, translators, composers, librettists, lyricists. **Description:** up to 12 scripts presented during 5-day festival; scripts given 8 hours of rehearsal culminating in public staged readings. **Financial arrangement:** free. **Guidelines:** full-length play that has not yet received an Equity production. **Application procedure:**

script, production history and resume. **Deadline:** 1 Mar 2005. **Notification:** 1 May 2005. **Dates:** Jun 2005.

FIRST STAGE

Box 38280; Los Angeles, CA 90038; (323) 850-6271, FAX 850-6295;
    email firststagela@aol.com; website www.firststagela.org
Dennis Safren, *Literary Manager*

Open to: playwrights, solo performers, screenwriters. **Description:** organization providing year-round developmental services using professional actors, directors and dramaturgs; weekly staged readings of plays and screenplays followed by discussions; bimonthly playwriting and screenwriting workshops; periodic dramaturgy workshops; annual short-play marathon; annual One-Act Play Contest with $300 first prize, $100 second and third prizes and videotaped staged reading for all winners, *deadline:* 30 Sept 2004 (send SASE for guidelines), *notification:* 1 Nov 2004. **Financial arrangement:** subscription of $190 a year or $55 a quarter for resident of Los Angeles, Orange or Ventura counties; $68 annual subscription for nonresident; nonmember may submit script for reading. **Application procedure:** script only. **Deadline:** ongoing. **Notification:** 2-6 months. **Dates:** year-round.

FLORIDA PLAYWRIGHTS' PROCESS

Altered Stages and Mahaffey Theater Foundation; 736 Scotland St;
    Dunedin, FL 34698; (727) 734-0880, FAX 734-0880;
    email flplaypro@yahoo.com
Elizabeth Brincklow, *Artistic Director*

Open to: playwrights. **Description:** up to 3 plays receive 3-4 months of workshops, rehearsals and staged readings, culminating in production with moderated audience discussion. **Financial arrangement:** $400 and maximum travel stipend of $250. **Guidelines:** playwright must be resident of FL, 19 years of age or older; unproduced and unpublished one-act or full-length play; cast limit of 6; maximum running time 2 hours; simple props and set. **Application procedure:** email or call for guidelines. **Deadline:** 8 Nov 2004. **Notification:** 31 Jan 2005. **Dates:** Feb-May 2005.

THE FRANK SILVERA WRITERS' WORKSHOP

Box 1791; Manhattanville Station; New York, NY 10027; (212) 281-8832,
    FAX 281-8839 (call first); email playrite@earthlink.net;
    website www.fsww.org
Garland Lee Thompson, *Founding Executive Director*

Open to: playwrights. **Description:** upper Manhattan- and Harlem-based program which includes Monday series of readings of new plays by new and established writers, followed by critiques; Saturday seminars conducted by master playwrights; staged readings; and 2-3 showcases and readers' theatre productions a year. **Financial arrangement:** $35 annual fee plus $10 per Saturday class; Monday-night readings free. **Guidelines:** interested in new plays by writers of all colors and backgrounds. **Application procedure:** attend Sep open house; submitting script and attending Monday-night session encouraged; call for information.

FREDERICK DOUGLASS CREATIVE ARTS CENTER WRITING WORKSHOPS

270 West 96th St; New York, NY 10025; (212) 864-3375,
FAX 864-3474 (call first); email fdcac@aol.com;
website www.fdcac.org
Kermit Frazier, *Acting President*

Open to: playwrights, screenwriters, television writers. **Description:** 4 cycles per year of 8-week beginning and advanced playwriting workshops; advanced workshops include readings; also film and television writing workshops; weekly meetings. **Financial arrangement:** $200 fee per workshop; author of play given staged reading receives $50. **Application procedure:** contact FDCAC for information. **Deadline:** Sep 2004 for 1st cycle; Jan 2005 for 2nd cycle; Apr 2005 for 3rd cycle; Jun 2005 for 4th cycle; call for exact dates.

GENESIUS THEATRE GUILD

520 8th Ave, Suite 329; New York, NY 10018; email info@genesiusguild.org;
website www.genesiusguild.org
Thomas Morrissey, *Artistic Director*

Open to: playwrights, translators, composers, librettists, lyricists, solo performers. **Description:** program offering range of developmental services including in-house readings, staged readings, and workshop and showcase productions; development process varies according to needs of script. **Financial arrangement:** free. **Application procedure:** synopsis or full script. **Deadline:** ongoing. **Dates:** year-round.

HAROLD PRINCE MUSICAL THEATRE PROGRAM

The Directors Company; 311 West 43rd St, Suite 307;
New York, NY 10036; (212) 246-5877, FAX 246-5882;
website www.thedirectorscompany.org
HPMTP Selection Committee

Open to: playwrights, composers, librettists, lyricists. **Description:** program supports creation, development and production of new musicals; writers and composers work collaboratively with director under guidance of program's artistic directors and Harold Prince; process includes monthly meetings, readings and presentation for invited audience in New York City. **Financial arrangement:** commissioning and optioning fees available. **Guidelines:** musicals in any stage of development; call for guidelines. **Application procedure:** full scripts accepted from agent or with professional recommendation; all others submit synopsis, 15-page dialogue sample and 6-song cassette or CD. **Deadline:** ongoing. **Notification:** 6-9 months.

HARVEST FESTIVAL OF NEW AMERICAN PLAYS

State Theater Company; Box 1566; Austin, TX 78767;
(512) 692-0509, FAX 472-7199;
email mpolgar@austintheatrealliance.org;
website www.austintheatrealliance.org
Michelle Polgar, *Associate Artistic Director*

Open to: playwrights. **Description:** 2-4 plays receive 2 weeks of rehearsals culminating in staged readings; plays considered for future full production. **Financial arrangement:** stipend, travel and housing. **Guidelines:** full-length play or adaptation not produced professionally; 1-submission limit. **Application procedure:** agent submission only. **Deadline:** 1 Mar 2005; no submission before 1 Dec 2004. **Notification:** 1 Sep 2005. **Dates:** Nov 2005.

HEDGEROW HORIZONS

146 West Rose Valley Rd; Wallingford, PA 19086; (610) 565-4211,
FAX 565-1672; email hedgerowtheatre@comcast.net
Walt Vail, *Literary Manager*

Open to: playwrights. **Description:** 5 full-length plays and 2 one-acts each given 1 rehearsal and 1 public reading. **Financial arrangement:** free. **Guidelines:** playwright must be resident of DE, PA or NJ; play not produced professionally. **Application procedure:** send SASE for guidelines. **Deadline:** 28 Feb 2005. **Notification:** 30 Apr 2005. **Dates:** 30 May 2005.

INNOVATIVE STAGES

Box 659; Bronxville, NY 10708; (914) 698-1052;
email info@innovativestages.com; website www.innovativestages.com
John Driver, *Co-Artistic Director*

Open to: playwrights, composers, librettists, lyricists. **Description:** 10 plays or musicals a year receive 3 script-in-hand readings followed by audience feedback. **Financial arrangement:** free. **Guidelines:** play or musical not previously produced in New York City; preference given to local writers; small cast preferred. **Application procedure:** first 15 pages of script, resume, synopsis and $10 fee; for musical, send sample CD; online submission preferred. **Deadline:** ongoing. **Notification:** 2-4 months.

THE LARK THEATRE COMPANY

939 Eighth Ave, Suite 301; New York, NY 10019; (212) 246-2676,
FAX 246-2609; email submissions@larktheatre.org;
website www.larktheatre.org
Miles Lott, *Literary Manager*

Open to: playwrights, translators, composers, librettists, lyricists. **Description:** organization providing developmental services for culturally diverse group of American and international plays. Playwrights Week: 8 plays receive 10-15 hours of rehearsal with actors, director and dramaturg, culminating in staged reading. Playwrights selected for Playwrights Week may have opportunity to participate in

Studio Retreat: 15 plays receive 20 hours of rehearsal with actors, director and dramaturg, culminating in staged reading followed by audience discussion; or BareBones: 7 plays receive workshop production. **Financial arrangement:** possible stipend for travel and housing. **Guidelines:** write for guidelines or download from web. **Application procedure:** script and $15 fee. **Deadline:** 31 Dec 2004; no submission before 1 Jun 2004. **Notification:** 8 months. **Dates:** Jun 2005.

LITTLE FESTIVAL OF THE UNEXPECTED
Portland Stage Company; Box 1458; Portland, ME 04104; (207) 774-1043,
FAX 774-0576; email literary@portlandstage.com;
website www.portlandstage.com
Tami Ramaker, *Managing Director*

Open to: playwrights. **Description:** 3-5 scripts given week of rehearsal and staged reading; some years reserved specifically for finalists of the Clauder Competition for New England Playwrights. **Financial arrangement:** $500 stipend; housing and some travel support. **Guidelines:** see website for complete guidelines. **Application procedure:** 10-page dialogue sample with cast breakdown and summary. **Deadline:** 1 Dec 2004. **Notification:** Feb 2005. **Dates:** late spring 2005.

LONG BEACH PLAYHOUSE NEW WORKS FESTIVAL
5021 East Anaheim St; Long Beach, CA 90804; (562) 494-1014,
FAX 961-8616; email lbph75@aol.com; website www.lbph.com
Elaine Herman, *Artistic Director/Literary Manager*

Open to: playwrights. **Description:** 4 plays chosen for annual staged reading attended by public and professional critics who provide written and oral feedback; playwright receives videotape of reading; plays may receive subsequent full production. **Financial arrangement:** $100 honorarium. **Guidelines:** unpublished, unproduced full-length plays. **Application procedure:** script, synopsis, character breakdown, submission form (download from web) and $10 fee. **Deadline:** 1 Nov 2004. **Notification:** Feb 2005. **Dates:** Mar-Jun 2005.

LORNA LITTLEWAY'S JUNETEENTH JAMBOREE OF NEW PLAYS
Box 3463; Louisville, KY 40201-3463; (502) 636-4200;
email juneteenthlegacy@aol.com
Lorna Littleway, *Founder/Producing Director*

Open to: playwrights. **Description:** 6 plays given professional staged reading during 3-week festival. **Financial arrangement:** free. **Guidelines:** plays which address the African-American experience and explore any of 5 themes: 19th-century African-American experience; pre- and Harlem Renaissance era; Caribbean/Native American influence on African-Americans; African-American youth and contemporary issues; and new images of women; young writers encouraged to apply. **Application procedure:** 4 copies of script and $15 fee (3 scripts and fee to Louisville address and

1 script to: 605 Water St, #21B; New York, NY 10002). **Deadline:** 15 Apr 2005; no submission before 15 Dec 2004. **Notification:** 30 Apr 2005. **Dates:** Jun 2005.

MANHATTAN PLAYWRIGHTS UNIT
338 West 19th St, #6B; New York, NY 10011-3982; (212) 989-0948
Saul Zachary, *Artistic Director*

Open to: playwrights, screenwriters. **Description:** developmental workshop meeting weekly for in-house readings and discussions of members' works-in-progress; end-of-season series of staged readings of new plays. **Financial arrangement:** free. **Guidelines:** produced or published writer. **Application procedure:** letter of inquiry, resume and SASE for response. **Deadline:** ongoing.

MARK TAPER FORUM KIRK DOUGLAS THEATRE DEVELOPMENTAL PROGRAMS
601 West Temple St; Los Angeles, CA 90012; (213) 972-8033;
        email scripts@ctgh.org; website www.taperahmanson.com
Pier Carlo Talenti, *Literary Manager*
(Also see entry in Production)

ASIAN THEATRE WORKSHOP (ATW)

Open to: playwrights, solo performers. **Description:** ongoing developmental program including Asian Pacific American Friends of Center Theatre Group (APAF) Reading Series; discussions with outside theatre artists; workshop productions. **Financial arrangement:** honorarium. **Guidelines:** Asian-Pacific playwright. **Application procedure:** script and resume. **Deadline:** ongoing.

BLACKSMYTHS

Open to: playwrights, solo performers. **Description:** ongoing developmental program including writers' group, staged readings and workshops. **Financial arrangement:** honorarium. **Guidelines:** African-American playwright; resident of Los Angeles area. **Application procedure:** script and resume. **Deadline:** ongoing.

LATINO THEATRE INITIATIVE (LTI)

Open to: playwrights, solo performers. **Description:** ongoing developmental program including staged readings and workshops. **Financial arrangement:** remuneration varies. **Guidelines:** Latino playwright. **Application procedure:** script and resume. **Deadline:** ongoing.

NEW WORK FESTIVAL

Open to: playwrights, solo performers. **Description:** 12-14 plays given 2 weeks development and an open public rehearsal. **Financial arrangement:** remuneration varies. **Guidelines:** unproduced, unpublished play. **Application procedure:** 5-10 sample pages, brief synopsis and resume. **Deadline:** 1 Mar 2005.

OTHER VOICES PROJECT

Open to: playwrights, solo performers. **Description:** ongoing developmental program including community and professional development; staged readings; workshops; Summer Chautauqua: biennial week-long seminar. **Financial arrangement:** remuneration varies. **Guidelines:** disabled playwright writing about disability; program designed to increase presence of disabled community in mainstream theatre. **Application procedure:** script and resume; call for guidelines for Summer Chautauqua. **Deadline:** call for information.

MUSICAL WRITERS' PLAYGROUND

(Formerly Musical Development Workshop)
215 West 75th St, Suite 3E; New York, NY 10023; (212) 502-3640,
  FAX (425) 671-1722; email musicalwriters@aol.com;
  website www.musicalwritersplayground.com
DJ Salisbury, *Artistic Director*

Open to: composers, librettists, lyricists. **Description:** 20 writers meet bimonthly for 1 year to present and develop new projects in a structured environment; established Broadway directors, producers, composers and lyricists brought in as guest speakers; 4 shows given Oct staged reading with cast and director for audience of producers, professional developmental organizations and directors. **Financial arrangement:** $300 annual membership fee; some scholarships available. **Application procedure:** application and work samples; call or download application from web. **Deadline:** 1 Dec 2002. **Notification:** 15 Jan 2003. **Dates:** Jan–Nov 2003.

THE NEW HARMONY PROJECT

Box 441062; Indianapolis, IN 46244; (317) 464-1103;
  website www.newharmonyproject.org
Joel Grynheim, *Project Director*

Open to: playwrights, composers, librettists, screenwriters. **Description:** 4-6 scripts given 2 weeks intensive development with professional community of directors, actors, producers, dramaturgs and musical directors. **Financial arrangement:** travel, room and board. **Guidelines:** narrative works that "emphasize the dignity of the human spirit and the worth of the human experience." **Application procedure:** script, 10-page dialogue sample of same script, resume, project proposal and statement of artistic purpose; for musicals also include 5 copies of CD. **Deadline:** 1 Oct 2004. **Notification:** 1 Mar 2005. **Dates:** 20 May–5 Jun 2005.

NEW PERSPECTIVES NEW PLAY DEVELOPMENT PROGRAM

750 Eighth Ave, #601; New York, NY 10036; (212) 730-2030,
  FAX 398-2561; email info@newperspectivestheatre.org;
  website www.newperspectivestheatre.org
Ariel Nazarian, *Director of New Play Development*

Open to: playwrights. **Description:** 5-10 plays chosen each year for range of developmental services from rehearsed staged readings with audience feedback to full workshop productions; development process varies according to needs of script; special interest in works by women and minority writers and/or works with a multicultural focus. **Financial arrangement:** free. **Guidelines:** full-length plays that "address critical social issues." **Application procedure:** 15-page dialogue sample, synopsis and character breakdown. **Deadline:** ongoing. **Notification:** 2-6 months from submission date. **Dates:** year-round.

NEW VISIONS/NEW VOICES

The Kennedy Center Youth and Family Programs; 2700 F Street NW; Washington, DC 20566; (202) 416-8880, FAX 416-8297; email yfp@kennedy-center.org; website www.kennedy-center.org/education/nvnv.html

Kim Peter Kovac, *Senior Program Director of Youth and Family Programs*

Open to: playwrights. **Description:** biennial program; up to 8 plays given rehearsals and staged readings. **Guidelines:** playwright must be sponsored by theatre; unproduced plays for young and family audiences; call for information and application. **Financial arrangement:** small stipend to assist with travel. **Application procedure:** sponsoring theatre submits completed application and supporting materials. **Deadline:** 1 Oct 2005. **Notification:** 1 Feb 2006. **Dates:** May 2006.

NEW VOICES PLAY DEVELOPMENT PROGRAM

Plowshares Theatre Company; 2870 East Grand Blvd, Suite 600; Detroit, MI 48202-3146; (313) 872-0279, FAX 872-0067; email plowshares@earthlink.net; website www.plowshares.org

Gary Anderson, *Producing Artistic Director*

Open to: playwrights, solo performers. **Description:** up to 6 plays-in-progress given 2 weeks of rehearsal with professional company of actors, directors and dramaturgs, culminating in 2 staged readings followed by audience discussion; program provides marketing assistance following development; possible future full production. **Financial arrangement:** $1000 to play chosen best of festival; some travel stipends available. **Guidelines:** African-American playwright; unproduced play addressing the African-American experience. **Application procedure:** 3 copies of script, synopsis, resume and bio. **Deadline:** ongoing. **Dates:** ongoing.

NEW YORK FOUNDATION FOR THE ARTS
FISCAL SPONSORSHIP PROGRAM

155 Avenue of the Americas, 14th Floor; New York, NY 10013-1507; (212) 366-6900, ext 223, FAX (646) 486-3285; email sponsor@nyfa.org; website www.nyfa.org/fs

Mary Six Rupert, *Program Officer*

Open to: playwrights, translators, composers, librettists, lyricists, solo performers, screenwriters, television and radio writers. **Description:** program provides fiscal sponsorship, financial services and technical assistance to individuals or organizations without not-for-profit status so that they can seek funds from foundations, corporations and individuals that require not-for-profit status in order to contribute funds. The program has two categories: Artists' Projects (individual artists or collaborating artists); and Emerging Organizations (emerging arts organizations in the process of obtaining not-for-profit status). Program does not offer grants or provide funding. **Financial arrangement:** as a service fee, NYFA retains a percentage of grants and contributions it receives on behalf of a project; $50-100 one-time processing fee. **Guidelines:** selection based on artistic excellence, uniqueness and fundability of project, and on artist's previous work and proven ability to complete proposed work. **Application procedure:** write for application and guidelines or download from web. **Deadline:** Nov 2004; May 2005; contact NYFA for exact dates. **Notification:** 8 weeks.

THE NEXT STAGE FESTIVAL OF NEW PLAYS
The Cleveland Play House; 8500 Euclid Ave;
 Cleveland, OH 44106-0189; (216) 795-7010, ext 207,
 FAX 795-7005
Seth Gordon, *Director of New Play Development*

Open to: playwrights. **Description:** annual mid-winter festival of 4-8 rehearsed readings over 1-month period; plays receive 3-4 rehearsal days with director, dramaturg and professional cast and 1-2 public readings with audience discussion; at least 1 play fully produced in following theatre season. **Financial arrangement:** stipend, travel and housing. **Guidelines:** unproduced full-length play or musical; must give theatre 90-day option on future production. **Application procedure:** letter of inquiry, brief synopsis, 10-page dialogue sample, resume, reviews and SASP for acknowledgement of receipt; include cassestte for musicals. **Deadline:** ongoing. **Notification:** 3-6 months. (See The Cleveland Play House in Production.)

NYC PLAYWRIGHTS LAB
Box 171; Peck Slip Station; New York, NY 10272; (212) 732-1020
Dina von Zweck, *Director of New Plays*

Open to: playwrights. **Description:** 10-session annual developmental workshop; writers meet weekly for readings of work-in-progress and critiques. **Financial arrangement:** free. **Guidelines:** playwrights must attend all 10 workshops. **Application procedure:** send SASE for guidelines and application. **Deadline:** 30 Apr 2005. **Notification:** 1 Aug 2005. **Dates:** Oct-Jan.

ONE ACTS IN PERFORMANCE
Polaris North, c/o Diane Martella; 1265 Broadway, Room 803;
 New York, NY 10001; (212) 684-1985
Diane Martella, *Treasurer/Co-Sponsor*

Open to: playwrights. **Description:** approximately every 6 months, 3-5 plays given brief rehearsal period, culminating in workshop production followed by informal audience discussion. **Guidelines:** unproduced one-act play not more than 30 minutes long; 4-character maximum; single set. **Financial arrangement:** free. **Application**

procedure: script with SASE for response. **Deadline:** ongoing. **Notification:** 6-8 weeks. **Dates:** year-round.

O'NEILL MUSIC THEATER CONFERENCE

O'Neill Theater Center; 305 Great Neck Rd; Waterford, CT 06385;
(860) 443-5378, FAX 443-9653; website www.oneilltheatercenter.org
Artistic Director

Open to: composers, librettists, lyricists. **Description:** developmental period of 3-4 weeks each summer at O'Neill Theater Center for new music-theatre works of all genres; some works developed privately in residence, others presented as public readings. **Financial arrangement:** stipend, travel, room and board. **Guidelines:** unproduced works-in-progress; commissioned and optioned work acceptable; adaptations acceptable if rights have been obtained. **Application procedure:** send SASE for guidelines and application form. **Deadline:** 3 Jan 2005. **Dates:** Jul–early Aug 2005.

O'NEILL PLAYWRIGHTS CONFERENCE

O'Neill Theater Center; 305 Great Neck Rd; Waterford, CT 06385;
(860) 443-5378, ext 300
Artistic Director

Open to: playwrights. **Description:** 4-week conference at O'Neill Theater Center, Waterford, CT; 12-15 plays developed and presented as staged readings. **Financial arrangement:** stipend, travel, room and board. **Application procedure:** send SASE in fall 2004 for guidelines. **Deadline:** 15 Oct 2004. **Notification:** Apr 2005. **Dates:** Jun–Jul 2005.

ORANGE COUNTY PLAYWRIGHTS ALLIANCE

Box 6927; Fullerton, CA 92834; (714) 962-7686; email firenbones@aol.com;
website www.ocpaplaywrights.org
Eric Eberwein, *Director*

Open to: playwrights. **Description:** ongoing developmental workshop meeting every 2 weeks; up to 12 scripts each year receive staged reading or possible production. **Financial arrangement:** $80 annual membership fee. **Guidelines:** residents of Orange County and greater Los Angeles area only. **Application procedure:** work sample and resume. **Deadline:** ongoing. **Notification:** 2 months.

ORLANDO SHAKESPEARE FESTIVAL'S PLAYLAB

Orlando-UCF Shakespeare Festival; 812 East Rollins St, Suite 100;
Orlando, FL 32803; (407) 447-1700 ext 249; FAX 447-1701;
email erich@shakespearefest.org;
website www.shakespearefest.org/playlab.htm
Eric Hissom, *PlayLab Director*

Open to: playwrights, composers, librettists, lyricists. **Description:** 6 plays chosen for development through year-long reading series; 2 plays selected for 2-week developmental program culminating in workshop production. **Financial**

arrangement: authors of plays selected for workshop production receive $300 stipend, travel, housing. **Guidelines:** unpublished full-length play or musical not professionally produced; plays must be based on or inspired by classic literature or historical figures, cast limit of 6; musicals must be adaptations of classic literature or Shakespeare, cast limit of 8. **Application procedure:** 10-page dialogue sample, 1-page synopsis, character breakdown, resume and letter of inquiry including email address; for musicals include cassette or CD of 4 songs. **Deadline:** 1 Mar 2005. **Notification:** 1 Aug 2005. **Dates:** year-round

PAGE 73 PRODUCTIONS, INC.

Box 800; New York, NY 10013; (212) 851–8997, FAX (646) 349–3481; email info@p73.org; website www.p73.org

Liz Jones, *Producing Director*

Open to: playwrights, composers, librettists, lyricists. **Description:** organization providing year-round developmental services; scripts may receive staged reading, workshop or showcase production; 1 playwright selected for fellowship. **Financial arrangement:** small stipend for work given showcase production; $2000 for fellowship. **Guidelines:** playwright whose work has not received major regional or New York production; musicals accepted only if complete. **Application procedure:** open submission for fellowship, guidelines on web; all others, script and resume submitted by agent or with professional recommendation only. **Deadline:** Mar 2005; exact date TBA; ongoing for fellowship. **Dates:** year-round.

PITTSBURGH NEW WORKS FESTIVAL

Box 42419; Pittsburgh, PA 15203; (412) 881–6888; email info@pittsburghnewworks.org; website www.pittsburghnewworks.org

Paige Pertz, *President*

Open to: playwrights. **Description:** 12 plays for adult audiences and 2 for young audiences given full production and 6 given staged reading by 20 collaborating theatre companies during annual 4-week fall festival. **Financial arrangement:** $50 stipend; $500 award for best play. **Guidelines:** unproduced one-act for young or adult audiences; no longer than 40 minutes; cast limit of 8; 1-submission limit in each category. **Application procedure:** 3 copies of script, $10 fee and SASE for response; call for guidelines or download from web. **Deadline:** 3 Apr 2005. **Notification:** mid-Jun 2005. **Dates:** Sep 2005.

PLAYFORMERS

20 Waterside Plaza, Apt 11G; New York, NY 10010; (212) 213–9835

John Fritz, *Executive Director*

Open to: playwrights. **Description:** playwrights' support group meets once a month for readings of works-in-progress and critiques. **Financial arrangement:** $15 initiation fee upon acceptance; $75 annual dues. **Guidelines:** playwright invited to attend meetings as guest before applying for membership. **Application procedure:** script and resume. **Deadline:** ongoing. **Dates:** Sep–Jun.

PLAYLABS

The Playwrights' Center; 2301 Franklin Ave;
  Minneapolis, MN 55406-1099; (612) 332-7481;
  email info@pwcenter.org; website www.pwcenter.org
Kristen Gandrow, *Director of Playwright Services*

Open to: playwrights, solo performers. **Description:** 3–4 new works given 2 weeks of development with playwright's choice of professional director, dramaturg and Twin Cities actors, culminating in staged reading followed by audience discussion. **Financial arrangement:** honorarium, travel, housing and per diem. **Guidelines:** U.S. citizen or permanent resident; writer must be available to attend entire conference; unproduced, unpublished play, solo performance piece or mixed-media piece; full-length works preferred. **Application procedure:** application and work sample; send SASE for application after 1 Oct 2004. **Deadline:** 1 Dec 2004. **Notification:** 1 May 2005. **Dates:** 6–20 Jul 2005.

THE PLAY PEN

The Asylum; Box 13380; Las Vegas, NV 89112; (702) 604-3417,
  FAX 650-0242; email asylum@asylumtheatre.org;
  website www.asylumtheatre.org
Sarah O'Connell, *Artistic Director*

Open to: playwrights. **Description:** 3 times a year, 3 plays-in-progress given 1 week of rehearsal each with resident company culminating in 1 public staged reading followed by audience discussion. **Financial arrangement:** $50 stipend and housing. **Guidelines:** play not produced professionally. **Application procedure:** script only. **Deadline:** ongoing. **Notification:** 1 May 2005. **Dates:** ongoing.

PLAYWRIGHTS' CENTER OF SAN FRANCISCO
STAGED READINGS

588 Sutter St, #403; San Francisco, CA 94102; (415) 820-3206,
  website playwrightscentersf.org
Producing Director: Staged Readings

Open to: playwrights. **Description:** developmental program meeting weekly for 1 staged reading, monthly for reading and discussion of works-in-progress. **Financial arrangement:** $40-60 annual membership fee. **Application procedure:** members only submit script, cast list and supporting materials; see website for guidelines. **Deadline:** ongoing.

PLAYWRIGHTS DEVELOPMENT PROGRAM

The Group at Strasberg; 7936 Santa Monica Blvd;
West Hollywood, CA 90046; (323) 650-7777;
website www.strasberg.com
Literary Manager

Open to: playwrights. **Description:** 3 plays per season given 2 weeks of rehearsal culminating in workshop production; plays considered for subsequent full production. **Financial arrangement:** small stipend, travel and housing. **Guidelines:** plays not previously produced; prefers works-in-progress. **Application procedure:** first 5 pages of script, synopsis, resume and $15 fee. **Deadline:** ongoing. **Notification:** ongoing. **Dates:** year-round.

PLAYWRIGHTS FORUM

Box 5322; Rockville, MD 20848; (301) 816-0569; email pforum@erols.com;
website www.erols.com/pforum/welcome.htm
Ernest Joselovitz, *President*

Open to: playwrights. **Description:** ongoing developmental program including 3-tier range of membership options: Forum 1, workshop program offering sessions of 6 biweekly meetings 3 times a year; Forum 2, professional playwriting group meeting biweekly; and Associate membership offering participation in many of Forum's auxiliary programs but not in workshops; depending on type of membership, members variously eligible for in-house and public readings, Musical Theatre Wing, mentorships, special classes, production observerships, free theatre tickets, internet activities, semiannual conference, organization's newsletter and handbook, and a commissioning program. **Financial arrangement:** for Forum 1, $100 per 15-week session; for Forum 2, $110 every 4 months; Associate membership, $30 fee per year; financial aid available. **Guidelines:** resident of mid-Atlantic area only; for Forum 2, prefers produced playwright or former Forum 1 participant willing to make long-term commitment; send SASE or visit website for further information. **Application procedure:** send SASE or call for information. **Deadline:** for Forum 1: 10 Sep 2004, 10 Jan 2005, 10 May 2005; for Forum 2: ongoing. **Notification:** 4 weeks.

PLAYWRIGHTS GALLERY

119 West 72nd St, Box 2700; New York, NY 10023; (212) 595-2582;
email info@woodstocktheatreco.com
Deborah Savadge, *Coordinator*

Open to: playwrights. **Description:** developmental workshop meeting bimonthly Sep-Jun; includes work-in-progress readings by resident actors; plays receive staged readings at 3-day festivals in fall and spring. **Financial arrangement:** playwrights share cost of space rental. **Application procedure:** 15-20-page work sample. **Deadline:** 1 Jul 2005. **Notification:** 1 Jan 2006.

PLAYWRIGHTS LAB

Pulse Ensemble Theatre; 266 West 37th St, 22nd floor; New York, NY 10018; (212) 695-1596; website www.pulseensembletheatre.org

Brian Richardson, *Company Manager*

Open to: playwrights, solo performers, screenwriters. **Description:** 4-month workshop meeting weekly culminating in public staged reading; possible production. **Guidelines:** experienced playwrights. **Financial arrangement:** $100 monthly fee. **Application procedure:** application, writing sample and professional recommendation. **Deadline:** ongoing. **Notification:** ongoing. **Dates:** year-round.

PLAYWRIGHTS' PLATFORM

Box 35151; Boston, MA 02135; email info@playwrightsplatform.org; website www.playwrightsplatform.org

Pat Brennan, *Artistic Director*

Open to: playwrights. **Description:** ongoing developmental program including weekly workshop held at Hovey Theatre, staged readings, summer festival of full productions, dramaturgical and referral services. **Financial arrangement:** participants encouraged to become members of organization ($35 annual dues). **Guidelines:** MA resident available for regular meetings only; unpublished, unproduced play; one-acts preferred. **Application procedure:** attend 2 readings; then, submit script with cast list. **Deadline:** ongoing.

PLAYWRIGHTS THEATRE OF NEW JERSEY
NEW PLAY DEVELOPMENT PROGRAM

Box 1295; Madison, NJ 07940; (973) 514-1787, ext 18; website www.ptnj.org

Peter Hays, *Literary Manager*

Open to: playwrights. **Description:** new plays developed through sit-down readings, staged readings and workshop productions; liaison with other producing theatres provided. **Financial arrangement:** playwright receives royalty. **Guidelines:** American playwright; unproduced play; send SASE or visit web for guidelines. **Application procedure:** 10-page dialogue sample, developmental history, if any, resume and SASP for acknowledgment of receipt. **Deadline:** 30 Jun 2005; no submission before 1 May 2005. **Notification:** 8 months. **Dates:** year-round.

PUERTO RICAN TRAVELING THEATRE PLAYWRIGHTS' UNIT

141 West 94th St; New York, NY 10025; (212) 354-1293, FAX 307-6769; email allenthe3rd@actorsfcu.net

Allen Davis III, *Director*

Open to: playwrights, solo performers. **Description:** 7-9-month workshops comprised of 2 units, 1 for professional playwrights, 1 for beginners; weekly meetings; spring staged reading series; City "In Sight" showcase production series. **Financial arrangement:** $100 fee per workshop cycle. **Guidelines:** resident of New York City area; Latino or other minority playwright or playwright interested in multicultural theatre. **Application procedure:** for professional unit, submit full-length play; beginners contact director. **Deadline:** 15 Sep 2004. **Notification:** within 4 weeks. **Dates:** Oct 2004-Jul 2005.

REMEMBRANCE THROUGH THE PERFORMING ARTS NEW PLAY DEVELOPMENT

Box 162446; Austin, TX 78716; (512) 329-9118; email RemPerArts@aol.com
Rosalyn Rosen, *Artistic Director*

Open to: playwrights. **Description:** 8 playwrights chosen annually for developmental workshops, culminating in staged readings or work-in-progress productions; plays subsequently given referral to nationally recognized theatres for world premieres. **Financial arrangement:** $350 fee per workshop. **Guidelines:** U.S. resident; concept or full-length play that has not received Equity production. **Application procedure:** email concept or send script, synopsis, resume and SASE. **Deadline:** ongoing.

THE RICHARD RODGERS AWARDS

American Academy of Arts and Letters; 633 West 155th St;
    New York, NY 10032-7599; (212) 368-5900, FAX 491-4615
Richard Rodgers Awards

Open to: playwrights, composers, librettists, lyricists. **Description:** 1 or more works a year given full production, studio/lab production or staged readings by not-for-profit theatre in New York City; writer(s) participate in rehearsal process. **Financial arrangement:** free. **Guidelines:** U.S. citizen or permanent resident; new work by writer/composer not already established in musical theatre; innovative, experimental material encouraged; 1-submission limit; previous submissions ineligible. **Application procedure:** send SASE for application and information. **Deadline:** 1 Nov 2004. **Notification:** Mar 2005.

RISK IS THIS...THE CUTTING BALL NEW PLAYS FESTIVAL

The Cutting Ball Theater; Intersection for the Arts; 446 Valencia St;
    San Francisco, CA 94103; (415) 419-3584; email rob@cuttingball.com;
    website: www.cuttingball.com
Rob Melrose, *Artistic Director*

Open to: playwrights. **Description:** 3 plays given 1 week of rehearsal with resident company of actors and directors, culminating in staged reading; plays considered for subsequent full production. **Financial arrangement:** $200 honorarium, travel and housing. **Guidelines:** playwright available for 1 week of rehearsal in Bay Area during Oct or Nov; prefers non-naturalistic plays with attention to language. **Application procedure:** script, resume and SASE for notification. **Deadline:** 4 Apr 2005. **Notification:** 1 Sep 2005. **Dates:** Oct-Nov 2005.

ROSELILY PRODUCTIONS AUDIENCE DEVELOPMENT READING SERIES

862-49th St; Brooklyn, NY 11220-2442

Laura Cosentino, *Founder and Artistic Director*

Open to: playwrights. **Description:** 2-4 plays or musicals selected for reading series and/or festival. **Financial arrangement:** $100 honorarium to play chosen best of reading series; possible publication. **Guidelines:** American playwright; prefers intergenerational and multicultural casts; each year has specific theme; send SASE for guidelines. **Application procedure:** script and SASE. **Deadline:** Oct 2004; exact date TBA. **Notification:** Nov 2004. **Dates:** year-round.

THE SAMUEL FRENCH OFF-OFF BROADWAY ORIGINAL SHORT PLAY FESTIVAL

45 West 25th St; New York, NY 10010-2751; (212) 206-8990, FAX 206-1429

Kenneth Dingledine, *Festival Coordinator*

Open to: playwrights. **Description:** festival production hosted by Love Creek Productions on Theatre Row in New York City; possible publication by Samuel French (see Publication). **Financial arrangement:** free. **Guidelines:** one-acts less than 35 minutes long only; play must have been developed and produced by theatre or college that has playwriting program; send SASE for application after Jan 2005. **Application procedure:** no submission by playwright; completed application submitted by organization producing work. **Deadline:** Apr 2005; exact date TBA. **Notification:** within 2 weeks. **Dates:** Jun 2005.

THE SCRIPTEASERS

3404 Hawk St; San Diego, CA 92103-3862; (619) 295-4040

Jonathan Dunn-Rankin, *Corresponding Secretary*

Open to: playwrights, screenwriters, television writers. **Description:** writers, directors and actors meet every other Friday evening in private home for cold readings of new scripts, followed by period of constructive criticism; 1 or 2 rehearsed staged readings a year presented at local theatres as showcases. **Financial arrangement:** donations of $1 accepted at each reading. **Guidelines:** guest writer must attend at least 2 readings before submitting script; unproduced script by new or established writer who is resident of San Diego County. **Application procedure:** write or call for guidelines. **Deadline:** ongoing.

SHENANDOAH INTERNATIONAL PLAYWRIGHTS

ShenanArts; 717 Quick's Mill Rd; Staunton, VA 24401;
(540) 248-1868, FAX 248-7728; email theatre@shenanarts.org;
website www.shenanarts.org

Robert Graham Small, *Artistic Director*

Kathleen Tosco, *Managing Director*

Open to: playwrights, screenwriters. **Description:** 4-week retreat for American and international writers at Pennyroyal farm in Shenandoah Valley; program geared to facilitate major rewrite or new draft of existing script; personal writing balanced by workshops and staged readings with professional company of dramaturgs, directors and actors. **Financial arrangement:** travel, room and board. **Guidelines:** competitive admission based on submitted work. **Application procedure:** 2 copies of completed draft of script to be worked on at retreat; personal statement of applicant's background as a writer; SASP for acknowledgment of receipt; write for guidelines or download from web. **Deadline:** 1 Feb 2005. **Notification:** after 10 Jun 2005. **Dates:** Jul–Aug 2005.

SOUTHERN APPALACHIAN PLAYWRIGHTS' CONFERENCE

Southern Appalachian Repertory Theatre; Box 1720; Mars Hill, NC 28754;
(828) 689-1384, FAX 689-1272; email sart@mhc.edu;
website www.sartheatre.com
William Gregg, *Artistic Director*

Open to: playwrights, composers, librettists, lyricists. **Description:** up to 5 writers selected to participate in annual 3-day spring conference at which 1 work by each writer is given reading and critiqued by panel of theatre professionals; 1 work may be selected for production as part of summer 2005 season. **Financial arrangement:** room and board; writer of work selected for production receives $1000 honorarium. **Guidelines:** unproduced, unpublished full-length play or musical; works that explore Southern Appalachian life, traditions and culture encouraged. **Application procedure:** script with author's name on title page only, synopsis, character breakdown and resume. **Deadline:** 30 Sep 2004.

SUMMERNITE

School of Theatre, Stevens Bldg; Northern Illinois University;
DeKalb, IL 60115-2854; (815) 753-1334, FAX 753-8415
Christopher Markle, *Artistic Director*

Open to: playwrights. **Description:** 2 plays chosen for full production; some plays chosen for periodic staged readings. **Financial arrangement:** royalties for plays chosen for production. **Guidelines:** special interest in large-cast full-length plays or translations not previously produced in Chicago area. **Application procedure:** agent submission only. **Deadline:** ongoing. **Notification:** 2 months. **Dates:** May–Aug 2005.

THE SUNDANCE INSTITUTE FEATURE FILM PROGRAM

8857 West Olympic Blvd; Beverly Hills, CA 90211; (310) 360-1981,
FAX 360-1969; website www.sundance.org

Open to: playwrights, screenwriters, filmmaking teams (e.g., writer/director). **Description:** program includes 5-day Screenwriters Labs each Jan and Jun offering participants one-on-one problem-solving sessions with professional screenwriters; 3-week Filmmakers Lab in Jun in which projects are explored through work with directors, writers, actors, cinematographers, producers, editors and other resource personnel; network/advisory service offers practical and creative assistance to selected projects. **Financial arrangement:** travel, room and board for at least 1 writer/filmmaker per project; possible room and board for additional members of team. **Guidelines:** "compelling, original, narrative feature film scripts (they can be based on a true story or be adaptations of plays, novels, short stories, etc.) which represent the unique vision of the writer and/or director"; special interest in supporting new talent committed to making their films independently and artists in transition (e.g., theatre artist who wants to work in film, writer who wants to direct); visit website for guidelines and application. **Application procedure:** application, cover letter, first 5 pages of screenplay, synopsis, bios of project participants and $30 fee; applicants who pass 1st round of selection will be asked to send full screenplay. **Deadline:** 1 May 2005. **Notification:** Jul 2005.

THE SUNDANCE THEATRE LABORATORY

8857 West Olympic Blvd; Beverly Hills, CA 90211; (310) 360-1981,
FAX 360-1975; email philip_himberg@sundance.org;
website www.sundance.org
Philip Himberg, *Producing Artistic Director, Sundance Theatre*
Robert Blacker, *Artistic Director, Sundance Theatre Labs*

Open to: playwrights, solo performers. **Description:** 7-8 scripts workshopped for 20 days. **Financial arrangement:** travel, room and board. **Guidelines:** full-length play, new adaptation and/or translation of classic material, musical, play for young audiences, solo piece; playwright-director teams encouraged. **Application procedure:** send SASE for guidelines and application. **Deadline:** 15 Dec 2004. **Notification:** Apr 2005. **Dates:** Jul 2005.

THE TEN-MINUTE MUSICALS PROJECT

Box 461194; West Hollywood, CA 90046;
website www.tenminutemusical.org
Michael Koppy, *Producer*

Open to: composers, librettists, lyricists, solo performers. **Description:** up to 10 brief pieces selected during annual cycle for possible inclusion in full-length anthology-musicals to be produced at Equity theatres in U.S. and Canada; occasionally some pieces workshopped using professional actors and director. **Financial arrangement:** $250 royalty advance with equal share of licensing royalties when produced. **Guidelines:** complete work with definite beginning, middle and end, 7-14 minutes long, in any musical style or genre; adaptations of strongly structured material in the public domain, or for which rights have been obtained, are encouraged; cast of 2-10, prefers 6-10; write for guidelines. **Application procedure:** script, lead sheets and cassette or CD of sung material. **Deadline:** 31 Aug 2005. **Notification:** 30 Nov 2005.

THEATRE WEST WRITERS WORKSHOP

3333 Cahuenga Blvd W; Los Angeles, CA 90068; (323) 851-4839,
FAX 851-5286; website www.theatrewest.org
Doug Haverty and Chris DiGiovanni, *Moderators*

Open to: playwrights, translators, librettists, lyricists. **Description:** weekly development workshop presenting 2 staged readings a year and limited-run workshop productions. **Financial arrangement:** $40 monthly fee. **Guidelines:** full-length plays, translations, adaptations and plays for young audiences; large-cast works encouraged. **Application procedure:** script and resume with SASE for response. **Deadline:** ongoing. **Notification:** 4 months. **Dates:** year-round.

UTAH SHAKESPEAREAN FESTIVAL
PLAYS-IN-PROGRESS SERIES
351 West Center St; Cedar City, UT 84720-2498; (435) 586-7880,
FAX 865-8003; email phillips@suu.edu; website www.bard.org
Aden Ross, *Director of Plays-in-Progress Series*

Open to: playwrights. **Description:** 4 plays receive up to 5 rehearsals with director and Festival actors, culminating in 2 staged readings. **Financial arrangement:** travel and housing provided. **Guidelines:** plays with no previous mainstage production only; classical themes encouraged. **Application procedure:** script only. **Deadline:** Dec 1 2004 (no submissions before 1 Jul 2004). **Notification:** 15 Mar 2005. **Dates:** Aug 2005.

THE WATERFRONT ENSEMBLE AND NEW JERSEY DRAMATISTS
Box 1486; Hoboken, NJ 07030; (201) 708-6535;
email njdramatists@hotmail.com; website www.waterfrontensemble.org
Pete Ernst, *Artistic Director*

Open to: playwrights, translators, solo performers. **Description:** playwright-driven company of actors, directors and playwrights that meets weekly to work on new plays in preparation for productions in New York and New Jersey; 25 one-acts and 3 full-length plays produced each year. **Financial arrangement:** suggested donation of $75 for 3 months. **Guidelines:** NY/NJ-area playwright. **Application procedure:** up to 30-page writing sample and resume. **Deadline:** ongoing. **Notification:** 4-12 months. **Dates:** year-round. **Special programs:** New Jersey All Ages Playwright Festival, *deadline:* 31 Mar 2005; *dates:* Jun 2005; call or write for more information.

WILLIAMSTOWN THEATRE FESTIVAL
229 West 42nd St, Suite 801; New York, NY 10036-7299;
(212) 395-9090, FAX 395-9099; website www.wtfestival.org
Michael Ritchie, *Producer*

Open to: playwrights, composers, librettists, lyricists. **Description:** 4 plays each season given public reading. **Financial arrangement:** travel and housing. **Guidelines:** play not professionally produced. **Application procedure:** agent submission only. **Deadline:** 15 Feb 2005; no submission before 1 Oct 2004. **Notification:** within 6-12 months.

WOMEN PLAYWRIGHTS SERIES

Centenary Stage Company; 400 Jefferson St;
Hackettstown, NJ 07840; (908) 979-0900, FAX 979-4297
email rustc@centenarycollege.edu; website www.centenarystagesco.org
Catherine Rust, *Program Director*

Open to: playwrights. **Description:** 1 play given 1 week of rehearsal with professional actors and director, followed by staged reading and possible mainstage production. **Financial arrangement:** $200 honorarium; room and board; 1 playwright each session receives travel. **Guidelines:** woman playwright; full-length play. **Application procedure:** 10-20-page writing sample, synopsis, letter of recommendation from field. **Deadline:** 1 Nov 2004. **Notification:** 30 Jan 2005. **Dates:** Apr 2005.

WOMEN'S WORK PROJECT

New Perspectives Theatre Company; 750 Eighth Ave, Suite 601;
New York, NY 10036; (212) 730-2030, FAX 730-2030;
email womenswork@newperspectivestheatre.org;
website www.newperspectivestheatre.org
Miriam Eusebio, *Women's Work Director*

Open to: playwrights. **Description:** up to 2 playwrights chosen for 6-9 month residency to develop full-length play. **Financial arrangement:** free. **Guidelines:** woman playwright; special interest in works by writers of color; unproduced full-length play. **Application procedure:** application and script; download application and guidelines from web. **Deadline:** 15 May 2005. **Notification:** 15 Aug 2005. **Dates:** year-round.

YOUNG PLAYWRIGHTS INC.

306 West 38th St, Suite 300; New York, NY 10018; (212) 594-5440;
email writeaplay@aol.com; website youngplaywrights.org

ADVANCED PLAYWRITING WORKSHOP
Advanced Playwriting Coordinator

Open to: playwrights. **Description:** weekly classes; guest lectures by prominent American playwrights; viewing of Broadway and Off-Broadway plays; development of new short play for public performance with professional actors and director. **Financial arrangement:** playwright must work minimal amount of office hours in lieu of tuition. **Guidelines:** New York City metropolitan area high school students. **Submission procedure:** application, 3-5-page writing sample, recommendation from teacher or mentor; call or email for application. **Deadline:** 1 Oct 2004. **Dates:** year-round.

URBAN RETREAT
Urban Retreat Coordinator

Open to: playwrights. **Description:** 1-week New York City retreat for writers aged 14-21; guest lectures by prominent American playwrights; one-on-one sessions with teaching artists; 3 intensive daily writing workshops; viewing of Broadway and Off-Broadway plays; development of new short play for public performance with professional actors and director. **Financial arrangement:** $1490 tuition includes meals, transportation in NYC, supervised housing and theatre tickets; limited financial aid available. **Guidelines:** playwright aged 14–21. **Application procedure:** application, 3-5-page writing sample, recommendation from teacher or mentor and $100 fee (applied to tuition; refundable if applicant does not attend); call or email for application. **Deadline:** 15 Apr 2005; 15 Apr 2006. **Dates:** Jul.

PART 2
CAREER
OPPORTUNITIES

Agents

Fellowships and Grants

Emergency Funds

State Arts Agencies

Colonies and Residencies

Membership and Service Organizations

AGENTS

I'm wondering whether or not I should have an agent. Where can I get information to help me decide?

Visit the Association of Authors' Representatives website at www.AAR-online.org to view their publications on the role of the literary agent, the canon of ethics, and their membership list. Also, see Useful Publications for books you may consult on the subject, ask your fellow playwrights, look at copies of scripts for the names of agents and make an intelligent guess as to whether they would be interested in representing your work.

How do I select the names of appropriate agents to contact?

All of the agents listed here represent playwrights. The Dramatists Guild also has a list of agents available to its members, and provides advice on relationships with agents (see Membership and Service Organizations). You may come across names that appear on none of these lists, but be wary, especially if someone tries to charge you a fee to read your script.

How do I approach an agent?

Do not telephone, do not drop in, do not send manuscripts. Write a brief letter describing your work and asking if the agent would like to see a script. Enclose your professional resume; it should show that you have had work produced or published, and make clear that you look at writing as an ongoing career, not an occasional hobby. If you're a beginning writer who's just finished your first play, you'd probably do better to work on getting a production rather than an agent.

ABRAMS ARTISTS AGENCY

275 7th Ave, 26th Floor; New York, NY 10001; (646) 486-4600
Beth Blickers, Morgan Jenness, Maura Testelbaum, *Agents*

ALAN BRODIE REPRESENTATION LTD.

211 Piccadilly; London W1J 9HF; England; 44-207-917-2871;
email info@alanbrodie.com; website www.alanbrodie.com
Alan Brodie, Sarah McNair, *Agents*

ANN ELMO AGENCY

60 East 42nd St; New York, NY 10165; (212) 661-2880
Mari Cronin, Letti Lee, *Agents*

THE BARBARA HOGENSON AGENCY, INC.

165 West End Ave, Suite 19C; New York, NY 10023; (212) 874-8084
Barbara Hogenson, *Agent*

BRET ADAMS LTD.

448 West 44th St; New York, NY 10036; (212) 765-5630
Bret Adams, Bruce Ostler, *Agents*

DOUGLAS & KOPELMAN ARTISTS, INC.

393 West 49th St, Suite 5G; New York, NY 10019; (212) 445-0160
Sarah Douglas, Charles Kopelman, *Agents*

THE DRAMATIC PUBLISHING COMPANY

311 Washington St; Box 129; Woodstock, IL 60098; (815) 338-7170;
email plays@dramaticpublishing.com; website www.dramaticpublishing.com
Linda Habjan, *Agent*

FARBER LITERARY AGENCY

14 East 75th St, 2E; New York, NY 10021; (212) 861-7075
Ann Farber, Seth Farber, *Agents*

FIFI OSCARD AGENCY, INC.

110 West 40th St, 16th Floor; New York, NY 10018; (212) 764-1100
Carolyn French, Carmen LaVia, Kevin McShane, Fifi Oscard,
Peter Sawyer, *Agents*

GAGE GROUP

14724 Ventura Blvd, Suite 505; Sherman Oaks, CA 91403; (818) 905-3800
315 West 57th St, Suite 408; New York, NY 10019; (212) 541-5250
Martin Gage, *Agent*

THE GERSH AGENCY

41 Madison Ave, 33rd Floor; New York, NY 10010; (212) 997-1818
John Buzzetti, Peter Hagan, Mike Lubin, Scott Yoselow, Kara Baker Young, *Agents*

GRAHAM AGENCY

311 West 43rd St; New York, NY 10036; (212) 489-7730
Earl Graham, *Agent*

GRANT SAVICH KOPALOFF AND ASSOCIATES

6399 Wilshire, Suite 414; Los Angeles, CA 90048; (323) 782-1854
Don Kopaloff, *Agent*

HARDEN-CURTIS ASSOCIATES

850 Seventh Ave, Suite 903; New York, NY 10019; (212) 977-8502
Mary Harden, *Agent*

INTERNATIONAL CREATIVE MANAGEMENT

40 West 57th St; New York, NY 10019; (212) 556-5600
Mitch Douglas, Patrick Herold, Buddy Thomas, Jarrien Steele, *Agents*

THE JIM FLYNN AGENCY

208 West 30th St, Suite 401; New York, NY 10001; (212) 868-1068
Jim Flynn, *Agent*

THE JOYCE KETAY AGENCY

630 9th Ave, Suite 706; New York, NY 10036; (212) 354-6825
Joyce P. Ketay, Carl Mulert, *Agents*

JUDY BOALS INC.

208 West 30th St, Suite 401; New York, NY 10001; (212) 868-0924
Judy Boals, *Agent*

THE LANTZ OFFICE

200 West 57th St, Suite 503; New York, NY 10019; (212) 586-0200
Robert Lantz, *Agent*

MARK CHRISTIAN SUBIAS AGENCY

331 West 57th St, #46; New York, NY 10019; (212) 445-1091
Mark Christian Subias, *Agent*

THE MARTON AGENCY, INC.

1 Union Square West, Suite 612; New York, NY 10003-3303; (212) 255-1908
Tonda Marton, Anne Reingold, *Agents*

PEREGRINE WHITTLESEY AGENCY

345 East 80th St, #31F; New York, NY 10021; (212) 737-0153
Peregrine Whittlesey, *Agent*

PINDER LANE & GARON-BROOKE ASSOCIATES

159 West 53rd St; New York, NY 10019; (212) 489-0880
Dick Duane, Robert Thixton, *Agents*

ROBERT A. FREEDMAN DRAMATIC AGENCY, INC.

1501 Broadway, Suite 2310; New York, NY 10036; (212) 840-5760
Robert A. Freedman, Selma Luttinger, Marta Praeger, *Agents*

ROSENSTONE/WENDER

38 East 29th St, 10th Floor; New York, NY 10016; (212) 725-9445
Ronald Gwiazda, Sonia Pabley, Howard Rosenstone, Phyllis Wender, *Agents*

STEPHEN PEVNER, INC.

382 Lafayette St, 8th Floor; New York, NY 10003; (212) 674-8403
Stephen Pevner, *Producer*

THE SUSAN GURMAN AGENCY, LLC

865 West End Ave, Suite 15A; New York, NY 10025; (212) 749-4618;
website www.gurmanagency.com
Susan Gurman, *Agent*

SUSAN SCHULMAN A LITERARY AGENCY

454 West 44th St; New York, NY 10036; (212) 713-1633

WILLIAM MORRIS AGENCY

1325 Ave of the Americas; New York, NY 10019; (212) 586-5100
Val Day, Peter Franklin, David Kalodner, Biff Liff, Roland Scahill, Susan Weaving, *Agents*

WRITERS & ARTISTS GROUP INTERNATIONAL

19 West 44th St, Suite 1410; New York, NY 10036; (212) 391-1112
William Craver, Christopher Till, *Agents*

FELLOWSHIPS
AND GRANTS

Can I apply directly to all the programs listed in this section?

No. A number of the grant programs we list must be applied to by a producing or presenting organization. However, you should be aware that these programs exist so that you can bring them to the attention of organizations with which you have a working relationship. All or most of the funds disbursed benefit the individual artist by covering commissioning fees, residencies and other expenses related to the creation of new works.

How can I enhance my chances of winning an award?

Apply for as many awards for which you qualify; once you have written the first grant proposal, you can often, with little additional work, adapt it to fit other guidelines. Some deadlines will fall outside the publication period of this biennial sourcebook. All deadlines reflect the next upcoming submission deadline for an organization at press time. Annual deadlines may stay the same from year to year but this is not an absolute—always obtain the latest information (an organization's website is the best place to check) before submitting. Use the Submission Calendar in the back of this book to help you plan your campaign. Start early. In the case of all programs for which you can apply directly, obtain the guidelines and application forms months ahead. Study the guidelines carefully and follow them meticulously. Don't hesitate to ask for advice and assistance from the organization to which you are applying. Submit a well-thought-out, clearly written, neatly typed application—and make sure it arrives in the organization's office by the deadline. (Never assume, without checking, that the deadline is the postmark date.)

THE ALFRED HODDER FELLOWSHIP

The Council of the Humanities; Joseph Henry House;
 Princeton University; Princeton, NJ 08544-5264;
 (609) 258-4717, FAX 258-2783;
 website www.princeton.edu/~humcounc

Open to: playwrights, translators. **Frequency:** annual. **Remuneration:** $54,000 fellowship (approximately). **Guidelines:** humanist in the early stage of career spends academic year at Princeton pursuing independent project; residency required; prefers individual outside of academia; send SASE for guidelines or download from web. **Application procedure:** maximum 10-page work sample (materials will not be returned), 2-3 page project proposal and resume. **Deadline:** 1 Nov 2004.

AMERICAN ANTIQUARIAN SOCIETY FELLOWSHIPS

185 Salisbury St; Worcester, MA 01609; (508) 471-2131, FAX 754-9069;
 email cmcrell@mwa.org; website www.americanantiquarian.org
James David Moran, *Director of Outreach*

Open to: playwrights, translators, composers, librettists, lyricists, solo performers, screenwriters. **Remuneration:** $1200 grant; up to $400 in travel reimbursement. **Guidelines:** fellowships to support historical research which will lead to production of imaginative, non-formulaic works dealing with pre-20th-century American history; prefers work for general public rather than for academic or educational audiences. **Application procedure:** application, work sample, letter of recommendation, resume and 5-page narrative describing project. **Deadline:** 5 Oct 2004. **Notification:** 15 Dec 2004.

THE AMERICAN-SCANDINAVIAN FOUNDATION

58 Park Ave; New York, NY 10016; (212) 879-9779, FAX 249-3444;
 email grants@amscan.org; website www.amscan.org
Fellowship Program

Open to: playwrights, translators, composers, librettists, lyricists. **Frequency:** annual. **Remuneration:** $3000-18,000 grant. **Guidelines:** U.S. citizen or permanent resident with undergraduate degree; grants and fellowships for research and study in Scandinavian countries. **Application procedure:** application, supplementary materials and $10 fee. **Deadline:** 1 Nov 2004. **Notification:** Mar 2005.

THE ARCH AND BRUCE BROWN FOUNDATION

31855 Date Palm Dr, PMB 503; Cathedral City, CA 92234;
 email ArchWrite@aol.com; website www.aabbfoundation.org
Arch Brown, *President*

Open to: playwrights, composers, librettists, lyricists, screenwriters. **Frequency:** award rotates triennially between fiction, short fiction and theatre. **Remuneration:** $1000 grant. **Guidelines:** work which presents gay and lesbian lifestyle in positive way, and which is inspired by historical person, culture, event or work of art; see website for guidelines. **Application procedure:** script and short note describing "historical inspiration" for the work; materials will not be returned. **Deadline:** postmarked by 30 Nov 2005. **Notification:** Apr 2006.

ARIZONA COMMISSION ON THE ARTS
PERFORMING ARTS FELLOWSHIP

417 West Roosevelt St; Phoenix, AZ 85003; (602) 255-5882, FAX 256-0282; email general@arizonaarts.org; website www.arizonaarts.org

Claire West, *Performing Arts Director*

Open to: playwrights, composers. **Frequency:** award rotates triennially among disciplines. **Remuneration:** $5000 fellowship. **Guidelines:** AZ resident 18 years of age or older who is not enrolled for more than 3 credit hours at college or university; see website for guidelines and application. **Application procedure:** application and work sample. **Deadline:** fall 2005 (contingent on funding), exact date TBA.

ARTISTS-IN-BERLIN PROGRAM

To obtain application only:
German Academic Exchange Service (DAAD);
871 United Nations Plaza; New York, NY 10017; (212) 758-3223,
FAX 755-5780; email daadny@daad.org; website www.daad.org

All applications and inquiries to:
Deutscher Akademischer Austauschdienst (DAAD);
Markgrafenstrasse 37; D-10117 Berlin, Germany; 49-030-202-2080,
FAX 49-030-204-1267; email bkp.berlin@daad.de;
website www.daad.de/berlin/

Open to: playwrights, composers, screenwriters. **Frequency:** annual. **Remuneration:** monthly grant to cover living costs and rent during 1-year residency in Berlin (6 months in exceptional cases); workspace provided or paid for; travel for writer and any members of immediate family who will be staying in Berlin for period of residency; health and accident insurance; in some cases specific projects such as readings or publications can be subsidized. **Guidelines:** to enable 15-20 internationally known and qualified young artists to pursue own work while participating in city's cultural life and making contact with local artists; must reside in Berlin for period of grant; German nationals and foreign writers who are resident in Germany ineligible; write for guidelines or download from web. **Application procedure:** application, samples of published work (no manuscripts), preferably in German, otherwise in English or French, for playwrights; scores, records, tapes or published work for composers. **Deadline:** 31 Dec 2004. **Notification:** spring 2005. **Dates:** residency begins between 1 Jan and 30 Jun 2005.

ARTIST TRUST

1835 12th Ave; Seattle, WA 98122; (206) 467-8734, FAX 467-9633;
email info@artisttrust.org; website www.artisttrust.org
Fionn Meade, *Director of Grant Programs*

FELLOWSHIPS

Open to: playwrights, composers, librettists, lyricists, screenwriters, radio and television writers. **Frequency:** biennial for theatre artists (award rotates among disciplines). **Remuneration:** $6000 grant. **Guidelines:** WA resident only; practicing professional artist of exceptional talent and demonstrated ability; award based on creative excellence and continuing dedication to artistic discipline; send SASE for guidelines (available mid-Apr 2005). **Application procedure:** application and work sample. **Deadline:** mid-Jun 2005; exact date TBA (20 Jun in 2003).

GAP (GRANTS FOR ARTIST PROJECTS)

Open to: playwrights, composers, librettists, lyricists, screenwriters, radio and television writers. **Frequency:** annual. **Remuneration:** grant up to $1400. **Guidelines:** WA resident only; grant provides support for artist-generated projects which can include (but is not limited to) the development, presentation or completion of new work; award based on quality of work and on creativity and feasibility of proposed project; send SASE for guidelines (available Dec 2004). **Application procedure:** application and work sample. **Deadline:** 25 Feb 2005.

ARTS INTERNATIONAL/THE FUND FOR U.S. ARTISTS AT INTERNATIONAL FESTIVALS AND EXHIBITIONS

251 Park Ave S, 5th Floor; New York, NY 10010; (212) 674-9744,
FAX 674-9092; email thefund@artsinternational.org;
website www.artsinternational.org/programs/index.htm
Kay Takeda, *Program Manager*

Open to: performing artists and organizations. **Frequency:** triannual. **Remuneration:** grants of up to $25,000 (most grants $1000-10,000) to cover expenses related to festival participation including travel, lodging, artist's fees and per diem. **Guidelines:** U.S. citizen or permanent resident who has been invited to international festival. **Application procedure:** application, work sample, proposal, bio, copy of invitation from festival, full budget showing all costs of participation in festival and festival's contribution to these costs. **Deadline:** 7 Sep 2004; 16 Jan 2005; 3 May 2005. **Notification:** 3 months. (See National Endowment for the Arts International Partnerships in this section.)

ASIAN CULTURAL COUNCIL
437 Madison Ave, 37th Floor; New York, NY 10022-7001;
(212) 812-4300, FAX 812-4299; email acc@accny.org;
website www.asianculturalcouncil.org

JAPAN-UNITED STATES ARTS PROGRAM
Open to: playwrights, composers, librettists, lyricists. **Frequency:** annual. **Remuneration:** amount varies. **Guidelines:** to support residencies in Japan for American artists for a variety of purposes, including creative activities (other than performances), research projects, professional observation tours and specialized training. **Application procedure:** application and project description. **Deadline:** 1 Feb 2005.

AURAND HARRIS CHILDREN'S THEATRE GRANTS AND FELLOWSHIPS
The Children's Theatre Foundation of America; 1114 Red Oak Dr;
Avon, IN 46123; (317) 272-9322;
website www.childrenstheatrefoundation.org
Dorothy Webb, *President*

FELLOWSHIPS
Open to: playwrights. **Frequency:** annual. **Remuneration:** $2500 maximum award. **Guidelines:** U.S. resident; funds to be used for specific projects or professional development of theatre artists who work in the area of children's theatre. **Application procedure:** write for guidelines. **Deadline:** 1 May 2005. **Notification:** 1 Sep 2005. (See listing for The Children's Theatre Foundation of America in Membership and Service Organizations.)

GRANTS
Open to: not-for-profit theatres. **Frequency:** annual. **Remuneration:** grant up to $3000. **Guidelines:** grant to assist in production costs of premiere of new play for children including expenses to enable playwright to participate in rehearsals and attend performances. **Application procedure:** write for guidelines. **Deadline:** 1 May 2005. **Notification:** 1 Sep 2005. (See listing for The Children's Theatre Foundation of America in Membership and Service Organizations.)

BUSH ARTIST FELLOWS PROGRAM
Bush Foundation; 332 Minnesota St, E-900; St. Paul, MN 55101;
(651) 227-5222; website www.bushfoundation.org
Julie Dalgleish, *Program Director*

Open to: playwrights, composers, screenwriters. **Frequency:** award rotates biennially among disciplines. **Remuneration:** $44,000 in equal monthly installments for 12-24 months. **Guidelines:** MN, ND, SD or western WI resident at least 25 years old who is not a student; playwright must have had at least 1 play given full production or workshop production; screenwriter must have had 1 public staged reading or workshop production, or screenplay sale or option. **Application procedure:** write for guidelines and application. **Deadline:** next deadline for playwrights, composers and screenwriters Oct 2004; exact date TBA. **Notification:** Apr 2005.

CINTAS FELLOWSHIPS

c/o Institute of International Education;
  U.S. Student Programs Division; 809 United Nations Plaza;
  New York, NY 10017-3580; (212) 984-5565, FAX 984-5325;
  email cintas@iie.org; website www.iie.org/cintas
Program Manager

Open to: playwrights. **Frequency:** biennial; award rotates among artistic disciplines. **Remuneration:** $10,000 paid in quarterly stipends. **Guidelines:** artist of Cuban decent or citizenship living outside of Cuba. **Application procedure:** call or visit website after Sep 2004 for guidelines. **Deadline:** exact date TBA.

CITY OF LOS ANGELES (C.O.L.A.) PERFORMING ARTS FELLOWSHIPS

City of Los Angeles Cultural Affairs Department;
  433 South Spring St, 10th floor; Los Angeles, CA 90013;
  (213) 473-8590, FAX 473-8352; website www.culturela.org
Arleen Chikami, *Arts Manager II*

Open to: composers, solo performers, performance artists. **Frequency:** annual. **Remuneration:** $10,000 grant. **Guidelines:** resident of L.A. County; minimum 15 years production/performance experience; not open to artists specializing in group presentations; funds to be used to create new solo work to be showcased by city in nonthematic presentation; write for guidelines or download from web. **Deadline:** 8 Oct 2004. **Notification:** 1 May 2005.

DOBIE-PAISANO FELLOWSHIP

University of Texas at Austin; J. Frank Dobie House;
  702 East Dean Keeton St; Austin, TX 78705; (512) 471-8542,
  FAX 471-9997; email aslate@mail.utexas.edu;
  website www.utexas.edu/ogs/paisano
Audrey Slate, *Director*

Open to: playwrights. **Frequency:** annual. **Remuneration:** living allowance to cover 6-month residency at 265-acre ranch; free housing; families welcome. **Guidelines:** native Texan, or playwright who has lived in TX for at least 3 years or has published work about TX; 2 writers selected each year. **Application procedure:** visit website. **Deadline:** 28 Jan 2005. **Notification:** May 2005.

THE DON AND GEE NICHOLL FELLOWSHIPS IN SCREENWRITING

Academy of Motion Picture Arts and Sciences; 1313 North Vine St;
  Los Angeles, CA 90028; (310) 247-3010;
  website www.oscars.org/nicholl
Greg Beal, *Program Coordinator*

Open to: playwrights, screenwriters. **Frequency:** annual. **Remuneration:** up to 5 fellowships of $30,000. **Guidelines:** playwright or screenwriter who has not worked as a professional screenwriter for theatrical films or television or sold screen or television rights for any original story, treatment, screenplay or teleplay; 1st-round selection based on submission of original screenplay or screen adaptation of writer's, or of two collaborators', own original work, 100-130 pages, written in standard screenplay format; write for guidelines after 1 Jan 2004. **Application procedure:** application, screenplay and $30 application fee; application may be downloaded from web. **Deadline:** 1 May 2004. **Notification:** Aug 2004 for 1st-round selection; late Oct 2004 for winners.

ELECTRONIC ARTS GRANT PROGRAM

Experimental Television Center; 109 Lower Fairfield Rd;
  Newark Valley, NY 13811; (607) 687-4341, FAX 687-4341;
  email etc@experimentaltvcenter.org;
  website www.experimentaltvcenter.org
Sherry Miller Hocking, *Program Director*

FINISHING FUNDS

Open to: media artists, including writers and composers, involved in creation of film, audio, video or computer-generated time-based works. **Frequency:** annual. **Remuneration:** up to $2000. **Guidelines:** resident of NY State; funds to be used to assist completion of work which is time-based in conception and execution; work must be presented as installation performance, on video, as website production or must utilize new technologies; write for guidelines. **Application procedure:** 3 copies of application, project description, work samples and resume. **Deadline:** 15 Mar 2005. **Notification:** 6-8 weeks.

PRESENTATION FUNDS

Open to: not-for-profit organizations presenting audio, film, video or computer-generated time-based works. **Frequency:** ongoing. **Remuneration:** grant of up to $900 to assist presentation of work and artist's involvement in activities related to presentation. **Guidelines:** NY State organization; event must be open to public; write for guidelines. **Application procedure:** individual may not apply; application and supporting materials submitted by organization well in advance of event. **Deadline:** ongoing. **Notification:** 15th of month following month of submission.

FULBRIGHT SENIOR SCHOLAR AWARDS
FOR FACULTY AND PROFESSIONALS

Council for International Exchange of Scholars (CIES);
    3007 Tilden St NW, Suite 5L; Washington, DC 20008–3009;
    (202) 686–7877, FAX 362–3442; email apprequest@cies.iie.org;
    website www.cies.org

Open to: scholars and professionals in all areas of theatre and the arts, including playwrights, translators, composers, librettists and lyricists. **Frequency:** annual. **Remuneration:** grant for university lecturing or research in one of more than 140 countries for 2–9 months; amount varies with country of award; travel; maintenance allowance for living costs of grantee and possibly family. **Guidelines:** U.S. citizen; Ph.D., MFA or comparable professional qualifications; university or college teaching experience for lecturing awards. **Application procedure:** application; application may be obtained from website. **Deadline:** 1 Aug 2005. **Notification:** up to 11 months, depending on country.

GEORGE BENNETT FELLOWSHIP

Phillips Exeter Academy; 20 Main St; Exeter, NH 03833–2460;
    website www.exeter.edu
Charles Pratt, *Coordinator, Selection Committee*

Open to: playwrights. **Frequency:** annual. **Remuneration:** academic-year stipend of $10,000; room and board for fellow and family. **Guidelines:** individual who is seriously contemplating or pursuing a career as a writer (in any genre) and who needs time and freedom from material considerations to complete a project in progress; committee favors playwrights who have not yet been produced commercially or at a major not-for-profit theatre; fellow expected to make self and talents available in informal and unofficial way to students interested in writing; send SASE for guidelines and application or visit website (no phone inquiries). **Application procedure:** application, work sample, statement concerning work-in-progress, names of 2 references and $5 fee. **Deadline:** 1 Dec 2004. **Notification:** 15 Mar 2005. **Dates:** Sep 2005–Jun 2006.

HARVARD UNIVERSITY RADCLIFFE INSTITUTE FOR ADVANCED STUDY FELLOWSHIPS

The Radcliffe Institute for Advanced Study; Fellowships Office;
    34 Concord Ave; Cambridge, MA 02138; (617) 496–1324,
    FAX 495–8136; email fellowships@radcliffe.edu;
    website www.radcliffe.edu/fellowships

Open to: playwrights, composers, librettists. **Frequency:** annual. **Remuneration:** up to $50,000 9-month fellowship. **Guidelines:** professionals of "demonstrated accomplishment and exceptional promise" to complete substantial project in their field; full-time appointment; fellow required to reside in Boston area and expected to present work-in-progress in scheduled event during year; office or studio space, auditing privileges and access to libraries and other resources at Harvard provided; call, write or visit website for guidelines and application. **Application procedure:** 4

copies of application and supporting materials. **Deadline:** 1 Oct 2004. **Notification:** Mar 2005. **Dates:** Sep 2005–Jun 2006.

THE JAPAN FOUNDATION
152 West 57th St, 39th Floor; New York, NY 10019; (212) 489–0299, FAX 489–0409; website www.jfny.org/jfny/index.html
Artist Fellowship Program

Open to: specialists in the fields of fine arts, performing arts, music, journalism and creative writing, including playwrights, composers, librettists, lyricists and screenwriters. **Frequency:** annual. **Remuneration:** monthly stipend of ¥370,000 (about $3050) or ¥430,000 (about $3550), depending on grantee's professional career; travel; other allowances. **Guidelines:** U.S. citizen or permanent resident; fellowship of 2-6 months, not to be held concurrently with another major grant, to support project substantially related to Japan. **Application procedure:** write for guidelines and application, stating theme of project, present position and citizenship. **Deadline:** 1 Dec 2004. **Notification:** mid-late Mar 2005. **Dates:** residency begins between 1 Apr 2005 and 31 Mar 2006.

JOHN SIMON GUGGENHEIM MEMORIAL FOUNDATION
90 Park Ave; New York, NY 10016; (212) 687–4470, FAX 697–3248; email fellowships@gf.org; website www.gf.org

Open to: playwrights, composers. **Frequency:** annual. **Remuneration:** 1-year fellowship (in 2003, 184 fellowships with average grant of $35,500). **Guidelines:** citizen or permanent resident of U.S. or Canada; recipient must demonstrate exceptional creative ability; grant to support research in any field of knowledge or creation in any of the arts under the freest possible conditions. **Application procedure:** write for guidelines. **Deadline:** 1 Oct 2004. **Notification:** Apr 2005.

JONATHAN LARSON PERFORMING ARTS FOUNDATION
Box 672; Prince Street Station; New York, NY 10012; (212) 529–0814, FAX 253–7604; email jlpaf@aol.com; website www.jlpaf.org
Nancy Kassak Diekmann, *Executive Director*

Open to: composers, librettists, lyricists, producing organizations. **Frequency:** annual. **Remuneration:** grants of $2500-15,000 for general or project support. **Guidelines:** professional musical theatre artists who have completed formal training and are committed to a career in musical theatre. **Application procedure:** 2 copies of application form and all listed attachments; download application from web. **Deadline:** 13 Sep 2004. **Notification:** Jan-Feb 2005.

THE KLEBAN AWARD

c/o New Dramatists; 424 West 44th St; New York, NY 10036;
(212) 757-6960; email newdramatists@newdramatists.org;
website www.newdramatists.org

Anita Gabrosek, *Kleban Award Administrator*

Open to: librettists and/or lyricists. **Frequency:** annual. **Remuneration:** TBA ($100,000 each to lyricist and librettist, paid in installments of $50,000 a year, in 2002-2003). **Guidelines:** applicant whose work has received a full or workshop production, or who has been a member or associate of a professional musical workshop or theatre group (e.g., ASCAP or BMI workshops; see Development); writer whose work has been performed on the Broadway stage for a cumulative period of 2 years ineligible; write for guidelines or download from web. **Application procedure:** application and work sample. **Deadline:** postmarked 15 Sep 2004. (See New Dramatists in Membership and Service Organizations.)

LUDWIG VOGELSTEIN FOUNDATION, INC.

Box 510; Shelter Island, NY 11964-0570;

Willi Kirkham, *Executive Director*

Open to: playwrights. **Frequency:** annual. **Remuneration:** grants of $1000-3500. **Guidelines:** individual grants for writers of merit who have no source of funding. **Application procedure:** work sample, resume, project proposal (include name, address, age and social-security number in upper right corner), copy of last IRS return and proposed budget; all materials should include writer's name on each page. **Deadline:** 16 Apr 2005 (writers' last initial A-M); 30 Apr 2005 (writers' last initial N-Z). **Notification:** Nov 2005.

MARIN ARTS COUNCIL INDIVIDUAL ARTIST GRANTS

650 Las Gallinas Ave, Suite C; San Rafael, CA 94903; (415) 499-8350,
FAX 499-8537; email lance@marinarts.org; website www.marinarts.org

Lance Walker, *Grants Coordinator*

Open to: playwrights, composers, screenwriters. **Frequency:** biennial. **Remuneration:** $4000-10,000 grant. **Guidelines:** Marin County resident; award based on strength of original work completed in past 3 years. **Application procedure:** application and work sample. **Deadline:** Jan 2005; exact date TBA. **Notification:** Jun 2005.

MEET THE COMPOSER GRANT PROGRAMS

75 9th Ave, Floor 3R, Suite 505; New York, NY 10011; (212) 645-6949;
FAX 645-9669; email mtrevino@meetthecomposer.org;
website www.meetthecomposer.org

Mark Treviño, *Director of Programs*

COMMISSIONING MUSIC/USA

Open to: theatre and music-theatre companies. **Frequency:** categories rotate annually. **Remuneration:** commissioning grant up to $30,000 to cover composer and librettist fees and copying costs. **Guidelines:** organizations that have been producing or presenting for at least 3 years; plans must involve full production of new work and a minimum of 4 performances for a single organization or a minimum of 6 for a consortium; for complete guidelines and application refer to MTC website. **Application procedure:** individuals may not apply; 1 host organization submits application and supporting materials; application may be from a single organization for grants up to $15,000 or from consortium of organizations for grants up to $30,000. **Deadline:** Nov 2005 for theatre; exact date TBA.

GLOBAL CONNECTIONS

Open to: not-for-profit organizations. **Frequency:** annually. **Remuneration:** $500–1500 per individual composer. **Guidelines:** provides financial assistance to composers traveling to another country to engage in a variety of activities surrounding the live performance of their music or traveling to another country for research and development of a new project or work; grants are based on the overall strength of the application and the level of the composer's participation in the proposed event. **Application procedure:** applications are submitted jointly by a composer and a hosting organization; composer and organization may not be based in the same country and one must be based in the U.S.; for guidelines and application refer to MTC website. **Deadline:** May 2005 (exact date TBA).

MEET THE COMPOSER FUND

Open to: theatre and music-theatre companies. **Frequency:** quarterly. **Remuneration:** up to $1000 appearance fee for composer actively participating in events featuring the performance of their music. **Guidelines:** awards based on the overall quality of application, level of composer participation and level of audience/community involvement; administered by Meet The Composer in New York and by four regional offices that comprise the National Affiliate Network; for complete guidelines and application refer to MTC website. **Application procedure:** varies from region to region; individuals may not apply; performing organizations apply on behalf of composer. **Deadline:** 1 Oct 2004; 2 Jan 2005; 1 Apr 2005; 1 Jun 2005.

NATIONAL ENDOWMENT FOR THE ARTS INTERNATIONAL PARTNERSHIPS

1100 Pennsylvania Ave NW, Room 704; Washington, DC 20506;
 (202) 682-5429, FAX 682-5024;
 website www.arts.gov/partner/international.html
Pennie Ojeda, *International Coordinator*

ARTSLINK PROJECTS

12 West 31st St; New York, NY 10001-4415;
 (212) 643-1985, ext 22, FAX 643-1996;
 email al@cecartslink.org; website www.cecartslink.org

Open to: playwrights, translators, composers, librettists, lyricists, solo performers.

Frequency: biennial; award rotates among disciplines. **Remuneration:** grant up to $10,000 (average grant $4500). **Guidelines:** U.S. citizen or permanent resident; to enable individual artist or groups of artists and arts organizations to work with their counterparts in Central Europe, Russia and Eurasia; mutually beneficial collaborative project that will enrich artist's work and/or create new work that draws inspiration from knowledge and experience gained in country visited; write for guidelines. **Application procedure:** application and supporting materials. **Deadline:** next deadline for playwrights: 15 Jan 2006. **Notification:** Apr 2006.

THE FUND FOR U.S. ARTISTS AT INTERNATIONAL FESTIVALS AND EXHIBITIONS

Arts International; 251 Park Ave S, 5th Floor; New York, NY 10010;
(212) 674-9744, FAX 674-9092; email thefund@artsinternational.org;
website www.artsinternational.org/programs/index.htm
Kay Takeda, *Program Manager*

Open to: performing artists and organizations. **Frequency:** triannual. **Remuneration:** grants of up to $25,000 (most grants $1000-10,000) to cover expenses related to festival participation including travel, lodging, artists' fees and per diem. **Guidelines:** U.S. citizen or permanent resident who has been invited to international festival. **Application procedure:** application, work sample, proposal, bio, copy of invitation from festival, full budget showing all costs of participation in festival and festival's contribution to these costs. **Deadline:** 7 Sep 2004; 16 Jan 2005; 3 May 2005. **Notification:** 3 months. (See Arts International in this section.)

UNITED STATES/JAPAN CREATIVE ARTISTS' FELLOWSHIPS

Japan/U.S. Friendship Commission; 1120 Vermont Ave NW, Suite 925;
Washington, DC 20005; (202) 418-9800; email artist@jusfc.gov;
website www.jusfc.gov

Open to: playwrights, translators, composers, librettists, lyricists. **Frequency:** annual. **Remuneration:** monthly stipend to cover housing, living expenses and modest professional support services; round-trip transportation for artist and family members; stipend to study Japanese language in U.S. if necessary. **Guidelines:** U.S. citizen or permanent resident; to enable established artist to pursue discipline in Japan for 6 consecutive months. **Application procedure:** write or call for guidelines and application materials or download from web. **Deadline:** 28 Jun 2005. **Notification:** Oct 2005. (See listing in Colonies and Residencies.)

NATIONAL ENDOWMENT FOR THE ARTS LITERATURE FELLOWSHIPS FOR TRANSLATORS

1100 Pennsylvania Ave NW, Room 720; Washington, DC 20506;
(202) 682-5034; website www.arts.gov

Open to: translators. **Frequency:** annual. **Remuneration:** $10,000-20,000 fellowship. **Guidelines:** previously published drama, verse, prose and poetry translators of exceptional talent; guidelines available Jan 2005. **Application**

procedure: visit website for 2007 guidelines and application. **Deadline:** Feb 2005 for 2006, Feb 2006 for 2007; exact dates TBA.

NATIONAL ENDOWMENT FOR THE HUMANITIES DIVISION OF PUBLIC PROGRAMS/HUMANITIES PROJECTS IN MEDIA

1100 Pennsylvania Ave NW; Washington, DC 20506;
(202) 606-8269, FAX 606-8557;
email publicpgms@neh.gov; website www.neh.gov
Margaret Scrymser, *Lead Program Analyst*

Open to: radio and television writers and producers. **Frequency:** annual. **Remuneration:** varies. **Guidelines:** support for planning, writing or production of, as well as consultation on, television and radio projects that "substantially draw their content from scholarship in the humanities and are aimed at a national or broad regional audience"; no adaptations of literary works. **Application procedure:** option to submit draft proposal before making formal application; call or visit website for guidelines. **Deadline:** 3 Nov 2004 for television planning, scripting and production grants; Mar 2005 for television consultation grants and radio consultation, development and production grants. **Notification:** late May 2005 for Nov deadline; late Jul 2005 for Mar deadline; exact dates TBA.

NATIONAL ENDOWMENT FOR THE HUMANITIES DIVISION OF RESEARCH PROGRAMS/COLLABORATIVE RESEARCH

1100 Pennsylvania Ave NW; Washington, DC 20506;
(202) 606-8461; FAX 606-8204; email mhall@neh.gov;
website www.neh.gov
Michael L. Hall, *Program Officer*

Open to: translators. **Frequency:** annual. **Remuneration:** amount varies according to project. **Guidelines:** U.S. citizen or resident for 3 years; money to support collaborative projects to translate into English works that provide insight into the history, literature, philosophy and artistic achievements of other cultures and that make available to scholars, students, teachers and the public the thought and learning of those civilizations; write for guidelines or download from web. **Application procedure:** application and supporting materials. **Deadline:** 1 Oct 2004. **Notification:** Jun 2005.

NATIVE ARTS PROGRAM VISITING ARTIST APPOINTMENTS

National Museum of the American Indian; Smithsonian Institution;
Cultural Resources Center; 4220 Silver Hill Rd; Suitland, MD 20746;
(301) 238-6624, ext 6353, FAX 238-3200;
email mccrackenm@si.edu; website www.americanindian.si.edu
Molly McCracken, *Community Services Outreach Assistant*

Open to: playwrights, translators, composers, librettists, lyricists, solo performers, screenwriters. **Frequency:** annual. **Remuneration:** $5000, travel, housing, 14-21-day visit to New York City, Boston, Philadelphia and Washington, D.C. **Guidelines:** Native

American of the Western Hemisphere; professional artist; no students; download guidelines from web. **Application procedure:** application form, work sample, 2 letters of recommendation, resume, 1-page artist statement, budget proposal and tribal identification. **Deadline:** 31 May 2005. **Notification:** Sep 2005.

NEW PLAY COMMISSIONS IN JEWISH THEATRE

National Foundation for Jewish Culture; 330 Seventh Ave, 21st Floor;
   New York, NY 10001; (212) 629-0500, ext 215, FAX 629-0508;
   email krunk@jewishculture.org; website www.jewishculture.org
Kristen L. Runk, *Associate Operations Director*

Open to: not-for-profit theatres. **Frequency:** annual. **Remuneration:** grant of $1000-5000. **Guidelines:** approximately 5 awards a year to North American theatres that have completed at least 2 seasons of public performances and are commissioning either a new full-length play, adaptation, work for young audiences, musical or opera dealing substantively with issues of Jewish history, tradition, values or contemporary life; theatre must commit to presenting at least a public workshop production and/or staged reading of work, followed by discussion with audience; funds may be applied to commissioning fee, playwright's residency expenses or workshop costs; write, call or email for guidelines. **Application procedure:** completed proposal, cover sheet and supporting materials, submitted by theatre. **Deadline:** 9 Sep 2004. **Notification:** Mar 2005. (See listing for The National Foundation for Jewish Culture in Membership and Service Organizations.)

NEW YORK FOUNDATION FOR THE ARTS (NYFA) ARTISTS' FELLOWSHIPS

155 Avenue of the Americas, 14th Floor; New York, NY 10013-1507;
   (212) 366-6900, ext 217, FAX 366-1778; email nyfaafp@nyfa.org;
   website www.nyfa.org
Penelope Dannenberg, *Director of Programs*

Open to: playwrights, composers, librettists, screenwriters. **Frequency:** award alternates biennially among disciplines. **Remuneration:** $7000 fellowship. **Guidelines:** NY State resident for 2 years prior to deadline; students ineligible. **Application procedure:** application and supporting materials; application seminars held each Sep. **Deadline:** next deadline for playwrights, composers, librettists and screenwriters postmarked early Oct 2005; exact deadline TBA.

NEW YORK THEATRE WORKSHOP PLAYWRITING FELLOWSHIP

New York Theatre Workshop; 83 East 4th St; New York, NY 10003;
   (212) 780-9037, FAX 460-8996
Ruben Polendo, *Artistic Associate*

Open to: playwrights. **Frequency:** annual. **Remuneration:** 2-4 stipends of approximately $3000. **Guidelines:** writer of color under 30 years of age and resident of New York City; must be available to attend monthly group meetings and 1-week summer retreat; writer must make 1-year commitment. **Application procedure:** one-act play or 20-page writing sample, artistic statement, resume and 2 letters of recommendation. **Deadline:** TBA; contact theatre in Jan 2005 for exact date. (See New York Theatre Workshop in Production.)

PEW FELLOWSHIPS IN THE ARTS

230 South Broad St, Suite 1003; Philadelphia, PA 19102;
(215) 875-2285, FAX 875-2276; website www.pewarts.org
Melissa Franklin, *Director*

Open to: playwrights, composers, screenwriters. **Frequency:** annual; award rotates among various disciplines. **Remuneration:** up to 12 $50,000 fellowships. **Guidelines:** to give artists living in Southeastern PA the opportunity to dedicate themselves wholly to the development of their work for up to 2 years; call or write for application and guidelines or download from web. **Application procedure:** application and work sample. **Deadline:** Dec 2004; exact date TBA.

PILGRIM PROJECT

156 Fifth Ave, Suite 400; New York, NY 10010; (212) 627-2288,
FAX 627-2184
Davida Goldman, *Secretary*

Open to: playwrights, solo performers, individual producers and theatre companies. **Frequency:** ongoing. **Remuneration:** grant of $1000-7000. **Guidelines:** grant toward cost of reading, workshop production or full production of play that deals with questions of moral significance. **Application procedure:** script only; write for further information. **Deadline:** ongoing.

THE PLAYWRIGHTS' CENTER GRANT PROGRAMS

2301 Franklin Ave E; Minneapolis, MN 55406-1099;
(612) 332-7481; email info@pwcenter.org;
website www.pwcenter.org
Carlo Cuesta, *Executive Director*

JEROME PLAYWRIGHT-IN-RESIDENCE FELLOWSHIPS

Open to: playwrights, solo performers. **Frequency:** annual. **Remuneration:** 4 1-year fellowships of $9000. **Guidelines:** U.S. citizen or permanent resident; emerging playwright whose work has not received more than 2 professional full productions; fellow must spend year in residence at Center, where fellow has access to developmental workshops, readings and other services; send SASE for guidelines. **Application procedure:** application and supporting materials. **Deadline:** 15 Sep 2004. **Notification:** 15 Jan 2005. **Dates:** 1 Jul 2005-30 Jun 2006.

MANY VOICES PLAYWRITING RESIDENCY AWARDS

Open to: playwrights, solo performers. **Frequency:** annual, contingent on funding. **Remuneration:** 8 awards consisting of $1250 stipend; playwriting class scholarship; 1-year Playwrights' Center membership; opportunity to participate in playwriting roundtables; dramaturgical assistance; workshop and public reading. **Guidelines:**

MN resident of color. **Application procedure:** send SASE for guidelines. **Deadline:** 31 Jul 2005. **Notification:** 15 Sep 2005. **Dates:** 1 Oct 2005–30 Jun 2006.

McKnight Advancement Grants

Open to: playwrights, solo performers. **Frequency:** annual. **Remuneration:** 3 grants of $25,000; up to $1500 per fellow for workshops and staged readings using Center's developmental program or for allocation to partner organization for joint development and/or production. **Guidelines:** U.S. citizen or permanent resident and legal MN resident since 1 Jul 2004; playwright of exceptional merit and potential who has had at least 2 plays fully produced by professional theatres; funds intended to significantly advance fellow's art and/or career and may be used to cover a variety of expenses, including writing time, residency at theatre or other arts organization, travel/study, production or presentation; fellow must designate 2 months of grant year during which he or she plans to participate actively in Center's programs, including weekly attendance at and critical participation in readings and workshops of other members' work; send SASE for guidelines after 1 Dec 2004. **Application procedure:** application and supporting materials. **Deadline:** 1 Feb 2005. **Notification:** 1 May 2005. **Dates:** 1 Jul 2005–30 Jun 2006.

McKnight National Playwriting Residency and Commission

Open to: playwrights, solo performers. **Frequency:** annual. **Remuneration:** $12,500 commission; $2500 to support the creation of a new work during 1-month residency; housing; and round-trip travel to Minneapolis. **Guidelines:** U.S. citizen or permanent resident, not MN resident; playwright must have had at least 2 works fully produced by professional theatres; work must have made a significant impact on contemporary theatre; must spend 1 month in residency at the Center, where playwright has access to developmental readings, workshops and other services; send SASE for guidelines. **Application procedure:** project description, writing sample and supporting materials; agent submission preferred. **Deadline:** 1 Dec 2004. **Notification:** 15 Feb 2005. **Dates:** 1 Jul 2005–30 Jun 2006.

Princess Grace Awards: Playwright Fellowship

Princess Grace Foundation–USA; 150 East 58th St, 25th Floor;
New York, NY 10155; (212) 317–1470, FAX 317–1473;
email cmg@pgfusa.com; website www.pgfusa.com
(Ms.) Toby Boshak, *Executive Director*

Open to: playwrights. **Frequency:** annual. **Remuneration:** $7500 grant; residency at New Dramatists in New York City (see listing in Membership and Service Organizations); inclusion of submitted script in New Dramatists' lending library and in its ScriptShare national script-distribution program for 1 year; representation and publication by Samuel French, Inc. (see listing in Publication). **Guidelines:** U.S. citizen or permanent resident; emerging artist at onset of career; award based primarily on artistic quality of submitted play and potential of fellowship to assist writer's growth; applcation available on web. **Application procedure:** application; unproduced, unpublished play (no adaptations); letter of recommendation and resume. **Deadline:** 31 Mar 2005.

TCG ARTISTIC PROGRAMS

Theatre Communications Group; 520 8th Ave, 24th Floor;
New York, NY 10018-4156; (212) 609-5900, FAX 609-5901;
email grants@tcg.org; website www.tcg.org

EXTENDED COLLABORATION GRANTS

Sheela Kangal, *Senior Artistic Programs Associate*

Open to: TCG member theatres, in collaboration with playwrights. **Frequency:** biannual. **Remuneration:** 12 grants of $5500. **Guidelines:** expands normal development resources of theatre by enabling playwright to develop work over an extended period of time in collaboration with director, designer, choreographer, composer and/or artist from another discipline; period of collaboration must exceed that which theatre would normally support; funds cover transportation expenses related to research and meetings among the collaborators; see website for guidelines. **Application procedure:** playwright may not apply; application submitted by artistic leader of TCG member theatre. **Deadline:** 25 Oct 2005; spring 2005 (exact date TBA).

NEA/TCG THEATRE RESIDENCY PROGRAM FOR PLAYWRIGHTS

Sheela Kangal, *Senior Artistic Programs Associate*

Open to: playwrights in association with not-for-profit professional theatres. **Frequency:** annual (contingent on funding). **Remuneration:** grant of $25,000 to playwright and $5500 Vivendi Universal Residency Award to host theatre (10 awarded in 2004). **Guidelines:** playwright must be citizen or permanent resident of U.S. at time of application and have had at least one play published or produced within the last 5 years; theatre must have history of developing new work, high artistic standards and a minimum operating budget of $150,000 in the most recently completed fiscal year; total of 6 months (132 days, not necessarily consecutive) must be dedicated to the development of new work with the host theatre; write or call for application and guidelines or download from web. **Application procedure:** intent to apply card, followed by application and supporting materials. **Deadline:** spring 2005 for intent to apply card, exact date TBA; summer 2005 for application, exact date TBA (7 Jul in 2004).

THE NEW GENERATIONS PROGRAM

Jennifer Werner, *Artistic Programs Associate*

Open to: not-for-profit professional theatres in association with theatre practitioners, including playwrights. **Frequency:** annual. **Remuneration:** individual receives mentorship from professional theatre artist for period of 2 years (8 awarded in 2004). **Guidelines:** program's focus is "cultivating and strengthening a new generation of theatre leadership"; see website for guidelines **Application procedure:** intent to apply card followed by preliminary proposal; only those selected by panel submit full application. **Deadline:** summer 2005 for intent to apply card, exact date TBA (6 Aug in 2004); summer 2005 for preliminary proposal, exact date TBA (16 Aug in 2004).

TCG/ITI Travel Grants

Jennifer Werner, *Artistic Programs Associate*

Open to: playwrights. **Frequency:** biannual. **Remuneration:** $2500 grant (15 awarded in 2003). **Guidelines:** program supports cultural exchange and artistic partnerships between professionals in U.S. and their counterparts in Russia and Eastern and Central Europe; grant covers transportation and living expenses essential to collaborative project, including research materials, communication costs, theatre tickets and/or services of interpreter. **Application procedure:** completed application. **Deadline:** 29 Oct 2004; spring 2005 (contingent on funding), exact date TBA (30 Apr in 2004).

Travel and Study Grant Program

c/o Jerome Foundation; 125 Park Square Ct; 400 Sibley St;
    St. Paul, MN 55101; (651) 224-9431, FAX 224-3439;
    website www.jeromefdn.org
Cynthia Gehrig, *President*

Open to: playwrights, composers, librettists and lyricists. **Frequency:** annual. **Remuneration:** grant up to $5000 for foreign or domestic travel. **Guidelines:** resident of MN; program supports periods of significant professional development through travel and study for independent professional artist or staff member of not-for-profit organization; write for guidelines. **Application procedure:** application, work sample and resume. **Deadline:** Mar 2005 (exact date TBA).

U.S. Department of State Fulbright U.S. Student Program at the Institute of International Education

809 United Nations Plaza; New York, NY 10017-3580;
    (212) 984-5330; website www.iie.org/fulbright

Open to: playwrights, translators, composers, librettists, lyricists. **Frequency:** annual. **Remuneration:** fellowship or grant; amount varies with country of award. **Guidelines:** specific opportunities for study abroad in the arts; write for brochure. **Application procedure:** application and supporting materials. **Deadline:** 21 Oct 2004. **Notification:** Jan 2005.

The Walt Disney Studios and ABC Entertainment Writing Fellowship Program

500 South Buena Vista St; Burbank, CA 91521-4016;
    (818) 560-6894; email abc.fellowships@abc.com;
    website www.abctalentdevelopment.com

Open to: screenwriters, television writers. **Frequency:** annual. **Remuneration:** 1-year salary of $50,000 for up to 12 writers; travel and 1-month housing for fellows from outside L.A. area. **Guidelines:** writers work full-time at developing their craft at the Walt Disney Studios in features or television division; no previous film or TV writing experience necessary; writer with Writers Guild of America credits eligible but should apply through the Guild's Employment Access at (213) 782-4648; call for guidelines and application or download from web. **Application procedure:** application and notarized standard letter agreement with resume, biography and writing sample (for feature division: screenplay approximately 120 pages long or full-length play; for TV division: 30-minute TV comedy or drama spec script based on a current cable or broadcast primetime show). **Deadline:** 31 May 2005. **Notification:** winter 2005 (finalists). **Dates:** fellowship year begins Jan 2006; exact date TBA.

WISCONSIN ARTS BOARD ARTIST FELLOWSHIP AWARDS

101 East Wilson St, 1st Floor; Madison, WI 53702; (608) 264–8191, FAX 267–0380; email mark.fraire@arts.state.wi.us; website www.arts.state.wi.us

Mark Fraire, *Grant Programs and Services Specialist*

Open to: playwrights, composers. **Frequency:** biennial. **Remuneration:** $8000 fellowship. **Guidelines:** WI resident for at least 1 year at time of application; artist must produce 1 public presentation of work as part of fellowship; visit website for guidelines and application. **Application procedure:** application and work sample. **Deadline:** 15 Sep 2004. **Notification:** Jan 2005.

EMERGENCY FUNDS

How do emergency funds differ from other sources of financial aid?

Emergency funds aid writers in severe temporary financial difficulties. Some funds give outright grants, others make interest-free loans. For support for anything other than a genuine emergency, turn to Fellowships and Grants.

THE AUTHOR'S LEAGUE FUND
31 East 28th St; New York, NY 10016; (212) 268-1208,
   FAX 564-8363
Sarah Heller, *Administrator*

Open to: playwrights. **Type of assistance:** interest-free loan; request should be limited to immmediate needs. **Guidelines:** published or produced working professional; must demonstrate real need. **Application procedure:** application and supporting materials. **Notification:** 2-4 weeks.

CARNEGIE FUND FOR AUTHORS
1 Old Country Rd, Suite 113; Carle Place, NY 11514

Open to: playwrights. **Type of assistance:** emergency grant. **Guidelines:** playwright who has had at least 1 play or collection of plays published commercially in book form (anthologies excluded); emergency which has placed applicant in substantial verifiable financial need. **Application procedure:** write for application form.

THE DRAMATISTS GUILD FUND
1501 Broadway, Suite 701; New York, NY 10036;
   (212) 391-8384, FAX 944-0420
Susan Drury, *Administrator*

Open to: playwrights, composers, librettists, lyricists. **Type of assistance:** interest-free grant; request should be limited to immediate needs. **Guidelines:** published or produced working professional; must demonstrate real need. **Application procedure:** application and supporting materials. **Notification:** 2-4 weeks.

MARY MASON MEMORIAL LEMONADE FUND
Theatre Bay Area, 870 Market St, Suite 375; San Francisco, CA 94102;
   (415) 430-1140, FAX 430-1145; email richard@theatrebayarea.org;
   website www.theatrebayarea.org/tba/lemonade.shtml
Richard Ryan, *Office Administrator*

Open to: playwrights, translators, lyricists, librettists, composers. **Type of assistance:** grants of up to $1000. **Guidelines:** resident of San Francisco Bay Area who has worked professionally or vocationally in theatre with minimum 2 years experience within the last 5; persons diagnosed with terminal or life-threatening illness; monies cannot be used for hospital expenses. **Application procedure:** call or email for application. **Notification:** 2-4 weeks. (See Theatre Bay Area in Membership and Service Organizations.)

PEN FUND FOR WRITERS & EDITORS WITH AIDS
PEN American Center; 568 Broadway; New York, NY 10012;
   (212) 334-1660 ext 101, FAX 334-2181; email motika@pen.org
Stephen Motika, *Coordinator*

Open to: playwrights, translators, librettists, lyricists, screenwriters, television writers, radio writers. **Type of assistance:** grant or interest-free loan of up to $1000. **Guidelines:** emergency assistance for published and/or produced writer who is HIV-positive and having financial difficulties. **Application procedure:** application, work sample, documentation of financial emergency and resume. **Notification:** 6-8 weeks.

PEN WRITERS FUND

PEN American Center; 568 Broadway; New York, NY 10012;
   (212) 334-1660 ext 101, FAX 334-2181; email motika@pen.org
Stephen Motika, *Coordinator*

Open to: playwrights, translators, librettists, lyricists, screenwriters, television writers, radio writers. **Type of assistance:** grant or interest-free loan of up to $500. **Guidelines:** emergency assistance for published and/or produced writer having financial difficulties. **Application procedure:** application, work sample, documentation of financial emergency and resume. **Notification:** 6-8 weeks.

STATE ARTS AGENCIES

What can my state arts agency do for me?

Possibly quite a bit—ask your agency for guidelines and study them carefully. State programs vary greatly and change frequently. Most have some sort of residency requirement, but eligibility is not always restricted to current residents, and may include people who were born in, raised in, attended school in or had some other association with the state in question.

What if my state doesn't give grants to individual artists?

A number of state arts agencies are restricted in this way. However, those with such restrictions, by and large, are eager to help artists locate not-for-profit organizations that channel funds to individuals. The New York State Council on the Arts, for example, is prohibited from funding individuals directly, and must contract with a sponsoring not-for-profit organization when it awards grants to individual artists. Yet NYSCA has a number of ways of supporting the work of theatre writers. The Literature Program funds translations and a number of other activities of interest to playwrights. The Individual Artists Program assists not-for-profit organizations in commissioning new theatre works. NYSCA also subgrants funds to the New York Foundation for the Arts (see Fellowships and Grants, and Development), which provides funds and project development assistance for individual artists.

At the least, every state has some kind of Artist-in-Education program; if you are able and willing to function in an educational setting you should certainly investigate this possibility.

ALABAMA STATE COUNCIL ON THE ARTS

201 Monroe St; Montgomery, AL 36130-1800; (334) 242-4076,
FAX 240-3269; email staff@arts.state.al.us; website www.arts.state.al.us
Al Head, *Executive Director*

ALASKA STATE COUNCIL ON THE ARTS

411 West 4th Ave, Suite 1E; Anchorage, AK 99501-2343;
(907) 269-6610, (888) 278-7424, FAX (907) 269-6601;
email aksca_info@eed.state.ak.us; website www.eed.state.ak.us/aksca
Charlotte Fox, *Executive Director*

AMERICAN SAMOA COUNCIL ON CULTURE, ARTS AND HUMANITIES

Box 1540; Office of the Governor; Pago Pago, AS 96799;
011-684-633-4347, FAX 011-684-633-2059;
website www.nasaa-arts.org/aoa/as.shtml
(Ms.) Le'ala E. Pili, *Executive Director*

ARIZONA COMMISSION ON THE ARTS

417 West Roosevelt St; Phoenix, AZ 85003; (602) 255-5882,
FAX 256-0282; email general@ArizonaArts.org;
website www.ArizonaArts.org
Shelley M. Cohn, *Executive Director*

ARKANSAS ARTS COUNCIL

1500 Tower Bldg; 323 Center St; Little Rock, AR 72201;
(501) 324-9766, 324-9150 (TTY), FAX 324-9207;
email info@arkansasarts.com; website www.arkansasarts.com
Joy Pennington, *Executive Director*

CALIFORNIA ARTS COUNCIL

1300 I St, Suite 930; Sacramento, CA 95814; (916) 322-6555,
(800) 201-6201, FAX (916) 322-6575; email cac@cwo.com;
website www.cac.ca.gov
Barry Hessenius, *Executive Director*

COLORADO COUNCIL ON THE ARTS

1380 Lawrence St, Suite 1200; Denver, CO 80204; (303) 866-2723,
FAX 894-2615; email coloarts@state.co.us; website www.coloarts.state.co.us
Renée Bouée, *Acting Executive Director*

CONNECTICUT COMMISSION ON THE ARTS
1 Financial Plaza; 755 Main St; Hartford, CT 06103;
(860) 566-4770, 566-6460 (TTY), (800) 411-1312, FAX (860) 566-6462;
email artsinfo@ctarts.org; website www.ctarts.org
Douglas C. Evans, *Executive Director*

DELAWARE DIVISION OF THE ARTS
Carvel State Office Bldg; 820 North French St; Wilmington, DE 19801;
(302) 577-8278, FAX 577-6561; email delarts@state.de.us;
website www.artsdel.org
Laura A. Scanlan, *Director*

DISTRICT OF COLUMBIA (DC) COMMISSION ON THE ARTS AND HUMANITIES
410 8th St NW, 5th Floor; Washington, DC 20004; (202) 724-5613,
727-3148 (TTY), FAX 727-4135; email cah@dc.gov; website dcarts.dc.gov
Anthony Gittens, *Executive Director*

FLORIDA DIVISION OF CULTURAL AFFAIRS
Department of State, 1001 DeSoto Park Dr; Tallahassee, FL 32301;
(850) 245-6470, FAX 245-6492; email infd@florida-arts.org;
website www.florida-arts.org
Linda Downey, *Program Director*

GEORGIA COUNCIL FOR THE ARTS
260 14th St, Suite 401; Atlanta, GA 30318; (404) 685-ARTS (2787),
685-2799 (TTY), FAX 685-2788; email gaarts@gaarts.org;
website www.gaarts.org
Susan S. Weiner, *Executive Director*

GUAM COUNCIL ON THE ARTS & HUMANITIES AGENCY
703 East Sunset Blvd; Tiyan, GU 96913-1549; (671) 475-2242,
FAX 472-2781; email kana1@kuentos.guam.net;
website www.guam.net/gov/kaha
Deborah J. Bordallo, *Executive Director*

STATE FOUNDATION ON CULTURE AND THE ARTS (HAWAII)
250 South Hotel St, 2nd Floor; Honolulu, HI 96813; (808) 586-0300,
586-0740 (TTY), FAX 586-0308; email sfca@sfca.state.hi.us;
website www.state.hi.us/sfca
Ronald K. Yamakawa, *Executive Director*

IDAHO COMMISSION ON THE ARTS
Box 83720; Boise, ID 83720-0008; (208) 334-2119, (800) 278-3863,
FAX (208) 334-2488; email cconley@ica.state.id.us;
website www2.state.id.us/arts
Dan Harpole, *Executive Director*

ILLINOIS ARTS COUNCIL
James R. Thompson Center; 100 West Randolph St, Suite 10-500;
Chicago, IL 60601; (312) 814-6750, FAX 814-1471;
email info@arts.state.il.us; website www.state.il.us/agency/iac
Richard C. Carlson, *Acting Executive Director*

INDIANA ARTS COMMISSION
150 West Market St, #618; Indianapolis, IN 46204; (317) 232-1268,
FAX 232-5595; email arts@state.in.us; website www.state.in.us/iac
Dorothy L. Ilgen, *Executive Director*

IOWA ARTS COUNCIL
600 East Locust; Des Moines, IA 50319-0290; (515) 281-6412,
242-5147 (TTY), FAX 242-6498; website www.iowaartscouncil.org
Anita Walker, *Executive Director*

KANSAS ARTS COMMISSION
700 Southwest Jackson, Suite 1004; Topeka, KS 66603-3761;
(785) 296-3335, FAX 296-4989; email KAC@arts.state.ks.us;
website arts.state.ks.us
David Wilson, *Executive Director*

KENTUCKY ARTS COUNCIL
Old Capitol Annex; 300 West Broadway; Frankfort, KY 40601-1980;
(502) 564-3757, (888) 833-2787, FAX (502) 564-2839;
email kyarts@ky.gov; website www.kyarts.org
Gerri Combs, *Executive Director*

LOUISIANA DIVISION OF THE ARTS
Box 44247; Baton Rouge, LA 70804-4247; (225) 342-8180,
FAX 342-8173; email arts@crt.state.la.us;
website www.crt.state.la.us/arts
Pam Bredux *Executive Director*

MAINE ARTS COMMISSION
193 State St; 25 State House Station; Augusta, ME 04333-0025;
(207) 287-2724, 287-2360 (TTY), FAX 287-2725;
email mainearts.info@maine.gov; website www.mainearts.com
Alden C. Wilson, *Executive Director*

MARYLAND STATE ARTS COUNCIL
175 West Ostend St, Suite E; Baltimore, MD 21230; (410) 767-6555,
333-4519 (TTY), FAX 333-1062; email msac@msac.org;
website www.msac.org
Theresa M. Colvin, *Executive Director*

MASSACHUSETTS CULTURAL COUNCIL
10 St. James Ave, 3rd Floor; Boston, MA 02116-3803;
(617) 727-3668, FAX 727-0044; email web@art.state.ma.us;
website www.massculturalcouncil.org
Mary Kelley, *Executive Director*

MICHIGAN COUNCIL FOR THE ARTS & CULTURAL AFFAIRS
702 West Kalamazoo; Box 30705; Lansing, MI 48909-8205;
(517) 241-4011, FAX 241-3979; email artsinfo@michigan.gov;
website www.michigan.gov/hal
Betty Boone, *Executive Director*

MINNESOTA STATE ARTS BOARD
Park Square Court; 400 Sibley St, Suite 200; St. Paul, MN 55101-1928;
(651) 215-1600, 215-6235 (TTY), (800) 866-2787, FAX (651) 215-1602;
email msab@arts.state.mn.us; website www.arts.state.mn.us
Robert C. Booker, *Executive Director*

MISSISSIPPI ARTS COMMISSION
239 North Lamar St, Suite 207; Jackson, MS 39201; (601) 359-6030,
(800) 582-2233 (TTY), FAX (601) 359-6008; website www.arts.state.ms.us
Timothy Hedgepeth, *Executive Director*

MISSOURI ARTS COUNCIL
111 North 7th St, Suite 105; St. Louis, MO 63101-2188;
(314) 340-6845, FAX 340-7215; email moarts@ded.mo.gov;
website www.missouriartscouncil.org
Norree Boyd, *Executive Director*

MONTANA ARTS COUNCIL

Box 202201; Helena, MT 59620-2201; (406) 444-6430,
FAX 444-6548; email mac@state.mt.us; website www.art.state.mt.us
Arlynn Fishbaugh, *Executive Director*

NEBRASKA ARTS COUNCIL

Joslyn Carriage House; 3838 Davenport St; Omaha, NE 68131-2329;
(402) 595-2122, FAX 595-2334; email cmalloy@nebraskaartscouncil.org;
website www.nebraskaartscouncil.org
Suzanne Wise, *Executive Director*

NEVADA ARTS COUNCIL

716 North Carson St, Suite A; Carson City, NV 89701; (775) 687-6680,
FAX 687-6688; website dmla.clan.lib.nv.us/docs/arts
Susan Boskoff, *Executive Director*

NEW HAMPSHIRE STATE COUNCIL ON THE ARTS

2 1/2 Beacon St, 2nd Floor; Concord, NH 03301-4974; (603) 271-2789,
(800) 735-2964 (TTY), FAX (603) 271-3584;
website www.state.nh.us/nharts
Rebecca L. Lawrence, *Director*

NEW JERSEY STATE COUNCIL ON THE ARTS

Box 306; 225 West State St; Trenton, NJ 08625; (609)292-6130,
633-1186 (TTY), FAX 989-1440; email njsca@arts.sos.state.nj.us;
website www.njartscouncil.org
David A. Miller, *Executive Director*

NEW MEXICO ARTS

Box 1450; Santa Fe, NM 87504-1450; (505) 827-6490,
(800) 879-4278, FAX (505) 827-6043; website www.nmarts.org
Loie Fecteau, *Executive Director*

NEW YORK STATE COUNCIL ON THE ARTS

175 Varick St, 3rd Floor; New York, NY 10014-4604; (212) 627-4455,
(800) 895-9838 (TTY), FAX (212) 620-5911; website www.nysca.org
Nicolette B. Clarke, *Executive Director*

NORTH CAROLINA ARTS COUNCIL

Department of Cultural Resources; Raleigh, NC 27699-4632;
(919) 733-2111, FAX 733-4834; email ncarts@ncmail.net;
website www.ncarts.org
Mary B. Regan, *Executive Director*

NORTH DAKOTA COUNCIL ON THE ARTS
1600 East Century Ave, Suite 6; Bismarck, ND 58503; (701) 328-7590,
FAX 328-7595; email comserv@state.nd.us; website www.state.nd.us/arts
Jan Webb, *Executive Director*

COMMONWEALTH COUNCIL FOR ARTS AND CULTURE (NORTHERN MARIANA ISLANDS)
Box 5553, CHRB; Saipan, MP 96950; (670) 322-9982, 322-9983,
FAX 322-9028; email galaidi@gtepacifica.net;
website www.nasaa-arts.org/aoa/nmar.shtml
Robert Hunter, *Executive Director*

OHIO ARTS COUNCIL
727 East Main St; Columbus, OH 43205-1796; (614) 466-2613,
FAX 466-4494; website www.oac.state.oh.us
Wayne P. Lawson, *Executive Director*

OKLAHOMA ARTS COUNCIL
Box 52001-2001; Oklahoma City, OK 73152-2001; (405) 521-2931,
FAX 521-6418; email okarts@arts.state.ok.us;
website www.oklaosf.state.ok.us/~arts
Betty Price, *Executive Director*

OREGON ARTS COMMISSION
775 Summer St NE, Suite 200; Salem, OR 97301-1284;
(503) 986-0082, 986-0123 (TTY), FAX 986-0260;
email oregon.artscomm@state.or.us;
website www.oregonartscommission.org
Christine T. D'Arcy, *Executive Director*

PENNSYLVANIA COUNCIL ON THE ARTS
Finance Bldg, Room 216; Harrisburg, PA 17120; (717) 787-6883,
(800) 654-5984 (TTY), FAX (717) 783-2538; website www.artsnet.org/pca
Philip Horn, *Executive Director*

INSTITUTE OF PUERTO RICAN CULTURE
Box 9024184; San Juan, PR 00902-4184; (787) 724-0700, FAX 724-8393;
email www@icp.gobierno.pr; website icp.gobierno.pr
Teresa Tió, *Executive Director*

RHODE ISLAND STATE COUNCIL ON THE ARTS
1 Capital Hill, 3rd Floor; Providence, RI 02408; (401) 222-3880,
222-7808 (TTY), FAX 422-3018; email info@risca.state.ri.us;
website www.risca.state.ri.us
Randall Rosenbaum, *Executive Director*

SOUTH CAROLINA ARTS COMMISSION
1800 Gervais St; Columbia, SC 29201; (803) 734-8696,
734-8983 (TTY), FAX 734-8526; website www.state.sc.us/arts
Suzette M. Surkamer, *Executive Director*

SOUTH DAKOTA ARTS COUNCIL
South Dakota State Library Bldg, 800 Governors Dr; Pierre, SD 57501;
(605) 773-3131, (800) 423-6665, FAX (605) 773-6962;
email sdac@state.sd.us; website www.state.sd.us/deca/sdarts
Dennis Holub, *Executive Director*

TENNESSEE ARTS COMMISSION
401 Charlotte Ave; Nashville, TN 37243-0780;
(615) 741-1701, FAX 741-8559; website www.arts.state.tn.us
Rich Boyd, *Executive Director*

TEXAS COMMISSION ON THE ARTS
Box 13406; Austin, TX 78711-3406; (512) 463-5535,
475-3327 (TTY), (800) 252-9415, FAX (512) 475-2699;
email front.desk@arts.state.tx.us; website www.arts.state.tx.us
Ricardo Hernandez, *Executive Director*

UTAH ARTS COUNCIL
617 East South Temple; Salt Lake City, UT 84102-1177;
(801) 236-7555, (800) 346-4128 (TTY), FAX (801) 236-7556;
website arts.utah.gov
Frank McEntire, *Director*

VERMONT ARTS COUNCIL
136 State St, Drawer 33; Montpelier, VT 05633-6001;
(802) 828-3291, (800) 253-0195 (TTY), FAX (802) 828-3363;
email info@vermontartscouncil.org;
website www.vermontartscouncil.org
Alexander L. Aldrich, *Executive Director*

VIRGINIA COMMISSION FOR THE ARTS
Lewis House, 2nd Floor; 223 Governor St; Richmond, VA 23219-2010;
(804) 225-3132, FAX 225-4327; email arts@arts.virginia.gov;
website www.arts.state.va.us
Peggy J. Baggett, *Executive Director*

VIRGIN ISLANDS COUNCIL ON THE ARTS
Box 103; St. Thomas, VI 00802; (340) 774-5984, FAX 774-6206;
email vicouncil@islands.vi; website www.nasaa-arts.org/aoa/vi.shtml
Beth Mahoney, *Executive Director*

WASHINGTON STATE ARTS COMMISSION
234 East 8th St SE; Box 42675; Olympia, WA 98504-2675;
(360) 753-3860, FAX 586-5351; email michellez@arts.wa.gov;
website www.arts.wa.gov
Kris Tucker, *Executive Director*

WEST VIRGINIA COMMISSION ON THE ARTS
1900 Kanawha Blvd E; Charleston, WV 25305-0300; (304) 558-0220,
558-3562 (TTY), FAX 558-2779; email richard.ressmeyer@wvculture.org;
website www.wvculture.org
Richard Ressmeyer, *Director of Arts*

WISCONSIN ARTS BOARD
101 East Wilson St, 1st Floor; Madison, WI 53702; (608) 266-0190,
267-9629 (TTY), FAX 267-0380; email artsboard@arts.state.wi.us;
website arts.state.wi.us/static
George Tzougros, *Executive Director*

WYOMING ARTS COUNCIL
2320 Capitol Ave; Cheyenne, WY 82002; (307) 777-7742, FAX 777-5499;
email ebratt@state.wy.us; website wyoarts.state.wy.us;
Rita Ortloff Basom, *Interim Director*

COLONIES AND RESIDENCIES

What entries make up this section?

Though artist colonies that admit theatre writers constitute the majority of the listings, there are other kinds of residencies, such as artist-in-residence positions at universities, listed here as well. You can also find listings in Development and the Fellowships and Grants sections that could be considered residencies. We have also included some "writers' rooms" where playwrights in need of a quiet place for uninterrupted work are welcome. Of course there are hotels and inns throughout the country that would be desirable for an artist seeking a quiet place to work, but we have chosen to limit our listings to those places set up as retreats for writers or that, in addition to reasonable lodging, provide services to benefit writers.

Note: annual deadlines may stay the same from year to year but this is not an absolute—always obtain the latest information (an organization's website is the best place to check) before submitting. You should assume that each deadline listed in this section is the date application materials must be *received*, unless stated otherwise.

ALDEN B. DOW CREATIVITY CENTER

Northwood University; 4000 Whiting Dr; Midland, MI 48640;
(989) 837-4478, FAX 837-4468;
email creativity@northwood.edu; website www.northwood.edu/abd

Open to: playwrights, translators, composers, librettists, lyricists, screenwriters. **Description:** 4 "Creativity Fellowships" each year for individuals working in any field, including the arts; 10-week summer residency at Northwood University, which provides environment for intense independent study; program includes interaction among fellows and formal presentation of work at end of program. **Financial arrangement:** travel stipend, room, board, $750 stipend for project costs. **Guidelines:** projects that are creative, innovative and unique; prefers 1 applicant per project; no accommodation for spouses, children or pets; write for brochure or visit website for more information. **Application procedure:** project description, work sample, resume and $10 application fee. **Deadline:** 31 Dec 2004. **Notification:** 1 Apr 2005. **Dates:** Jun-Aug 2005.

ALTOS DE CHAVON

c/o Parsons School of Design; 66 Fifth Ave, #604A; New York, NY 10011;
(212) 229-5370, FAX 229-8988; email altos@earthlink.net
Carmen Lorente, *Program Coordinator*

Open to: playwrights, composers, screenwriters. **Description:** residencies of 3½ months for 15 artists a year, 1-2 of whom may be writers or composers, at not-for-profit arts center located in tropical Caribbean surroundings 8 miles from town of La Romana in the Dominican Republic; efficiency studios or apartments with kitchenettes; small individual studios nearby; small visual-arts-oriented library. **Financial arrangement:** $100 nonreturnable reservation fee; resident pays rent of $400 per month and provides own meals (estimated cost $20 a day). **Guidelines:** prefers Spanish-speaking artists who can use talents to benefit community, and whose work relates to Dominican or Latin American context; residents may teach workshops and are expected to contribute to group exhibition/performance at end of stay; write for further information. **Application procedure:** letter explaining applicant's interest in program, work sample and resume. **Deadline:** 15 Jul 2005. **Notification:** 1 Aug 2005. **Dates:** residencies start 1 Feb 2006, 1 Jun 2006, 1 Sep 2006.

ATLANTIC CENTER FOR THE ARTS

1414 Art Center Ave; New Smyrna Beach, FL 32168; (386) 427-6975,
(800) 393-6975, FAX (386) 427-5669;
email program@atlanticcenterforthearts.org;
website www.atlanticcenterforthearts.org
Paul Markunas, *CEO*
Nicholas Conroy, *Program Director*

Open to: playwrights, composers. **Description:** 5 3-week workshops each year offering writers, choreographers, media, visual and performing artists opportunity of concentrated study with internationally known Master Artists-in-Residence. **Financial arrangement:** housing which includes private room and bath and access to communal studio; weekday meals provided. **Application procedure:** Master Artist specifies submission materials and selects participants; visit website or call for more information. **Deadline:** 3 months before residency. **Notification:** 2 months before residency. **Dates:** exact dates TBA; see website.

BLUE MOUNTAIN CENTER

Box 109; Blue Mountain Lake, NY 12812; (518) 352-7391;
    email bmc1@telenet.net; website www.bluemountaincenter.org
Ben Strader

Open to: playwrights, composers, librettists, lyricists, solo performers. **Description:** 4-week residencies for 14 writers, composers and visual artists at center in Adirondack Mountains. **Financial arrangement:** free room and board. **Guidelines:** artist whose work is aimed at a general audience and reflects social concerns. **Application procedure:** send SASE for information or see website. **Deadline:** 1 Feb 2005. **Notification:** early Apr 2005. **Dates:** mid-Jun–Oct 2005.

BYRDCLIFFE ART COLONY

The Woodstock Guild; 34 Tinker St; Woodstock, NY 12498-1233;
    (845) 679-2079, FAX 679-4529; email wguild@ulster.net;
    website www.woodstockguild.org
Artists Residency Program

Open to: playwrights, translators, librettists, lyricists, solo performers, screenwriters. **Description:** 4-week residencies for writers, composers and visual artists at historic 300-acre colony in the Catskill Mountains, 1½ miles from Woodstock village center, 90 miles north of New York City; private room and separate individual studio space in Villetta Inn, spacious turn-of-the-century mountain lodge; common dining room and living room; residents provide own meals, using community kitchen. **Financial arrangement:** resident pays fee of $600 per session. **Guidelines:** proof of serious commitment to field of endeavor is major criterion for acceptance; professional recognition helpful but not essential; send SASE for further information. **Application procedure:** application, work sample, project description, resume, reviews and articles if available, contact information for 2 references and $5 fee. **Deadline:** 1 Apr 2005 (applications received after deadline considered for space still available). **Notification:** 15 May 2005. **Dates:** Jun–Sep 2005.

CAMARGO FOUNDATION

125 Park Square Ct; 400 Sibley St; St. Paul, MN 55101-1928;
    website www.camargofoundation.org
Ellen Guettler, *U.S. Secretariat*

Open to: playwrights, translators, composers. **Description:** 11 concurrent residencies, most for scholars and teachers pursuing projects relative to Francophone culture, but also including 1 for writer, 1 for composer and 1 for visual artist, at estate in ancient Mediterranean fishing port 30 minutes from Marseilles; furnished apartments; music studio available for composer. **Financial arrangement:** $3500 stipend; free housing; residents provide own meals. **Guidelines:** resident outlines project to fellow colony members during stay and writes final report; families welcome when space available. **Application procedure:** write for guidelines and application. **Deadline:** 15 Jan 2005. **Notification:** 30 Apr 2005. **Dates:** Sep–Dec 2005; Jan–May 2006.

CENTRUM CREATIVE RESIDENCIES PROGRAM

Fort Worden State Park; Box 1158; Port Townsend, WA 98368;
(360) 385-3102, FAX 385-2470; website www.centrum.org
Sally Rodgers, *Residency Program Facilitator*

Open to: playwrights, translators, composers, librettists, lyricists, solo performers, screenwriters, television writers. **Description:** creative residencies for writers, composers, poets, visual artists and choreographers at center near Victorian seaport in 440-acre Fort Worden State Park; self-contained cabins near beach and hiking trails; separate studio space. **Financial arrangement:** free. **Guidelines:** artist who has clear direction and some accomplishment in field; artist who wants to explore new style, medium or genre; download guidelines from web. **Application procedure:** application, project description, work sample and resume. **Deadline:** 1 Sep 2004. **Notification:** 31 Nov 2004. **Dates:** Jan–May 2005; Sep–Nov 2005.

DJERASSI RESIDENT ARTISTS PROGRAM

2325 Bear Gulch Rd; Woodside, CA 94062-4405; (650) 747-1250,
FAX 747-0105; email drap@djerassi.org; website www.djerassi.org
Dennis O'Leary, *Executive Director*
Judy Freeland, *Residency Coordinator*

Open to: playwrights, translators, composers, librettists, lyricists, solo performers, screenwriters. **Description:** 4-week residencies for writers, choreographers, composers, media, visual and interdisciplinary artists and performers concurrently at 600-acre ranch in Santa Cruz mountains 1 hour south of San Francisco; interdisciplinary projects encouraged; collaborative projects considered. **Financial arrangement:** free room and board. **Guidelines:** emerging or established artist whose work has clear direction. **Application procedure:** application, sample of published work or work-in-progress, resume and $25 fee; send SASE for application or download from web. **Deadline:** 15 Feb 2005. **Notification:** 15 Aug 2005. **Dates:** Mar–Nov 2006.

DORSET COLONY FOR WRITERS

Box 510; Dorset, VT 05251-0510; (802) 867-2223, FAX 867-0144;
email theatre@sover.net; website www.dorsetcolony.org
John Nassivera, *Executive Director*

Open to: playwrights, composers, librettists, lyricists. **Description:** residencies of 1 week-1 month at house located in historic village in southern VT. **Financial arrangement:** resident pays $150 per week for housing; meals not provided; large, fully equipped kitchen. **Guidelines:** artist must demonstrate seriousness of purpose and have record of professional achievement (readings or productions of works); collaborative teams may apply; work sample may be requested from less established artist. **Application procedure:** letter of inquiry with description of proposed project and desired length and dates of stay; resume. **Deadline:** open. **Notification:** 3 weeks. **Dates:** 1 Oct–30 Nov; 1 Apr–13 May.

THE HALL FARM CENTER FOR ARTS AND EDUCATION

392 Hall Dr; Townshend, VT 05353; (802) 365-4483;
    email info@hallfarm.org; website www.hallfarm.org
Scott Browning, *Director*

Open to: playwrights, translators, composers, librettists, lyricists, solo performers, screenwriters, television writers. **Description:** 1 week–1 month residencies for 4-5 artists per session on 220 acre farm in southeastern Vermont; private rooms with separate studios; communal barn includes dining room, library and office space. **Financial arrangement:** free. **Application procedure:** application, work sample, project description, letter of recommendation, resume and $20 fee. **Deadline:** 1 Feb 2005. **Notification:** Apr 2005. **Dates:** Jun–Sep.

THE HAMBIDGE CENTER FOR CREATIVE ARTS AND SCIENCES

Box 339; Rabun Gap, GA 30568; (706) 746-5718, FAX 746-9933;
    email center@hambidge.org; website www.hambidge.org

Open to: playwrights, translators, composers, librettists, lyricists. **Description:** residencies of 2 weeks–2 months for professionals in all areas of arts and humanities on 600 acres in northeast GA mountains; 8 private cottages with bedroom, kitchen, bathroom and studio/work area; evening meal provided Tues-Fri. **Financial arrangement:** resident pays minimum of $125 per week toward total cost plus refundable $50 cleaning fee. **Guidelines:** visit website or send SASE for guidelines. **Application procedure:** application, work sample, resume, bio, 3 letters of recommendation from professionals in applicant's field and $20 fee; download application from web. **Deadline:** 1 Oct for spring and summer residencies; 1 May for fall and winter residencies (applications received after deadline considered for space still available). **Notification:** 2-3 months. **Dates:** Feb–Dec.

HAWTHORNDEN CASTLE INTERNATIONAL RETREAT FOR WRITERS

Lasswade, Midlothian; Scotland EH18 1EG; 44-131-440-2180
Administrator

Open to: playwrights. **Description:** residencies of 4 weeks for playwrights, poets and novelists at medieval castle on secluded crag overlooking valley of the River Esk 8 miles south of Edinburgh; 5 writers in residence at any one time; fully furnished study-bedroom; communal breakfast and dinner, lunch brought to writer's room; typewriter rental and use of excellent libraries in Edinburgh can be arranged. **Financial arrangement:** free room and board. **Guidelines:** author of at least 1 published work. **Application procedure:** write for application and further information. **Deadline:** 30 Sep 2004. Notification: mid-Jan 2005. **Dates:** Feb-Dec 2005.

HEADLANDS CENTER FOR THE ARTS

944 Fort Barry; Sausalito, CA 94965; (415) 331-2787,
FAX 331-3857
Kathryn Reasoner, *Executive Director*

Open to: playwrights, composers, librettists, lyricists, screenwriters, television writers. **Description:** residencies of 1-3 months for artists in all disciplines at center in national park on 13,000 acres of coastal wilderness across the bay from San Francisco; accommodation in 4-bedroom house with communal kitchen; meals provided Sun-Thur; 11-month "live-out" residencies available for Bay Area artists only, providing studio space, 2 meals a week and access to center's facilities but no housing; all residents encouraged to interact with fellow artists in other media and with the environment. **Financial arrangement:** free housing for artist from outside Bay Area; studio space for Bay Area artist. **Guidelines:** CA, NC, NJ or OH residents only; students ineligible. **Application procedure:** call or write for information (applications available Apr 2005). **Deadline:** 6 Jun 2005. **Dates:** Mar-Nov 2006.

HEDGEBROOK

2197 Millman Rd; Langley, WA 98260; (360) 321-4786;
website www.hedgebrook.org

Open to: playwrights, librettists. **Description:** residencies of 2 weeks for women writers of diverse cultural backgrounds working in all literary genres; 6 individual cottages on 48 wooded acres on Whidbey Island, near Seattle; writer furnishes own computer; Hedgebrook sponsors, in collaboration with Seattle Repertory Theater, the Women Playwrights Festival, an annual residency specifically for women playwrights; see website for details. **Financial arrangement:** free room and board. **Guidelines:** woman writer of any age, published or unpublished; women of color encouraged to apply. **Application procedure:** application, project description, work sample and $15 fee; send SASE for application. **Deadline:** fall 2004 for 2005 session; exact date TBA. **Notification:** 2 months. **Dates:** Feb-Nov.

HELENE WURLITZER FOUNDATION OF NEW MEXICO

Box 1891; Taos, NM 87571; (505) 758-2413, FAX 758-2559;
email HWF@taosnet.com
Michael Knight, *Director*

Open to: playwrights, composers, screenwriters. **Description:** 11 studio/apartments available to writers, composers, poets and visual artists; length of residency flexible, usually 3 months. **Financial arrangement:** free housing and utilities; resident provides own meals; no financial aid. **Application procedure:** application, project description, work sample and resume; send SASE for application. **Deadline:** 18 Jan 2004. **Dates:** residencies available year-round, but only on limited basis 1 Oct-31 Mar 2004.

ISLE ROYALE NATIONAL PARK ARTIST-IN-RESIDENCE

800 East Lakeshore Dr; Houghton, MI 49931;
  (906) 482-0984 (general information), 487-7152 (Greg Blust),
  FAX 482-8753; email greg_blust@nps.gov;
  website www.nps.gov/volunteer/air.htm

Open to: playwrights, composers, lyricists, solo performers. **Description:** 1 artist at a time housed for 2-3 weeks in cabin on remote island on Lake Superior; no electricity; resident must bring 2-3-week supply of food. **Financial arrangement:** free housing. **Guidelines:** writer with artistic integrity, ability to live in wilderness environment and to relate to park through their work; must donate 1 work to park and communicate experience of residency through programs for public. **Application procedure:** application, project description, work sample and resume. **Deadline:** 16 Feb 2005. **Notification:** 15 Apr 2005. **Dates:** Jun–Sep 2005.

THE JOHN STEINBECK WRITER'S ROOM

Long Island University–Southampton Campus Library;
  Southampton, NY 11968; (631) 287-8382, FAX 287-4049;
  email library@southampton.liu.edu
Robert Gerbereux, *Library Director*

Open to: playwrights. **Description:** small room, space for 4 writers; carrel, storage space, access to reference material in room and to library. **Financial arrangement:** free. **Guidelines:** writer working under contract or with specific commitment. **Application procedure:** application. **Notification:** 1 week. **Dates:** year-round.

KALANI OCEANSIDE RETREAT, INSTITUTE FOR CULTURE AND WELLNESS

RR2 Box 4500; Pahoa–Beach Road, HI 96778-9724; (808) 965-7828,
  FAX 965-0527; email kalani@kalani.com; website www.kalani.com
Richard Koob, *Director*

Open to: playwrights, translators, composers, librettists, lyricists, solo performers, screenwriters, television writers. **Description:** up to 20 artists share four 500-1000-square-foot studio spaces for 2-week to 2-month residencies at 113-acre coastal resort spa with private rooms, resturaunt and shared or private baths. **Financial arrangement:** artist eligible for 50% discount on regular daily room rates of $110–240; meals available at resort restaurant, artist pays per meal or $43 per day. **Guidelines:** any artist with demonstrated ability to complete projects. **Application procedure:** application, project description, work sample and resume with $10 fee. **Deadline:** open. **Notification:** within 1 week of receipt of application. **Dates:** ongoing, but discounted rates more likely available May–Nov.

LANESBORO RESIDENCY PROGRAM FELLOWSHIPS

Cornucopia Arts Center; Box 152; Lanesboro, MN 55949; (507) 467-2446,
FAX 467-4446; email cac2446@acegroup.cc;
website www.lanesboroarts.org
Sara Decker, *Administrative Director*

Open to: playwrights, composer, librettists, lyricists, screenwriters, television writers. **Description:** 4-6 residencies of 1, 2 or 4-weeks in small MN town with historic Main Street, 200-foot bluffs, trout river and bike trail; active arts and cultural community; artist spends minimum 6-8 hours working in community as part of their proposed project. **Financial arrangement:** $500-2500 stipend. **Guidelines:** innovative and creative projects which further artists' work and promote meaningful community experience; send SASE for application and guidelines. **Application procedure:** application form, work sample, 1-page community project description, resume, artist statement and 2 letters of reference. **Deadline:** 15 June for residencies Sep-Jan; 15 Oct for residencies Feb-Aug. **Notification:** 2 months. **Dates:** Sep-Jan; Feb-Aug.

LEDIG HOUSE INTERNATIONAL WRITERS' COLONY

55 Fifth Ave; 15th Floor; New York, NY 10003; (212) 206-6060,
FAX 206-6114; email artomi55@aol.com; website www.artomi.org
David Knowles, *Executive Director*

Open to: playwrights, translators, screenwriters, television writers. **Description:** residencies of 2 weeks-2 months in the spring and fall for writers of all genres at 150-acre farm in upstate NY with library and computer access; private sleeping and work space; communal living and dining rooms; all meals provided. **Financial arrangement:** free room and board. **Guidelines:** published and unpublished writers proficient in English; call or fax for guidelines. **Application procedure:** project description, work sample, resume and letter of recommendation with SASE for notification. **Deadline:** 30 Nov annually. **Notification:** 31 Dec annually. **Dates:** spring session 1 Apr-15 Jun 2005; fall session 19 Aug-31 Oct 2005.

LEIGHTON STUDIOS FOR INDEPENDENT RESIDENCIES

The Banff Centre; Box 1020, Station 28; 107 Tunnel Mountain Dr;
Banff, Alberta; Canada T1L 1H5; (403) 762-6180, (800) 565-9989,
FAX (403) 762-6345; email arts_info@banffcentre.ab.ca;
website www.banffcentre.ca
Office of the Registrar

Open to: playwrights, translators, composers, librettists, lyricists, performance artists, screenwriters, television writers. **Description:** residencies of 1 week-3 months for writers and composers at studios situated in mountains of Banff National Park; 8 furnished studios, each with washroom, kitchenette, Macintosh G3 laptop or G4 desktop with printing capabilities, CD/cassette player and internet and email access; living accommodations (single room with bath) on Centre's main campus; nearby access to all amenities of Centre, including dining room, library and recreation complex. **Financial arrangement:** resident pays approximate daily cost of $110 Canadian (about $70 U.S.) for studio, room and meals; discount on studio cost available for those who demonstrate need. **Guidelines:** established or emerging artist who demonstrates sustained contribution to own field and shows evidence of significant achievement. **Application procedure:** write or email for application and further information or download from web. **Deadline:** open; apply at least 6 months before desired residency. **Dates:** year-round.

THE MACDOWELL COLONY

100 High St; Peterborough, NH 03458-2485; (603) 924-3886,
   (212) 535-9690, FAX (603) 924-9142;
   email info@macdowellcolony.org; website www.macdowellcolony.org
Cheryl Young, *Executive Director*

Open to: playwrights, composers, screenwriters. **Description:** residencies of up to 2 months for writers, composers, visual artists, video/filmmakers, architects and interdisciplinary artists at 450-acre estate; free room, board and exclusive use of studio; studios and common areas accessible for those with mobility impairments. **Financial arrangement:** voluntary contributions accepted; travel grants available; writers in need of financial assistance are eligible for grants of up to $1000 to relieve financial burdens related to their stay at the Colony. **Guidelines:** admission based on talent. **Application procedure:** application, work samples, project description, names of 2 professional references and $20 fee; collaborating artists must apply separately; send SASE, call or visit website for application. **Deadline:** 15 Sep 2004 for 1 Jan-30 Apr 2005; 15 Jan 2005 for 1 May-31 Aug 2005; 15 Apr 2005 for 1 Sep-31 Dec 2005. **Notification:** 2 months. **Dates:** year-round.

MARY ANDERSON CENTER FOR THE ARTS

101 St. Francis Dr; Mount St. Francis, IN 47146; (812) 923-8602,
   FAX 923-0294; email maca@iglou.com;
   website www.maryandersoncenter.org
Debra Carmody, *Executive Director*

Open to: playwrights, translators, composers, librettists, lyricists. **Description:** residencies of 1 week-3 months for 7 writers and visual artists concurrently at center on beautiful 400-acre wooded site with lake, 15 minutes from Louisville, KY; private studio/bedroom, communal kitchen and dining room. **Financial arrangement:** resident pays fee of $60 a day for room and board; possibility of funded residencies or work exchange program; write for information. **Guidelines:** formal education and production credits are not requirements but will be taken into consideration when applications are reviewed. **Application procedure:** application, project description, work sample, resume and 2 references. **Deadline:** open. **Notification:** 1 month. **Dates:** year-round.

THE MILLAY COLONY FOR THE ARTS

454 East Hill Rd; Box 3; Austerlitz, NY 12017-0003;
  (518) 392-3103; email nikkihayes@millaycolony.org;
  website www.millaycolony.org
Nikki Hayes, *Executive Assistant*

Open to: playwrights, composers, screenwriters. **Description:** 1-month residencies for up to 6 writers, composers, photographers, filmmakers and visual artists concurrently at 600-acre estate in upstate NY; studio space and separate bedroom; colony accommodates artists with disabilities. **Financial arrangement:** free room, board and studio space. **Application procedure:** application and supporting materials; send SASE or email application@millaycolony.org for application. **Deadline:** 1 Nov 2004. **Notification:** 1 Feb 2005. **Dates:** Apr-Nov.

MONTANA ARTISTS REFUGE

Box 8; Basin, MT 59631; (406) 225-3500; email mar@mt.net;
  website www.montanarefuge.org
Joy Lewis, *Residency Coordinator*

Open to: playwrights, translators, composers, librettists, lyricists, solo performers, screenwriters, television writers. **Description:** 1-month-1-year residencies for 3-5 artists of all disciplines, located in a former gold camp in the midst of the Rocky Mountains, approximately 12 miles from the Continental Divide; Basin has 250 residents, two restaurant/bars, café/espresso shop, post office and town park; artists housed in 3 fully equipped apartments, all with kitchens and private phones. **Financial arrangement:** resident pays $395-550 per month; meals not provided; financial aid available for up to full rent. **Guidelines:** send SASE for guidelines or download from web. **Application procedure:** application, work sample, project description and resume. **Deadline:** 15 Aug for Jan-Apr; 15 Jan for May-Aug; 15 May for Sep-Dec.

NEW YORK MILLS ARTS RETREAT

24 North Main Ave; New York Mills, MN 56567; (218) 385-3339;
  email nymills@uslink.net; website www.kulcher.org
Heather Humbert Price, *Arts Retreat Coordinator*

Open to: playwrights, composers, librettists, lyricists, solo performers, screenwriters. **Description:** 1 artist at a time housed for 2-4 weeks in small farming community in north central Minnesota; housing in small one-bedroom home; resident provides own meals. **Financial arrangement:** Jerome Foundation Fellowships stipend of $1500 for 4-week residency or $750 for 2-week residency, placing special emphasis on opportunities for artists of color. **Guidelines:** emerging artist of demonstrated ability; must donate minimum 8 hours during residency to community outreach, most often teaching in area schools. **Application procedure:** application, project description, work sample, resume and 2 letters of recommendation. **Deadline:** 1 Oct 2004; 1 Apr 2005. **Notification:** 8 weeks after deadline. **Dates:** Jan-Jun; Jul-Dec.

NORCROFT

Box 218; Lutsen, MN 55612; (800) 770-0058; website www.norcroft.org

Kay Grindland, *Managing Director*

Open to: playwrights, translators, librettists, screenwriters, television writers. **Description:** 4 concurrent residencies of 1-4 weeks for women writers in all genres at remote lodge on shores of Lake Superior; private bedroom and separate individual "writing shed." **Financial arrangement:** free housing; groceries provided, resident does own cooking. **Guidelines:** women only; artist whose work demonstrates an understanding of and commitment to feminist change; download application from web. **Application procedure:** application, 5-page writing sample and one essay each on feminism and commitment to writing. **Deadline:** 1 Oct 2004. **Notification:** 1 Apr 2005. **Dates:** May-Oct 2005.

RAGDALE FOUNDATION

1260 North Green Bay Rd; Lake Forest, IL 60045;
    (847) 234-1063, ext 206; email mosher@ragdale.org;
    website www.ragdale.org

Melissa Mosher, *Director of Admissions*

Open to: playwrights, composers, librettists, performance artists. **Description:** residencies of 2 weeks-2 months for writers, composers and visual artists from the U.S. and abroad on property situated on edge of 55-acre prairie, 1 mile from town center. **Financial arrangement:** resident pays $105 a week for room and board; partial or full fee waivers awarded on basis of financial need. **Guidelines:** admission based on quality of work submitted. **Application procedure:** application, description of work-in-progress, work sample, resume, 2 references and $30 fee; request guidelines via email, phone, SASE or by visiting website. **Deadline:** 15 Jan for Jun-Dec; 1 Jun for Jan-Apr. **Notification:** 15 Apr for Jan deadline; 1 Sep for Jun deadline. **Dates:** year-round except for May, 1 week in Oct and last 2 weeks in Dec.

ROCKY MOUNTAIN NATIONAL PARK
ARTIST-IN-RESIDENCE PROGRAM

1000 Highway 36; Estes Park, CO 80517; (970) 586-1206;
    website www.nps.gov/romo

Information Office

Open to: playwrights, composers, lyricists, solo performers. **Description:** 2-week residencies for 1 artist at a time in renovated historic furnished cabin overlooking meadow and stream with Rocky Mountains in distance; 1 bedroom, kitchen, living/dining room, bathroom and porch; artist gives 2 45-minute public presentations. **Financial arrangement:** free housing; resident provides own meals; must donate 1 appropriate work within 1 year of residency. **Guidelines:** professional artist. **Application procedure:** 6 copies of application and intent of residency, work sample, 6 copies of resume with list of professional works; write or call for application. **Deadline:** 1 Dec 2004; no submission before 15 Oct 2004. **Notification:** Mar 2005, exact date TBA. **Dates:** Jun-Sep 2005.

STUDIO FOR CREATIVE INQUIRY
Carnegie Mellon University; College of Fine Arts;
Pittsburgh, PA 15213-3890; (412) 268-3454, FAX 268-2829;
email mmbm@andrew.cmu.edu; website www.cmu.edu/studio/
Marge Myers, *Associate Director*

Open to: playwrights, translators, composers, librettists, lyricists, solo performers, screenwriters, television writers. **Description:** residencies of 6 months-3 years concurrently for artists in all disciplines; residency provides studio facility located in Carnegie Mellon's College of Fine Arts building, including office and meeting space, work area, computers, sound and video editing equipment; fellows may also use resources of university, including library. **Financial arrangement:** stipend; assistance in finding housing in community. **Guidelines:** writer able to use science and technology in work, interested in taking leadership role in collaborative projects and able to relate work to larger community. **Application procedure:** concept proposal, work sample and resume; admission based on quality of work, clear statement of intention, experience with collaboration and project feasibility. **Deadline:** open. **Notification:** 2 months. **Dates:** year-round.

THE TYRONE GUTHRIE CENTRE
Annaghmakerrig; Newbliss; County Monaghan;
Ireland; 353-47-54003, FAX 353-47-54380;
email thetgc@indigo.ie; website www.tyroneguthrie.ie
Sheila Pratschke, *Resident Director*

Open to: playwrights, composers, librettists, lyricists, screenwriters, television writers. **Description:** residencies of 1 week-6 months for artists in all disciplines at former country home of Tyrone Guthrie, set amid 450 acres of forested estate overlooking large lake; private apartments; music room, rehearsal/performance space and extensive library. **Financial arrangement:** non-Irish artists pay about 2550 EURO (about $3170) a month for housing and meals; self-catering houses also available at reasonable rents; fees may be negotiable depending on factors such as length of stay, nature of project, involvement with Irish artists or institutions, etc. **Guidelines:** artist must show evidence of sustained dedication and a significant level of achievement; prefers artist with clearly defined project; artist teams (e.g., writer/director, composer/librettist) welcome. **Application procedure:** write for application and further information. **Deadline:** open. **Dates:** year-round.

UCROSS FOUNDATION RESIDENCY PROGRAM
30 Big Red Ln; Clearmont, WY 82835; (307) 737-2291,
FAX 737-2322; email ucross@wyoming.com;
website www.ucrossfoundation.org
Sharon Dynak, *Executive Director*

Open to: playwrights, translators, composers, librettists, lyricists. **Description:** residency of 2 weeks-2 months at "Big Red," restored historic site in the foothills of the Big Horn Mountains; 8 concurrent residencies for writers, composers and visual artists; opportunity to concentrate on own work without distraction and to present work to local communities, if desired. **Financial arrangement:** free room, board and studio space. **Guidelines:** admission based on quality of work and commitment; send SASE for application and further information. **Application procedure:** application, project description and work sample. **Deadline:** 1 Oct for Feb–Jun; 1 Mar for Aug–Dec. **Notification:** 8 weeks. **Dates:** year-round except Jan and Jul.

THE U.S./JAPAN CREATIVE ARTISTS' PROGRAM

Japan–U.S. Friendship Commission; 1110 Vermont Ave NW,
    Suite 800; Washington, DC 20005; (202) 418-9800,
    FAX 418-9802; email jusfc@jusfc.gov; website www.jusfc.gov
Eric J. Gangloff, *Executive Director*

Open to: playwrights, composers, librettists, lyricists, solo performers, screenwriters, television writers. **Description:** residencies of 6 continuous months for 3–5 artists each year; residents find own housing in location of their choice in Japan. **Financial arrangement:** monthly stipend of ¥400,000 (about $3670) plus ¥100,000 (about $920) for housing and ¥100,000 (about $920) for professional expenses; free travel and pre-departure Japanese language instruction. **Guidelines:** U.S. citizen or permanent resident; mid-career professional artist with compelling reason to work in Japan and whose work "exemplifies the best in U.S. art"; visit website for application and further information. **Application procedure:** application, work sample and resume. **Deadline:** 26 Jun 2005.

VIRGINIA CENTER FOR THE CREATIVE ARTS

154 San Angelo Dr; Amherst, VA 24521; (434) 946-7236,
    FAX 946-7239; email vcca@vcca.com; website www.vcca.com
Director

Open to: playwrights, translators, composers, librettists, lyricists, screenwriters. **Description:** residencies of 2 weeks–2 months for writers, composers and visual and performance artists at 450-acre estate in Blue Ridge Mountains; separate studios and bedrooms; all meals provided. **Financial arrangement:** resident pays suggested minimum of $30 a day for room and board or as means allow; financial status not a factor in selection process. **Guidelines:** admission based on achievement or promise of achievement. **Application procedure:** application, work sample, resume and 2 recommendations. **Deadline:** 15 Sep for Feb–May; 15 Jan for Jun–Sep; 15 May for Oct–Jan. **Notification:** 3 months. **Dates:** year-round.

WILLIAM FLANAGAN MEMORIAL CREATIVE PERSONS CENTER

Edward F. Albee Foundation; 14 Harrison St;
    New York, NY 10013; (212) 226-2020;
    website www.pipeline.com/~jtnyc/albeefdtn.html

Open to: playwrights, translators, composers, librettists, screenwriters. **Description:** 1-month residencies for up to 5 writers, composers and visual artists concurrently at "The Barn" in Montauk, Long Island. **Financial arrangement:** free housing.

Guidelines: admission based on talent and need; write or visit website for further information. **Application procedure:** application, script (recording for composers) and supporting materials. **Deadline:** 1 Apr 2005; no submission before 1 Jan 2005. **Notification:** May 2005. **Dates:** 1 Jun-1 Oct 2005.

WILLIAM INGE CENTER FOR THE ARTS

Box 708; Independence, KS 67301; (620) 331-4100, ext 4216;
FAX 331-9022; email bpeterson@ingecenter.org;
website www.ingecenter.org
Peter Ellenstein, *Artistic Director*

Open to: playwrights. **Description:** residencies of 8-9 weeks for 2 writers at a time at William Inge's family home in small Midwestern town; private bedroom in historic 1920s-era home, shared bath; playwrights share teaching of 1 college class and 1 high-school class 10-12 hours a week and receive at least 1 rehearsed reading of work.. **Financial arrangement:** $4000 stipend, travel; meals not provided. **Guidelines:** playwrights with teaching experience and whose work has had several professional productions. **Application procedure:** writing sample, project description, resume (with references and teaching experience), 1-page bio, 3 letters of recommendation from professional theatres or play development centers, availability over next 2 years and letter of inquiry. **Deadline:** ongoing. **Notification:** 10 weeks.

WRITERS & BOOKS GELL CENTER OF THE FINGER LAKES

c/o Writers & Books; 740 University Ave; Rochester, NY 14607;
(585) 473-2590, ext 103, FAX 442-9333; website www.wab.org
Kathy Pottetti, *Gell Center Director of Operations and Programming*

Open to: playwrights, translators, librettists, lyricists, solo performers, screenwriters, television writers. **Description:** private bedroom and bath plus shared living, dining and kitchen area available in house surrounded by 23 acres of woodlands; residents provide own meals. **Financial arrangement:** resident pays $35 a day. **Application procedure:** write or call for application. **Deadline:** open. **Notification:** 1 week. **Dates:** year-round.

THE WRITERS ROOM

740 Braodway, 12th Floor; New York, NY 10003; (212) 254-6995,
FAX 533-6059; website www.writersroom.org
Donna Brodie, *Executive Director*

Open to: playwrights, translators, composers, librettists, lyricists. **Description:** large room with 40 desks separated by partitions, space for 400 writers each quarter; open 24 hours a day year-round; kitchen, lounge and bathrooms, storage for files and laptops, small reference library; monthly readings. **Financial arrangement:** $75 application fee; $300-500 semi-annual fee (6-month period). **Guidelines:** writer, emerging or established, must show seriousness of intent. **Application procedure:** application and references; all inquiries by mail or through website (no visits without appointment).

THE WRITERS' STUDIO

The Mercantile Library Association; 17 East 47th St;
New York, NY 10017; (212) 755-6710, FAX 758-1387;
email info@mercantilelibrary.org

Harold Augenbraum, *Director*

Open to: playwrights, composers. **Description:** carrel space for 17 writers in not-for-profit, private lending library of 175,000 volumes; storage for personal computers, library membership. **Financial arrangement:** $200 fee for 3 months, renewal possible for up to 1 year. **Guidelines:** open to all writers; unpublished writer must submit evidence of serious intent. **Application procedure:** application and work sample or project outline, interview with library director.

YADDO

Box 395; Saratoga Springs, NY 12866-0395; (518) 584-0746,
FAX 584-1312; email yaddo@yaddo.org; website www.yaddo.org

Admissions Committee

Open to: playwrights, composers, performance artists, screenwriters. **Description:** residencies of 2 weeks-2 months for artists in all genres, working individually or as collaborative teams of up to 3 persons, at 19th-century estate on 400 acres; approximate total of 200 residents a year (15 concurrently Sep-May, 34 concurrently May-Labor Day). **Financial arrangement:** free room, board and studio space. **Guidelines:** admission based on review by panels composed of artists in each genre; quality of work submitted is major criterion; send 55¢ SASE for application and further information. **Application procedure:** application, work sample, resume, 2 letters of support, $20 fee and SASP for acknowledgment of receipt. **Deadline:** 15 Jan 2005 for mid-May 2005-Feb 2006; 1 Aug 2005 for 1 Nov 2005-mid-May 2006. **Notification:** 1 Apr 2005 for Jan deadline; 1 Oct 2005 for Aug deadline. **Dates:** year-round except early Sep.

MEMBERSHIP AND SERVICE ORGANIZATIONS

What's included here?

A number of organizations that exist to serve either the American playwright or a wider constituency of writers, composers and arts professionals. Some have a particular regional or special-interest orientation; some provide links to theatres in other countries. Taken together, these organizations represent an enormous range of services available to those who write for the theatre, and it is worth getting to know them.

THE ALLIANCE OF LOS ANGELES PLAYWRIGHTS
7510 Sunset Blvd, #1050; Los Angeles, CA 90046-3418;
   (323) 957-4752; email ALAPnews@aol.com;
   website www.laplaywrights.org
Dan Berkowitz and Jon Dorf, *Co-Chairs*

Founded in 1993, ALAP is a support and service organization dedicated to addressing the professional needs of the Los Angeles playwriting community. ALAP's programs and activities include the Playwrights Expo, which brings together L.A. playwrights and dozens of representatives of local and national theatres; the series In Our Own Voices, in which members read from and share their work; the annual Playreading Festival in which local theatres present rehearsed readings of members' plays; a bimonthly New Works Lab, featuring table readings of plays in development; a website with a catalog of members' scripts; the C. Bernard Jackson Award, given in recognition of individuals and organizations that nurture, develop and support L.A. playwrights; symposia and panel discussions; networking and social events; and a hotline listing upcoming events. ALAP's publications include the bimonthly *NewsFlash*, which keeps members posted on upcoming events; and an annual membership directory. Annual dues are $35.

THE ALLIANCE OF RESIDENT THEATRES/NEW YORK
575 Eighth Ave, Suite 17S; New York, NY 10018; (212) 244-6667,
   FAX 714-1918; email questions@art-newyork.org
   website www.offbroadwayonline.com
Virginia P. Louloudes, *Executive Director*

The Alliance of Resident Theates/New York (A.R.T./New York), founded in 1972, is the service organization for Off-Broadway theatre, currently serving nearly 400 not-for-profit theatres and related organizations throughout the five boroughs of New York City. In recent years, A.R.T./New York has established itself as a provider of management-related technical assistance, a grantmaker to small and emerging theatres, a provider of low-cost office and rehearsal space, a developer and producer of audience initiatives and an advocate for the arts at the state and local levels.

ALTERNATE ROOTS
1083 Austin Ave; Atlanta, GA 30307; (404) 577-1079,
   FAX 577-7991; email info@alternateroots.org;
   website www.alternateroots.org
Kim Waters, *Managing Director*

Founded in 1976, Alternate ROOTS is a service organization run by and for southeastern artists. Its mission is to support the creation and presentation of original art in all its forms that is rooted in a particular community of place, tradition or spirit. It is committed to social and economic justice and the protection of the natural world, and addresses these concerns through its programs and services. ROOTS now has more than 200 individual members across the country, including playwrights, directors, choreographers, musicians, storytellers and new vaudevillians, and representatives of diverse performing and presenting organizations. ROOTS makes artistic resources available to its members through workshops; creates appropriate distribution networks for the new work being generated in the region via touring, publications and liaison activity; and provides opportunities for enhanced visibility and financial stability via publications and periodic performance festivals. Opportunities for member playwrights include readings and peer critiques of works-in-progress at the organization's annual meeting. Membership is open to all artists whose work is consistent with the goals of ROOTS; members are accepted throughout the year. The organization's meetings and workshops are open to the public and its newsletter is available to the public for a small fee. Annual membership dues are $50 for members, $75 for board members; $20 introductory membership available, see website.

AMERICAN INDIAN COMMUNITY HOUSE
708 Broadway, 8th Floor; New York, NY 10003; (212) 598-0100,
 FAX 598-4909; website www.aich.org
Jim Cyrus, *Performing Arts Director*

American Indian Community House was founded in 1969 to encourage the interest of all U.S. ethnic groups in the cultural contributions of the American Indian, and to foster intercultural exchanges. The organization now serves the Native American population of the New York City region through a variety of social, economic and educational programs, and through cultural programs which include theatre events, an art gallery and a newsletter. Native Americans in the Arts, the performing arts component of the Community House, is committed to the development and production of works by Indian authors, and presents staged readings, workshops and full productions in The Circle, their in-house performance space. The Community House also sponsors several other performing groups, including Spiderwoman Theatre, Coatlicue Theatre Company, Off the Beaten Path, the Thunderbird American Indian Dancers, the Silver Cloud Singers and the jazz-fusion and traditional singing group Ulali. A showcase for Native American artists is presented to agents and casting directors once a year.

AMERICAN MUSIC CENTER (AMC)
30 West 26th St, Suite 1001; New York, NY 10010-2011;
 (212) 366-5260, ext 10, FAX 366-5265; email center@amc.net;
 website www.amc.net
Richard Kessler, *Executive Director*

Founded in 1939, the American Music Center provides numerous programs and services for composers, performers and others interested in contemporary American classical music and jazz. The Composer Assistance Program helps composers pay for extracting performance materials, creating media for electronic works and obtaining licenses to use text that is in copyright. The American Music Center Collection at the New York Public Library for the Performing Arts (see listing this section) contains more than 60,000 scores and recordings, including a large collection of opera and music-theatre works, available to the public. The AMC provides information on competitions, publishers, performing ensembles, composers and other areas of interest in new music, and offers a catalog entitled *Opportunities in New Music.* Its website, NewMusicBox (www.newmusicbox.org), is a free monthly online publication that includes interviews, samples of new recordings, an open forum for discussion and much more. Members receive the monthly "Opportunity Update"; are able to post scores and recordings on their "online library" (www.newmusicjukebox.org), which includes a database searchable by composer, title, instrumentation and keywords; and receive discounts for the AMC's professional development programs and on all AMC publications. Membership is open to the public. Annual dues are $55 for individuals ($35 for students and senior citizens); organization membership also available.

AMERICAN TRANSLATORS ASSOCIATION (ATA)

225 Reinekers Ln, Suite 590; Alexandria, VA 22314-2840;
    (703) 683-6100, FAX 683-6122; email ata@atanet.org;
    website www.atanet.org
Walter W. Bacak, Jr., *Executive Director*

Founded in 1959, the ATA is a national not-for-profit association which seeks to promote recognition of the translation profession; disseminate information for the benefit of translators and those who use their services; define and maintain professional standards; foster and support the training of translators and interpreters; and provide a medium of cooperation with persons in allied professions. Members receive the monthly *ATA Chronicle*, a membership directory and inclusion in the online *Directory of Translating and Interpreting Services.* ATA holds an annual conference and sponsors several honors and awards (see American Translators Association Awards in Prizes). Active membership is open to U.S. citizens and permanent residents who have professionally engaged in translating or closely related work and have passed an ATA certification examination or demonstrated professional attainment by other prescribed means. Those who meet these professional standards but are not U.S. citizens or residents may hold corresponding membership; other interested persons may be associate members. Interested persons should contact ATA for a membership application, or visit the ATA website. Annual dues are $60 for associate-students; $120 for active, corresponding and associate members; $150 for institutions; and $300 for corporations.

ASCAP (AMERICAN SOCIETY OF COMPOSERS, AUTHORS AND PUBLISHERS)

1 Lincoln Plaza; New York, NY 10023; (212) 621-6234, FAX 621-6558;
    website www.ascap.com
Michael A. Kerker, *Director of Musical Theatre*

ASCAP is a not-for-profit organization whose members are writers and publishers of musical works. It operates as a clearinghouse for performing rights, offering licenses that authorize the public performance of all the music of its composer, lyricist and music publishing members and collects license fees for these members. ASCAP also sponsors workshops for member and nonmember theatre writers (see ASCAP

Musical Theatre Workshop in Development). Membership in ASCAP is open to any composer or lyricist who has been commercially recorded or regularly published.

ASSITEJ/USA (INTERNATIONAL ASSOCIATION OF THEATRE FOR CHILDREN AND YOUNG PEOPLE)

724 Second Ave S; Nashville, TN 37210; (615) 254-5719, FAX 254-3255; email usassitej@aol.com; website www.assitej-usa.org

Steve Bianchi, *Membership Director*

Founded in 1965, ASSITEJ/USA is a national service organization promoting the power of professional theatre for young audiences through excellence, collaboration and innovation across cultural and international boundaries. Members include theatres, institutions and individuals concerned about the theatre, young audiences and international goodwill. Members receive *Theatre for Young Audiences Today*, published 2 times annually, and priority consideration for participation in national and international events. Membership costs $30 a year for students, $35 for retirees, $50 for libraries, $65 for individuals, $125-375 for organizations (depending on size of budget).

ASSOCIATION FOR JEWISH THEATRE

c/o Winnipeg Jewish Theatre; C402-123 Doncaster; Winnipeg, MB R3N2B2; Canada; (204) 477-7518, FAX 477-7516; email Kayla@wjt.ca; website www.afjt.com

Kayla Gordon, *Past President*

Founded in 1987, the Association for Jewish Theatre is dedicated to promoting the development and production of plays relevant to Jewish life and values. AJT acts to promote the visibility and viability of those theatres dedicated to a Jewish mission. Membership is open to theatres, as well as individual artists, who have shown a commitment to Jewish theatre. Services include annual conference (reduced fee for members), new play showcases at conferences, free tickets to member theatre productions, publication of semiannual newsletter, networking opportunities and assistance in coordinating cooperatively developed projects. Annual dues range from $35-100 depending on theatre budget and individual financial situation; dues are reevaluated by board each year.

ASSOCIATION FOR THEATRE IN HIGHER EDUCATION (ATHE)

Box 69; Downers Grove, IL 60515-0069; (888) 284-3737, FAX (630) 964-1941; email nericksn@aol.com; website www.athe.org

Nancy Erickson, *Administrative Director*

Founded in 1986, ATHE is an organization composed of individuals and institutions that provides leadership for the profession and promotes excellence in theatre education. Membership services include insurance benefits; scholarships; annual professional awards, including the Jane Chambers Playwriting Award (see Prizes); and assistance with issues such as tenure and alternate employment opportunities. The annual conference convenes theatre scholars, educators and professionals from all over the world to participate in workshops, performances, plenary sessions and group meetings. ATHE publishes several periodicals of interest to the theatre professional, including *ATHENEWS*, a newsletter that includes a list of teaching positions available at member organizations; *Theatre Topics*, a semiannual journal; *Theatre Journal*, a quarterly journal; a membership directory and pamphlets on various topics such as assessment guidelines for higher education theatre programs and tenure. There are 5 annual membership levels: students, $50; retirees, $80; individuals, $105; 2-person households, $155; organizations, $195. Members receive all publications.

ASSOCIATION OF HISPANIC ARTS

220 East 10th St, 3rd floor; New York, NY 10029; (212) 876-1242,
FAX 727-1285; email ahanews@latinoarts.org;
website www.latinoarts.org
Frank Puig, *Executive Director*

Founded in 1975, AHA is a multidisciplinary organization which supports Hispanic arts organizations and individual artists with technical assistance. Its quarterly publication, *AHA! Hispanic Arts News*, features articles on the local and national arts community, including artists' profiles and a calendar of events. AHA's website lists up-to-date information on events, opportunities and happenings in the arts community.

ASSOCIATION OF INDEPENDENT VIDEO AND FILMMAKERS (AIVF)

304 Hudson St, 6th Floor; New York, NY 10013; (212) 807-1400,
FAX 463-8519; email info@aivf.org; website www.aivf.org
Elizabeth Peters, *Executive Director*

AIVF is a national membership organization serving over 5,000 independent filmmakers. Its mission is to increase the creative and professional opportunities for independent video and filmmakers and to enhance the growth of independent media. In addition to publishing *The Independent Film & Video Monthly*, AIVF provides advice and referral services; informative seminars and networking events; trade discounts; group health insurance plans; online resources and advocacy for media arts issues.

THE ASSOCIATION OF WRITERS & WRITING PROGRAMS (AWP)

Mail Stop 1E3; George Mason University; Fairfax, VA 22030; (703) 993-4301,
FAX 993-4302; email awp@gmu.edu; website www.awpwriter.org
David Fenza, *Executive Director*

Founded in 1967, AWP is a not-for-profit organization serving the needs of writers, college and university writing programs, and students of writing by providing information services, job placement assistance, publishing opportunities, literary arts advocacy and forums on all aspects of writing and its instruction. Writers' Conferences & Centers (WC&C), an association of 80 nonacademic conferences for writers, is now a division of AWP. Writers not affiliated with colleges and universities but who support collective efforts to improve opportunities are also represented by AWP. The *Writer's Chronicle*, published 6 times annually and available for $20 a year, includes listings of publishing opportunities, grants, awards and fellowships; interviews with writers; and essays on writing technique. The *AWP Official Guide to Writing Programs* (11th edition, $28.45 including shipping) offers a listing of writing programs and a section on writing conferences, colonies and centers.

AUSTIN SCRIPT WORKS (ASW)

Box 9787; Austin, TX 78766; (512) 454-9727;
email info@scriptworks.org; website www.scriptworks.org
Christina J. Moore, *Producing Director*

Founded in 1997, Austin Script Works is a playwright-driven organization which provides support for playwrights at all stages in the writing process. ASW's programs include salon readings, staged readings, workshops, one-act commissions, writing retreats, online services and support for full productions. Associate Membership ($35 annually) is open to anyone. Benefits of Associate membership include participation in salon readings and the 10-minute playwriting retreat; the opportunity to apply for staged readings and 10-minute play showcase productions; and discounts to all ASW events. Core membership ($50 annually) is open only to playwrights living in the central Texas region. Playwrights are selected for a 4-year period based on script submission. Core members receive all benefits of Associate members and are also eligible to apply for small stipends, commissions and extended workshop opportunities.

BLACK THEATRE NETWORK (BTN)

7226 Virginia Ave; St. Louis, MO 63111; (314) 352-3771;
website www.blacktheatre.org
Gregory Horton, *President*

Black Theatre Network (BTN) is a national network of professional artists, scholars and community groups founded in 1986 to provide an opportunity for the interchange of ideas; publish information regarding black theatre activity; provide an annual national forum to view and discuss black theatre; and encourage and promote black dramatists and the production of plays about the black experience. BTN members are eligible to attend national conferences and workshops and receive complimentary copies of all BTN publications, which include the quarterly *Black Theatre Network News*, listing conferences, contests, BTN business matters and national items of interest; *Black Theatre Directory*, which contains more than 800 listings of black theatre artists, scholars, companies, higher education programs and service organizations; *Dissertations Concerning Black Theatre: 1900–1994*, a listing of Ph.D. theses; and *Black Theatre Connections*, a quarterly listing of jobs in educational and professional theatre, and other career development opportunities. *Black Voices*, a catalog of works by black playwrights, is available from BTN for $20. Annual dues are $35 for retirees and students, $75 for individuals, $110 for organizations.

BMI (BROADCAST MUSIC INCORPORATED)

320 West 57th St; New York, NY 10019-3790; (212) 586-2000,
FAX 262-2824
Jean Banks, *Senior Director, Musical Theater and Jazz*

BMI, founded in 1940, is a performing rights organization which acts as a steward for the public performance of the music of its writers and publishers, offering licenses to music users. BMI monitors music performances and distributes royalties to those whose music has been used. Any writer whose songs have been published and are likely to be performed can join BMI at no cost. BMI also sponsors a musical theatre workshop (see BMI-Lehman Engel Musical Theatre Workshop in Development).

The BMI Foundation (President, Ralph Jackson) was established in 1984 to provide support for individuals in furthering their musical education and to assist organizations involved in the performance of music and music training.

CENTRE FOR CREATIVE COMMUNITIES

118 Commercial St; London E1 6NF; England; 44-20-7247-5385,
FAX 44-20-7247-5256; email info@creativecommunities.org.uk;
website www.creativecommunities.org.uk
Jennifer Williams, *Executive Director*

Founded in 1978, the Centre for Creative Communities is an independent research and policy center that believes in working and thinking innovatively across borders, disciplines and sectors. It is dedicated to promoting inclusive community development through creativity and learning. CCC conducts research, organizes conferences and produces a free monthly electronic newsletter. The Centre maintains a website and a specialized arts, education and community-development library open to the public by appointment. CCC is not a grant-giving organization.

THE CENTRE FOR INDIGENOUS THEATRE

401 Richmond St W; Suite 205; Toronto, Ontario; M5V 1X3; Canada;
(416) 506-9436; FAX 506-9430; email citmail@indigenoustheatre.com;
website www.indigenoustheatre.com
J.L. Watson, *Managing Director*

The Centre for Indigenous Theatre grew out of the Native Theatre School, established in 1974 by the late James H. Buller. It was Buller's vision to create an environment that would nourish the creative aspirations of Aboriginal people and inspire a new generation of writers, actors and directors. In 1994, The Centre for Indigenous Theatre was born and in 1998, the program expanded to include a one-year, full-time, post-secondary training program. Today, CIT offers a full-time three-year program as well as two summer programs that bring together classical theatre training and traditional teachings to support and enrich voices through self-exploration, song, story and performance. CIT distributes a biannual newsletter, which describes school and student activities. Memberships are $25 Canadian ($16 U.S.).

CHICAGO ALLIANCE FOR PLAYWRIGHTS (CAP)

Theatre Building; 1225 West Belmont; Chicago, IL 60657-3205;
(773) 929-7367, ext 60, FAX 327-1404;
email info@chicagoallianceforplaywrights.org;
website www.chicagoallianceforplaywrights.org
Joanne Koch, *President*

The Chicago Alliance for Playwrights is a service organization founded in 1990 to establish a network for Chicago-area playwrights and others committed to the development of new work for the stage. Members of the coalition include Chicago Dramatists (see listing below), Chicago Writers Bloc, Columbia College Theatre/Music Department and Theatre Building Chicago (see Production). CAP sponsors writers forums and publishes a directory of Chicago-area playwrights and their principal works. Annual dues are $25 for individuals, $100 for groups.

CHICAGO DRAMATISTS

1105 West Chicago Ave; Chicago, IL 60622-5702; (312) 633-0630,
FAX 633-0840; email newplays@chicagodramatists.org;
website www.chicagodramatists.org
Russ Tutterow, *Artistic Director*

Founded in 1979, Chicago Dramatists is dedicated to the development of playwrights and new plays. It employs a variety of year-round programs to nurture the artistic and career development of both established and emerging playwrights, including play readings, productions, classes, workshops, symposia, festivals, talent coordination, marketing services, collaborative projects with other theatres and referrals to producers.

The Resident Playwright program seeks to nurture the work and careers of Chicago-area dramatists who will potentially make significant contributions to the national theatre repertory. At no charge, Resident Playwrights benefit from Chicago Dramatists' fullest and longest-term support (a 3-year, renewable term), with complete access to all programs and services. Admittance to the program is selective, with emphasis on artistic and professional accomplishment or potential. Interested playwrights should contact Chicago Dramatists for full information and details of the application procedure, which includes the submission of 2 plays, a resume and letters of recommendation and intent. *Deadline:* 1 Apr each year (no submission before 1 Mar).

The Playwrights' Network provides any U.S. playwright the opportunity to form an association with Chicago Dramatists. For an annual fee of $110, Network playwrights receive written script critiques, consideration for all programs and productions, class discounts, free admittance to events and other benefits.

Classes and the quarterly 10-Minute Workshop are open to all playwrights. Website and quarterly flyers announce events and programs, and include application and submission procedures.

THE CHILDREN'S THEATRE FOUNDATION OF AMERICA (CTFA)

1114 Red Oak Dr; Avon, IN 46123; (317) 272-9322

Dorothy Webb, *President*

Founded in 1958, The Children's Theatre Foundation of America (CTFA) is a not-for-profit organization which seeks to advance the artistic and professional interests of theatre and theatre education for children and youth by funding proposals of artists and scholars working in those fields. In the past CTFA has funded playwriting grants, scholarships, research, performances and lectures, theatre festivals, conferences, symposia, publications and crisis-management assistance. CTFA also administers the annual Aurand Harris Children's Theatre Grants and Fellowships (see Fellowships and Grants), as well as awarding a Medallion for significant achievement in the field of children's theatre.

COLORADO DRAMATISTS

Box 40516; Denver, CO 80204; (303) 675-6500;

  email khopkins@qwestinternet.net, mccbacon@earthlink.net

Kathleen Hopkins and Jeff Chacon, *Co-Chairs*

Founded in 1981 as a regional playwright organization, Colorado Dramatists is dedicated to assisting playwrights in all levels of script development, from inception to production; creating a mutually beneficial relationship with the local theatre community; promoting the production of new plays; increasing audience awareness and participation with original works; and establishing a national reputation for the work of regional playwrights. Colorado Dramatists offers opportunity for playwrights to workshop their plays in a small group setting and then see the final play produced as a staged reading in the Public Readings program. Additional benefits include participation in local play festivals, rehearsal space, mentoring, internal competitions, assistance with outside productions and professional workshops dealing with playwriting and production. Members receive the *Colorado Dramatists Newsletter*. Membership dues are $15 for a limited time, senior and student memberships are $10.

CORPORATION FOR PUBLIC BROADCASTING

401 9th St NW; Washington, DC 20004-2037; (202) 879-9600,

  FAX 879-9700; website www.cpb.org

Robert T. Coonrod, *CEO and President*

Founded in 1967, the Corporation for Public Broadcasting, a private not-for-profit organization funded by Congress, promotes and helps finance public television and radio. CPB provides grants to local public television and radio stations; conducts research in audience development, new broadcasting technologies and other areas. The corporation helped establish the Public Broadcasting Service. It supports public radio programming through programming grants to stations and other producers, and television programming by funding proposals made by stations and independent producers.

THE DRAMATISTS GUILD OF AMERICA, INC.

1501 Broadway, Suite 701; New York, NY 10036; (212) 398-9366,
FAX 944-0420; email tstratton@dramaguild.com

John Weidman, *President*

The Dramatists Guild of America, founded more than 75 years ago, is the only professional association governed by and established to advance the rights of playwrights, composers and lyricists. The Guild has more than 6000 members worldwide, from beginning writers to Broadway veterans. Membership benefits include a business affairs toll-free hotline, which offers advice on all theatre-related topics, including options, commissions, copyright procedures and contract reviews; model production contracts, which provide the best protection for the writer at all levels of production; collaboration, commission and licensing agreements; seminars led by experienced professionals concerning pressing topics for today's dramatist; access to a national health insurance program and a group term life insurance plan; free/discounted tickets to Off-Broadway/Broadway performances; and a meeting room that can accommodate more than 50 people for readings and backers auditions, available for a nominal rental fee. The Guild has 4 levels of membership: 1. Active ($150 a year): writers who have been produced on Broadway, Off-Broadway or on the mainstage of a LORT theatre; 2. Associate ($95 a year): theatrical writers who have been produced in other venues or who have completed a full script; 3. Student ($35 a year): full-time students; 4. Estate ($125 a year): representatives of the estates of deceased authors.

Members receive *The Dramatists Guild Newsletter,* issued 6 times a year, with up-to-date business affairs articles and script opportunities; *The Dramatist,* a magazine that contains interviews as well as articles on all aspects of theatre; *The Dramatists Guild Resource Directory,* a biannual collection of contact information on producers, agents, contests, workshops and production companies. The periodicals are available to nonwriters on a subscription basis: Individual Subscribers ($25 a year): individuals receive *The Dramatist* only; Institutional Subscribers ($135 a year): educational institutions, libraries and educational theatres receive all 3 periodicals and have access to audiotapes of Guild seminars; Professional Subscribers ($200 a year): producers and agents receive all 3 periodicals.

EDUCATIONAL THEATRE ASSOCIATION

2343 Auburn Ave; Cincinnati, OH 45219; (513) 421-3900;
FAX 421-7077; email info@edta.org; website www.edta.org

Michael Peitz, *Executive Director*

The Educational Theatre Association is an international not-for-profit professional association for theatre educators and an honorary society for their students. Its mission is to promote and strengthen theatre in education. The Association focuses efforts on student development, teacher training and advocacy. It operates the International Thespian Society, an honorary organization for high school students; sponsors the International Thespian Festival for students, an annual convention for teachers; sponsors the Professional Development Institutes, a middle school theatre forum; and provides various awards and scholarship programs. The Association publishes *Dramatics* (see Publications), a monthly magazine; and *Teaching Theatre*, a quarterly journal. Membership is available to individuals and for active participants in chartered middle school or high school troupes of the International Thespian Society.

THE FIELD

161 Sixth Ave; New York, NY 10013; (212) 691–6969,
   FAX 255–2053; email info@thefield.org;
   website www.thefield.org
Diane Vivona, *Executive Director*

The Field, founded in 1986, is a not-for-profit organization dedicated to helping independent performing artists develop artistically and professionally through a variety of performance opportunities, workshops, services and publications. The Field does not engage in curatorial activity; all artists are eligible to participate in its programs. Of special interest to New York metropolitan area playwrights wishing to produce their own work are programs such as Fielday, a showcase of 12-minute work; and Fieldwork, 10-week workshops for works-in-progress, guided by trained facilitators, culminating in performances. Writers should also note Artward Bound, free 10-day summer residencies at various rural locations on the East Coast for multidisciplinary groups of 6–10 artists with at least 3 years professional experience; transportation, room and board, rehearsal space, workshops and career guidance seminars all provided; send resume and application. Applications are due 1 Apr each year. The application is available on The Field's website after 1 Mar. The Field assists artists with many aspects of producing their work, including grant writing, fundraising, project management, securing performance and rehearsal space, and cooperative promotional efforts. Publications include a monthly member newsletter; the *Self-Production Guide; Funding Guide for Independent Artists; Space Chase Guide to Performance and Rehearsal Spaces*, a listing of local performance spaces throughout New York City as well as out-of-town festivals, residencies and artist colonies. All programs are available to members and nonmembers; members receive all publications, discounts on programs and may use The Field as an umbrella organization, falling under its not-for-profit status. Annual membership costs $85; individual programs range in cost from $25–125. Field programs are also offered in many other cities; see their website for a complete list.

FIRST STAGE

Box 38280; Los Angeles, CA 90038; (323) 850–6271,
   FAX 850–6295; email firststagela@aol.com;
   website www.firststagela.org
Dennis Safren, *Literary Manager*

Founded in 1983, First Stage is a service organization for playwrights that holds staged readings, which are videotaped for the author's archival purposes; conducts workshops; provides referral services for playwrights; and publishes *First Stage Newsletter*. Services are free to nonmembers, except for workshops, which are available to members only. Membership dues are $55 per quarter or $190 per year; $68 per year for nonlocal members.

THE FOUNDATION CENTER
National Libraries:
1627 K St NW; Washington, DC 20006; (202) 331-1400;
79 Fifth Ave; New York, NY 10003; (212) 620-4230, FAX 807-3677;
    website www.fdncenter.org
Field Offices:
312 Sutter St; San Francisco, CA 94108; (415) 397-0902;
    Hurt Bldg, Suite 150, Grand Lobby; 50 Hurt Plaza;
    Atlanta, GA 30303; (404) 880-0094;
    1422 Euclid, Suite 1600; Cleveland, OH 44115; (216) 861-1934
Judith Margolin, *Vice President, Public Services, New York Library*

The Foundation Center is a nationwide service organization established and supported by foundations to provide a single authoritative source of information on foundation giving. It disseminates information on foundations through a public service program and through such publications as *The Foundation Directory, Directory Part 2,* and *Foundation Grants to Individuals,* available in print and online, which lists scholarships, fellowships, residencies, internships, grants, loans, awards, prizes and other forms of assistance available to individuals from approximately 6000 grantmakers. The center maintains 5 libraries and a national network of more than 213 cooperating collections. For the name of the collection nearest you or for more information about the center's programs, call (800) 424-9836 or visit the website.

THE FUND FOR WOMEN ARTISTS
Box 60637; Florence, MA 01062; (413) 585-5968, FAX 586-1303;
    email info@womenarts.org; website www.womenarts.org
Martha Richards, *Executive Director*

The Fund for Women Artists was founded in 1994 with the belief that women artists have the power to change the way women are perceived in our society. The Fund supports the creation and appreciation of art that reflects the full diversity and complexity of women's lives and advocates to increase the employment opportunities available to women artists. The Fund is currently raising funds to begin offering fellowships to women artists in December 2004. The Fund also publishes free electronic newsletters: *Advocacy E-News,* a funding e-newsletter for theatre artists and a funding e-newsletter for film and video artists. The publications provide subscribers with information regarding new and current grant programs, calls for proposals and calls for new works. Any female artist can create a free profile page on the Women Arts Network at www.womenarts.org.

GREENSBORO PLAYWRIGHTS' FORUM

c/o City Arts; 200 North Davie St, Box #2; Greensboro, NC 27401;
(336) 335-6426, FAX 373-2659;
email stephen.hyers@greensboro-nc.gov;
website www.playwrightsforum.org

Stephen D. Hyers, *Director*

GPF was founded in 1993 to facilitate a monthly gathering for playwrights to discuss works in progress, share knowledge and encourage each other's artistic growth. Programs include cold and staged readings of member's plays and the annual North Carolina New Play Project open to NC playwrights; winner receives $500 and workshop production; *deadline:* mid-Jul. GPF also provides members with studio space for play development and publishes *New Play Catalog*, which lists plays written by members. Membership is open to anyone. Annual dues are $25.

HATCH-BILLOPS COLLECTION

491 Broadway, 7th Floor; New York, NY 10012-4412;
(212) 966-3231, FAX 966-3231 (call first);
email hatchbillops@worldnet.att.net

James V. Hatch, *Executive Secretary*

Founded in 1975, the Hatch-Billops Collection is a not-for-profit research library specializing in black American art and theatre history. It collects and preserves primary and secondary resource materials in the black cultural arts; provides tools and access to these materials for artists and scholars, as well as the general public; and develops programs in the arts which use the collection's resources. The library's holdings include 1800 oral-history tapes; theatre programs; approximately 300 unpublished plays by black American writers from 1858 to the present; files of clippings, letters, announcements and brochures on theatre, art and film; slides, photographs and posters; and more than 4000 books and 400 periodicals. The collection also presents a number of salon interviews and films, which are open to the public; and publishes transcriptions of its annual "Artist and Influence" series of salon interviews, many of which feature playwrights. The collection is open to artists, scholars and the public by appointment only at a rate of $5 per hour.

HISPANIC ORGANIZATION OF LATIN ACTORS (HOLA)

Clemente Soto Vélez Cultural Center; 107 Suffolk St, 3rd Floor;
New York, NY 10002; (212) 253-1015, FAX 253-9651;
email holagram@hellohola.org; website www.hellohola.org

Manuel Alfaro, *Executive Director*

Founded in 1975, HOLA is a not-for-profit arts service organization for Hispanic performers and theatre artists. HOLA provides information, a 24-hour hotline, casting referral services, professional seminars and workshops. The organization publishes a biennial *Directory of Hispanic Talent: HOLA Pages* (including an online version) and a newsletter, *La Nueva Ola*, which lists job opportunities, grants and contests of interest to Hispanic artists. Members pay annual dues of $65.

INDEPENDENT FEATURE PROJECT (IFP)

104 West 29th St, 12th Floor; New York, NY 10001-5310;
(212) 465-8200, FAX 465-8525; email ifpny@ifp.org;
website www.ifp.org
Michelle Byrd, *Executive Director*

The Independent Feature Project (IFP), a not-for-profit membership-supported organization, was founded in 1979 to encourage creativity and diversity in films produced outside the established studio system. The IFP produces the IFP Market, which features 300 American independent features, shorts, works-in-progress, documentaries and feature scripts. The IFP and IFP/West publish *Filmmaker*, a quarterly magazine. IFP also sponsors a series of screenings, professional seminars and industry showcases, including a conference on screenplay development. Group health insurance, production insurance, discounts, a Resource Program, publications and a series of transcripts of previous seminars and workshops are available to members. Membership dues start at $100 a year ($65 for students).

INSTITUTE FOR CONTEMPORARY EAST EUROPEAN DRAMA AND THEATRE

The City University of New York Graduate Center; 365 5th Ave;
New York, NY 10016-4307; (212) 817-1869; email seep@gc.cuny.edu
Daniel C. Gerould, *Director*

The Institute for Contemporary East European Drama and Theatre, under the auspices of the Martin E. Segal Theatre Center, publishes a triquarterly journal, *Slavic and East European Performance: Drama, Theatre, Film*, which is available by subscription ($10 a year, $15 foreign) and includes articles about current events in the East European and Slavic theatre, as well as reviews of productions and interviews with playwrights, directors and other theatre artists. The Institute also has available 2 annotated bibliographies of English translations of Eastern European plays written since 1945: *Soviet Plays in Translation* and *Polish Plays in Translation* ($5 each, $6 foreign). The institute is interested in hearing of published or unpublished translations for possible listing in updated editions of these bibliographies; translators may submit descriptive letters or scripts.

INSTITUTE OF OUTDOOR DRAMA

CB #3240; University of North Carolina; Chapel Hill, NC 27599-3240;
(919) 962-1328, FAX 962-4212; email outdoor@unc.edu;
website www.unc.edu/depts/outdoor/
Scott J. Parker, *Director*

The Institute of Outdoor Drama, founded in 1963, is a research and advisory agency of the University of North Carolina. It serves as a communications link between producers of existing outdoor dramas and is a resource for groups, agencies or individuals who wish to create new outdoor dramas or who are seeking information on the field. The institute provides professional consultation and conducts feasibility studies; holds annual auditions for summer employment in outdoor drama; sponsors conferences, lectures and symposia; and publishes a quarterly newsletter, as well as information bulletins. Writers should note that the institute maintains a roster of available artists and production personnel, including playwrights and composers. It seeks to interest established playwrights and composers in participating in the creation of new outdoor dramas, and to encourage and advise new playwrights who wish to write for this specialized form of theatre.

INTERNATIONAL THEATRE INSTITUTE–U.S. CENTER
Theatre Communications Group; 520 8th Ave, 24th Floor;
New York, NY 10018-4156; (212) 609-5900, FAX 609-5901;
email iti@tcg.org; website www.tcg.org
Joan Channick, *Director*

Now operating centers in 90 countries, ITI was founded in 1948 by UNESCO "to promote the exchange of knowledge and practice in the theatre arts." The U.S. Center of ITI became part of Theatre Communications Group in November 1999. ITI assists both foreign theatre visitors in the U.S. and American theatre representatives traveling abroad. TCG/ITI Travel Grants, funded by the Trust for Mutual Understanding, offer $2500 grants for American theatre artists to travel to Russia or Central Europe (see website for program guidelines). The International Theatre Institute/Martha W. Coigney Collection, a reference library which documents theatrical activity in 146 countries and houses over 12,700 plays from 97 countries, is now housed at the New York Public Library for the Performing Arts, where it will be available to the public in 2005. American playwrights, as well as other theatre professionals, will be able to use the collection to make international connections; to consult foreign theatre directories for names of producers, directors or companies with a view to submitting plays abroad; and to research the programs and policies of theatres or managements.

THE INTERNATIONAL WOMEN'S WRITING GUILD
Box 810, Gracie Station; New York, NY 10028-0082;
(212) 737-7536, FAX 737-9469; email iwwg@iwwg.com;
website www.iwwg.com
Hannelore Hahn, *Executive Director*

The International Women's Writing Guild, founded in 1976, is a network of international women writers. Playwrights, television and film writers, songwriters, producers and other women involved in the performing arts are included in its membership. Workshops are offered throughout the U.S. and annually at a week-long writing conference/retreat at Skidmore College in Saratoga Springs, NY. Members may also submit playscripts to theatres who have offered to read, critique and possibly produce IWWG members' works. *Network*, a 32-page newsletter published 6 times a year, provides a forum for members to share views and to learn about playwriting contests and awards, and theatre- and TV-related opportunities. The guild offers contacts with literary agents, as well as health insurance and other services to its members. Annual dues are $45.

LA STAGE ALLIANCE

644 South Figueroa St; Los Angeles, CA 90017; (213) 614-0556,
   FAX 614-0561; email info@lastagealliance.com;
   website www.lastagealliance.com

A not-for-profit membership association of more than 200 performing arts groups, LA Stage Alliance was founded in 1975 to unite, represent and promote theatre in southern CA. LA Stage Alliance administers the annual Ovation Awards; publishes *LA Stage*, southern CA's Performing Arts magazine; produces the *LA Stage Times*, a cooperative advertising opportunity in the *Los Angeles Times*; operates LA Stage Tix, online half-price ticketing; and provides information and referral services for members. Asssociate membership opportunities are also available to individuals, professionals and businesses interested in supporting theatre.

LEAGUE OF CHICAGO THEATRES/LEAGUE OF CHICAGO THEATRES FOUNDATION

228 South Wabash, Suite 900; Chicago, IL 60604; (312) 554-9800,
   FAX 922-7202; email info@chicagoplays.com;
   website www.chicagoplays.com

Founded in 1979, the League of Chicago Theatres/League of Chicago Theatres Foundation is a member organization which advocates for the business and artistic needs of the Chicago theatre community. It operates as an information clearinghouse; offers vendor discounts, including a cooperative advertising program; conducts the Annual Theatre CommUNITY Conference; markets "Play Money" Theater Gift Certificates; implements marketing initiatives such as the award-winning Sears Theater Fever; and sells half-price theatre tickets through its 7 Hot Tix locations. Publications include the bimonthly *Theater Guide* and *Chicagoplays* theatre programs. Theatre companies, producers and presenters incorporated for at least one year and located within 50 miles of Chicago may be eligible to join.

LEAGUE OF PROFESSIONAL THEATRE WOMEN/NEW YORK

35 West 64th St, #4D; New York, NY 10023; (646) 505-1822,
   FAX (914) 764-4280; website www.theatrewomen.org
Sheilah Roe, *President*

Founded in 1979, the league is a not-for-profit organization of theatre professionals providing programs and services which promote women in all areas of professional theatre; create industry-related opportunities for women; and highlight contributions of theatre women, past and present. Through its salons, seminars, educational programs, social events, awards and festivals, the league links professional theatres with theatre women nationally and internationally and provides an ongoing forum for ideas, methods and issues of concern to the theatrical community and its audiences. Programs include the Lee Reynolds Award, given annually to a woman or women whose work for, in, about or through the medium of theatre has helped to illuminate the possibilities for social, cultural or political change; the Oral History

Project, which seeks to chronicle and document the contribution of significant theatre women; a membership directory; and panels discussing topics of interest to women theatre professionals with well-known experts in the field. Regular monthly meetings enable members to network, initiate programs and serve on committees. To be eligible for membership in the league, playwrights, composers, librettists and lyricists must have had a work presented in a professional production in the U.S. or Canada; or in a New York City theatre under Equity's Basic Minimum Contract, excluding showcases; or at least 2 productions presented in a resident theatre, as defined under Equity's Minimum Basic Contract for Resident Theatres. All other theatre professionals must meet criteria listed in brochure. Annual dues are $100.

LITERARY MANAGERS AND DRAMATURGS OF THE AMERICAS (LMDA)

Box 728, Village Station; New York, NY 10014; (212) 561-0315;
  email lmdanyc@hotmail.com; website www.lmda.org
DD Kugler, *President*

LMDA, the professional service organization for American and Canadian literary managers and dramaturgs, was founded in 1985 to affirm, examine and develop these professions. Among the programs and services it offers to members are: a university caucus and a student caucus which act as liaisons between training programs and the profession; an advocacy caucus, which examines and reports on current working conditions; an annual conference each June; discussion and announcement listservs and job postings. Publications include: the quarterly *LMDA Review*, the *LMDA Script Exchange*, the *Production Notebooks* (2 volumes), employment Guidelines, a guide to training programs, a sourcebook for teachers of dramaturgy and an annual bibliography; most of these publications are availble through the LMDA website. Voting membership is open to dramaturgs and literary managers; associate membership is open to playwrights, artistic directors, literary agents, educators and other theatre professionals. Dues are $25 for students, $45 for associate members, $60 for voting members, $130 for institutional members.

LUMINOUS VISIONS

267 West 89th St; New York, NY 10024; (212) 724-7059, FAX 581-3964
Carla Pinza, *Co-Founder*

Founded in 1976, Luminous Visions is a multicultural, not-for-profit organization dedicated to developing the creative skills of film and television writers, directors and actors seeking employment within the English-speaking film and television mainstream. Luminous Visions offers year-round youth workshops to develop acting, writing and musical talent in students ages 6-17. The organization sponsors a weekly workshop for writers, an annual Writers Forum and a spring Staged Reading Festival.

MARY ANDERSON CENTER FOR THE ARTS

101 St. Francis Dr; Mount Saint Francis, IN 47146; (812) 923-8602,
FAX 923-0294; email maca@iglou.com;
website www.maryandersoncenter.org
Debra Carmody, *Executive Director*

The Mary Anderson Center, founded in 1989, is a not-for-profit organization dedicated to providing artists with a quiet place where they can concentrate and work on their craft. Named after the 19th-century actress from Louisville who rose to become an international celebrity, the center is located on 400 acres in southern Indiana. The center's goal is to provide retreats and residencies for artists in many disciplines (see the organization's entry in Colonies and Residencies). As part of its outreach effort to the Midwest and the nation, the center sponsors symposia, conferences and other gatherings which explore, in a multidisciplinary mode, topics of interest to society and to artists. Contributors to the center receive a quarterly newsletter featuring center activities and news of area artists.

MEET THE COMPOSER

75 9th Ave, Floor 3R, Suite C; New York, NY 10023; (212) 645-6949,
FAX 645-9669
Heather Hitchens, *President*

Founded in 1974, Meet The Composer is a national service organization whose mission is to increase opportunities for composers by fostering the creation, performance, dissemination and appreciation of their music. With support from foundations, corporations, individual patrons and government sources, Meet The Composer designs programs that support composers writing in all styles of music: classical, jazz, folk, electronic, symphonic, opera, dance, experimental, etc. Through a variety of programs, Meet The Composer provides composer fees to not-for-profit organizations that perform, present and commission original works. Applications to all Meet The Composer programs are submitted by sponsoring organizations, not individual composers. Its programs include: Commissioning Music/USA, Music Alive, the Fund for Small Ensembles and the Meet The Composer Fund (see Meet The Composer Grant in Fellowships and Grants).

MUSE OF FIRE THEATRE COMPANY

475 West 57th St, Suite 24C2; New York, NY 10019;
(212) 397-2757, FAX 397-2757; email glenn.english2@verizon.net;
website www.museoffiretheatreco.org
Glenn English and Vivian Paxton, *Co-Artistic Directors*

Founded in 1999, Muse of Fire Theatre Company is a not-for-profit organization dedicated to developing and producing original plays by American playwrights. With a resident company of actors, directors and playwrights, Muse of Fire seeks to promote new playwriting and develop new audiences, particularly young audiences. Its programs include an ongoing readers workshop which offers staged readings of new plays, the Muse Writers Workshop (open to members only) and the Sirens One Act Festival, dedicated to promoting work by women writers. The organization publishes the quarterly *Muse of Fire Newsletter.* Writers interested in becoming a part of Muse of Fire should submit writing sample, bio and letter of inquiry.

NATIONAL ALLIANCE FOR MUSICAL THEATRE

520 8th Ave, Suite 301; New York, NY 10018; (212) 714-6668,
    FAX 714-0469; email info@namt.net; website www.namt.net
Kathy Evans, *Executive Director*

The National Alliance for Musical Theatre, founded in 1985, is the national service organization for musical theatre. Its membership includes theatres, booking and presenting organizations, universities and individual producers. Located throughout 33 states and 6 countries, member companies vary substantially in size, structure and purpose, reflecting the increasing diversity of the field. Their common bond is a shared commitment to preserving and enhancing musical theatre. Cumulatively, NAMT's 140 member organizations have more than 739,000 subscribers, more than $562 million in operating revenues and an annual attendence of more than 13 million people. As part of its services, NAMT organizes two annual conferences, maintains a website, surveys the membership on various industry issues and publishes a weekly electronic newletter and membership directory. NAMT also produces an annual Festival of New Musicals in New York City for the discovery, development and advancement of the musical theatre art form. Submissions for the Festival are accepted every year in January and February. In addition, NAMT has a Producer-Writer Initiative Program (PWI), which awards six grants to NAMT Member theatres, who apply on behalf of their organization and a musical theatre writing team with whom the members wish to work. Every theatre will receive $3000 to help fund the writing team's minimum seven-day residency.

THE NATIONAL AUDIO THEATRE FESTIVALS (NATF)

115 Dikeman St; Hempstead, NY 11550; (516) 483-8321;
    FAX 538-7583; website www.natf.org
Sue Zizza, *Executive Director*

Founded in 1979, The National Audio Theatre Festivals is a national resource center for audio theatre. NAFT hosts the annual Audio Theatre Workshop, a week-long hands-on intensive at Southwest Missouri State University in West Plains, Missouri. NATF is a membership-based professional and educational not-for-profit arts organization, whose services include providing information and referral services and technical assistance to interested individuals and groups; distributing educational materials; and publishing a newsletter and an online *Audio Dramatists Directory,* a guide to current audio artists, producers, programmers and professional resources. NATF also holds an annual script contest to identify and promote emerging and established audio script writers (see NATF Script Competition in Prizes). Winning scripts may be produced during one of a series of audio theatre workshops held each year. Membership fees vary.

THE NATIONAL FOUNDATION FOR JEWISH CULTURE

330 Seventh Ave, 21st Floor; New York, NY 10001; (212) 629-0500,
FAX 629-0508; email nfjc@jewishculture.org;
website www.jewishculture.org
Richard A. Siegel, *Executive Director*

Founded in 1960, The National Foundation for Jewish Culture (NFJC) is the central cultural agency of the American Jewish community. The NFJC, dedicated to the enhancement of Jewish life in America through the support and promotion of the arts and humanities, provides programs and services to cultural institutions, local communities and individual artists and scholars in every region of the country. The NFJC serves as advocate and coordinator for the fields of Jewish culture through its Council of American Jewish Museums and Council of Archives and Research Libraries in Jewish Studies; sponsors grants and awards to artists, scholars and major cultural institutions such as YIVO, Leo Baeck Institute, American Jewish Historical Society, Histadrut Ivrit and the Jewish Publication Society of America; promotes an understanding and appreciation of contemporary Jewish life and culture through conferences, symposia, publications, media productions, traveling exhibitions, residencies and performances; and presents the annual Jewish Cultural Achievement Awards recognizing outstanding contributions to Jewish life in America through the arts and scholarship. (See listing for New Play Commissions in Jewish Theatre in Fellowships and Grants.)

THE NATIONAL LEAGUE OF AMERICAN PEN WOMEN, INC.

1300 17th St NW; Washington, DC 20036-1973; (202) 785-1997,
FAX 452-6868; email nlapw1@juno.com;
website www.americanpenwomen.org
Wanda A. Rider, *National President*

Founded in 1897, NLAPW is a national membership organization for professional women writers, composers and visual artists. It holds local monthly meetings, annual State Association meetings, a Mid-Administration Congress, the National Biennial Convention and a National Art Show, and sponsors the Mature Woman Scholarship Award. Members receive the bimonthly magazine *The Pen Woman* and a national roster. Annual national dues are $30; dues for individual branches are separate and vary.

THE NATIONAL THEATRE WORKSHOP OF THE HANDICAPPED

535 Greenwich St; New York, NY 10013; (212) 206-7789, FAX 206-0200;
email admissions@ntwh.org; website ntwh.org
Rick Curry S.J., *Founder and Artistic Director*

Founded in 1977, the National Theatre Workshop of the Handicapped (NTWH) is a not-for-profit organization founded to provide persons with disabilities the opportunity to learn the communication skills necessary to pursue a life in professional theatre and to enhance their opportunities in the workplace. NTWH advocates for persons with physical disabilities in the theatre and offers a forum for dramatic literature on themes of disability. NTWH runs the Playwrights Workshop, a

2-week program held each spring for 4 playwrights to develop new works in residence at NTWH-Crosby, a fully accessible residential facility in Belfast, ME; selected works are fully produced later. NTWH also offers professional instruction in acting, singing, voice, movement, playwriting and fine arts at the NTWH studio in New York City.

NEW DRAMATISTS

424 West 44th St; New York, NY 10036; (212) 757-6960,
    FAX 265-4738; email newdramatists@newdramatists.org;
    website www.newdramatists.org
Todd London, *Artistic Director*

Founded in 1949, New Dramatists is the nation's oldest playwright development center, designed to provide member playwrights with the resources they need to create plays for the American theatre. Rather than producing plays, New Dramatists aids playwrights in the development of their craft through play readings and workshops; dramaturgy; a resident director program; musical theatre development and training; ScriptShare (a national script distribution program); fellowships, awards and prizes; a free ticket program for Broadway and Off-Broadway productions; writing spaces and accommodations; and photocopying. All services are provided free of charge to members.

In addition, New Dramatists hosts several playwright exchanges, including the Brooks Atkinson Exchange/Max Weitzenhoffer Fellowship to the Royal National Theatre, England; the Sumner Locke Elliott Exchange to the Australian National Playwrights Centre; and Interplay, a 6-playwright exchange with Hungary, Serbia and the Czech Republic.

Membership is open to emerging playwrights living in the greater New York area, and to those living outside the area who demonstrate a willingness to regularly travel to New York and actively participate in this community of artists. Playwrights interested in applying for membership should write for guidelines.

NEW ENGLAND THEATRE CONFERENCE (NETC)

PMB 502; 198 Tremont St; Boston, MA 02116-4750;
    (617) 851-8535; email mail@NETConline.org;
    website www.NETConline.org

Founded in 1952, New England Theatre Conference is a membership organization including playwrights, teachers, students and theatre professionals, but not exclusively for the New England theatre community. Services include an annual conference, publication of a member directory and annual summer theatre auditions. NETC also administers both the John Gassner Memorial Playwriting Award and Aurand Harris Memorial Playwriting Award (see Prizes). The organization publishes *New England Theatre Journal* and *NETC News*. Membership dues are $30 for students, $45 for individuals, $95 for groups.

NEW PLAYWRIGHTS FOUNDATION

c/o 608 San Vicente Blvd, #18; Santa Monica, CA 90402;
(310) 393-3682; website www.newplaywrights.org
Jeffrey Lee Bergquist, *Artistic Director*

Founded in 1968, New Playwrights Foundation is a service organization for writers working in theatre, film, television and video. The foundation runs developmental workshops, holds readings, produces video and film projects and assists members in furthering their careers. Membership in NPF is limited to a maximum of 15 writers who must be able to attend meetings in Santa Monica every other Thursday night. Candidates for membership attend 3 meetings before submitting copyrighted materials to be reviewed by the group. Annual membership dues are $25.

THE NEW YORK PUBLIC LIBRARY FOR THE PERFORMING ARTS

40 Lincoln Center Plaza; New York, NY 10023-7498;
(212) 870-1639, FAX 870-1868; email rtaylor@nypl.org;
website www.nypl.org
Bob Taylor, *Curator, The Billy Rose Theatre Collection*

Founded in 1931, The Billy Rose Theatre Collection, a division of the Library for the Performing Arts, is open to the public (ages 18 and over) and contains material on all aspects of theatrical art and the entertainment world, including stage, film, radio, television, circus, vaudeville, burlesque and numerous other genres. The Theatre on Film and Tape Archive (TOFT) is a special collection of moving images of theatrical productions recorded during performance, as well as informal dialogues with important theatrical personalities. Tapes are available for viewing by appointment (call 212-870-1642) to students, theatre professionals and researchers.

NON-TRADITIONAL CASTING PROJECT, INC.

1560 Broadway, Suite 1600; New York, NY 10036; (212) 730-4750,
FAX 730-4820; email info@ntcp.org; website www.ntcp.org
Sharon Jensen, *Executive Director*

Founded in 1986, the Non-Traditional Casting Project is a not-for-profit organization which addresses and seeks solutions to the problems of racism and exclusion in the theatre and related media, particularly those which involve creative personnel: including, but not limited to, actors, directors, writers, designers and producers. The project works to advance the creative participation of artists of color and artists with disabilities through both advocacy and specific projects. Key NTCP programs include Artist Files Online, a national talent bank; roundtable discussions with industry leaders; National Diversity Forum; and a national Consulting and Information Program. Writers of color and/or with disabilities, who are citizens or residents of the U.S. or Canada and have had at least one play given a professional production or staged reading should send a resume for inclusion in Artist Files Online, indicating their cultural identification and, in the case of disabled artists, any accommodation they may use; those interested in contacting listed artists will call the artists or their agents directly.

NORTH CAROLINA WRITERS' NETWORK

Box 954; Carrboro, NC 27510; (919) 967-9540, FAX 929-0535;
    email mail@ncwriters.org; website www.ncwriters.org
Linda Hobson, *Executive Director*

Founded in 1985, North Carolina Writers' Network (NCWN) is an independent literary arts service organization serving writers at all stages of development. NCWN provides workshops, conferences, readings, literary competitions, a resource center and library, a critiquing and editing service and a summer writers-in-residence program. NCWN members receive *Writers' Network News*, a 24-page bimonthly newsletter, a range of consultation services and discounts on all NCWN programs and events. Annual membership dues are $55 ($40 for seniors and students).

NORTHWEST PLAYWRIGHTS GUILD

Box 1728; Portland, OR 97207; (503) 452-4778;
    email bjscript@teleport.com; website www.nwpg.org
Bill Johnson, *Office Manager*

Founded in 1982, Northwest Playwrights Guild is an information clearinghouse and support group for playwrights. The guild sponsors public readings, holds workshops and produces regional conferences on theatre, which include the full production of original scripts. The guild publishes the quarterly, *Script*, containing articles on theatre in the Northwest; and update newsletters, providing information on script opportunities. Membership dues are $25 a year.

PEN AMERICAN CENTER

568 Broadway; New York, NY 10012; (212) 334-1660,
    FAX 334-2181; email pen@pen.org; website www.pen.org
Michael Roberts, *Executive Director*

Founded in 1921, PEN is an international association of writers; the American Center is the largest of the 130 centers that comprise International PEN. The 2800 members of PEN American Center are established North American writers and translators, and literary editors. PEN activities include the Freedom-to-Write program; monthly symposia, readings and other public events; a prison writing program; and a translator-publisher clearinghouse. Among PEN's annual prizes and awards are The Gregory Kolovakos Award, PEN-Book-of-the-Month Club Translation Prize, the PEN/Laura Pels Foundation Award for Drama (see Prizes) and Writing Awards for Prisoners. The PEN Writers Fund and the PEN Fund for Writers & Editors with AIDS assist writers (see Emergency Funds). PEN's publications include *Grants and Awards Available to American Writers*, a biennially updated directory of prizes, grants, fellowships and awards (2004-2005 edition to be published in fall 2004); *PEN America*, a biannual literary journal; The *PEN Prison Writing Information Bulletin* and *A Handbook for Literary Translators*, available for free on the website.

PHILADELPHIA DRAMATISTS CENTER (PDC)

3500 Lancaster Ave; Philadelphia, PA 19104; (215) 735-1441;
email pdc@usner.org; website www.phillydramatists.org
Ed Shockley, *Artistic Director*

Philadelphia Dramatists Center, founded in 1994, is a community of scriptwriters that provides resources for the artistic and professional development of its members. PDC unites writers and collaborative artists to enhance their craft and provides a number of services, including: writers' circles; staged readings; workshops; an active group of directors and actors to aid in development of work; and discounted tickets to local theatres. Annual membership dues are $40 for individuals; $20 for students.

THE PLAYWRIGHTS' CENTER

2301 Franklin Ave East; Minneapolis, MN 55406-1099; (612) 332-7481;
email info@pwcenter.org; website www.pwcenter.org
Polly Carl, *Producing Artistic Director*

The Playwrights' Center, founded in 1971, is a service organization for playwrights. Its programs include developmental services (cold readings and workshops using an Equity acting company); fellowships; exchanges with theatres and other developmental programs; PlayLabs (see Development); playwriting classes; and the Many Voices program, designed to provide awards, education and lab services to new and emerging playwrights of color. The Center annually awards 4 Jerome Playwright-in-Residence Fellowships, for which competition is open nationally; 1 McKnight National Residency and Commission; 3 McKnight Advancement Grants open to Minnesota playwrights; 3 McKnight Theater Artist Grants; and 8 Many Voices Artist in Residency opportunities for Minnesota playwrights of color (see Fellowships and Grants). A broad-based center membership is available to any playwright or interested person. Benefits of general membership for playwrights include discounts on classes, applications for all center programs and eligibility to apply for the script-development readings and workshops.

THE PLAYWRIGHTS CENTER SAN FRANCISCO

588 Sutter St, #430; San Francisco, CA 94102; (415) 820-3206;
email pcsf@playwrightscentersf.org;
website www.playwrightscentersf.org
(Ms.) Jody Hanley, *Chair*

The Playwrights Center San Francisco, founded in 1980, is a membership organization devoted to helping playwrights develop their scripts from initial concept to staged reading with professional actors and direction. The Center provides readings of entire scripts, as well as "Scene Nights," where each playwright may have up to 10 pages read by group members. The Center also provides its members with a weekly e-newsletter with announcements and current opportunities. Membership also includes a personal email address, resume hosting, discounts and voting privileges. Annual dues are $40-60 for email and resume services (see website for details). The Center is committed to never turning away a member for financial reasons. A limited number of "waivers" are available for those who cannot afford the annual fee; those interested should come to a Tuesday night event.

PLAYWRIGHTS FOUNDATION

Box 460357; San Francisco, CA 94146; (415) 626-0453, ext 110;
email info@playwrightsfoundation.org;
website www.playwrightsfoundation.org
Amy Mueller, *Artistic Director*

Founded in 1976, the Playwrights Foundation actively fosters the inception and development of new plays by diverse playwrights throughout the U.S. They produce the annual Bay Area Playwrights Festival (see Development), and are engaged in numerous projects that support and encourage the creativity of playwrights. Their multi-tiered programs establish collaborations, focus on creative process and promote world-premiere productions of contemporary theatre through co-commissions and producing partnerships.

PLAYWRIGHTS THEATRE OF NEW JERSEY

Box 1295; Madison, NJ 07940; (973) 514-1787, FAX 514-2060;
website www.ptnj.org
John Pietrowski, *Artistic Director*

Founded in 1986, the Playwrights Theatre of New Jersey is both a service organization for playwrights of all ages and a professional developmental theatre. In addition to its New Play Development Program (see Development), PTNJ cosponsors, with the New Jersey Council on the Arts, the New Jersey Writers Project, a statewide program which teaches prose, poetry and dramatic writing in schools. Specialized programs include a playwriting-for-teachers project; adult playwriting classes; children's creative dramatics classes; playwriting projects, which include work in housing projects, with senior citizens, teenage substance abusers and court-appointed youth, persons with physical disabilities; a playwriting-in-prisons initiative; and a program that teaches Spanish-language prose, poetry and dramatic writing. Young playwrights festivals are held in Madison and Newark, in addition to a statewide festival which is part of the New Jersey Young Playwrights Program. Gifted and talented playwriting symposia, hosted by well-known playwrights, provide intensive 2-day experiences for up to 60 students from various school districts.

PLAZA DE LA RAZA

3540 North Mission Rd; Los Angeles, CA 90031; (323) 223-2475,
FAX 223-1804; email information@plazadelaraza.org;
website www.plazadelaraza.org
Rose Cano, *Executive Director*

Founded in 1970, Plaza de la Raza is a cultural center for the arts and education, primarily serving the surrounding community of East Los Angeles. Plaza de la Raza conducts classes in drama, dance, music and the visual arts; provides resources for teachers in the community; and sponsors special events, exhibits and performances.

PROFESSIONAL ASSOCIATION OF CANADIAN THEATRES

215 Spadina Ave, Suite 210; Toronto, Ontario; Canada; M5T 2C7;
(416) 595-6455, FAX 595-6450; email info@pact.ca;
website www.pact.ca
Lucy White, *Executive Director*

PACT is a member-driven organization that serves as the collective voice of professional Canadian theatres. For the betterment of Canadian theatre, PACT provides leadership, national representation and a variety of programs and practical assistance to member companies, enabling members to do their own creative work. PACT publishes *The Theatre Listing*, an annual directory of English-language Canadian theatres, rehearsal and performance spaces, government agencies and arts service organizations; *Artsboard*, the monthly bulletin of employment opportunities in the arts in Canada; and various studies and research papers available from their website. PACT also hosts an annual theatre conference each spring.

THE PURPLE CIRCUIT

921 North Naomi St; Burbank, CA 91505; (818) 953-5096;
email purplecir@aol.com; website www.buddybuddy.com/pc.html/
Bill Kaiser, *Coordinator*

The Purple Circuit, founded in 1991, is a network of gay, lesbian, queer, bisexual and transsexual theatres, producers, performers and "Kindred Spirits" (theatres which are not exclusively gay or lesbian in orientation but are interested in producing gay or lesbian material on a regular basis). The Purple Circuit Hotline (818-953-5072) provides information on gay and lesbian shows currently playing in CA, advises travelers on shows around the U.S. and abroad, and provides information for playwrights, journalists and others interested in promoting gay/lesbian/bisexual/transgender theatre and performance. The Purple Circuit publishes news, information and articles of interest to its constituency on its website. *The Purple Circuit Directory* lists theatres and producers around the world that are interested in presenting gay, lesbian, bisexual and transsexual works.

THE SONGWRITERS GUILD OF AMERICA

1560 Broadway, Suite 1306; New York, NY 10036; (212) 768-7902,
FAX 768-9048; email ny@songwritersguild.com;
website www.songwritersguild.com
Administration Office:
1500 Harbor Blvd; Weehawken, NJ 07086; (201) 867-7603
Los Angeles Office:
6430 Sunset Blvd, Suite 705; Hollywood, CA 90028; (323) 462-1108
Nashville Office:
1222 16th Ave, Suite 25; Nashville, TN 37212; (615) 329-1782
George Wurzbach, *National Projects Director*

Founded in 1931, The Songwriters Guild is a voluntary national association run by and for songwriters; all officers and directors are unpaid. Among its many services to composers and lyricists, the guild provides a standard songwriter's contract and reviews this and other contracts on request; collects writers' royalties from music publishers; maintains a copyright renewal service; conducts songwriting workshops and critique sessions with special rates for members; issues news bulletins with essential information for writers; and offers a group medical and life insurance plan. Full members of the guild must be published songwriters and pay dues on a graduated scale from $70–400. Unpublished songwriters may become associate members and pay dues of $70 per year.

S.T.A.G.E. (SOCIETY FOR THEATRICAL ARTISTS' GUIDANCE AND ENHANCEMENT)

Box 214820; Dallas, TX 75221; (214) 630-7722, FAX 630-4468;
  email stage_tx@swbell.net; website www.stage-online.org
Jeff Fenter, *Operations Manager*

Founded in 1981, S.T.A.G.E. is a not-for-profit membership organization which serves as an information clearinghouse and provides training and education for the theatre, broadcast and film industries in north central Texas. The society maintains a library of plays, theatre texts and resource information; offers counseling on agents, unions, personal marketing and other career-related matters; posts job opportunities; maintains a callboard for regional auditions in theatre and film; and sponsors an actor's showcase, Noon Preview. Members of S.T.A.G.E. receive audition postings via email. Annual dues are $80, $45 for volunteers.

STAGESOURCE

88 Tremont St, Suite 714; Boston, MA 02108; (617) 720-6066,
  FAX 720-4275; email info@stagesource.org;
  website www.stagesource.org
Jeffrey Poulos, *Executive Director*

Founded in 1985, StageSource, the Alliance for Theatre Artists and Producers, is a not-for-profit arts service organization committed to providing leadership and resources for the advancement of theatre in the Greater Boston/New England area. Its membership includes more than 190 producing organizations and 1900 individual theatre artists. StageSource hosts annual Equity and non-Equity auditions, an annual theatre town meeting and a community social event, The Party. Its other programs include: group health insurance for freelance theatre artists; the Professional Development Series, offering career development and master classes in art and business; a Playwrights Alliance, focusing on needs of area playwrights; a Talent Bank, a library of resumes and headshots; and a 2-for-1 ticket discount program to more than 60 Greater Boston area theatres. A weekly e-newsletter features job, audition and workshop opportunities; news; and free and discount ticket offers. StageSource publishes a quarterly calendar, *The Stage Page*, and a biannual regional theatre guide, *The Source: The Greater Boston Theatre Resource Guide*. Membership is open to individuals, theatres and producing organizations. Annual dues for individuals are $50 for students and renewing members, $100 for new members, $100-425 for theatres and producing organizations, based on operating budget.

THEATRE BAY AREA (TBA)

870 Market St, Suite 375; San Francisco, CA 94102;
(415) 430-1140, FAX 430-1145; email tba@theatrebayarea.org;
website www.theatrebayarea.org

Founded in 1976, TBA is a resource organization for San Francisco Bay Area theatre workers. Its membership includes 3200 individuals and more than 370 theatre and dance companies. Its programs include TIX Bay Area, San Francisco's half-price ticket booth; TIX By Mail, half-price tickets online; professional workshops; and communications and networking services. Membership includes a subscription to *Theatre Bay Area Magazine*, a monthly magazine featuring articles, interviews and essays on the northern CA theatre scene, as well as information on play contests and festivals, and listings of production activity, workshops, classes, auditions, jobs and services. TBA also publishes *Theatre Directory of the Bay Area*, which includes entries of local theatre companies; the *Performance and Rehearsal Space Directory of the Bay Area*, with listings of rehearsal and performance spaces; *Sources of Publicity*; and *Management Memo*, a monthly e-newsletter for theatre administrators and artistic directors. The website includes a playbill calendar, online tickets and sample magazine articles. Annual dues are $61.

THEATRE COMMUNICATIONS GROUP

520 8th Ave, 24th Floor; New York, NY 10018-4156; (212) 609-5900,
FAX 609-5901; email tcg@tcg.org; website www.tcg.org
Ben Cameron, *Executive Director*

Founded in 1961, Theatre Communications Group (TCG) offers a wide array of services in line with its mission: to strengthen, nurture and promote the not-for-profit professional American theatre. TCG's programs and services encompass 5 primary areas of activity: artistic programs, including grants to artists and theatres; management programs, including conferences, research and management training; international programs, including the U.S. Center of the International Theatre Institute; advocacy, serving as the primary national advocate for the field, in conjunction with the American Arts Alliance; and publications.

TCG has 17,000 individual members, including theatre professionals, educators and students, and a network of 430 member theatres nationwide, representing a wide range of institutional sizes, structures and aesthetics.

TCG's artistic programs available to playwrights include the NEA/TCG Theatre Residency Program for Playwrights, also supported in part by the Ford Foundation's NewWorks program, which provides $25,000 grants to help playwrights create new works and strengthen relationships with theatres, which also receive $4500 when they host a playwright; Extended Collaboration Grants, funded by Met Life Foundation, which help theatres offer playwrights extended developmental work with other collaborators; and the New Generations Program, funded by the Doris Duke Charitable Foundation and The Andrew W. Mellon Foundation, which offers full-time mentorships in resident professional theatres. (See TCG Artistic Programs in Fellowships and Grants. Program guidelines are also available on TCG's website.) TCG also administers the invitation-only AT&T:OnStage program, which supports productions of new plays and musicals.

In addition to *American Theatre* magazine, which provides an up-to-date perspective on theatre throughout the country and includes the full texts of five new plays annually, other TCG publications of interest to theatre writers include *Theatre Directory*, which provides complete contact information for 430 U.S. not-for-profit professional theatres and related organizations; *Stage Writers Handbook: A Complete Business Guide for Playwrights, Composers, Lyricists and Librettists*, by Dana Singer; *The Production Notebooks: Theatre in Process*, Volumes I and II, edited by Mark Bly; *Stage Directors Handbook: Opportunities for Directors and Choreographers*, edited by the SDC Foundation; and *ArtSEARCH*, a biweekly bulletin of job opportunities in the arts which is available online or in print. TCG also publishes plays and musicals, theatre-related books, and resource books on the not-for-profit professional theatre. (For further information, see the Publications and Useful Publications chapters of this book. A complete publications catalog is available from TCG and on TCG's website.)

Individual members receive a free subscription to *American Theatre* magazine, discounted tickets to performances at theatres nationwide and discounts on all TCG books, including TCG distribution titles. Other benefits include discounts on car rentals and eligibility for a no-fee affinity credit card. Individual memberships are available for $39.95 a year, $20 for students. (See the TCG membership application in the back of this book.)

THE THEATRE MUSEUM

1E Tavistock St; London WC2E 7PA; England;
44-207-943-4700, FAX 44-207-943-4777;
website www.theatremuseum.vam.ac.uk

Founded in 1987, the Theatre Museum, a branch of the Victoria & Albert Museum, is Britain's national museum of the performing arts. In addition to its regular displays, which feature 400 years of the history, technology, art and craft of theatre, and its special exhibitions, the museum houses the U.K.'s largest archive of performing arts materials, including play texts, photographic and biographical files, theatre programs and reviews, and books about the theatre. The museum's education department runs workshops and study days on theatre practice for children, students, teachers and adult groups. The museum also runs a program of celebrity interviews, seminars and events.

THEATRE PROJECT

45 West Preston St; Baltimore, MD 21201; (410) 539-3091, FAX 539-2137;
email office@theatreproject.org; website www.theatreproject.org
Anne Cantler Fulwiler, *Producing Director*

Founded in 1971, the Theatre Project, also known as Baltimore Theatre Project, offers established and emerging performing artists a supportive environment to develop and present their work. Theatre Project productions provide Baltimore with a professional international center for diverse artistic voices. Artists receive visitor housing; technical, promotional and front-of-house support; and opportunities to meet with other artists. Additional services include workshops, roundtables, seminars, open auditions and a shared database of Baltimore-area affiliated artists.

VOLUNTEER LAWYERS FOR THE ARTS

1 East 53rd St, 6th Floor; New York, NY 10022-4201;
   (212) 319-2787, ext 1 (administrative office and Art Law Hotline),
   FAX 752-6575; email vlany@vlany.org; website www.vlany.org
Elena M. Paul, *Executive Director*

Founded in 1969, VLA provides pro bono legal services, education and advocacy to the New York arts community. Through public advocacy, VLA frequently acts on issues vitally important to the arts community, freedom of expression and the First Amendment being areas of special expertise and concern. VLA provides legal assistance to more than 6000 clients each year through a variety of ways, including pro bono case placements for low-income artists and not-for-profit arts organizations; the VLA Legal Clinic; the Edmond de Rothschild Foundation Nonprofit Assistance Program; and the Art Law Line, a legal hotline. VLA operates a membership program for artists. Membership benefits include discounts on VLA workshops and publications, invitations to member events, access to the VLA Art Law Line, access to the members-only VLA Legal Clinic, discounts on staff consultations and mediate art services, and access to VLA's Speaker's Bureau and Board Bank. Programs of special interest to playwrights include workshops on copyright and contracts. VLA can also make referrals to similar organizations nationwide.

WOMEN'S THEATRE ALLIANCE (WTA)

2936 North Southport; Chicago, IL 60657-4120; (312) 408-9910;
   email wtachicago@aol.com; website www.wtachicago.org
Katie Carey Govier, *President*

Founded in 1992, the Women's Theatre Alliance (WTA) is dedicated to the development of dramatic works by, for and/or about women and to the promotion of women's leadership within the Chicago theatre community. Programs of special interest to playwrights include the Play Development Workshop and New Plays Festival, which unites women writers with a director and actors for a development process culminating in a 2-week festival of staged readings; Solo Voices, which facilitates the creation of one-woman shows and performance pieces; and the Salon Series, an informal presentation of new work offering social networking opportunities. WTA also publishes a monthly newsletter. Membership is open to women and men. Annual dues are $25.

WRITERS GUILD OF AMERICA, EAST (WGAE), AFL-CIO

555 West 57th St; New York, NY 10019; (212) 767-7800,
 FAX 582-1909; website www.wgaeast.org
Mona Mangan, *Executive Director*

WGAE is the union for writers in the fields of motion pictures, television and radio who reside east of the Mississippi River (regardless of where they work). The union negotiates collective bargaining agreements for its members and represents them in grievances and arbitrations under those agreements. The guild gives annual awards; sponsors a foundation, which currently teaches film writing to disadvantaged high school students; and offers a 10-year script registration service. WGAE participates in reciprocal arrangements with the International Affiliation of Writers Guilds and with its sister union, Writers Guild of America, west. The guild publishes a bi-monthly newsletter, which is available to nonmembers by subscription; and a quarterly journal, *On Writing.*

WRITERS GUILD OF AMERICA, WEST (WGAW)

7000 West 3rd St; Los Angeles, CA 90048-4329; (323) 951-4000,
 FAX 782-4800; website www.wga.org
John McLean, *Executive Director*

WGAw is the union for writers in the fields of motion pictures, television, radio and new media who write both entertainment and news programming. It represents its members in collective bargaining and other labor matters. It publishes a monthly magazine, *Written By.* The guild registers material, including screen- and teleplays, books, plays, poetry and songs (call 323-782-4500). The WGAw library is open to the public Mon–Fri (call 323-782-4544).

YOUNG PLAYWRIGHTS INC.

306 West 38th St, Suite 300; New York, NY 10018; (212) 594-5440;
 email writeaplay@aol.com; website youngplaywrights.org
Sheri M. Goldhirsch, *Artistic Director*

Young Playwrights Inc. (YPI), founded in 1981 by Stephen Sondheim, is America's only not-for-profit professional theatre devoted solely to playwrights ages 18 years or younger. The producer of the annual Young Playwrights Festival, YPI's mission is to identify and develop promising young writers, while encouraging self-expression through playwriting and its integration into the basic curriculum. YPI serves as an advocate for young writers regardless of ethnicity, physical ability, sexual orientation or economic status, and works to ensure that their voices are acknowledged by a diverse community of artists and theatregoers. Contests include the Young Playwrights Festival National Playwriting Competition and the WRITE A PLAY! NYC Contest (see Prizes). Programs include the Young Playwrights Writers Conference; Urban Retreat, a summer playwriting program in NYC (see Development); Advanced Playwriting Workshop, a weekly after-school seminar; WRITE A PLAY! Workshops, which bring playwriting into the classroom; and WRITE A PLAY! Teacher Training Institute, a curriculum-based professional development program.

PART 3
RESOURCES

Useful Publications

Online Resources

Submission Calendar

Special Interests Index

General Index

USEFUL PUBLICATIONS

This is a selective listing of the publications that we think most usefully supplement the information given in the *Sourcebook*. Note that publications of interest to theatre writers are also described throughout this book, particularly in the chapter introductions, in the Membership and Service Organizations listings, and in the Online Resources chapter. We have purposely left out any "how to" books on the art of playwriting because we do not want to promote the concept of "writing-by-recipe." Pricing and ordering information may change after this book goes to press, so it would be wise to confirm details before ordering a publication.

AMERICAN THEATRE

Theatre Communications Group; 520 8th Ave, 24th Floor;
New York, NY 10018-4156; (212) 609-5900, FAX 609-5902;
email custserv@tcg.org; website www.tcg.org

1-year subscription/TCG membership $39.95; single issue $5.95. This magazine, published 10 times per year, provides comprehensive coverage of all aspects of theatre. *American Theatre* regularly features articles and interviews dealing with theatre writers and their works, and publishes the complete texts of 5 new plays a year. Schedules for more than 400 theatres are published in each issue, and a special Season Preview issue prints upcoming season schedules each October. Selected feature articles and season schedules are posted on the website monthly.

BACK STAGE

770 Broadway, 4th Floor; New York, NY 10003;
email backstage@backstage.com; website www.backstage.com

1-year subscription $95, 2 years $149; single issue $2.95, $5.95 by mail. This performing arts weekly includes industry news; national coverage; reviews; columns, including "Playwrights' Corner"; and occasional features on playwriting. The primary focus is on casting; script solicitation, workshops and classes for playwrights are also advertised.

HOLLYWOOD SCRIPTWRITER

Box 10277; Burbank, CA 91510; (310) 530-0000;
email editorial@hollywoodscriptwriter.com;
website www.hollywoodscriptwriter.com

1-year subscription (6 issues) $30 US, $38.70 Canada, $47.00 all other international. This 24-page trade paper contains interviews and articles giving advice to playwrights and screenwriters, and a "Markets for Your Work" section. A list of back issues with a summary of the contents of each issue is available; call for information.

INSIGHT FOR PLAYWRIGHTS

2206 Washington St; Merrick, NY 11566-3543
email info@insightforplaywrights.com;
website www.insightforplaywrights.com

1-year print subscription (12 issues) $45, email subscription $35. This monthly marketing newsletter for playwrights provides submission guidelines for theatres, residencies, publishers, grants, festivals and contests, and lists special programs for women writers, and more; visit website for sample issue.

LITERARY MARKET PLACE 2004

Information Today, Inc; 630 Central Ave; New Providence, NJ 07974;
(800) 409-4929, Customer Service: 300-9868, FAX (908) 771-8736;
email custserv@infotoday.com; website www.literarymarketplace.com

2003. 2088 pp, $299 (plus 21% postage and handling and sales tax where applicable) paper. Also available on the web at www.literarymarketplace.com (various fee options and subscription rates are provided). This directory of the North American book publishing industry gives contact information for book publishers and those in related fields, and includes 2 "Names & Numbers" indexes totaling more than 600 pages. The 2005 LMP is due out in Nov 2004.

PROFESSIONAL PLAYSCRIPT FORMAT GUIDELINES AND SAMPLE

Feedback Theatrebooks; Order Department: P.O. Box 174;
Brooklin, ME 04616; (207) 359-2781, FAX 359-5532;
email feedback@hypernet.com

2nd ed, 2001. 42 pp, $9.95 (plus $5.50 shipping via UPS and sales tax where applicable) paper. This booklet provides updated and expanded instructions for laying out a script in a professional manner; includes "Margin and Tab Setting Guide" and sample pages of script.

SONGWRITER'S MARKET

Writer's Digest Books; 4760 East Galbraith Rd; Cincinnati, OH 45236;
(513) 531-2690, ext 1423, FAX 531-2686;
email songmarket@fwpubs.com; website www.writersdigest.com

2004. 520 pp, $24.99 (plus $3 shipping and handling and sales tax where applicable) paper. This annually updated directory, which lists contact information for more than 1700 song markets, includes a section on musical theatre. It also lists associations, contests and workshops of interest to songwriters. The 2005 edition is due out in summer 2004.

STAGE DIRECTIONS MAGAZINE

250 West 57th St, Suite 420; New York, NY 10107;
(212) 265-8890, ext 35, FAX 581-6217;
email carmstrong@lifestylemedia.com;
website www.stage-directions.com

1-year subscription (12 issues) $26, 2 years $48; single issue $4.99. This magazine provides information for theatre professionals about new plays and musicals, new products, industry-related news, as well as information regarding lighting, sound, costumes, scenery and makeup.

STAGE WRITERS HANDBOOK: A COMPLETE BUSINESS GUIDE FOR PLAYWRIGHTS, COMPOSERS, LYRICISTS AND LIBRETTISTS

Theatre Communications Group; 520 8th Ave, 24th Floor;
New York, NY 10018-4156; (212) 609-5900, FAX 609-5901;
email custserv@tcg.org; website www.tcg.org

1997. 328 pp, $18.95 (plus $5 postage and handling for 1 book, ¢.50 for each additional book) paper. This comprehensive guide, written by the former Executive Director of The Dramatists Guild, covers such topics as copyright (updated 2004), collaboration, underlying rights, marketing and self-promotion, production contracts, representation (agents and lawyers), publishers, authors' relationships with directors, and videotaping and electronic rights.

THE STUDENT'S GUIDE TO PLAYWRITING OPPORTUNITIES

Box 519; Dorset, VT 05251; (802) 867-2223; FAX 867-0144;
email theatre@sover.net; website www.theatredirectories.com

3rd ed, 2002. 135 pp, $18.95 (exact price and handling costs TBA) paper. This guide is a compendium of academic (undergraduate/graduate) and professional programs, which includes submission opportunities and essays on playwriting.

THEATRE DIRECTORY 2004-05

Theatre Communications Group; 520 8th Ave, 24th Floor;
New York, NY 10018-4156; (212) 609-5900, FAX 609-5901;
email custserv@tcg.org; website www.tcg.org

2004. 256 pp, $13.95 (plus $5 postage and handling for 1 book, ¢.50 for each additional book) paper. TCG's annually updated directory provides complete contact information for more than 420 not-for-profit professional theatres, including new TCG theatres that join after this *Sourcebook* is published, and more than 60 arts resource organizations. Includes special interest, personnel and state index for all theatres.

THEATRE PROFILES 12

Theatre Communications Group; 520 8th Ave, 24th Floor;
New York, NY 10018-4156; (212) 609-5900, FAX 609-5901;
email custserv@tcg.org; website www.tcg.org

1996. 254 pp, $22.95 (plus $5 postage and handling for 1 book, ¢.50 for each additional book) paper. The 12th volume of this biennial series contains artistic profiles, production photographs, financial information and repertoire information for the 1993-95 seasons of 257 theatres. Theatre Profiles project encompassing theatre seasons 1996-2002 is available via website.

U.S. COPYRIGHT OFFICE PUBLICATIONS

Copyright Office; Library of Congress; 101 Independence Ave SE;
Washington, DC 20559-6000; (202) 707-3000, 707-6737 (TTY);
email copyinfo@loc.gov; website www.copyright.gov

There are many ways to receive free informational circulars and registration forms: through the website obtain all copyright registration forms, informational circulars and general copyright information; the Publications Hotline (202-707-9100) processes requests circulars and forms (if interested in registering a dramatic work request packet FL-119); the Fax-on-Demand service (202-707-2600) permits one to request up to three circulars. Application forms are not available via fax. Copyright information specialists can answer questions Monday–Friday 8:30 A.M. to 5:00 P.M. at (202) 707-3000.

THE WRITER

c/o Kalmbach Publishing Co; 21027 Crossroads Circle; Box 1612;
Waukesha, WI 53187-1612; (262) 796-8776, FAX 798-6468;
email editor@writermag.com; website www.writermag.com

1-year subscription (12 issues) $29, 2 years $54, 3 years $78. This monthly magazine publishes market news, prize announcements, events, feature interviews with authors and articles on the process of writing.

ONLINE RESOURCES

What's here and what's not.

Now that nearly every organization, theatre and otherwise, has established an internet presence, our goal in presenting Online Resources in *Dramatists Sourcebook* is to spotlight sites that offer useful information distinct from opportunities already included elsewhere in the book. Many URLs from local playwrights' home pages, community playwrights' forums and college playwriting courses appear in the far reaches of search engine results. In the interest of accuracy and longevity, we have opted to include a select menu of sites that are mainstays of the internet playwriting community—sites with free content and broad professional appeal.

As you well know, empires are destroyed in a day in the online world: the site you landed on this morning might not exist by the time you check back tomorrow. Or worse yet, it might exist but not have been updated for the last five years. Take the time to assess the editorial merit and accuracy of the site. What we present here is a guide to the best that's currently available, which you can also use to measure the quality of new ventures.

AISLE SAY

www.aislesay.com/index.html

Description: no-frills compilation of reviews of professional and community theatre productions from around the country written by local theatre critics. The writing style and quality of the reviews vary significantly, but the coverage is thorough and fair. **Site includes:** reviews, links to critics' biographies and index of additional sources for reviews.

AMERICANTHEATER WEB

www.americantheaterweb.com

Description: database where theatres around the country post their production schedules. The listings are not comprehensive but the collection of theatres is diverse. **Site includes:** theatre headlines, current production listings by region, small bookstore, chat, newsletter and free email.

ARTS JOURNAL

www.artsjournal.com

Description: chronicle of feature articles on arts and culture from more than 180 English-language newspapers, magazines and publications. Direct links to the most interesting or important stories are posted every weekday beginning at 8 A.M. EST. Stories from sites that charge for access are excluded, as are sites that require visitors to register, with the exception of the *New York Times*. **Site includes:** articles sorted by discipline and date, newsletter, weekly email updates, classifieds and related links.

ARTSLYNX INTERNATIONAL ARTS RESOURCES

www.artslynx.org

Description: compilation of international links for a great variety of artistic disciplines. **Site includes:** multitude of links and resource pages on many topics, from mime to makeup artistry to playwriting.

ARTS RESOURCE NETWORK

www.ArtsResourceNetwork.org

Description: portal for Seattle arts community. **Site includes:** links to organizations and information, online community for artists and a newsletter.

ASIAN AMERICAN THEATRE REVUE

www.aatrevue.com/AATR-1.html

Description: hub for Asian-American theatre. **Site includes:** news, calendar, list of Asian-American playwrights and their plays; directory of Asian-American theatre companies; reviews; library of anthologies, individual authors and critical perspectives; bulletin boards and related links.

BARTLEBY.COM
www.bartleby.com

Description: online version of Bartleby's bookstore, which provides searchable databases of reference materials free of charge. **Site includes:** unlimited access to *Columbia Encyclopedia, Sixth Edition; American Heritage Dictionary, Fourth Edition; Roget's II: The New Thesaurus; American Heritage Book of English Usage; Simpson's Contemporary Quotations; Bartlett's Familiar Quotations; King James Bible; Oxford Shakespeare; Gray's Anatomy; Strunk's Elements of Style* and *World Fact Book.*

CAMBRIDGE DICTIONARIES ONLINE
dictionary.cambridge.org

Description: *Cambridge Dictionary* online. **Site includes:** full access to *Cambridge International Dictionary;* international dictionary of idiom, international dictionary of phrasal verbs, *Learner's Dictionary* of English and others.

CITYSEARCH
www.citysearch.com

Description: nationwide, city-specific entertainment guide for arts, events, restaurants, etc., by city, date or subject. **Site includes:** database of cities by neighborhood and zip code and links to local services.

THE ENCYCLOPEDIA MYTHICA
www.pantheon.org/mythica.html

Description: capsule definitions and explanations from world mythology, folklore and legend. **Site includes:** lists of more than 5700 articles, 300 illustrations, maps and genealogy tables from more than 25 cultures.

INTERNET BROADWAY DATABASE
www.ibdb.com

Description: IBDB is the official database for Broadway production information culled from the League of Resident Theatre's archives. **Site includes:** several search options including keyword search, category search (shows, people, theatre or season) or date search (date range, day or current production).

INTERNET MOVIE DATABASE
www.imdb.com

Description: comprehensive searchable database containing information about film, video and made-for-TV movies. **Site includes:** movie and TV news; U.S. movie show times searchable by date, city, state and zip code; photo galleries; IMDB staff and user recommendations; independent film index; new releases and user favorites.

IN TRANSLATION
www.intranslation.com.ar

Description: central database of Spanish to English theatre translations that can be downloaded in their entirety. **Site includes:** database of Spanish to English theatre translations listed by author; alphabetical listing of translators; resources section and calendar of events, conferences, workshops and deadlines.

KMC: A BRIEF GUIDE TO INTERNET RESOURCES IN THEATRE AND PERFORMANCE STUDIES
www.stetson.edu/csata/thr_guid.html

Description: selected list of theatre resources compiled by Ken McCoy, Associate Professor of Communication Studies and Theatre Arts at Stetson College. **Site includes:** list of McCoy's most used sites, resources searchable by theatre subject, listservs, newsgroups and other guides.

NATIVE AMERICAN AUTHORS
www.ipl.org/div/natam/

Description: information about contemporary Native North American authors including playwrights. **Site includes:** searchable database of writers with bibliographies of their published works and biographical information, and links to interviews, online texts and tribal websites.

NATIVE AMERICAN WOMEN PLAYWRIGHT'S ARCHIVE
staff.lib.muohio.edu/nawpa/

Description: catalog of writing by Native American women playwrights. **Site includes:** playwright's directory, online exhibit of Spiderwoman Theater, bibliography of Native American women's theatre, author's roundtable, archive of *NAWPA* newsletters, listings of recent programs and productions, and related links.

NEW YORK THEATRE WIRE
www.nytheatre-wire.com

Description: source for what's playing on New York City stages. **Site includes:** articles, publication information, Broadway and Off-Broadway listings, reviews, museum directory and classifieds.

NYFA SOURCE
www.nyfa.org

Description: national database of grants, awards, services and publications for artists. **Site includes:** calendar of grant and award deadlines; lists of services, fellowships, organizations and publications; job listings for artists; tutorials; artist news and other services.

NYTHEATRE.COM

www.nytheatre.com

Description: source for New York theatre that gives equal attention to Broadway, Off- and Off-Off-Broadway. **Site includes:** listings, articles, reviews, interviews, venue information, not-for-profit theatre news and other features.

THE OFF-OFF BROADWAY REVIEW

www.oobr.com

Description: no-frills publication detailing the theatre of Off-Off-Broadway. **Site includes:** reviews, listings, archives and information about the Midtown International Theatre Festival and the Lower East Side Festival of the Arts.

PLAYBILL ONLINE

www.playbill.com

Description: expanded version of *Playbill*'s print publication including information about Broadway and Off-Broadway. **Site includes:** news from the U.S., Canada and international theatre communities; Broadway and Off-Broadway listings; online ticket sales; feature articles; job bank and links.

PLAYS AND PLAYWRIGHTS

groups.yahoo.com/group/playsandplaywrights

Description: discussion group for playwrights. **Site includes:** discussion comprised of 45–300 messages per month on plays and playwriting, production information, submission and grant opportunities, teaching and professional development; discussion can be viewed online or emailed to participants.

THE PLAYWRIGHTING SEMINARS

www.vcu.edu/artweb/playwriting/seminar.html

Description: online textbook by playwright Richard Toscan which covers the craft and business of playwriting. **Site includes:** seminar topics such as content, film, structure, working, script format and business; quotes from established playwrights and a reading list.

PLAYWRIGHTS ON THE WEB

www.stageplays.com/writers.htm

Description: international database of playwrights and their websites. **Site includes:** plays listed alphabetically by author and genre, playwrights' discussion forum, newsletter, callboard and links.

THEATREMANIA
theatermania.com

Description: portal featuring theatre news and information from major cities around the country and some international locations. **Site includes:** theatre ticket services, listings organized by city, feature and news articles, links to theatre festivals and awards, theatre store and membership information.

THE U.S. COPYRIGHT OFFICE
www.copyright.gov

Description: branch of the Library of Congress. **Site includes:** general copyright information, copyright records, publications including forms in downloadable format, and legislation and copyright links.

WOMEN OF COLOR, WOMEN OF WORDS
www.scils.rutgers.edu/~cybers/home.html

Description: information site on accomplished women playwrights of color, especially African-Americans. **Site includes:** writers' bios, list of completed works, directory of libraries and research centers with an African-American focus, list of critical/biographical resources, links to theatres that produce multicultural work, directory of dissertations on featured playwrights, recommended books on African-American theatre history and egroup for African-American women playwrights.

WRITEEXPRESS ONLINE RHYMING DICTIONARY
www.writeexpress.com/online2.html

Description: online rhyming dictionary. **Site includes:** searchable database by end, last, double, beginning and first syllable rhymes.

WRITERSDIGEST.COM
THE 101 BEST WEB SITES FOR WRITERS
www.writersdigest.com/101sites/2004_index.asp

Description: well-indexed list of web resources for writers. **Site includes:** links to search engines, media news and reference, job sites, the writing life, self- and e-publishing, and writers' organizations.

WWW VIRTUAL LIBRARY THEATRE AND DRAMA
vl-theatre.com

Description: library of international theatre resources updated daily. **Site includes:** links to academic/training institutions, book dealers, conferences for theatre scholars, online play archives, online journals, mailing lists, monologues/plays in print, newsgroups, theatre books in print, theatre companies, theatre image bank, and theatre syllabus bank.

WWW.YOURDICTIONARY.COM

www.yourdictionary.com

Description: index of online dictionaries. **Site includes:** dictionaries (of varying completion and quality) in 260 languages, multilingual dictionaries, specialty English dictionaries, thesauri and other vocabulary aids, language identifiers and guessers, index of dictionary indices, web of online grammar and web of linguistic fun.

YAHOO THEATRE INDEX

dir.yahoo.com/Arts/Performing_Arts/Theatre

Description: index of theatre-related sites. **Site includes:** information on many topics including playwrights and plays.

SUBMISSION CALENDAR

Included here are all specified deadlines; the more general submission dates for theatres listed in Production are not included. Deadlines listed reflect the next upcoming submission deadline as provided at press time. Some deadlines may fall outside the years covered by this book, so it is always important to confirm a deadline before submitting work. There are always important deadlines that are not available at press time and so cannot be included here.

SEPTEMBER

1 Anna Zornio Memorial Children's Theatre Playwriting Award, 121

1 Centrum Creative Residencies Program, 239

1 Regent University Theatre One-Act Play Competition, 147

1 Santa Fe Performing Arts New Playwrights Competition, 149

7 Fund for U.S. Artists at Int'l Festivals and Exhibitions (1st deadline), 216

9 New Play Commissions in Jewish Theatre, 218

10 National New Play Award, 142

10 Playwrights Forum (1st deadline), 189

12 Arizona Commission on the Arts Fellowships, 207

13 Jonathan Larson Performing Arts Foundation, 213

15 Jerome Playwright-in-Residence Fellowships, 219

15 Kleban Award, 214

15 MacDowell Colony (1st deadline), 244

15 Puerto Rican Traveling Theatre Playwrights' Unit, 190

15 Virginia Center for the Creative Arts (1st deadline), 248

15 Wisconsin Arts Board Artist Fellowship Awards, 223

20 Susan Smith Blackburn Prize, 152

30 Attic Theatre Ensemble's One-Act Marathon, 123

OCTOBER

NOVEMBER

DECEMBER

JANUARY

1 BTW Unbound, 20

1 Nantucket Short Play Festival and Competition, 141

1 Sketchbook Festival, 150

2 Kumu Kahua Theatre Playwriting Contest, 136

2 Meet The Composer Fund (2nd deadline), 215

3 O'Neill Music Theater Conference, 186

5 TADA!'s One-Act Playwriting Contest, 153

10 Playwrights Forum (2nd deadline), 189

14 PEN/Laura Pels Foundation Award for Drama, 145

15 Ashland New Plays Festival, 173

15 Bay Area Playwrights Festival (full-length plays), 174

15 Camargo Foundation, 238

15 Jewel Box Playwrighting Award, 133

15 MacDowell Colony (2nd deadline), 244

15 Montana Artists Refuge (2nd deadline), 245

15 Ragdale Foundation (1st deadline), 246

15 Reva Shiner Full-Length Play Contest, 148

15 Source Theatre Company 2005 Literary Prize, 151

15 Summerfield G. Roberts Award, 152

15 Virginia Center for the Creative Arts (2nd deadline), 248

15 Yaddo (1st deadline), 250

16 Fund for U.S. Artists at Int'l Festivals and Exhibitions (2nd deadline), 216

18 Helene Wurlitzer Foundation of New Mexico, 241

21 TheaterFest Regional Playwriting Festival, 153

24 Grawemeyer Award for Music Composition, 155

28 Dobie-Paisano Fellowship, 210

31 Baker's Plays High School Playwriting Contest, 124

31 Dubuque Fine Arts Players National One-Act Playwriting Contest, 128

31 James D. Phelan Award in Literature, 132

31 McLaren Memorial Playwriting Competition, 139

31 Short Grain Contest, 149

Contact for exact deadline during this month:

Frederick Douglass Writing Workshops (2nd deadline), 179

Marin Arts Council Individual Artist Grants, 214

FEBRUARY

MARCH

APRIL

15 John Gassner Award, 133
15 Lorna Littleway's Juneteenth Jamboree, 181
15 MacDowell Colony (3rd deadline), 244
15 VSA Arts Playwright Discovery Award, 156
15 Young Playwrights Inc. Urban Retreat, 196
16 Ludwig Vogelstein Foundation–last initial A–M, 214
23 Appalachian Festival of Plays & Playwrights, 122
30 Little Theatre of Alexandria One-Act Playwriting Competition, 137
30 Ludwig Vogelstein Foundation–last initial N–Z, 214
30 NYC Playwrights Lab, 185
Contact for exact deadline during this month
Frederick Douglass Writing Workshops (3rd deadline), 179
Off-Off Broadway Original Short Play Festival, 192

MAY

1 Aurand Harris Children's Theatre Grants and Fellowships, 209
1 Aurand Harris Memorial Playwriting Award, 123
1 BMI Musical Theatre Workshop (librettists), 174
1 Don and Gee Nicholl Fellowships in Screenwriting, 211
1 Dorothy Silver Playwriting Competition, 128
1 EcoDrama Playwright Festival, 129
1 Hambidge Center for Creative Arts and Sciences (2nd deadline), 240
1 HRC's Annual Playwriting Contest, 131
1 Met Life Foundation Nuestras Voces, 139
1 Sundance Institute Feature Film Program, 193
3 Fund for U.S. Artists at Int'l Festivals and Exhibitions (3rd deadline), 216
10 Playwrights Forum (3rd deadline), 189
15 German Literary Translation Prize, 121
15 Lewis Galantiere Literary Translation Prize, 121
15 Montana Artists Refuge (3rd deadline), 245
15 Virginia Center for the Creative Arts (3rd deadline), 248
15 Women's Work Project, 196
15 Writer's Digest Writing Competition, 157
31 Buntville Crew, 125
31 Native Arts Program Visiting Artist Appointments, 217
31 Walt Disney Studios and ABC Entertainment Writing Fellowship, 222
Contact for exact deadline during this month:
Global Connections, 215

JUNE

JULY

AUGUST

SPECIAL INTERESTS INDEX

Here is a guide to entries which indicate a particular or exclusive interest in certain types of material, or which contain an element of special interest to writers in certain categories. Under Young Audiences, Media, Multimedia, Performance Art and Solo Performance, we list every entry of interest to writers in these fields. In the cases of Adaptations, Musicals, One-acts and Translations, there are numerous theatres willing to consider these types of material; we list here only those theatres and other organizations that give major focus to them. The Multicultural category is for those organizations expressing general interest in muticultural works. Under African-American, Asian-American, Hispanic/Latin-American and Native American Theatre, we have included only those organizations specifically seeking work by or about people from these ethnic groups. The Student/College Submission category refers to college writing students or students in an affiliated writing program. Young Playwrights is a special interest category for playwrights 18 or under.

AFRICAN-AMERICAN THEATRE

ASIAN-AMERICAN THEATRE

COMEDY

DISABILITIES: Theatre for and by people with disabilities

EXPERIMENTAL THEATRE

MEDIA (film, radio, television)

MULTICULTURAL THEATRE

MULTIMEDIA

MUSICAL THEATRE

NATIVE AMERICAN THEATRE

ONE-ACTS AND SHORT PLAYS

PERFORMANCE ART

RELIGIOUS/SPIRITUAL THEATRE

SOLO PERFORMANCE

STUDENT/COLLEGE SUBMISSIONS

TRANSLATIONS

YOUNG PLAYWRIGHTS PROGRAMS

GENERAL INDEX

Remember the two alphabetizing principles used throughout the book: First, entries beginning with a person's name are alphabetized by the first name rather than the surname. However, you can find these entries indexed by both names. Hence you will find the Robert J. Pickering Award for Playwriting Excellence under R and P. Regardless of which way "theatre" is spelled in an organization's title, it is alphabetized as if it were spelled "re," not "er."

325

K

VLA (Volunteer Lawyers for the Arts), 281

Vogel Award in Playwriting, The Paula, 136

Vogelstein Foundation Inc., Ludwig, 214

Volunteer Lawyers for the Arts (VLA), 281

VS Theatre Company, 113

VSA Arts Playwright Discovery Award, 156

W

Wagner College Theatre, 151

Walnut Street Theatre, The, 113

Walt Disney Studios and ABC Writing Fellowship Program, The, 222

Ward Prize for African-American Playwrights, Theodore, 154

Washington State Arts Commission, 235

Waterfront Ensemble, The, 195

Watertower Theatre, Inc., 113

Weissberger Award, L. Arnold, 137

Weissberger Theater Group, 114

Weitzenhoffer Fellowship/Brooks Atkinson Exchange, Max, 272

Wellfleet Harbor Actors Theater, 114

Welty New Play Series, Eudora, 70

Wender/Rosenstone, 204

West Coast Ensemble, 114

West Coast Ensemble Contests, 156

West Coast Ensemble Full-Length Play Competition, 156

West Coast Ensemble Musical Stairs, 156

West Coast Playwrights Alliance, 80

Westcliffe Center for the Performing Arts, 144

Western Stage, The, 114

Westport Country Playhouse, 115

West Virginia Commission on the Arts, 235

WGAE (Writers Guild of America, East), 282

WGAW (Writers Guild of America, West), 282

White Memorial National Children's Playwriting Contest, Jackie, 132

Whittlesey Agency, Peregrine, 204

Wichita Falls Backdoor Players, Inc., 173

Wichita State University, 157

Wichita State University Playwriting Contest, 157

Will Geer Theatricum Botanicum, 115

William Flanagan Memorial Creative Persons Center, 248

William Inge Center for the Arts, 249

William Morris Agency, 204

Williams/New Orleans Literary Festival One-Act Play Competition, Tennessee, 153

Williamstown Theatre Festival, 115, 195

Willows Theatre Company, 116

Wilma Theater, The, 116

Windows on the Works, 98

Wings Theatre Company, Inc., 116

Winnipeg Jewish Theatre, 255

Wisconsin Arts Board, 235

Wisconsin Arts Board Artist Fellowship Awards, 223

Wolk Award, Christopher Brian, 172

Women and Theatre Program, 132

Women Arts Network, The, 263

Women of Color, Women of Words, 295

Women Playwrights Festival, 241

Women Playwrights Series, 196

Women's Project & Productions, 117

Women's Theatre Alliance (WTA), 281

Women's Work Project, 196

Woodstock Fringe, 117

Woodstock Fringe Festival of Theatre and Song, 117

Woodstock Fringe Playwrights Unit, 117

Woodstock Guild, The, 238

Woolly Mammoth Theatre Company, 117

Worcester Foothills Theatre Company, 118

WorkingStages, 34

ABOUT THEATRE COMMUNICATIONS GROUP

Theatre Communications Group (TCG), the national organization for the American theatre, offers a wide array of services in line with its mission: to strengthen, nurture and promote the professional not-for-profit American theatre. Artistic programs support theatres and theatre artists by awarding grants ($3 million in 2003–2004), and offer career development programs for artists. Management programs provide professional development opportunities for theatre leaders through workshops, conferences, forums (including teleconferences and online) and publications, as well as industry research on the finances and practices of the American not-for-profit theatre. Advocacy, conducted in conjunction with the dance, presenting and opera fields, includes guiding lobbying efforts and providing theatres with timely alerts about legislative developments. The country's leading independent press specializing in dramatic literature, TCG's publications include *American Theatre* magazine, the *ArtSEARCH* employment bulletin, plays, translations and theatre reference books. As the U.S. Center of the International Theatre Institute, a worldwide network, TCG supports cross-cultural exchange through travel grants and other assistance to traveling theatre professionals. Through these programs, TCG seeks to increase the organizational efficiency of its member theatres, cultivate and celebrate the artistic talent and achievements of the field, and promote a larger public understanding of and appreciation for the theatre field. TCG serves over 430 member theatres nationwide.

THEATRE COMMUNICATIONS GROUP

Ben Cameron, *Executive Director*

2004–2005 BOARD OF DIRECTORS

Paula Tomei, *President*
South Coast Repertory

Gary Anderson, *Vice President*
Plowshares Theatre Company

Oskar Eustis, *Vice President*
Trinity Repertory Company

Nancy Keen Roche, *Treasurer*
Center Stage

Jeff Church, *Secretary*
The Coterie Theatre

Susan V. Booth
Alliance Theatre

Carlyle Brown
Playwright

Carol Brown
Pittsburgh Cultural Trust

Peter DuBois
The Public Theater

Todd Haimes
Roundabout Theatre Company

Danny Hoch
Actor, Playwright, Director

Melanie Joseph
The Foundry Theatre

Jayne Baccus Khalifa
Minneapolis Civil Rights Department

Martha Lavey
Steppenwolf Theatre Company

Robert H. Leonard
Virginia Tech

Todd London
New Dramatists, Inc.

Abel López
GALA Hispanic Theatre

Catherine Maciariello
Andrew W. Mellon Foundation

Ellen McLaughlin
Actor, Playwright

Susan Medak
Berkeley Repertory Theatre

Benjamin Moore
Seattle Repertory Theatre

Charles Newell
Court Theatre

Paul Nicholson
Oregon Shakespeare Festival

Daniel Renner
Denver Center Theatre Company

Rosalba Rolón
Pregones Theater

Timothy J. Shields
Milwaukee Repertory Theater

Molly Smith
Arena Stage

Susan Trapnell
ACT Theatre

Susan Tsu
Carnegie Mellon University

Chay Yew
Playwright, Director

TCG is proud to publish the following authors:

Jon Robin Baitz	Peter Hall	Lynn Nottage
Augusto Boal	Karen Hartman	Sarah O'Connor
Anne Bogart	Tina Howe	Robert O'Hara
Eric Bogosian	David Henry Hwang	John O'Keefe
Lee Breuer	Adrienne Kennedy	Suzan-Lori Parks
Peter Brook	Harry Kondoleon	Reynolds Price
Jo Carson	Lisa Kron	Alvin H. Reiss
Aimé Césaire	Tony Kushner	Ronald Ribman
Joseph Chaikin	Tina Landau	José Rivera
Ping Chong	Robert Lepage	Sarah Ruhl
Caryl Churchill	Kristin Linklater	Carl Hancock Rux
Pearl Cleage	Romulus Linney	David Savran
Constance Congdon	Craig Lucas	Christopher Shinn
Culture Clash	Charles Ludlam	Nicky Silver
Nilo Cruz	Eduardo Machado	Dana Singer
E. L. Doctorow	Emily Mann	Stephen Sondheim
Declan Donnellan	Donald Margulies	Tadashi Suzuki
The Five Lesbian	Richard Maxwell	Alfred Uhry
Brothers	Ellen McLaughlin	Paula Vogel
Dario Fo	Conor McPherson	Naomi Wallace
Richard Foreman	Sherrill Myers	Michael Weller
Athol Fugard	Richard Nelson	Thornton Wilder
Philip Kan Gotanda	Danny Newman	August Wilson
Spalding Gray	Marsha Norman	George C. Wolfe
Jessica Hagedorn		

To order books, visit our website: www.tcg.org
Catalog available upon request

TCG INDIVIDUAL MEMBERSHIP

.s a *Sourcebook* user, you're invited to become an Individual Member of **Theatre Communications Group**— the national organization for the merican Theatre and the publisher of *American Theatre* magazine.

As an Individual Member of TCG, you'll get inside information about theatre performances around the country, as well as substantial discounts on tickets to performances and on publications about the theatre. Plus, as the primary advocate for not-for-profit professional theatre in America, TCG will ensure that your voice is heard in Washington. We invite you to join us today and receive all of TCG's benefits!

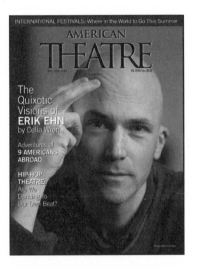

MEMBERS RECEIVE A FREE SUBSCRIPTION TO *AMERICAN THEATRE* AND THESE SPECIAL BENEFITS

- A FREE subscription to *American Theatre*—10 issues...5 complete playscripts... artist profiles...in-depth coverage of contemporary, classical and avant-garde performances...special issues in October (Season Preview) and January (Theatre Training).
- Discounts on tickets to performances at participating theatres nationwide.
- 15% discount on resource materials including *Theatre Directory, ArtSEARCH* and *Dramatists Sourcebook*—all musts for the theatre professional or the serious theatregoer.
- A FREE catalog of TCG publications.
- 10% discount on all books from TCG and other select theatre publishers.
- Your personalized Individual Membership card.
- Opportunity to apply for a no-fee TCG Credit Card.
- Special discounts for Hertz Rent A Car.

JOIN NOW AND SAVE

TCG MEMBERS SAVE ON ALL TCG RESOURCES AND BOOK

Stage Writers Handbook

By Dana Singer

Singer gathers the information and ideas stage writers need to conduct their careers in a businesslike manner, with all the protections the law provides. Subjects covered include copyright, collaboration, underlying rights, marketing, self-promotion and more.
PAPER $18.95

Dramatists Sourcebook

The *Sourcebook* contains more than 950 opportunities for playwrights, translators, composers, lyricists and librettists. Included are details for script-submission procedures for 380 professional theatres, 137 prizes, and scores of publishers, fellowships, residencies and development programs.
PAPER $21.95

Theatre Directory

This pocket-sized directory contains information for over 430 not-for-profit professional theatres and related organizations. Artistic and Managing Directors, board chairmen, along with business and box-office phone numbers, email and website addresses are included and more. **PAPER $13.95**

The Production Notebooks

Theatre in Process, Volume Two

Edited with an Introduction by Mark Bly

Four of the finest dramaturgs offer comprehensive histories of the development of four major productions, *The First Picture Show, Shakespeare Rapid Eye Movement, In the Blood* and *Geography.* **PAPER $18.95**

The Playwright's Voice

American Dramatists on Memory, Writing and the Politics of Culture

Interviews by David Savran

This volume of interviews with contemporary playwrights celebrates the art and talent of fifteen of the theatre's most important artists, including: Edward Albee, Jon Robin Baitz, Philip Kan Gotanda, Holly Hughes, Tony Kushner, Terrence McNally, Suzan-Lori Parks, José Rivera, Ntozake Shange, Nicky Silver, Anna Deavere Smith, Paula Vogel, Wendy Wasserstein, Mac Wellman and George C. Wolfe. **PAPER $16.95**

THESE FINE BOOKS AND OTHERS AVAILABLE FROM TCG.

VISIT OUR ONLINE BOOKSTORE AT WWW.TCG.OR

TCG MEMBERS SAVE 15%
ON A SUBSCRIPTION TO ArtSEARCH

ArtSEARCH

The National Employment Bulletin
for the Arts

Looking for a job in the arts?

ArtSEARCH PROVIDES HUNDREDS OF
JOB OPPORTUNITIES FROM ENTRY-LEVEL
TO UPPER MANAGEMENT IN 5 MAJOR
CATEGORIES.

Administration, Artistic, Education, Production/Design, Career Development

A subscription includes access to ArtSEARCH online at www.tcg.org and the
twice-monthly bulletin sent to subscribers via first-class mail.

ANNUAL SUBSCRIPTION RATES (23 ISSUES)
U.S.: Individual: $60, Individual TCG Member: $51
Institutional: $150, TCG Member Theatre: $75
6-month (online only) Individual: $40, Individual TCG Member: $34

*Online only rates available to Canada and overseas. For print edition Canadian and
overseas subscription rates contact custserv@tcg.org.*

**Call TCG Customer Service at (212) 609-5900, use the order form in this book,
or order online at www.tcg.org.**

SUBSCRIBE TODAY!

Take Advantage NOW and SAVE!
Become a TCG INDIVIDUAL MEMBER and Receive Extraordinary Benefits

☐ **YES**, I would like a one-year Individual Membership to TCG, which includes a subscription to *American Theatre*.

    ☐ Individual Membership ~~$39.95~~ $29.95

    ☐ Student Membership (enclose copy of ID) $20.00

☐ I prefer a two-year membership.

    ☐ Individual Membership ~~$79.90~~ $70.00

Not only would I like to become a member, but I would like to take advantage of my discounts right now!
(Discount prices are only good if you are a member. If you are not a member, please use the full price for your order.)

☐ Please begin my one-year subscription to *ArtSEARCH*.

    Individual one year ☐ ~~$60.00~~ $51.00   Individual 6-month ☐ ~~$40.00~~ $34.00

    Institutional ☐ $150.00   TCG Member Theatre ☐ $75.00

☐ **TOTAL ORDER** _____

To order, send this form to: TCG Order Dept., 520 Eighth Ave., 24th Floor, New York, NY 10018-4156. You may also call (212) 609-5900, fax (212) 609-5901, email custserv@tcg.org, or visit our website www.tcg.org. For credit card orders, please include your billing address if it is different than your mailing address.

☐ Check is enclosed. ☐ Please charge my credit card: ☐ VISA ☐ MC ☐ AMEX

NAME _____

OCCUPATION/DATE _____

ADDRESS _____

CITY _____ STATE _____ ZIP _____

*PHONE/FAX/EMAIL _____

CARD# _____ EXP. DATE _____

SIGNATURE _____

* All orders must have telephone number

For Individual Membership outside the U.S., $60 per year (U.S. currency only, drawn from a U.S. bank). Allow 6-8 weeks from receipt of order.

[Mkt. code: DS█]